Untangling

Bosnia
and
Hercegovina

A Search for Understanding

Gale A. Kirking

A Real World Press Book
Madison, Wisconsin

Designed and Published with
Grote Publishing
634 West Main Street, Suite 207
Madison, WI 53703-2634
(608) 257-4640

            Library of Congress Cataloging-in-Publication Data
Kirking, Gale A., 1958-
    Untangling Bosnia and Hercegovina : [a search for understanding] / Gale
    A. Kirking.
        p. cm.
    Includes bibliographical references and index.
    ISBN 0-9663436-3-8
    1. Bosnia and Hercegovina--Description and travel. 2. Kirking, Gale A.,
    1958---Journeys--Bosnia and Hercegovina. I. Title.

    DR1671 .K57 2000
    914.974204'3--dc21   99-049836

Printed in the United States of America.

10 9 8 7 6 5 4 3 2 1

This book is printed on acid-free paper.

To my parents.

I will be as honest as I can be, as honest as anyone ever could be, for I have begun to doubt that sincerity and honesty are one and the same. Sincerity is the certainty that we speak the truth (and who can be certain of that?), but there are many kinds of honesty, and they do not always agree with one another.

— Ahmed Nuruddin
(from *Death and the Dervish* by Meša Selimović)

A journey is a person in itself; no two are alike. And all plans, safeguards, policing, and coercion are fruitless. We find after years of struggle that we do not take a trip; a trip takes us...In this a journey is like marriage. The certain way to be wrong is to think you control it.

— John Steinbeck
(from *Travels with Charley*)

Contents

Acknowledgments

While the agonies and joys of writing a book accrue predominantly to the author, rare must be the writer who does not benefit from the assistance and encouragement of others. Numerous friends, family members and generous acquaintances have given me great and diverse support. My thanks go out to all of you.

I would like especially to thank Bryan McNeely, Milan Radovich, and Alan Henson, who reviewed the manuscript in its entirety. Their suggestions and criticisms were extremely valuable. The manuscript was greatly improved by their inputs.

A number of individuals reviewed excerpts from the manuscript at early stages and gave me useful feedback that helped me to continue moving productively forward. They include Pavel Kříž, Tom Buhler, Peter Posker, Donna Legoo, Le Verne and Jean Kirking, Brian Bertha and Alan Henson. Thanks also to Trey Whalley for assistance in proofreading and to Bryan McNeely for the final proofing. I am grateful to Mary-Carel Verden and her staff at Grote Publishing for their assistance and patience.

Undoubtedly, there were some well-intended suggestions and criticisms by which I did not abide out of plain stubbornness but which, had I done so, would have improved the text. I am wholly responsible for all defects and errors of fact, grammar or style which may have found their way into this book, as I am for any views which might be regarded as controversial.

Much of this book was written at Pine Knoll Farm, the Wisconsin family farm of my upbringing and where my parents continue to reside. During the weeks I spent working there, my mother and father were extraordinarily supportive in innumerable ways.

This project would never have come to pass were it not for the several years of inspired and inspiring teaching from which I benefited while a history student at the University of Wisconsin–Madison under the late Michael Boro Petrovich. Professor Petrovich's love of learning and appreciation for the mélange of the world's peoples and cultures will remain an essential influence throughout my life.

Preface

Bosnia and Hercegovina is a beautiful, fascinating and, of course, extraordinarily tragic place.[1] It is today also quite mysterious. The country exists in a moral twilight that is neither the darkness of war nor the full light of peace. Truth, goodness and fairness are sometimes not easily distinguished in such duskiness from falsehood, evil and injustice. This setting gives rise to unfortunate and complicating effects upon otherwise normal people and upon their relations with one another. The results are sadly intriguing to observe.

Over the past year, my mind scarcely has known a waking moment when it was not occupied by the puzzle that is Bosnia and Hercegovina. This state of affairs was of my own making, for I had fixed upon an objective to reach a personal understanding of the country. *Untangling Bosnia and Hercegovina* reflects that effort.

Nearly three years after the Dayton peace accord had ended the wars in Bosnia and Hercegovina, I was interested to see how the people and country were getting on. I traveled there intending to learn what I could of day-to-day realities and about prospects for the future. I wanted to formulate opinions that would be based on real understanding.

I gathered the core material for this book while traveling in Bosnia and Hercegovina during two momentous periods. The first occasion, in September of 1998, was at the time of the final campaign, voting and aftermath of a general election. This was only the second such election since the Dayton peace had been negotiated in late-1995. An earlier general election, in 1996, had been a cobbled-together affair that by no stretch of the imagination could have been called free and fair. The 1998 vote was an important test to see if democratic institutions could function. It was also a measure of public support for the nationalist parties, which, arguably, have taken positions and actions disastrous for the country.

My next visit, in March 1999, was at a time when Serb nationalists were all astir. The international community's leading official in Bosnia

---

[1] I should comment about the name of the country that is the subject of this book. Its full name is (Republic of) Bosnia and Hercegovina. I have resisted the temptation simply to call it "Bosnia," as that, after all, is not the country's name. The hyphenated form— Bosnia-Hercegovina— is commonly seen but is not technically correct. I have reserved this hyphenated form for: 1) references to the former Yugoslav republic that lay within the same boundaries as does today's independent country of Bosnia and Hercegovina, and 2) earlier historical references to that same geographic territory.

and Hercegovina had just fired the president of the country's Serb entity who had been democratically elected in September. Furthermore, an international arbitrator had just stripped Serb officials of control over a key city. Croat nationalists, too, were worked up at that time. They were pressing to create their own Croat ministate within Bosnia and Hercegovina, and one of their leading officials was mortally wounded in a car-bomb attack while I was in the country. Meanwhile, there was concern about a deteriorating situation in nearby Kosovo. One week after that follow-up visit NATO began bombing Serbian targets and Serb forces launched a vicious ethnic-cleansing campaign in Kosovo.

From the outset, I was determined that I would speak in Bosnia and Hercegovina first and foremost with ordinary people rather than to seek out journalists' usual fare of politicians, diplomats, aid workers and assorted experts. I felt that such an approach would result in a more authentic reflection of reality. Actual experience confirmed that this grassroots focus was indeed appropriate.

Although I tried during my journeys to speak with something like a cross-section of regular people in different parts of the country, I do not pretend that the conversations summarized here constitute a wholly representative sample of views in Bosnia and Hercegovina. It is much easier, for example, to speak with the more open, tolerant and peaceable members of society than with those citizens characterized less by those attributes. Despite my efforts to do so, I frankly found it fairly difficult to approach the most intolerant and energetically hateful people. Fortunately, a few of them found me.

Any individual's observations and conclusions are unique. I do not claim a monopoly on the truth. Indeed, in Bosnia and Hercegovina there are many variants of truth. If you read what I have written and reach different conclusions, I will not be disappointed.

Untangling Bosnia and Hercegovina is not intended to be a book about the wars of Yugoslav succession. It is not primarily an analysis of the breakdown of what once was Yugoslavia. Neither is this a history book. Nevertheless, there is some description of the wars. I discuss somewhat the breakdown of Yugoslavia. A fair bit of history is woven in here and there. One cannot comprehend Bosnia and Hercegovina today by examining it completely outside the context of its past.

This is not journalism. I am a former journalist, though, so my method and style undoubtedly reflect that. As in my journalism days, I try to make sure that the things presented as facts are indeed factual. What I do in *Untangling Bosnia and Hercegovina* that I did not do as a journalist is to include my intuitive perceptions and opinions. It was important to use all of my senses—including the sixth one that is intuition—in order fully to absorb and communicate the situation in Bosnia and Hercegovina.

This is not a scholarly study. I endeavor to minimize my use of footnotes, adding these only when I feel source attribution particularly important or when something needs to be said but could distract the reader from the flow of the main text were it included there. The book is not structured as a formal analysis, and it is targeted especially to the general reader.

Finally, I have not aimed to fit *Untangling Bosnia and Hercegovina* into the travelogue genre (if such a thing exists) or any other particular category. It is what it is.

That said, the main body of the book is nonetheless a narrative based upon two journeys. This narrative is preceded by a substantial introductory section, which I call "Thinking about Bosnia and Hercegovina." The several short introductory chapters lay out some basic facts and explanations that will help the reader better to appreciate the narrative that follows. I thought arranging this material at the front of the book was a more reasonable approach than to try and work all of that background into the main text. Depending upon your prior knowledge and disposition, you might just choose initially to skip over this introductory material, coming back to it as you feel it necessary or desirable to do so.

To write a book about current events is to take aim at a moving target. At some point, one must draw a line and say, "My story stops here." I am doing so today. Change is coming but terribly slowly to Bosnia and Hercegovina. Many of the stories and observations that I share here will remain relevant for a long time. Some are timeless and even speak to us of things that are fundamental to our species. With respect to my objective, I feel that I now can hold opinions about Bosnia and Hercegovina that are founded in reasonable understanding. I hope *Untangling Bosnia and Hercegovina* helps you also to comprehend better this sometimes enigmatic but always important country and its region.

Gale A. Kirking
30 July 1999

Notes on Pronunciation

I have not attempted to transform the spellings of people and place names from their Serbo-Croatian forms into some sort of English equivalent. Experience suggests that to do so contributes more to confusion than to clarity. The language is written in basically the same Latin alphabet as are English, German, French and Spanish. Serbo-Croatian uses diacritical marks to create several special letters from other Latin characters. The sounds of these letters are easily learned and are consistently applied. Although regional differences exist within the former Yugoslavia, and the "color" of vowels and "hardness" of consonants can vary slightly depending upon how letters are combined with others and their positions in a word, these differences are subtle and unimportant to the nonspecialist.

The Serbo-Croatian alphabet has 30 characters. These are presented below in three groups: 1) vowels, 2) consonants written and pronounced as in English, and 3) consonants written and/or pronounced differently than in English. Do not be intimidated by the alphabet or by Serbo-Croatian names. After all, if you pronounce the names of people and cities even close to correct, you will be far ahead of most people.

1) Vowels:

a indicates "**ah**" as in otter or father
e indicates "**eh**" as in bet or well
i indicates "**ee**" as in me or keep or jolly
o indicates "**oh**" as in flow or open
u indicates "**oo**" as in fool or shoe or flu

2) Consonants written and pronounced the same as in English:

b, d, f, g (as in **g**ood), **k, l, m, n, p, s, t, v, z**

3) Consonants written and/or pronounced differently than in English:

c indicates "**ts**" as in Betsy or Fritz
č indicates "**ch**" as in church or itch
ć also indicates "**ch**" as in church or itch
dž indicates "**j**" as in George or jewel

dj also indicates "**j**" as in George or jewel; (depending upon usage and regional dialect, **dj** can indicate the "d" and consonantal "y" sounds run together, as in bad yam)

h indicates "**kh**" as in Bach

j indicates the consonantal "**y**" as in yellow or yam

lj indicates the "**l**" and consonantal "**y**" sounds run together, as in full yam

nj indicates the "**n**" and consonantal "**y**" sounds run together, as in fun yam

r is slightly rolled or trilled, as in Spanish usage

š indicates "**sh**" as in sheep or chute

ž indicates "**zh**" as in pleasure

The accent or stress in Serbo-Croatian can be on any syllable of a word except the last one. In the case of two-syllable words, then, it is easy. The city of Mostar must be pronounced MOH-stahr (where capitalization indicates the stressed syllable). Knowing how to pronounce the name of the Yugoslav president, Slobodan Milošević (SLOH-boh-dahn Mee-LOHSH-eh-veech) is not so obvious.

A few words are particularly important and troublesome, so I will mention them here. **Hercegovina** (hehr-tseh-GOH-vee-nah) is the southern region of the country Bosnia and Hercegovina. The word **Croat** is pronounced KROH-aht, and **Bošnjak** is BOHSH-nyahk.

Maps

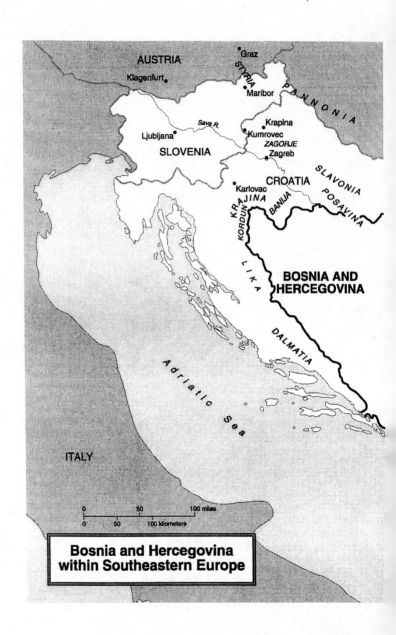

Bosnia and Hercegovina
within Southeastern Europe

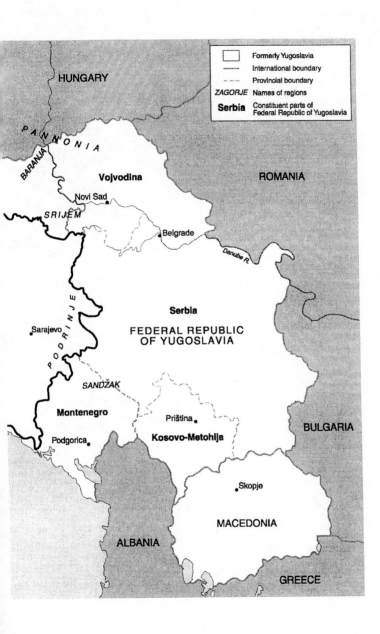

CROATIA

Bihać

Banja
Luka

Bosanski
Petrovac

Ključ

Mrkonjić
Grad

Drvar

Jajce

UK Operational Zone

Glamoč

Adriatic Sea

**Post-Dayton
Zones of Control**

Local and International Forces

0   25   50 miles

0   25   50 kilometers

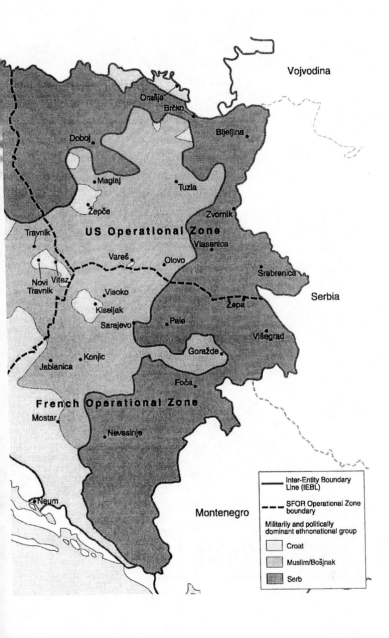

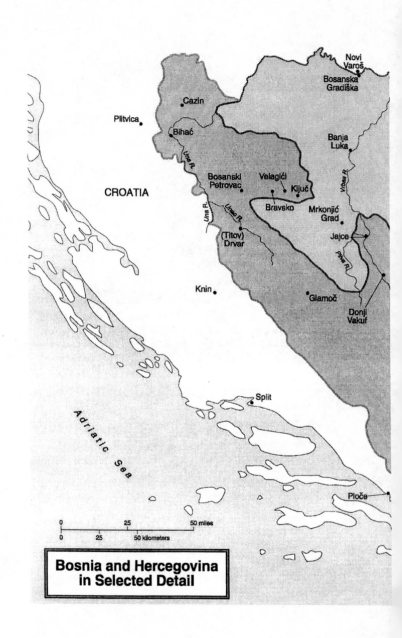

**Bosnia and Hercegovina
in Selected Detail**

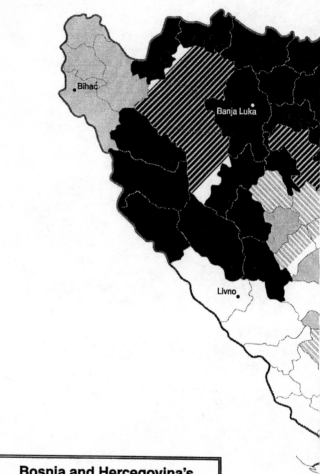

**Bosnia and Hercegovina's
Former Ethnographic Structure**

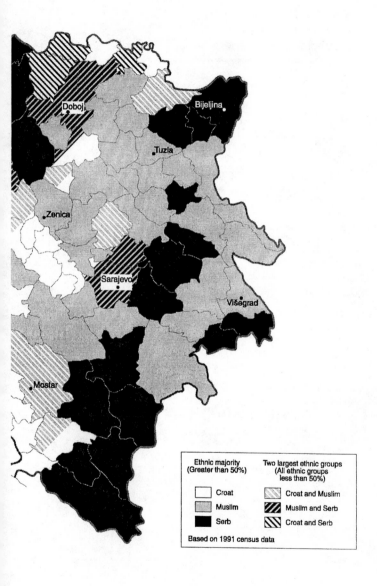

Ethnic majority
(Greater than 50%)

Two largest ethnic groups
(All ethnic groups
less than 50%)

Croat

Croat and Muslim

Muslim

Muslim and Serb

Serb

Croat and Serb

Based on 1991 census data

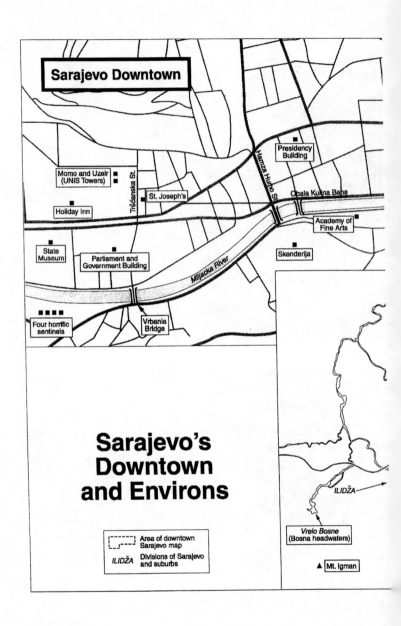

Sarajevo Downtown

Momo and Uzeir
(UNIS Towers)

Trćanska St.

St. Joseph's

Presidency
Building

Hamza Humo St.

Opala Kulina Bana

Holiday Inn

Academy of
Fine Arts

State
Museum

Parliament and
Government Building

Miljacka River

Skenderija

Four horrific
sentinels

Vrbania
Bridge

Sarajevo's
Downtown
and Environs

Area of downtown
Sarajevo map

ILIDŽA   Divisions of Sarajevo
and suburbs

ILIDŽA

Vrelo Bosne
(Bosna headwaters)

▲ Mt. Igman

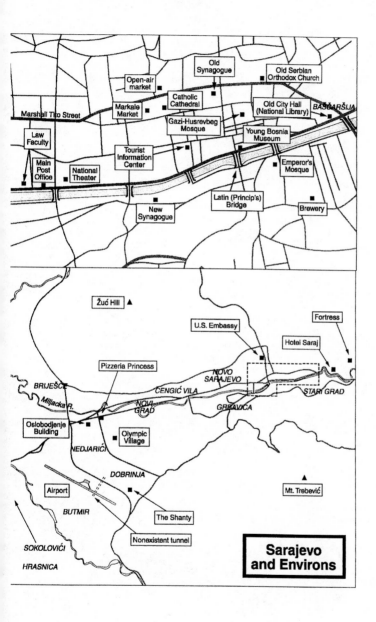

Old Synagogue

Old Serbian Orthodox Church

Open-air market

Catholic Cathedral

Old City Hall (National Library)

BAŠČARŠIJA

Marshall Tito Street

Markale Market

Gazi-Husrevbeg Mosque

Young Bosnia Museum

Law Faculty

Tourist Information Center

Main Post Office

National Theater

Emperor's Mosque

New Synagogue

Latin (Princip's) Bridge

Brewery

Žuć Hill ▲

U.S. Embassy

Fortress

Hotel Saraj

Pizzeria Princess

NOVO SARAJEVO

BRIJEŠĆE

ČENGIĆ VILA

STARI GRAD

Miljacka R.

NOVI GRAD

GRBAVICA

Oslobodjenje Building

NEDJARIĆI

Olympic Village

DOBRINJA

Mt. Trebević ▲

Airport

BUTMIR

The Shanty

SOKOLOVIĆI

Nonexistent tunnel

Sarajevo and Environs

HRASNICA

Prologue:
Innocence Abroad

I had only just arrived in Zagreb, Croatia's capital city. It was my first visit. Perceiving that I was a bit bewildered, another youngish man on the streetcar kindly offered me his assistance. He, like me, as it turned out, had come in on the overnight train from Paris. Coincidentally, too, we were on our way to the same hotel. After checking in, we agreed to meet in the evening and go together into the old town for drinks.

This visit to Yugoslavia, in summer 1990, was a relatively minor stopover on a trip to Russia, Ukraine, Belarus and Poland. Momentous changes were occurring in the Soviet Union and former Soviet Bloc. I was intent upon witnessing these up close. Yugoslavia seemed no more than a sideshow in those days, and, frankly, I was not paying it much attention. I did not yet realize how close that country was to coming apart or what that would mean to the rest of Europe and the world when it did.

The friendly stranger from the streetcar had been born in France into a Croatian family. He presented me that evening an animated discursion in mixed French, English and Serbo-Croatian. The longer we spoke, the more eccentric I found his character to be. Actually, he mostly spoke and I mostly listened.

He was in Zagreb on business—to do market research. His business plan was to wholesale pornography to Croat retailers who were selling into a growing market, since controls over such activities were becoming less restrictive. The commercial strategy hinged upon an assumption that the Croatian market for smut would be less sensitive to timeliness than was the French market. He, therefore, would buy prurient overstock accumulated in French publishers' warehouses and sell it for very reasonable prices (but with a lucrative markup) into Croatia.

A passionate nationalist, this member of the Croat diaspora spoke of Croatia's long and glorious history. He told me of how Croatian President Franjo Tudjman and his Croatian Democratic Union (HDZ) had been very successful in the spring election. I heard about the origin and symbolic importance of the *šahovnica*, the red-and-white checkerboard crest that Tudjman and his HDZ had put onto the Croatian flag. There was a controversy at the time as to whether or not the *šahovnica* should be worn on policemen's uniforms. Ethnic-Serb policemen in Croatia strongly objected to the idea, as they, along with other Croatian Serbs, associated that symbol with the World War II Croatian fascists known as *Ustaše*.

The *Ustaše* were not so bad, my new acquaintance insisted. Much worse were the Serb *Četniks*. Perhaps the *Ustaše* killed some Serbs, he allowed, but the *Četniks* killed many more Croats and other innocents. On the subject of killing, the youngish man insisted that most of what one reads in books about the World War II Holocaust is much exaggerated. There were not nearly so many Jews killed as is reported. He carried on about that last subject for quite awhile.[2]

Toward the end of the evening, a conflict began to brew on the other side of the table-lined and narrow plaza upon which we were seated. There was no physical violence, just the threat of violence. A husky, bearded fellow was in verbal confrontation with several others who were together at a table. The burly man was on his feet. It seemed he had had a few drinks all right, and he was ready to take on the whole tableful of those who were taunting him.

A couple policemen came by, the showdown broke up, and the bearded man moved along. The Croat-Frenchman was quite unhappy to see it end so peacefully. He had been getting more and more agitated as the scene had played itself out. He kept saying things along the line of: "It's only just starting now, but something is going to happen. People are being careful so far, but you will see. Something big is going to happen." I did not really know what he was talking about. To me, this looked like the beginning of a typical brawl between rednecks, fueled by a volatile but not acutely dangerous mix of too much testosterone and alcohol. My new acquaintance scarcely was thinking and talking about the tempest in a teapot that was brewing a few yards away. He was looking well beyond that and saw a real and violent storm brewing on a much grander scale.

I just figured I had met up with a wacko and did not take his vague premonitions very seriously.

•   •   •   •

There already was a lot of armed fighting in former Yugoslavia by the time I moved to Prague, Czechoslovakia in summer 1992, and the warfare had spread into Bosnia and Hercegovina. I was nearer to the conflict now than were most Americans, and I even took an interest stronger than average. I had studied Balkan history at university and even had struggled through two years of Serbo-Croatian language classes. Still, I did not think deeply about the Yugoslav crisis at that time. The increasingly violent struggle over the rocky chunks of a crumbling Yugoslavia seemed far away and easy to dismiss as hopelessly beyond the strategic interest and influence of the US.

---

[2] In addition to his being a nationalist politician, a former Communist and Yugoslav army officer who had fought with Tito's Partisans, Franjo Tudjman is a historian. He is known for arguing in his writings that Serbs have exaggerated the numbers of *Ustaše* killings in order to undermine Croatian interests.

Besides, I was trying to learn some Czech and to build a career and life in what was for me a new and rapidly changing country.

Within a few months, Czechoslovakia would itself come apart, albeit without violence. The Czech Republic and Slovakia's "velvet divorce" occurred without a referendum and seemed as much as anything to reflect an irreconcilable conflict between two egotistical politicians: the arrogant Czech academician turned politician Vaclav Klaus and the Slovak communist turned demagogic nationalist Vladimir Mečiar. The 1990s were a time when conceited men (they were mostly men, after all) helped tear apart formerly communist countries while dazed proletariats looked on and hoped all would work out for the best.

Serbs, Croats and Slavic Muslims were showing up in my Czech language courses. Yugoslavs were opening restaurants and small businesses in Prague and elsewhere. As the term "ethnic cleansing" found its way into every European language, refugees from former Yugoslavia began appearing in European cities.

•   •   •   •

When I left my job on 31 March 1998, I did so with a plan to take a year off for travel, study and personal assessment. One activity for this sabbatical year was to drive the length of the Croatian coastline to Dubrovnik. I had wanted to do this for about 15 years. In the days when that idea had first come into my head, Yugoslavia was still regarded by many as a sort of socialist paradise. Tito, Yugoslavia's strong and charismatic leader since World War II, had just died in 1980. That had been cause for some concern as to the country's future, but few in the West had yet been willing or able to see the extent to which Yugoslavia already was straining under centrifugal forces and decay.

During spring 1998, as I am reading up on background, refreshing my language skills and planning my travel through Slovenia and Croatia, I find my attention and interest migrating increasingly to Bosnia and Hercegovina. Alpine Slovenia will be pleasant and the Adriatic seacoast beautiful, of course, but postwar Bosnia and Hercegovina, it seems to me, will be fascinating.

I will end my Croatian trip with a one-day drive the length of Bosnia and Hercegovina from Dubrovnik, through Mostar and Sarajevo, up the Bosna River valley, then across the Sava River to Croatia. This windshield survey will convince me to return in a few weeks' time. I intend to travel about and to stay long enough to really learn something.

Introduction:
Thinking about Bosnia and Hercegovina

A Vulnerable Land

If the former Yugoslavia could be said to have had a heart, it lay somewhere in Bosnia-Hercegovina. Probably, that heart was Sarajevo. If there was a "Yugoslav Idea" of Croats, Serbs, Slavic Muslims and ethnically assorted others living together in toleration, and perhaps even harmony, within a compact and shared space, then that idea had its highest expression in Bosnia-Hercegovina.

I do not speak of the Yugoslav heart and idea in order to romanticize nostalgically about Sarajevo, Bosnia-Hercegovina, or the former Yugoslavia. Their pasts and wasted potential have been fully mourned, eulogized and embellished elsewhere. This excursion into Bosnia and Hercegovina seeks not drama and sentimentality, after all, but understanding. Nevertheless, it would have been no great exaggeration to see in colorful Bosnia and Hercegovina a near microcosm of Yugoslavia. It was precisely here, too, that the forces of competing South Slavic nationalisms could have been expected to collide most explosively.

As the Cold War had come to its end, Yugoslavia, like the Soviet Union and Warsaw Pact, had been in danger of crumbling into its component parts. Pinned between the heaviest pieces of the Yugoslav structure, Bosnia-Hercegovina was seriously imperiled. Its relative poverty, ethnonational diversity and history added to that vulnerability.

Bosnia-Hercegovina was a complicated place even before it was hit by the whirlwind wars of Yugoslav succession that raged through much of the early-1990s. Those wars left more than 200,000 people dead, more than a million others displaced from their homes, and most of Bosnia and Hercegovina's housing stock, industrial plants and countryside devastated at best or totally destroyed at worst. We should not expect to find that the wars did much to reduce that complexity.

We will travel into a torn and tangled web of historical controversy, cultural diversity, complex human relations, and rugged geography. If we are to take away from this journey a fuller and more accurate appreciation for today's reality in Bosnia and Hercegovina, then we need some background that will help us to appreciate what we will encounter. This part of *Untangling Bosnia and Hercegovina* provides such a background and, I hope, will stimulate our thinking.

•　　•　　•　　•

The more complex is a question and its context the greater is the need to simplify. Greater, too, is the temptation to oversimplify. Such was the case when it came to explaining events in Yugoslavia and in Bosnia-Hercegovina early in the 1990s. Popular in the West was the simple notion that this was a country and region torn by ancient and deeply ingrained hatreds between irreconcilable ethnic groups. This view was taken to justify outside countries' standing clear from (or even nudging forward) Yugoslavia's bloody disintegration. According to that sentiment, those Yugoslavs had to be left to fight amongst themselves until there would be clear winners and losers, until territorial issues were resolved once and for all, and until all parties to the fighting had exhausted themselves. Some nationalist forces within former Yugoslavia also promoted this view—both to their local and foreign audiences.

Later, more sophisticated explanations gained popularity. Yugoslavia's economic decline through the 1980s had created conditions inviting an internal struggle for limited resources and wealth. That had been accompanied by political deterioration, which gave rise to a competition also for political power. Because the Cold War had ended, meanwhile, the West no longer needed a united and independent Yugoslavia to stand as a moderate-communist counterbalance to the Soviet Bloc. Demagogic political leaders were taking advantage of internal strife and external disregard to satiate their own urges for power. Brandishing the powerful tool that is nationalism, they were duping the masses into differentiating and segregating themselves, turning upon one another, and, along the way, assisting political leaders to carve out their own states and fiefdoms. Eventually, outright warfare created opportunities for the most ruthless elements of society (including some nationalist politicians) to enrich themselves. This situation created incentives for those gaining from the hostilities to continue and to intensify the cycles of violence.

To speak in terms of "ancient hatreds" between the peoples of Bosnia and Hercegovina is perhaps not entirely accurate. It would be wrong, though, to deny that there have been very real ethnonational divides and that there are deep historical roots to the conflicts. Roman Catholicism, Orthodoxy and Islam have struggled amongst themselves for the Balkan people's souls and identities for centuries. For hundreds of years, too, various states and political entities have entered the fray, and often these were united with religious forces. Conflicts based in nationalist struggles emerged more recently in history, but these, too, are connected to the distant past.

•   •   •   •

Through the next several short chapters, we will briefly survey this land, its people and the neighborhood. We will consider how Serbs,

Croats and Bosnia and Hercegovina's Slavic Muslims perceive their own and one another's identities. We will touch upon Bosnia and Hercegovina's and former Yugoslavia's importance in European and global politics and diplomacy. Finally, while packing the car, so to speak, we will review how Yugoslavia came apart, how Bosnia and Hercegovina was put on a course toward war, and what others in the world tried to do about it. Then we will be ready to experience today's Bosnia and Hercegovina.

Geography and People

South Slavs and Their Neighbors

Until it all began coming apart in the summer of 1991, Bosnia-Hercegovina was one of six republics that together constituted Yugoslavia. The others were Serbia, Croatia, Montenegro, Slovenia and Macedonia. The largest of these, Serbia, had included two autonomous provinces: Kosovo and Vojvodina. The two provinces remain within Serbia today, although their autonomy effectively was revoked in 1989.

Yugoslavia's name means "the land of the South Slavs." The country was created on 1 December 1918 from pieces of the dismantled Austro-Hungarian and Ottoman (Turkish) empires. These two empires, which between them had contained virtually all the lands inhabited by South Slavs, disintegrated as a result of World War I.[3] The victorious great powers (i.e., Britain, France, Italy and the US) determined that the South Slavs and their lands would be united into a single country. "Yugoslavism," which is the concept of bringing all South Slavs into a single state, was not entirely imposed by outsiders, though. The idea also had supporters among the South Slavs themselves. Originally, this new state was not named Yugoslavia. Rather, it was called the "Kingdom of Serbs, Croats and Slovenes."

After World War I, South Slavic political and intellectual leaders generally regarded it as advantageous to unite their related groups into a single state. Not all these ethnonational leaders, though, had the same motivations. Serbia and the Serbs were the largest territory and people. The Ottoman Turks had controlled Serbia from the 14th to the 19th centuries. Throughout the 19th century, Serbia increasingly had shaken itself out of the Turkish yoke, established itself as a kingdom, and eventually achieved international recognition as an independent state. Serbia's independence made it unique among these South Slavic territories at the close of World War I.[4] In that not all Serbs had lived in the territory known as Serbia, Yugoslavia and Yugoslavism allowed for all the Serbs to be brought into a single state. The most arrogant of

---

[3]Serbia and Montenegro were internationally recognized as being independent from the Ottoman Empire already as of 1878.

[4]To simplify the discussion, I am here ignoring Montenegro. Essentially a second Serb-populated state, Montenegro never was fully controlled by the Ottoman Turks. Neither was it merged with Serbia to create a larger state.

Serbs saw South Slav unity as a way to make territorial gains by diplomatic and political means. Serb leaders expected to dominate the new state, and Serbs did just that.

Slovenes, by contrast, lived in a very small area. Italy and Austria also wanted that territory, and the Slovenes' claims were weakened by the fact that never in their history had they had any political entity of their own. Joining Yugoslavia was their best protection against being divided up between the Italians and Austrians.

The territory of Macedonia, meanwhile, was coveted by all of its neighbors. At that time, Macedonian ethnonational identity was only weakly developed and not much recognized by the world at large. Within what might be termed this "first" Yugoslavia, Macedonia was generally referred to as "South Serbia," although Serbs constituted only a fraction of its population.

At the start, Yugoslavism looked like a good deal, too, for Croats and Croatia. (There was, though, also a movement rallying for an independent Croat state, and, as we shall see, this force was not subdued within the new state.) It gave them an opportunity to get out from under their traditional overlords, the Hungarians and Austrians. Croats had not intended, though, to be bullied about by Serbs in this new country. Forming Yugoslavia created an arena within which Croat and Serb nationalisms would duke it out during the 20th century. Croatia and Serbia were the fighters' corners; Bosnia and Hercegovina constituted the center ring. In the first Yugoslavia, Bosnia and Hercegovina were regarded merely as geographic regions that were inhabited by a mixture of Serbs, Croats and Muslims. There was plentiful room for debate as to whether the Slavic Muslims there were really Islamicized Croats, Islamicized Serbs or something more unique.

Today, just two of the six republics—Serbia (with Kosovo and Vojvodina) and Montenegro—remain in a state entity calling itself Yugoslavia. Bosnia and Hercegovina, Croatia, Slovenia and Macedonia all are independent countries.

Before the wars of Yugoslavia succession, the country's population of 23.5 million was distributed (by republic and province) as follows: Serbia (proper), 5.8 million; Croatia, 4.7 million; Bosnia-Hercegovina, 4.4 million; Macedonia, 2.1 million; Vojvodina, 2 million; Slovenia, 1.9 million; Kosovo, 1.9 million and Montenegro, 0.6 million.

•   •   •   •

The 1995 Dayton peace agreement, which ended the warfare in Bosnia and Hercegovina, gave international recognition to the fact that the 1992–1995 wars there had effectively divided that country into two entities. These are known as the "Federation of Bosnia and Hercegovina" and "Republika Srpska."[5] The Federation includes 51% of Bosnia and Hercegovina's territory while Republika Srpska takes in the remaining 49%. In theory, there is a central government for all of Bosnia and Hercegovina. In practice, the two entities largely conduct their own affairs. Republika Srpska's politicians are especially reluctant to participate in the so-called "joint" governing institutions.

Located on the very edge of what once was Yugoslavia, Slovenia was the first republic formally to leave Yugoslavia, and its independence is today secure. Slovenia is small, ethnically homogeneous and has its own language. That country has no expansionist ambitions, and its Austrian and Italian neighbors no longer seriously expect to carve off any parts of Slovenia for themselves.

Macedonia's situation is more precarious. Also rather small, Macedonia is surrounded by Albania, Greece, Bulgaria and Serbia (including Kosovo). It has an ethnically mixed population and its neighbors harbor various claims on Macedonia's territory and people. If the neighbors ever begin fighting over Macedonia, the world will see a very ugly free-for-all.

Macedonia and Slovenia mark the southeastern and northwestern extremes of former Yugoslavia. Linguistically, too, they stand a bit to the side from the other South Slavs. Unlike the other South Slavs within the territory of the former Yugoslavia, the Slovenes and Macedonians have languages of their own.[6] By contrast, there is a single dominating language in Serbia, Croatia, Montenegro and Bosnia and Hercegovina. This language is generally known (outside of these countries themselves, anyway) as Serbo-Croatian. It is different from, but related to, Slovenian and Macedonian. Broadly speaking, all Serbo-Croatian speakers live together. Each of the four countries in the Serbo-Croatian language zone has a common border with each of the others. It is within this core of former Yugoslav republics that most of the blood has been shed during the wars of Yugoslav succession. Each of the four has feuded with each of the others. Bosnia and Hercegovina has found itself, literally, in the middle of it all.

---

[5] I will also refer to the Federation of Bosnia and Hercegovina variously as "the Federation," the Croat-Muslim Federation" and the "Muslim-Croat Federation." Republika Srpska is sometimes referred to as the "Bosnian Serb Republic," although I have not chosen to use that term.

[6] The Macedonian language is very closely related to Bulgarian.

Although it has a major language in common, this Serbo-Croatian zone is populated by three major ethnonational groups, two smaller ethnic populations and one or two groups of ambiguous ethnic identity. The largest group consists of Serbs. As of today, the Serbs reside primarily in Serbia, in Montenegro and in the Republika Srpska entity of Bosnia and Hercegovina. Serbs are much less dispersed among the others today than they were before the wars of Yugoslav succession. Croats, the second-largest group, live especially in Croatia and in the Federation entity of Bosnia and Hercegovina.

The third ethnonational group is made up of Slavic Muslims within Bosnia and Hercegovina. These days, Muslims within the Federation entity of Bosnia and Hercegovina are encouraged by their nationalist leaders to identify themselves as "Bošnjaks." The Bošnjak population is today concentrated in the Federation. During the wars of Yugoslav succession, tens of thousands went there when they were driven from their homes in what is now Republika Srpska. Many Slavic Muslims fled abroad, leaving former Yugoslavia territory altogether. Some are now returning, but many will never come back to live.

The minor ethnic groups are important in the broader, regional context but are not directly relevant to understanding Bosnia and Hercegovina. In Kosovo, a formerly autonomous province of Serbia, the majority of people are ethnic Albanians. These Kosovar Albanians speak a non-Slavic language (Albanian) and are not closely related to Slavs by blood. Although most Kosovar Albanians share the Islamic religious heritage with Bosnia and Hercegovina's Slavic Muslims, the two groups are otherwise unrelated. Vojvodina, the other formerly autonomous province of Serbia, has a large minority population of ethnic Hungarians. They are not Slavs, and their Hungarian language is unrelated to South Slavic languages.

Another group of Muslims has traditionally lived in a region known as Sandžak, which is a broad band of territory straddling the Montenegro-Serbia border. Historically, this Sandžak strip has connected the Slavic Muslim territory of Bosnia and Hercegovina with the ethnic-Albanian Muslim territory of Kosovo. Other Muslims may regard their coreligionists within Sandžak as neither Bošnjak nor Kosovar.

The ethnonational identity of Montenegrins also can be ambiguous. Generally speaking, the Montenegrins are Serbs, but they have also a competing Montenegrin identity. Through much of their history, Montenegrins have been cut off from other Serbs. They evolved an independent, tribal society within their extremely mountainous land.

While other Serbs and South Slavs were subjugated by Ottoman Turks, Hungarians and Austrians, the Montenegrins fiercely and (as a practical matter) successfully defended their independence. Some of them might regard themselves as belonging to a super strain of Serbs.

Bosnia and Hercegovina on the Map

Let us now turn our focus back to Bosnia and Hercegovina and its situation. According to the 1991 census, taken just before Yugoslavia disintegrated, its population consisted of 44% Muslims, 31% Serbs, 17% Croats and 8% people identifying themselves as "Yugoslav" or others. Although demographic estimates are now not very precise, the wars during the 1990s probably reduced the proportion of Muslims and increased that of Serbs in Bosnia and Hercegovina. More Muslims than Serbs were killed or driven out, and many Serbs who fled Croatia ended up in Republika Srpska. The proportions of Serbs and Muslims in the country's total population may now be nearly equal. Given such diversity and ethnic overlap with neighboring republics, it is hardly surprising that Bosnia-Hercegovina's situation was precarious in a crumbling Yugoslavia.

As seen on the map, Croatia has the shape of two jaws spread wide but solidly gripping two sides of the almost triangular territory of Bosnia and Hercegovina. Croatia looks to be all mouth and no body; it can hold on but cannot swallow. Croatia's gaping maw presses Bosnia and Hercegovina against Serbia and Montenegro (which together continue to call themselves Yugoslavia).

Within Bosnia and Hercegovina the raggedly shaped Muslim-Croat Federation and Republika Srpska look like two giant amoebas, each of which is trying to engulf the other. Where the amoebas' membranes press together delineates the so-called Inter-Entity Boundary Line (IEBL). To see them on the map, Republika Srpska would appear now to be the stronger positioned vis-á-vis the Federation in the contest for each to devour the other. Republika Srpska squashes against the Federation's core and presses the Croat-Muslim entity hard against Croatia's lower jaw.

Let us not, though, carry this analogy too far. In wartime, in fact, Serb nationalist forces once controlled nearly three-quarters of Bosnia and Hercegovina territory, not just half. The Dayton peace agreements drew the IEBL. This internal boundary largely reflects the military situation on the ground after Croat-Muslim forces, in 1995 offensives, took away from the Serbs much that the Serb nationalists had militarily gained earlier in the fighting. Republika Srpska is smaller and much weaker than it once was. A better analogy then, perhaps, is to see

Republika Srpska as consisting of two lobes—a western lobe and an eastern one. The Federation presses in between these lobes and nearly splits Republika Srpska's mass into two at its slenderest spot.

In purely geographic (but not political) terms, Bosnia and Hercegovina consists of the two regions that give the country its name. Much of the outside world, of course, has come to use the simpler name Bosnia for the entire country. Bosnian Muslims have a tendency to do so, as well. Naturally, Hercegovinians do not appreciate that very much. Hercegovina is the southern tip of the country that, roughly speaking, lies below Lake Jablanica. Bosnia is the larger portion to the north.

Known at the time as "Hum," this southern region had been annexed into the medieval Bosnian state in the 14th century. So, perhaps there is some justification for calling the combined territory Bosnia. On the other hand (and when one speaks of historical boundaries in the Balkans there is almost always an "on the other hand"), Hum was renamed Hercegovina because, in the 15th century, its local ruler had taken the title of *herceg* (meaning "duke"). He had done so to emphasize his independence from the Bosnian state.

As one learns about the wars of Yugoslav succession and, in particular, the struggles relating to Bosnia and Hercegovina, the names of other smaller regions lying within these countries often come up. Among these are Krajina, Dalmatia, Banija, Lika, Kordun, Slavonia, Posavina, Srijem (called "Srem" by Serbs), Baranja and Sandžak. All of these have their own histories and were ravaged by fighting and/or massive and coerced migrations during the recent wars. We will not consider each of these here, but all are shown on a map at the front of the book.

Physical Geography and Economy

Smaller than the State of West Virginia, Bosnia and Hercegovina is a rather tiny country with few natural economic advantages. Mountains and rivers are the most important defining elements of its physical geography. For the most part, where mountains do not cover the country it is nevertheless hilly or has high elevation. In most areas, the mountains and hills are forested. There are a few areas that are relatively level or with lower elevations, but these are exceptions to the rule. Major cities and the most fertile soils are in river valleys. The many rivers endow the country with great hydroelectric potential. Other major industries include mining, forest products, agriculture and manufacturing. There are many farms, but these are mostly small and traditionally not highly productive. With its rugged, natural beauty, Bosnia and Hercegovina would seem to have substantial potential for tourism. But that industry has never been well developed. In Yugoslav days, tourism had been especially associated with neighboring Croatia, which controls most of the Adriatic seacoast.

Wars during the 1992–1995 period lay waste to much of the country's economic potential. Many mines and factories do not operate at all now, and others do so only at very low levels of output. Manufacturing operations were badly damaged in the fighting, are starved for investments in new technologies or have lost their markets. Bosnia-Hercegovina had depended largely upon the integrated Yugoslav market, but that mostly crumbled away with the collapse of the country and of the individual republics' economies.[7] Already in Yugoslav times, Bosnia-Hercegovina had ranked among the poorer of the republics, along with Macedonia, Montenegro and, especially, the province of Kosovo. That these poorer areas of the country had been drawing investment resources for their economic development away from the relatively wealthier republics (in particular, from Slovenia and Croatia) had been a source of resentment and contributed to Yugoslavia's collapse. Centrally targeted investments in Bosnia-Hercegovina had emphasized defense-related industries. This could be justified on grounds of military strategy as well as of economic development. Because historical experience had shown that rugged Bosnia-Hercegovina would be particularly difficult for an invading enemy to capture, the republic had figured prominently in defense planning.

As a general matter today, foreign investors would not yet consider Bosnia and Hercegovina sufficiently stable such that they would commit large investments to the country. Reforms to create suitable legal structures (such as to protect property rights) are not yet completed. State-owned enterprises have not yet been privatized (although mass privatization programs for large enterprises are beginning during 1999 in both the Federation and Republika Srpska).[8]

---

[7]Tiny Slovenia, which was always more productive and wealthier relative to the other Yugoslav republics, is exceptional in that it continues to do well economically.

[8]As in several other formerly communist countries, citizens in Bosnia and Hercegovina are to receive vouchers that they can use to bid for shares in enterprises being privatized. The vouchers also may be used to buy state-owned apartments. The sell-off of state assets has been repeatedly postponed.

The potential for unrest and even renewed fighting poses too great a risk for foreign investors.

Tens of thousands of acres of Bosnia and Hercegovina's agricultural land has remained uncultivated since the wars ended. Farms have been abandoned by their owners, houses and barns destroyed, livestock killed and farm equipment ruined. Agriculture is discouraged, too, by the fact that several hundred thousand landmines remain in the ground across the country.

On the plus side, Bosnia and Hercegovina has a relatively well-developed system of roads (although no superhighways) that are in reasonably good repair. There is substantial private enterprise in the retail and small-scale business sectors. Earnings repatriated to Bosnia and Hercegovina from refugees working abroad must be considerable. Indeed, to go abroad as "guest workers" in Germany and other foreign countries was common practice even in communist times. Nevertheless, slow growth and high unemployment in western Europe was reducing opportunities to work abroad already in the 1980s. In that Yugoslavia was a surplus-labor country and opportunities to work abroad amounted to a sort of safety valve, diminished job openings in western Europe also contributed to economic decline and rising tensions in Yugoslavia's final years.

In short, Bosnia-Hercegovina was before the wars a republic with limited economic resources and a surplus workforce. In the independent country, and in spite of a much-reduced population, that situation continues to exist.

Ethnonational Identities

Defining Names and Terms

Whatever their original causes, the wars of Yugoslav succession and their aftermath are generally viewed in terms of multiple struggles between ethnic or national groups.[9] The terminology used in reference to those groups can get confusing. We should sort it out at the outset.

Within Bosnia and Hercegovina, the relevant groups include Croats, Serbs and Slavic Muslims. There is a fourth major group, too: people who do not want to be identified with any ethnic or national tag. Perhaps they were born of mixed marriages; maybe they just refuse to be associated with efforts to divide people into mutually exclusive groups. People in this fourth group may prefer to be known simply as "Bosnians" or, if they are from the south, even as "Hercegovinians." These are geographic names and carry no ethnic or national meaning. A few people may wish to think of themselves as "Yugoslavs," although that term has fallen particularly out of favor.

We sometimes refer to "Bosnian Croats" and "Bosnian Serbs" in order to distinguish ethnic Croats and Serbs living in Bosnia and Herce-govina from those in the neighboring countries of Croatia and Serbia. The terms are generally accurate but not always well regarded locally.[10]

References to Bosnia and Hercegovina's Slavic Muslims create more confusion. Sometimes, we see and hear these Muslims referred to simply as "Bosnians." In that case, the intent generally is to differentiate them from Serbs and Croats, whether the latter be from Bosnia and Hercegovina, Croatia, Serbia or elsewhere. It is not accurate, though, to use the term "Bosnian" as a synonym for "Slavic Muslim of Bosnia or Hercegovina," and I will never use the term Bosnian in that way in this book. It is not too surprising that this inaccurate term has come into use in the West, as nationalistic Muslims have in some sense also encouraged that usage locally.

---

[9] The argument can be made that all of this violence was more than anything due to a drive by a minority of intolerant nationalists and powermongers to impose their will on a majority that would prefer just to live in an unsegregated and tolerant society. I recognize that view, but my intent here is to provide some definition without getting into the polemics.

[10] I say "generally" (but not always precisely) because some of these "Bosnian" Serbs or Croats actually are Hercegovinian.

There are two terms in the local language meaning Bosnian. These are "*Bosanac*" and "*Bošnjak.*" *Bosanac* is the geographic term, which translates very properly into English as "Bosnian." There is no simple translation of *Bošnjak* into English, however. It is the word that Bosnia and Hercegovina's Slavic-Muslim nationalists have anointed as the politically correct term to use for members of their group. At least until the world gets accustomed to the term Bošnjak, we will still sometimes hear the word Bosnian used in English to refer to Bosnia and Hercegovina's Slavic Muslims.

So, who are these Serbs, Croats and Bošnjaks? How are they different from one another? How are they similar? If they are fighting one another, or if war is being waged in their collective names, they must be distinguishable one from another, right? Do they constitute "ethnic groups" or "nations" or something else? These are key questions, and this chapter will address them.

There is an entire literature written by (and for) academic specialists who focus upon what does and does not constitute an ethnic group, a nation or some other form or level of group identity. For the majority of us who are not interested in academic hair-splitting, we can get by just fine with a less precise terminology. I will generally use the term "ethnonational" to refer to these groups. Let us assume simply that "ethnic group" is a simpler form, or stage, of group identity and that "nation" is a more developed one. Members of an ethnic group recognize that because of their common race, language or other factors, they all belong to a single group. If a group constitutes a nation, some of its leading members are sure to be saying their group ought to have a state (or country) of its own, if it does not have one already.[11]

The groups known as Croats, Serbs and Bošnjaks all can be placed somewhere along that group-identity continuum between ethnic group and nation. Each is probably at a different place, with Bošnjaks closer to the ethnic end and Serbs nearest the national end.

Some defining characteristics of group identity are generally agreed upon. These may (but do not necessarily in every case) include: 1) a shared racial origin or blood relationship, 2) a language in common, 3)

---

[11]Because it corresponds with local usage, I will occasionally use the term "nation" also in reference to these groups. In former Yugoslavia, people use the term "*nacija*" to indicate group identity. Asked one's *nacija*, a person is likely to answer "Catholic," "Orthodox" or "Muslim." This term may be translated into English as "nation," but its meaning locally is not quite the same as either of the English-language terms ethnicity or nationality.

a unifying religion, 4) a shared historical experience, which may include national myths, 5) a common living space, 6) a political consciousness and urge for statehood, 7) an actual state under the group's own control, although it may be occupied also by other, minority or less powerful groups, and 8) a common set of customs, folk traditions and higher cultural achievements.

Let us examine each of the three groups in terms of these group-identity criteria.

Racial Origin

Croats, Serbs and Bošnjaks all are generally regarded as Slavs, but that should not be taken to mean they are in any sense pure-blooded. Their Slavic origins were not in the Balkans where they live today.

In the remote and obscure past, where history melts into prehistory, tribes of people known as Illyrians lived in the western Balkan Peninsula and in what is today Bosnia and Hercegovina. Illyrians were not Slavs. They were ancestors of the non-Slavic people that today are called Albanians.

During the early decades of the Christian era, while the ancient Romans spread their empire over the western Balkan Peninsula, the Slavic tribes still were far away from what would one day be the land of the South Slavs. The Slavs were developing and differentiating themselves in their primordial homeland, in a space roughly corresponding to the area where today's countries of Ukraine, Belarus and Poland join. These Slavic tribes began spreading beyond their incubative habitat as early as the 5th and 6th centuries. By the 7th century, they had migrated well to the north, west and south.

The Slavic tribes further differentiated themselves as they migrated in their various directions, settled into new homelands, and blended into their own cultures the elements of other cultures. There emerged from this differentiating process the West Slavs (including Poles, Slovaks and Czechs), East Slavs (Russians, Ukrainians and Belorussians) and South Slavs (Croats, Serbs, Slovenes, Bošnjaks, Macedonians and Bulgarians).

Slavs began arriving and spreading through the Balkan Peninsula in the 6th century. We scarcely can identify these first Slavs to arrive by any meaningful names. To some extent they mixed their genetic material both with that of their new Balkan neighbors and with that of other races with which they were associated during their migrations. One can, however, identify tribes that might be differentiated as Croats or Serbs settling on the western side of the peninsula in the 7th and 8th centuries. At that time, their self-identities probably had more to do with their own tribal groups than with larger groups that would have called themselves Croats and Serbs. They were concentrated at first along and not far inland from the Adriatic coast. The Croats and Serbs were in quite close proximity to one another and spoke variants of a single language. Croats were generally farther north and the Serbs farther south. Meanwhile, there still were plenty of Slavs of mixed descent about from earlier migrations. Still other Slavs, who were neither Croats nor Serbs, were migrating into the area which we today call Slovenia.

In a development unrelated to these early migrations, some of those known today as Serbs probably had ancestors who were not Slavs at all, but who rather were Vlachs. The Vlachs belonged to another ancient race that is related to the Romanians. Vlachs were nomadic shepherds and, when they were Christianized, generally became Orthodox rather than Catholic. When they settled among the South Slavs, their identity tended to blend with that of the Serbs, who also were Orthodox.

In any case, there was probably much genetic blending going on throughout the Balkan Peninsula in the centuries of and following the Slav immigrations. To generalize, then, there is a certain degree of blood relationship, but it probably links Serbs, Croats and Bošnjaks to one another about as much as it sets them apart from one another.

Common Language

Serbs, Croats and Bošnjaks all speak Serbo-Croatian. Croats tend, though, to call this language Croatian, Serbs to call it Serbian and Bošnjaks to call it Bosnian.[12] Linguists with nationalist inclinations claim there are distinct Serbian, Croatian and Bošnjak languages. Although that really is not true today, they are working to create that reality.

Serbo-Croatian can be, and is, written in two wholly different alphabets. In Serbia, a Cyrillic alphabet similar to that used in Russia and Ukraine is used. Serbs in Bosnia and Hercegovina may also prefer to write in Cyrillic, especially in these days of heightened nationalism. Croats and Bošnjaks use the Latin alphabet. This is the same lettering system as is used to render English and other west European languages

---

[12]As with the *Bosanac-Bošnjak* distinction in reference to people, there are two distinct terms regarding language that may be translated into English as "Bosnian." One term suggests there is—or should be—a unique language for Bošnjaks, another suggests there is—or should be—a Bosnian language that would cut across ethnonational differences and be spoken by all people of Bosnia and Hercegovina.

but with some additional characters. In Yugoslav days, all schoolchildren were taught both alphabets. That is no longer the general rule.

In modern Serbo-Croatian one may identify three major dialects, one consisting of three important subdialects. All are mutually comprehensible. Before the wars of Yugoslav succession, just two among these five major variants were widely spoken in Bosnia-Hercegovina: the *Jekavsko* and *Ikavsko* subdialects of the *Štokavski* dialect. The other *Štokavski* subdialect, known as *Ekavsko*, is dominant in Serbia proper. Serbs in Bosnia-Hercegovina did not speak *Ekavsko*. Nevertheless, Serb nationalists generally assert that *Ekavsko* is the genuine Serbian language rather than just a dialect or subdialect. From the viewpoint of linguistic classification, this claim is nonsense.

Croats in and around Zagreb (within Croatia proper) speak a dialect of Serbo-Croatian called *Kajkavski*. In Croatia's Istrian and Dalmatian regions, though, the third dialect (the fifth variant overall), known as *Čakavski*, is spoken.[13] As virtually no Croats in Bosnia-Hercegovina traditionally spoke either *Kajkasvski* or *Čakavski*, but rather one of the same *Štokavski* dialects as did their Muslim and Serb neighbors, it is even more difficult for Croat nationalists to invent or lay claim to a unique national language than it is for Serb nationalists to do so.

The Cyrillic alphabet, then, can be a group-identifying characteristic for Serbs. Otherwise, language has more to do with the region in which one lives than to one's ethnonational identity. Linguistic reconstruction, education and conscious effort by those who speak the language would be required for the three groups to evolve distinct languages.

Unifying Religions

Religion may be the most important characteristic distinguishing the three groups. Serbs are by tradition Orthodox Christian. There has been a strong Serbian Orthodox Church since the early-13th century. Unlike Catholicism (from which the Orthodox or Byzantine Church broke in the Great Schism of 1054), Orthodoxy has national churches and no supreme pope. Russians, Greeks and others also have national Orthodox churches.

Although many Serbs are not religious today, they do recognize the Serbian Orthodox Church as an important repository of their

---

[13]Serbo-Croatian dialects are named according to the word for "what" that is used in each. Thus, in most areas "what" is rendered as "*što*," although elsewhere it is "*kaj*" or "*ča*." To explain the subdialects of *Štokavski* is more complicated. Let it suffice just to look at the spellings of the word meaning "milk" in the *Ekavsko*, *Jekavsko* and *Ikavsko* subdialects, respectively: *mleko, mlijeko* and *mliko*.

national identity. There is a strong spiritual element to Serbian nationalism. This reflects a long historical connection between church and state. The church canonized as saints the early Serbian rulers, and it preserved the Serbian identity through nearly five centuries that the Ottoman Turks ruled over Serb lands.

Croats are by tradition Catholic. Indeed in Bosnia and Hercegovina the term "Catholic" is synonymous with "Croat," just as "Orthodox" is synonymous with "Serb." In that there is but one pope and the Roman Catholic hierarchy very much centers on its leader in the Vatican, the Croats cannot have a national church the way the Serbs do. Whereas Serb identity lives within a national church, Catholicism is only one very important element in the Croatian identity. Imbued with nationalist fervor, though, Croatian Catholic leaders can be quite assertive and sometimes act quite independently from Rome

Catholicism links Croatia to the religious and cultural traditions of the Roman and Austro-Hungarian empires.[14] Among those traditions is hostility to the Byzantine and Orthodox world. A split between the Roman Catholic West and Orthodox Christian East traces back to the fourth-century founding of Constantinople (today's Istanbul) as the capital of the Eastern Roman Empire. Constantinople had been created as the eastern capital in an administrative reform intended to make the Roman Empire more manageable. The dividing line became more rigid as the years passed, however, and the cultural and political entities on both sides became more defined and defiant in their separateness. Ultimately, the Eastern Roman Empire evolved into the entirely separate Byzantine Empire. Differences, particularly those religious in nature, hardened into outright animosities. The dividing line between Roman and Byzantine empires, and therefore between Orthodox and Catholic Christendoms, cut from north to south straight through what would one day be Yugoslavia (bisecting also Bosnia and Hercegovina). The breach between the churches and cultures never has been mended.

In the 20th century, antagonism between Catholicism and Russian-fostered, atheistic communism has reinforced this division. This is demonstrated, for example, by a case in which the conflict had the effect to promote a Croat cardinal, Alojzije Stepinac, to national hero. Although his reputation was badly tainted by his support of Croatia's Nazi-backed *Ustaše* regime during World War II, Stepinac (who was then an

---

[14]In that Protestantism is an offshoot of Catholicism, Croats' Catholicism links them more generally to the entire Western Christian tradition.

archbishop) is highly regarded by Croats and the Vatican for his postwar resistance to communism and the sufferings he endured in defending the faith. His symbolic place in the Croat identity was assured when Pope John Paul II beatified Stepinac on a visit to Zagreb in October 1998.

Islam is the traditional faith of the Bošnjaks. But, relative to Catholicism and Orthodoxy, Islam has a shorter history (less than 600 years) in Bosnia and Hercegovina. The distant ancestors of today's Muslim Slavs, then, were likely either Catholic, members of an independent Bosnian Church or Orthodox. Both Croat and Serb nationalists have argued that these Bošnjaks really are Croats or Serbs and that, therefore, Croatia or Serbia has a claim, on the bases of ethnicity and history, to justify annexing Bosnia and Hercegovina (or partitioning it between Croatia and Serbia).

To counter Serbian and Croatian claims on Bosnia and Hercegovina territory, the engineers of *Bošnjaštvo*, or Bošnjak nationalism, argue that Bošnjaks existed even before the Ottoman Turks brought Islam to Bosnia and Hercegovina.

Deep and Intertwined Historical Roots

Bošnjaks, Serbs and Croats all can trace unbroken histories for their own ethnonational groups back to and beyond medieval states. These three medieval states emerged and expanded at various times. Each would include some lands that at other times lay within the other two. None of these were what could be called "national" states in the modern sense. The concepts of nations and of nation-states came much later. Rather, these were decentralized and rather transient entities. They were assembled from various lands by conquest, by diplomacy (including negotiated marriages between ruling families) and by cutting deals with the assorted local lords on those lands. When the strong leaders that had created or held together these entities died or otherwise fell out of the picture, the medieval states would consequently shrink dramatically, be absorbed into neighboring states or disappear entirely.

Croats Built First, Then Were Absorbed

A Croatian state was beginning to take shape in the 9th century. The Croats were by that time already Christianized, and their souls were under the care of the Roman church. That state reached its greatest expanse in the reign of King Tomislav, who ruled in the early-10th century. Croatia had its ups and downs over the next couple centuries. Finally, in 1102, the leading noble families signed onto an agreement with the Hungarian King that effectively ended Croatia's independence. The agreement granted Croatia a right to self-rule within the Hungarian Kingdom, but the Hungarians were often lax about honoring their end of the bargain. Until Yugoslavia was created at the end of World War I, then, Croatia remained within the Hungarian Kingdom. At its greatest expanse, the Croatian state had included most of present-day Croatia and Bosnia (but not Hum/Hercegovina).

Serb State Founded on Orthodoxy

Croatia was already firmly within the Hungarian grasp by the time the Serbian state began to take shape during the 1180s under a ruler named Stefan Nemanja. Nemanja established not only a state but also a dynasty that would continue to build that state for the next two centuries. This *Nemanjić* dynasty also founded and built the Serbian Orthodox Church, although the Serbs had been Christianized much earlier under Byzantine rule. One of Nemanja's sons, a monk, founded the Serbian church and later was canonized as St. Sava. Stefan Nemanja eventually abdicated to another son and also became a monk. He, too, was canonized by the church that his son had established. The *Nemanjić* dynasty created an enduring tradition of close cooperation between church and state. Successive *Nemanjić* rulers regularly allocated some of their wealth to erecting church buildings and monasteries. The Church reciprocated by sanctifying the *Nemanjić* dynasty and incorporating its memory into Serbian Orthodox traditions.

Many religious buildings of the *Nemanjić* era exist still today in what is northern Kosovo. At various times and at its greatest expanse, the Serbian medieval state took in much of what is today Serbia, Kosovo, Albania, Macedonia, Greece, Montenegro and Hercegovina, as well as small portions of Croatia and Bosnia. The 14th-century's Stefan Dušan was the greatest state builder in the *Nemanjić* line. After Dušan's death, though, his empire came apart. In the late-14th century and into the 15th, these lands increasingly were incorporated into the expanding empire of the Ottoman Turks.

The historically not very accurate story of one particular battle over Serb-held lands is burned into the Serbs' national memory. It is the 1389 battle of Kosovo Polje. Serbs regard this battle as marking the point in time when Serbia lost its statehood to the Turks. That loss was to be avenged and never forgotten. The myth is greater than the reality, though, as are myths generally. Kosovo Polje was not the most important battle against the Turks, it probably was more like a draw than a loss for the Serb side, and it was not a purely Serb-Turk battle.

Bošnjaks Point to Bosnian Kingdom

Among the non-Serbs fighting at Kosovo Polje were soldiers sent by King Tvrtko, who by that time ruled a Bosnian state that took in most of what is today Bosnia, all of Hercegovina, and portions of Croatia, Montenegro and Serbia. *Bošnjaštvo* theorists lean pretty strongly upon demonstrating a historical continuity between Tvrtko's state and modern Bosnia and Hercegovina.

This Bosnian state had begun to take shape and to assert itself under one Ban Kulin, who ruled late in the 12th century. Hungary, which considered that territory to lie within its sphere of influence, did not much appreciate Kulin's presumptuousness to rule alone. Kulin was Catholic and, nominally, at least, so was his state. But Orthodoxy existed there, too. Sometime during the 13th century an independent Bosnian Church also asserted itself. Thereafter, neighboring Catholic rulers and churchmen continually would accuse the Bosnians of heresy.

Stjepan Kotromanić, who ruled in the 14th century, is notable for having annexed Hum, thereby bringing a considerable Orthodox population into the medieval state. Indeed, Kotromanić probably was originally Orthodox himself, although he later converted to Catholicism and also tolerated the Bosnian Church. During his reign, Kotromanić invited the Franciscan order of Catholics into Bosnia in order to improve the functioning and practices of the church. If ever there were a leader of Bosnia and Hercegovina particularly tolerant of religious diversity, it would seem to have been Kotromanić.

The abovementioned Tvrtko was a son of Kotromanić. Like his father, Tvrtko continued to expand the territory under his rule. Although the Bosnian state reached its greatest expanse under Tvrtko, Bosnia and Hercegovina, like Serbia, fell under Turkish rule during the 15th century.

While there is general agreement that the state created under Kulin, Kotromanić and Tvrtko was predominantly populated by Slavs, there has been much argument since the 19th century as to whether those were Croats, Serbs or some other brand of Slavs. *Bošnjaštvo* theorists are prone to argue that these were principally descendents of the "undifferentiated" Slavs that had migrated to the Balkan Peninsula ahead of the Croats and Serbs.

Ottomans Cultivated Separate Identities

The centuries of Ottoman rule over Serbia, Bosnia and Hercegovina actually strengthened the Serb identity, helped to forge a Bošnjak identity, and preserved the potential for the Catholics in Bosnia and Hercegovina to identify with their coreligionists beyond the frontier in Croatia (which was not under Ottoman control but remained within the Hungarian Kingdom and later the Austro-Hungarian Empire). That is because the Ottoman administrative system did not greatly interfere with the religious practices of those over whom it ruled.

Under the Ottoman Empire's *millet* system, religious communities were allowed to thrive. Religious leaders were made responsible for certain local governing functions within their own communities. There were tax advantages and other benefits for embracing Islam, but the Ottoman state had no general policy of forced conversion. Nonetheless, a high proportion of its subjects living within Bosnia and Hercegovina, as well as in Kosovo and Albania, did convert. Not all Muslims in Bosnia and Hercegovina became wealthy landowners under the Ottomans, but the privileged landowning class there was predominantly Muslim. This could not have had a positive effect on relations between the Muslims and their Catholic and Orthodox neighbors.

The Ottomans established Orthodox and Jewish *millets* within the South Slav lands. The Orthodox *millet* was rather favored early on, but that favoritism diminished when Orthodox Russia began seriously to threaten the Ottoman Empire in the 18th century. Catholics did not have their own *millet*. They nevertheless were granted charters legalizing their communities, which were to be administered by the Franciscans. It was not lost on the Ottomans that the Catholics within their empire naturally had interests in common with neighboring Austria and Hungary, two states posing constant threats to the Ottoman Empire.

Within the Ottoman Empire, then, it was always very clear who was who, and the distinctions were made upon the basis of religion. That differentiation was reinforced further in that the various religious communities forbade intermarriage between groups. This system of separate but (especially in Bosnia and Hercegovina) interspersed communities created an environment in which members of each group collectively could define themselves vis-á-vis those of the other groups.

Slavic Muslims, certainly not yet known as Bošnjaks, were commonly referred to in those days as "Turks." They were a favored class but on the whole a minority in comparison to the Serbs. It must have been a jolt when the Ottoman Turks eventually lost control over

Bosnia and Hercegovina. Surrounded by Christians, the Muslims could no longer count on a ruling power more or less on their side. The Orthodox constituted a large but second-class group. Their tradition and folk epics reminded them of what they had lost in 1389, and the Serbs sometimes strongly resisted Turkish rule. Catholics in Bosnia and Hercegovina, an even smaller group and whose clergy had links to Croatia, may have felt their natural cultural ties were more with Catholics beyond the border than with the Muslims and Serbs in neighboring villages.

Common Living Space

At the beginning of the 1990s, none of these three ethnonational groups really were concentrated in living spaces that they could call wholly their own. But their situations in this regard differed strikingly one from another.

Croats in Croatia, Bosnia and Hercegovina

Before the wars, more than three-quarters of Yugoslavia's 4.6 million Croats lived in Croatia proper. Most of the remaining Croats lived in Bosnia-Hercegovina, where they numbered nearly 800,000. Croats were most concentrated on the western side of Bosnia-Hercegovina but were mixed also with Serbs and, especially, Muslims. There also were important Croat communities in central and northern Bosnia. A smaller but significant number of Croats were in Serbia's Vojvodina, adjacent to Croatia's eastern border.

More than three-fourths of Croatia's total population was at that time made up of Croats. Serbs constituted the main minority group in Croatia, numbering about 600,000. By the time the fighting ended in Croatia in 1995, all but about 150,000 of these Serbs had been driven out or had left of their own accord. Croatia's population today is probably more purely Croat than it ever has been. The western edge of Bosnia and Hercegovina (bordering on Croatia) is now mixed Croat-Muslim, with the proportion of Croats rising dramatically as one moves south.

Wars Concentrated Serbs

So long as Yugoslavia existed, Serbs lived within a single country but were much more dispersed across the republics than were Croats. Before the recent wars, approximately three-quarters of Yugoslavia's more than 9 million Serbs and Montenegrins resided in the territory which today still calls itself Yugoslavia. Serbs constituted strong majorities in Serbia and in Montenegro, a slight majority in Vojvodina and a small minority in Kosovo (only about 10% of the population versus 90% that was ethnic Albanian). At that time, roughly 15% of Yugoslavia's total Serb population lived in Bosnia and Hercegovina and another 6% in Croatia.

Prior to the 1991–1995 wars, the Serb population within Bosnia and Hercegovina was widely dispersed and living among Croats and Muslims. Serbs were most concentrated in northwestern Bosnia, in eastern Hercegovina (adjacent to Montenegro) and (mixed with Muslims) in much of eastern Bosnia. In Croatia, Serbs constituted majorities in the region known as Banija and in several other areas. The latter generally were areas adjacent to similarly large Serb-populated areas in Bosnia and Hercegovina. Substantial Serb concentrations had existed also in Croatia's eastern Slavonia, adjacent to Vojvodina.

Following the 1992–1995 wars and the Dayton peace agreement, Serbs within Bosnia and Hercegovina find themselves concentrated into the Republika Srpska entity. Many Serbs that had been expelled from Croatia also live now in Republika Srpska, while others have gone farther on to Serbia. Croats and Muslims mostly have been driven out of Republika Srpska territory. The Muslims of eastern Bosnia (with the exception of a small enclave in and around the city of Goražde) were exterminated or expelled. Thus, Serbs in Bosnia and Hercegovina are no longer much dispersed among Croats and Muslims but live in a smaller and ethnically more homogeneous zone.

Bosnia and Hercegovina Only Bošnjak Homeland

As members of former Yugoslavia's three main groups of Muslims have little affinity for their coreligionists from within the other two, the Bošnjaks constitute a distinct group.[15] Numbering nearly 2 million, Bošnjaks constituted a plurality but not a majority in Bosnia-Hercegovina. Bošnjaks are today interspersed among Croats in the Federation. While Croats and Serbs within Bosnia and Hercegovina can relate their identities to the adjoining countries of Croatia and Serbia, there is no real equivalent adjacent homeland for the Bošnjaks. Their only home is Bosnia and Hercegovina.

Although Serbs, Croats and Muslims were much interspersed across prewar Bosnia-Hercegovina, there nonetheless was substantial

---

[15]In addition to the Slavic Muslims of Bosnia and Hercegovina, the Sandžak Muslims (who are primarily Slavs) and the Kosovar Albanians, there is a small but substantial population of Muslims in Macedonia. Some Macedonian Muslims are Slavs and others are ethnic Albanians. Bosnia and Hercegovina also has a small group of Muslim Gypsies.

separation on a local basis. The ethnonational groups tended to live in their own communities. This self-segregation was particularly evident in rural areas, but existed also to various extents even in the largest cities, including Sarajevo.

Political Consciousness and Nation-Statehood

National identities and strivings for nation-statehood are phenomena arising especially during the late-18th and 19th centuries, taking on ideological forms in the wake of the French Revolution. Like many other nations (or potential nations), Serbia and Croatia, within the Ottoman and Austro-Hungarian empires, respectively, had their own national awakenings; their intellectual and political elites began to contemplate statehood separate from their imperial masters. Serbs and Croats could look back through time to once-powerful medieval states for inspiration. The Serbian Orthodox Church had preserved historical memory, and the Croatian nobility, even under the Hungarians, had held onto some small vestiges of self-rule. Serb and Croat intellectuals began to investigate and to think deeply about their collective histories, their unique folk cultures, and the potential to develop a standard literary language from one or another local vernacular.

No substantial Bošnjak or multiethnic-Bosnian group identity would emerge until the 20th century. When such developments did begin, and as has been particularly obvious also in the Bošnjak movement of the 1990s, they would occur in response to intensifying Croatian and Serbian nationalisms and political consciousness.

Serb political leaders, intellectuals and mercantile interests moved first, fastest and furthest in pressing forward Serb national development. Two Serb uprisings against their Turkish overlords during the period 1804–1814, along with continuing efforts in following years, brought first autonomy and then independence and expansion for a Serbian Kingdom. The leaders of the two rebellions came from competing ruling families: the Karadjordjevićes and the Obrenovićes. Collapse of the Austro-Hungarian and Ottoman empires in World War I opened new possibilities for South Slav national developments.

Serb King for First Yugoslavia

A member of the Karadjordjević family was named to head a constitutional monarchy in the newly created Kingdom of Serbs, Croats and Slovenes. Nationalist political infighting, in particular between Croat and Serb political figures, eventually caused a frustrated King Aleksandar to abrogate the constitution in 1929, to rename the country as the Kingdom of Yugoslavia and to rule it as a dictatorship. Ethnonationally torn Yugoslavia, it seemed, was not suited to democracy. One of the last straws that broke the back of the parliamentary experiment had been the murder or wounding of five Croat deputies within the parliamentary chamber. The assailant, a Montenegrin deputy, was an extreme Serb nationalist. Later, in 1934, a Croat nationalist organization, headquartered in already fascist Italy and dedicated to establishing an independent Croatian state, arranged to have Aleksandar assassinated.[16]

On the radical fringe, at least, Croatian political nationalism was already well developed and aggressive by the time of Aleksandar's assassination. This is somewhat ironic in that the earliest efforts in 19th-century Croatia to build a national consciousness had aimed to bridge the gaps between the South Slavs by diminishing the distinctions between Croats, Serbs and others. Yugoslavism and Serb-Croat rivalry were counterflowing currents, as they would be, too, during the life of the second Yugoslavia that emerged from World War II.

The Muslims of Bosnia-Hercegovina in this first Yugoslav state could see they had much to lose in the conflict that was being fought out in the collective names of their Orthodox and Catholic neighbors. They had gotten a taste of that earlier when, with the World War I defeat of the Ottoman Empire, their Christian neighbors had robbed and killed a good many Muslims. There had been an economic, or social-class, motivation for much of this vengeance, as the major landowners had been Muslim and many Christians were their serfs. Nevertheless, the violence had been directed also towards poorer Muslims, who were associated in the minds of some Croats and many Serbs with the former, and defeated, Ottoman oppressors.

The Yugoslav Muslim Organization (YMO), founded in 1919, became the leading political party speaking for Bosnia-Hercegovina's Muslims. In 1920, an election was held to select delegates to a constituent assembly that would shape the new South Slavic state. Voting was along ethnic lines, and the YMO's position as a powerful force to be courted by Croat and Serb parties was thereafter assured. That Muslims threw their support behind a uniquely Muslim political party foreshadowed what would occur 70 years later, when the first

---

[16]The actual assassin was a Macedonian and associated with a revolutionary group in Macedonia.

democratic elections were held in Bosnia-Hercegovina within a fatally weakened Yugoslavia.

Analogous also to the situation in the 1990s was the necessity for Muslims in multiethnic Bosnia-Hercegovina to confront the questions as to where they should fit into the new state and what manner of state organization would best serve their interests. The very name of this new Kingdom of Serbs, Croats and Slovenes did not recognize the Muslims' importance—or even their existence. Serb leaders wished after World War I to organize a centralized state. That best suited their ethnonational interests since Serbs were spread about this South Slav living space. Croat leaders wanted to create a federation of autonomous entities with boundaries drawn on an ethnonational basis.

The danger in federation was that the Muslims of Bosnia-Hercegovina would see their territory and rather weakly formed identity absorbed into a Croat entity or a Serb entity or be divided between the two. In a sense, the YMO got the best of both worlds. A centralized state was created, although it was subdivided into 33 provinces with limited local government. Six provinces were created within the historical boundaries of Bosnia-Hercegovina, and so its integrity as a single but multiethnic unit was basically maintained. But it did not last long.

Bosnia-Hercegovina's integrity was broken when the frustrated King Aleksandar later reorganized the Kingdom. It was soon to be violated even more brutally.

Bosnia-Hercegovina Divided, Absorbed, Restored

Yugoslavia would enter into World War II already divided. As the storm clouds of renewed war gathered in Europe, Croat nationalists made ever more threatening demands that there be an autonomous Croatia within Yugoslavia. Without consulting Bosnia-Hercegovina's Muslims, Serb and Croat leaders reached an agreement in 1939 to create an autonomous Croatian *Banovina* that would include Croatia and approximately one-third of Bosnia. The extreme *Ustaše* were not satisfied with that arrangement, however. They wanted complete Croatian independence and all of Bosnia-Hercegovina. Within less than two years, the *Ustaše* would have it their way. When Germany declared war on Yugoslavia in 1941, the Independent State of Croatia was immediately established. The new state was to be administered by the *Ustaše* under protection of the Italian and German military forces. It included all of Bosnia and Hercegovina.

The independent Croatia did not survive. When Yugoslavia was recreated after World War II, Bosnia-Hercegovina's historic borders were again recognized and it became one of the six Yugoslav republics. The republic's Muslims once more resided within a single political unit, but this was a multiethnic and not a Bošnjak entity. There has never been a recognized Bošnjak state. There scarcely could be so long as Croats, Serbs and Muslims were thoroughly mixed within Bosnia-Hercegovina. Still, from Yugoslavia's birth there existed a weak but real collective political consciousness among Bosnia-Hercegovina's Muslims.

Communists Experiment with Nationalism

Communists ruled the second Yugoslavia. They officially recognized five constituent nationalities: Croats, Serbs, Slovenes, Macedonians and Montenegrins. Muslims, whether in Bosnia-Hercegovina or elsewhere, were seen as a separate group but without a specifically national identity. The communists' early hope, however, was that ethnonational differences would disappear over time and that all the country's citizens would eventually come to see themselves as Yugoslavs. That did not happen, and in the mid-1960s a new view became official ideology. The new perspective was that ethnonational differences did exist and would continue but that the groups could cooperate and thrive together within a pluralist, socialist state.

As Yugoslav policy on nationalities evolved, so, too, did the official classification of Muslims. In the 1948 census, most Muslims stated their identity as "Uncategorized." There was no census category for "Muslims." In the 1953 census, though, citizens were given the choice to declare themselves as "Yugoslavs," and most of the Muslims in Bosnia-Hercegovina so identified themselves. The 1961 census, then, allowed them to declare themselves as "ethnic Muslims," but only in the 1981 census were they given the opportunity to declare themselves as "Muslims in the national sense." These official identities were equally open to Muslims elsewhere (e.g., in Sandžak, Kosovo and Macedonia), so the changes in census category did not directly bolster a separate Bošnjak identity.

New (Dis)Order after Tito

The first multiparty elections in 1990, however, did reinforce that identity. By that time, the Republics of Croatia and Slovenia had already elected nationalists to their republic governments. Theirs had been the first Yugoslav elections to put other parties in competition with the communists. Yugoslavia had not yet come apart at that time, but individual republics were increasingly assertive, the central government was steadily weakening, and the Yugoslav League of Communists was fading as a political force.

In Bosnia-Hercegovina, three nationalist parties emerged and garnered the most votes in the 1990 election. For the most part, voting followed ethnonational lines. These same three parties continue to dominate politics in today's Bosnia and Hercegovina. The Muslim party was created first. It was called the Party of Democratic Action (known as "SDA" for its initials in Serbo-Croatian). SDA was, and remains, headed by Alija Izetbegović. The Croat party is the Croatian Democratic Union (HDZ). This is a branch of the party by the same name that is the leading political force in neighboring Croatia, where it is headed by Croatian President Franjo Tudjman. The Serb Democratic Party (SDS) elected as its president Radovan Karadžić.

This overwhelming and, arguably, spontaneous political subdivision leads one to question just how much the people really accepted nonethnic "Yugoslav" or "Bosnian" identities at the close of the Tito era. As of 1990, many—and perhaps most—people in Bosnia-Hercegovina clearly regarded their ethnonational identities as somehow politically better self-defining than were any ethnically blind political ideologies. Of course, the main ideologies competing with nationalisms in 1990 were variations on the discredited theme of communism.

Questioning Brotherhood and Unity

Under Tito, there had existed a slogan and ideology of interethnic relations that went by the name of "Brotherhood and Unity." It held that Yugoslavia's various ethnic groups and nations were committed to respect one another and work together toward a common good. A skeptic might point out that communists had many slogans—and that people rejected them all just as soon as the strong arm of the state and party stopped forcing them down their throats.

The subject of Brotherhood and Unity is a controversial one. Yugoslavia's disintegration may seem evidence enough that Yugoslavs scarcely had internalized Brotherhood and Unity as an axiomatic and immutable rule by which to conduct their personal and civic lives. Nevertheless, some intellectuals and academics in the West had come to regard Brotherhood and Unity as substantive. Along with some diplomats and journalists, these specialists had been among those with the greatest exposure to Titoist Yugoslavia. Some tended rather to romanticize that country. They were influenced by their friendships and exposure to Yugoslav intellectuals they had met in Belgrade, Zagreb, Sarajevo, Ljubljana and on their own university campuses. There was a lot of Yugoslav idealizing when I was at university during the late-1970s and into the 1980s. For one to suggest in such circles today that maybe Brotherhood and Unity was never much more than another empty communist slogan is to touch a raw nerve.

Customs, Traditions, Cultural Achievements

In the final analysis, a Serb is a Serb, a Croat is a Croat, and a Bošnjak is a Bošnjak because each recognizes and feels himself or herself to be so. Consciousness of one's group identity is reinforced every day by the symbols, customs and rituals that comprise a group's cultural *milieu*. These might include the way one greets one's neighbor, prepares food or courts a potential mate. Group identity can be manifest in the folk song one sings when working in the fields, in the embroidery on a blouse, in the color of a sash, in the name given to a child, in what one drinks to celebrate a small or great achievement. The style in which a man builds his house, the way a woman cares for her baby, and the traditions that govern how an extended family organizes its activities—these also can reinforce group identity.

Although their cultures have much in common, Serbs, Croats and Bošnjaks each have cultural elements of their own that distinguish them from one another. Some anthropologists believe that differences in everyday customs (as occur, for example, in manners of dress, spoken expressions and dietary habits) reflect an effort, conscious or unconscious, for members of one group actively to differentiate themselves from members of other groups. These differences are sometimes subtle and even invisible to outsiders. Some elements of traditional culture, it should be noted, reflect more local or regional uniqueness than they do specifically ethnic differences. Some customs prominent in the villages are forgotten when villagers move to the cities, settle into a more modern life and blend more with other groups.

The subject of everyday cultural differences in Bosnia and Hercegovina is very broad and complex. Several worthwhile books dealing with one or more groups are mentioned in the bibliography.[17]

In addition to their customs and traditions, the Croats, Serbs and Bošnjaks also can claim association with what we might call "higher"

---

[17]Consider in particular the works cited that are by Bringa, Lodge, Halpern, Sivric, Lockwood and Mihailovich.

culture. By this, I refer to the likes of literature, performance arts, painting, sculpture and special contributions to the various spheres of science and ideas. Higher culture often builds upon folk culture. Melodies from traditional songs are incorporated into symphonies, for example. Folk legends are transformed into plays, operas and formalized literature. Literary language is formed from vernacular speech. Traditional costumes, festivals, myths and legendary heroes may be immortalized in paintings and in sculptures. All of Bosnia and Hercegovina's ethnonational groups can claim—rightly and proudly—that they have made important contributions in the areas of higher culture.

Physics of Ethnonational Interaction

Ethnonational identity is part natural phenomenon and part deliberate human creation. However they are formed, group identities emerge most rapidly and distinctively when groups somehow compete with one another. The more groups clash, the sharper may be the distinctions.

That, it seems to me, is as natural in human society as is the perpetual and predictable motion of the planets, moons and sun within our solar system. In his third law of motion, Isaac Newton, the 17th-century scientist, revealed that bodies in motion influence one another. When one body exerts a force on another, that second body also exerts an equal and opposite force upon the first. The larger body will change more slowly under that equal force and the smaller body more quickly, but each will necessarily affect the other. So it goes also, I believe, when groups of human beings interact.

Pressed by Turkish rule within the huge Ottoman Empire, Serb nationalism grew quickly. Austro-Hungarian domination likewise stimulated Croat identity. The pressure of many smaller nations, meanwhile, contributed to both empires' slow but sure deterioration. Once the Muslims of Bosnia and Hercegovina were cut loose from the empire that had protected them and they confronted Croat, Serb and Austrian forces, their ethnonational identity had necessarily to solidify lest it be destroyed altogether. So, too, the Serb-Croat rivalry must have its effect on both of those groups.

We will soon see up close just how these ethnonational groups interact with one another, with that fourth group of people who reject nationalism, and with the international community that aims to see Bosnia and Hercegovina rebuilt. In that complex interplay lies the future of Bosnia and Hercegovina as a state and society.

Cohesion and Disintegration

Geopolitics and the South Slavs

Location and volatility long have given give the South Slavic territories a geopolitical importance greater than their size or direct economic significance might indicate. Prior to World War I, remember, these lands had been divided between the Austro-Hungarian and Ottoman empires. The Russian Empire also took an interest in the region. Russia's interest reflected an affinity for the Serbs and neighboring Bulgarians, who were fellow Slavs and Orthodox. Perhaps more importantly, though, that concern was due to the Russian Empire's rivalry with the Austro-Hungarian and Ottoman empires and its desire to occupy non-Balkan lands currently held by those other empires but bordering upon the Russian Empire.

Through the 19th century, the Ottoman Empire was steadily crumbling due to its internal decrepitude and external pressures. Austria-Hungary, too, was past its imperial prime. It only was a matter of time until both empires would come apart. Marked by fracture lines between East and West, Europe and Asia, Catholicism and Orthodoxy, Christianity and Islam, the Balkan Peninsula was bound to experience internationally momentous events.

In 1875, there were uprisings in Hercegovina and then in Bosnia against the Muslim landlords. Subsequently, Serbia and Montenegro declared war on the Ottoman Empire. Then Russia invaded the Ottoman Empire. The Ottomans lost this Russo-Turkish War. In the war's wake, Austria was allowed in 1878 to occupy Bosnia-Hercegovina and Sandžak, although these remained nominally within the Turkish empire. This was a blow to Serbia and to a grand design for creating a unified South Slavic state under Serbian rule. Serb nationalists were angrier still when Austria formally annexed Bosnia and Hercegovina in 1908.

Some voices in Austria-Hungary called for a quick but decisive war against Serbia before its nationalist agitators stirred up too much trouble among the other Slavs within the Austro-Hungarian Empire. The 1914 assassination in Sarajevo of the visiting heir to the Austro-Hungarian throne provided the pretext to declare war on Serbia. This set off a chain of events that activated military alliances and plunged Europe into the general conflagration that was World War I.

Following World War I (and again after World War II), a combination of internal and external forces created Yugoslavia, held it together for a time, and ultimately tore it apart. The first Yugoslavia was conceived in the spirit of national self-determination. The hope after World War I was that if more homogeneous nation-states were created in Europe then the continent would be more in harmony and less likely to tear itself apart again. In fact, Yugoslavia was itself neither homogeneous nor harmonious.

During the interwar period, South Slav nationalisms became steadily stronger and more aggressive—both within Yugoslavia and without. Particularly active in Italy and elsewhere abroad were the Croatian *Ustaše* and the Internal Macedonian Revolutionary Organization (VMRO). Some members of VMRO wanted autonomy for Macedonia within Yugoslavia, others sought unification with Bulgaria, but all opposed Serb rule.

Although the chaos and violence were great there, in the big picture Yugoslavia was a relatively minor theater of war during World War II. The Yugoslav army and central government surrendered quickly. Germany and Italy divided the country amongst themselves early on and gave some pieces to their allies, Hungary and Bulgaria. There were two important resistance organizations, known as the *Četniks* and the Partisans. The *Četniks* were led by Colonel Draža Mihailović, who was the armed forces minister for the Yugoslav government in exile. Made up primarily of Serbs, the *Četniks* opposed Croats and the *Ustaše*, as well as communists. The Partisans were ethnically broader based. This group was led by Josip Broz Tito, a charismatic communist, who would emerge from World War II as the father of the second Yugoslavia.

Allied forces (in particular, Britain and the USSR) vacillated in their support for *Četniks* or Partisans, depending upon which group appeared most effective in diverting German and Italian soldiers, attention and resources from the other fronts. Meanwhile, Partisans, *Ustaše* and *Četniks* fought one another and committed atrocities that remain burned into people's memories to this day. Much of the most vicious and ethnonationally motivated violence occurred in Bosnia-Hercegovina.

Tito's Yugoslavia in the Cold War

During the Cold War that followed World War II, Tito's Yugoslavia enjoyed a pivotal position between East and West. Bosnia-Hercegovina and the Muslim Slavs played a special role during that period.

Tito and his Yugoslav communists dramatically broke with Stalin and Moscow in 1948. They had refused to be bullied, to see Stalin and Moscow make light of their wartime accomplishments, and to subordinate Yugoslav policies and interests to Soviet direction and whims. The US and West welcomed and fostered this breech in the communist world, offering

Yugoslavia economic aid, membership in international organizations and respectability. The main objective was to weaken Soviet hegemony in the central and eastern European states that the USSR had come to dominate after World War II. Tito played this hand for all it was worth.

Also during this period, Yugoslavia was a founder and leader of the Non-Aligned Movement (NAM). Established by Third World countries during the 1950s, the NAM members chose not to harness their foreign policies to either Soviet or US superpower interests. Since a number of NAM members were Islamic countries, Muslims in Bosnia-Hercegovina were helpful in building relations in the Third World.

As the Cold War wound down and the 1980s gave way to the 1990s, Yugoslavia no longer could depend upon the US, Western Europe and NATO countries for handouts and other support. The Soviet menace had lost its frightfulness. What's more, with communist governments dropping left and right, even the Yugoslav communists—previously favored for their moderation—no longer seemed so laudable or even important.

Yugoslavia Comes Apart

South Slav observers sometimes quipped during the Cold War that Tito was perhaps the only real Yugoslav. He had been president for life. There were concerns that with his death would come also Yugoslavia's demise. Tito expired in 1980. Ailing Yugoslavia lingered on for another decade, but nearly all of its vital systems were failing: The economy was stumbling and gasping. A reformed central government and communist party were losing their grip. Cancers of nationalism were spreading slowly at first but threatening to hasten their growth. Meanwhile, the West grew less willing to provide life support.

Symptoms of Yugoslavia's languishing economy during the 1980s included falling real incomes, high (but sometimes stop-and-go) inflation, poor export performance, high foreign debt and rising unemployment. The causes were manifold: An experiment in socialist enterprise management called "worker self-management" (for which Yugoslavia was renowned) was proving a failure. Borrowing from abroad had been too easy previously; now it became much more difficult. Recession in Europe diminished opportunities for surplus workers to go to Germany and other countries to earn money that they could send back home. There were poor investment decisions and corruption. Cooperation between the Yugoslav republics broke down in the areas of regional development, structural reforms and other economic matters. Where a collective will to address and solve problems was needed, there were instead quarrels and obstructionism.

Prior to his death, Tito had sought to develop a political and governing structure that would discourage the rise of a single, dictatorial successor who might not be so benevolent and broadly Yugoslav in his outlook. A 1974 constitutional reform had created a more confederal system. All of the six republics and two autonomous provinces had seen their status as constituent units of Yugoslavia more clearly defined. Greater decision-making authority had been devolved to the republic and province levels. A collective presidency had been created, and it was to have a member from each of the eight constituent entities. All decisions at the highest, or central, level were to be made by consensus. That, in practice, gave each republic and province veto power over collective initiatives.

This constitutional reform had negative effects, and these became more apparent and severe when all the provisions kicked in after Tito's death. It enabled communist officials at the republic level to gather more power into their hands. Each republic fought increasingly for its own parochial interests. Republic leaders resisted efforts by the center to act for the collective good if that meant compromising on local concerns. For example, wealthier and export-oriented republics (e.g., Slovenia and Croatia) resisted sharing their profits and export earnings with poorer entities (e.g., Kosovo, Montenegro and Bosnia-Hercegovina) that were in need of investments for their economic development. The consensus rule and parochialism stymied central decision-making.

In various ways, the new constitutional order inspired nationalism. Empowered and with greater freedom of action, wealthy and ethnically homogeneous Slovenia began to contemplate following an even more independent course. Serbian nationalists, on the other hand, reacting negatively to the partially decentralized system, argued that it unfairly limited their largest ethnonational group's influence to less than its due.

In short, economic factors, constitutional shortcomings and international diplomatic neglect had fatally weakened Yugoslavia; Serb, Slovene and Croat nationalisms were the explosive substances that would combine to blow the country apart.[18]

---

[18]To simplify the story, I have not mentioned here Kosovar Albanian nationalism, even though it also is important. That Serb nationalism is so intense partially reflects its heated struggle against Kosovar Albanian nationalism. In a Serbian recentralizing effort, the Serbian constitution was amended in 1989 to revoke Kosovo autonomy. In 1990, the Kosovar Albanians proclaimed an independent republic. That

Wars of Yugoslav Succession

Yugoslavia was torn not by a single war during the 1991–1995 period, but by several interrelated and sometimes overlapping wars. The first was essentially a Slovene-Serb fight. It occurred over a 10-day period after Slovenia declared independence on 25 June 1991. In the end, about 50 people died and the war over Slovenia's secession did not amount to much. Serbian President Slobodan Milošević had been pressing for more centralized power in Yugoslavia while Slovenian President Milan Kučan was maneuvering for even greater autonomy.[19] As there were virtually no Serbs in Slovenia anyway, and since Slovenia had only hampered efforts to boost Serb influence, Milošević and Serb nationalists cared little about losing Slovenia.

Croatia was a different story. That republic, which declared independence on the same day as did Slovenia, had a large Serb minority. Croatian Serbs already had declared autonomy for several regions within Croatia and sporadic armed clashes had occurred. Warfare spread and intensified gradually but steadily over the summer and into the autumn of 1991. This was, on the one hand, a fight for independence against the Yugoslav National Army (JNA). On the other, it was a contest against Serb-autonomist forces that were taking over large patches of Croatian territory.

A cease-fire was agreed in November 1991 and a United Nations Protection Force (UNPROFOR) moved in after several months' delay. UN forces encountered continuing difficulties between Serbs and Croats in and around the four so-called "UN protected areas." Fighting flared several times; cease-fires were negotiated and broken. The cease-fires and UNPROFOR postponed the day of reckoning until Croatia was strong enough militarily to resolve the situation to its best advantage. In 1995, two massive and furious Croat offensives, known as operations Flash (*Bljesak*) and Storm (*Oluja*), cleared the protected areas of their Serb occupants. Only a portion of Croatia's eastern Slavonia remained under Serb control. Croatia recovered eastern Slavonia in an agreement

---

independence never was internationally recognized. Slovenia, still within Yugoslavia but itself seeking greater autonomy or even independence, supported the Kosovar Albanians and criticized Serbian leaders for their antidemocratic methods.

[19]Milošević was president of Serbia through the wars in Slovenia, Croatia and Bosnia and Hercegovina, as well as during the early implementation phase of the Dayton accords. He was elected president of Yugoslavia in 1997. As a practical matter, his powers as president of Serbia or of Yugoslavia are about the same.

negotiated at Dayton, Ohio in autumn 1995. The Dayton talks were devoted to making peace in Bosnia and Hercegovina, but the Croat-Serb agreement on eastern Slavonia was a side deal.

In Bosnia and Hercegovina, full-scale warfare began when the European Community recognized the country's independence on 6 April 1992.[20] Not surprisingly considering its position and diversity, the wars in Bosnia and Hercegovina were more complex than was that in Croatia. These wars included: 1) a contest between Serb nationalists and the rest of Bosnia and Hercegovina's population (in particular, its Muslims), 2) a war between the new country's Croats and Muslims, 3) a conflict between rival Muslim groups, and 4) a Serb-Croat struggle that had spilled over from Croatia.

Serb nationalists in all republics had seen Yugoslavia as their Greater Serbia, a country within which the entire Serb nation could live. Although they necessarily shared Yugoslavia with various South Slavs and other groups, Serbs at least constituted the largest ethnonational group therein. Losing Slovenia did not diminish this abstract Greater Serbia. But to see Croatia, Bosnia and Hercegovina secede, that Serb nationalists would regard as disastrous.

Well before war broke out in Bosnia and Hercegovina, assorted pockets and patches of Serb-dominated territory within the country began to declare autonomy and their determination not to be taken out of Yugoslavia. In January 1992, Bosnian Serb politicians proclaimed that a Serb republic (Republika Srpska) existed henceforth within Bosnia and Hercegovina. No matter what the Muslims and Croats chose to do,

---

[20]The US would recognize Bosnia and Hercegovina the following day. While granting recognition may, on its surface, seem innocuous enough, this was highly contentious and momentous at the time. A sequence of premature and, arguably, ill-conceived recognitions may be regarded as one of Europe's several important diplomatic failures in regard to the Yugoslav situation. Observers criticize Germany and its foreign minister at the time, Hans-Dietrich Genscher, for railroading through European recognition of Slovenia and Croatia in 1991. At a time that some in the EC were working to preserve Yugoslav unity, Germany undermined those efforts by threatening to break EC ranks and unilaterally to recognize Slovenian and Croatian independence. Germany's overt support for Croatian and Slovenian independence reminded Serbs of how Nazi Germany had backed the murderous *Ustaše* regime during World War II. Genscher and Germany did not recognize—or perhaps did not care—that their actions spelled almost certain disaster for Bosnia and Hercegovina. Once a course had been set for Yugoslavia's disorderly disintegration, Croat and Serb nationalists were bound to try and tear Bosnia and Hercegovina apart.

this Serb republic, incorporating the far-flung autonomous regions, intended to remain part of Yugoslavia.

When and where the wars in Bosnia and Hercegovina began is debatable. Within days of a 1 March 1992 referendum on independence for Bosnia and Hercegovina, Bosanski Brod, a Sava River town on the northern border with Croatia, came under Serb attack. On 1 April, the Serb paramilitary leader known as Arkan brought his ferocious band of thugs from eastern Croatia into the northeast Bosnian city of Bijeljina. Arkan's Tigers terrorized Bijeljina and, a few days later, captured nearby Zvornik then slaughtered truckloads of its Muslim civilians.[21] On 6 April, the day independence was recognized, Serb snipers in the top floors of Sarajevo's Holiday Inn opened fire on peace demonstrators, killing several.

By May 1992, Sarajevo was solidly besieged by Serb nationalist forces. The JNA had been withdrawn from Bosnia and Hercegovina, which meant in practice that the Serb forces there were transformed into a Bosnian Serb Army. Ethnic cleansing of the Muslim population was in full swing, and the Bosnian Serb Army was well on its way to capturing some 70% of Bosnia and Hercegovina territory.

In September 1992, the UN voted to send peacekeepers into Bosnia and Hercegovina and declared the country's airspace a no-fly zone. UNPROFOR II moved into Sarajevo. The fighting continued. Serb forces were well armed, having taken over JNA armaments. Because of an international arms embargo against all sides, Muslim forces scarcely were armed at all. In 1993, the UN declared as "safe areas" several enclaves where Muslims had collected. These proved far from safe.

Fierce fighting between Croats and Muslims broke out during spring 1993 in central Bosnia. Early on, they had allied with one another to fight the Serbs. Over time, Serb gains and ethnic cleansing crowded Bosnia and Hercegovina's Muslims and Croats together into a smaller and tighter space. Meanwhile, Croat forces became well armed while Bošnjak fighters still had few weapons. Serb and Croat leaders probably were discussing how to partition Bosnia and Hercegovina. The result was a Croat-Muslim war within a war.

---

[21]"Arkan" is the *nom de guerre* of Željko Ražnjatović, a feared yet popular Serb paramilitary leader and indicted war criminal. Ražnjatović and his stealthy private army (known as the "Tigers") are regarded to be among the most vicious of the ethnic cleansers. Reportedly, Arkan had a career in the dusky domain of international espionage and criminality even before he came into the only slightly brighter world of Serb-nationalist paramilitary and political activity. War-time pillage and smuggling almost certainly have made Ražnjatović very wealthy.

Although the Croat political and military leaders were playing both sides in this bloody game, by early-1994 they were convinced to formalize an alliance with the Muslims by creating the Muslim-Croat Federation. Strong pressure from the US and European Union (EU) had more to do with bringing the Croats around than did any other motivation: If Croatia and Croatians did not wish to be portrayed as pariahs like Serbia and the Serbs, and if Tudjman and company cared about prospects for joining Europe, then they had best to change their ways—or at least put on a decent appearance of doing so.

Diplomatic and Peace Processes

Dealing with the Yugoslav imbroglio was supposed to be Western Europe's big chance to show that it could take care of sticky situations in its own backyard with minimal US participation. In the end, though, superpower intervention was needed. Europe demonstrated it still had far to go before it would be ready to tend to such matters. The EU and NATO members simply could not sing out of the same diplomatic hymnbook. Nor did Western Europe have the joint-military and functioning institutional mechanisms to address the situation. The US (which early on in the Yugoslav crisis had its hands full with a war in Iraq and Kuwait), UN and European Community (soon to be EU) failed to recognize the gravity of the situation until it was getting out of hand.

None of this is to say that the international community did not make serious efforts along the way. It certainly did, but the Yugoslav crisis quickly took on the character of a treacherous free-for-all and quagmire. Moreover, most responsibility for what has happened—and is happening—there lies not with foreign countries but with people inside of former Yugoslavia.

Let us look briefly at the major diplomatic landmarks that marked the road through violence and toward an imperfect peace.

Brioni Accord

The first peace deal negotiated under EC sponsorship, known as the Brioni Accord, scarcely bears mentioning except that it marks a beginning point for international involvement. Formally, it ended the 10-day war for Slovene independence. In fact, Kučan and Milošević had worked out an understanding in advance of the meeting in early-July 1991. Although Croatia and Slovenia already had declared their independence, they now agreed to wait through a three-month cooling-off period before implementing that independence.

Carrington Plan

In late-summer 1991, Lord Peter Carrington, an experienced British diplomat, was assigned the task by the EC President to bring together Yugoslavia's feuding leaders. Slovenia's independence was virtually a done deal by that time and fighting was raging between Serbs and Croats in Croatia. The aim was to have the parties agree upon a comprehensive and peaceful settlement relating to all republics and peoples in what had been Yugoslavia. The plan was to freeze the republic borders, to guarantee rights for minorities in all republics, and to keep the six republics (some of which might be independent states) in some sort of loose association. Events were by this time running well ahead of orderly diplomacy. The effort demonstrated the extent of disunity and naiveté within Western Europe. German Foreign Minister Hans-Dietrich Genscher axed the Carrington Plan once and for all when he bullied other EC members prematurely to recognize Slovenia and Croatia as independent.

Lisbon Accord

For better or worse, Yugoslavia was on a course toward dissolution. The international diplomatic focus in early-1992 turned toward preventing a war in—and over—Bosnia-Hercegovina, Kosovo and Macedonia. Taking the ill-advised recognition of Slovenia and Croatia one step farther, the EC offered international recognition also to Bosnia-Hercegovina, Macedonia and Montenegro. A precondition was that each republic stage a referendum on independence. Macedonians already had voted overwhelmingly to go it alone. Montenegrins would vote to remain with Serbia in Yugoslavia. Bosnia-Hercegovina's referendum was set for 29 February and 1 March.

In February, just days before the referendum in Bosnia-Hercegovina, there was an EC-sponsored meeting in Lisbon of that republic's Serb, Croat and Muslim political leaders. The EC put two agreements on the table. The first would have the parties agree that a future, independent Bosnia and Hercegovina would exist within the republic's current borders. The second was that the future country would be divided into cantons. That division would be roughly along ethnonational lines, but it would have been impossible to divide Bosnia and Hercegovina into ethnically pure cantons without relocating hundreds of thousands of people.

The leaders accepted the agreements in Lisbon. But the Croats' HDZ and Muslims' SDA rejected cantonization shortly after they got home. The referendum took place, recognition was granted, the Lisbon agreements were ignored, and the country exploded into war.

Vance-Owen Plan

In September 1992, a new and permanent International Conference on the Former Yugoslavia (ICFY) was convened in Geneva, Switzerland. It was cochaired by Cyrus Vance, a US diplomat and lawyer acting in this instance as the UN envoy, and David Owen, a British politician and peace envoy for the EC. The conference agreed that Bosnia and Hercegovina should not be broken into separate states, although it could be subdivided into cantons or provinces under the authority of a single, central government. Vance-Owen proposed to create much larger cantonal or provincial units in comparison to the cantonal patchwork envisioned in the Lisbon Accord.

Presented in January 1993, the plan envisioned subdividing Bosnia and Hercegovina into 10 cantons. These would have been created in consideration of existing and historical ethnonational demographics. The cantons would have had considerable scope for individual self-rule, and a central government in Sarajevo would have had limited powers.

Three of the cantons would have been predominantly Muslim, three with Serb majorities, and two mainly Croat. Sarajevo would have been a thoroughly mixed canton, with the three groups sharing power. The 10th canton, which was to take in much of central Bosnia, was a bone of contention. This would have been a Croat-majority canton but with a large proportion of Muslims.

Croat leaders signed onto the plan immediately because it was a better deal for them than they might have imagined. Muslim leaders eventually signed the agreement but fully anticipated that the Bosnian Serbs would reject it. And reject it they did since Vance-Owen did not grant the Serbs all that they already had taken militarily.

Vance and Owen did not intend for their cantonization plan to create nine ethnonational mini-dictatorships. Once the Croats and Muslims had signed on, though, Croat forces began asserting what they regarded as their right to rule. The 10th canton, taking in much of central Bosnia with its large Muslim minority, was whipped up into a vicious conflagration.

Owen-Stoltenberg Plan

With Vance-Owen in the dustbin and Croats fighting Muslims in central Bosnia in anticipation of future subdivision, the UN and EU mediators began thinking in terms of a country broken into three ethnonational entities. (Thorvald Stoltenberg, a Norwegian diplomat, had replaced Vance as UN cochair of the ICFY when the latter resigned in 1993). Critics of the ICFY's general approach accuse the EU and UN of creating—or at least reinforcing—the notion that the fight in Bosnia and Hercegovina was a straightforward ethnonational conflict between Croats, Serbs and Muslims. The approach was indifferent to the fact that many people in that country wished to regard themselves as Bosnians (or Hercegovinians) without regard to ethnic identity. The ICFY proposed solutions that reflected the separatist view, promoting division rather than unity.[22] The Owen-Stoltenberg Plan, presented in August 1993, was another step in that direction.

Owen-Stoltenberg proposed that Bosnia and Hercegovina be divided into three confederated republics. This Union of Republics of Bosnia and Hercegovina would consist of: a Serb Republic with 52% of the territory, a Croat republic with 18%, and a Muslim/Bosnian republic taking in 30% of the territory.

This was a last-ditch effort by a frustrated negotiating team. The proposal essentially recognized war gains and played into the hands of Croatian President Tudjman and Serbian President Milošević. They intended this as a first step toward ultimately annexing their portions of Bosnia and Hercegovina into their respective countries. Not waiting for the plan to be approved by all sides, Croat nationalists went ahead and proclaimed their Croatian Republic of Herceg-Bosna. The Serb side, of course, had declared its republic long ago. There was no such thing as a Bosnian, or Bošnjak, republic. Bosnia and Hercegovina's president, Alija Izetbegović, and most other Muslims had been thinking (and hoping) all along to preserve a unified and multiethnic country.

Although Owen-Stoltenberg died on the vine, its negotiation had some important and not altogether positive effects. Owen-Stoltenberg promoted development of a Bošnjak national consciousness, and it invited territorial fighting between Croats and Muslims. What's more, the plan exacerbated a split in the Muslim camp. Because Izetbegović backed away from Owen-Stoltenberg, the ICFY negotiators supported his political opponent, Fikret Abdić, who soon proclaimed an autonomous province in a Muslim area of northwestern Bosnia.

Washington Agreement and Contact Group Plan

By early-1994, it was clear that a new approach was in order. Two major developments occurred. First, Croats and Bosnia and Hercegovina's Muslims declared a cease-fire and then created the Muslim-Croat Federation. Second, a new diplomatic team and initiative, known as the Contact Group, took over from the ICFY and put forth a new plan.

---

[22]The counterargument can be made that ending a war is a practical matter that cannot address every idealistic nicety. Voting largely along ethnonational lines in their 1990 elections, Bosnians and Hercegovinians in the majority had themselves taken a huge step to promote the idea of ethnonational division. Moreover, Serb and Croat nationalists defined the fighting in those terms, and their views and influence were strong. Once the fires of nationalism were in full rage, voices advocating tolerance, diversity and pluralism were but weakly heard over the nationalist din.

Muslims had strengthened their fighting forces and were beginning to make progress against the Croats. Meanwhile, the US and UN were threatening sanctions on Croatia if Tudjman did not abandon anti-Muslim military activity and withdraw the Croatian Army from Bosnia and Hercegovina. The so-called Washington Agreement of March 1994 shifted the military balance in Bosnia and Hercegovina as Croats and Muslims, through their Federation, united in their efforts to defeat Serb forces and even to recover lost territory.

In April, the Contact Group came together in Geneva. This included representatives of the US, Russia, Germany, France and the United Kingdom. The Contact Group put forward a plan that: 1) recognized the existing borders of Bosnia and Hercegovina and 2) allocated 51% of the territory to the Muslim-Croat Federation and 49% to the Serb side. The Croats agreed immediately to the plan. With some convincing, the Muslim side also was brought on board. Strong pressure was brought to bear not only on the Bosnian Serbs but also on Milošević in Belgrade. If the Serbs refused to sign on, the threat implied, it might be necessary selectively to lift the arms embargo in favor of the Muslims and Croats.

Bosnian Serbs emphatically rejected the Contact Group's terms, and the threats resonated with an all too familiar hollow ring. The Contact Group would hold together, though, and key elements of its plan would be carried into the Dayton peace negotiations in 1995.

Dayton Peace Accords

Something was bound to give in 1995. Militarily and diplomatically, it was push come to shove time. In early-May, Croat forces launched Operation Flash. Disregarding the UN, they retook Serb-held territories in Croatia and drove out the Serb population. In July, Serb forces overran the UN "safe areas" of Srebrenica and Žepa in eastern Bosnia. Thousands of Muslims were slaughtered and thousands more driven out. Emboldened by Serb actions in the east, Krajina Serbs attacked Bihać, a UN safe area in the northwest. In August, Croat forces launched Operation Storm, retaking Serb-held areas in Krajina, smashing the Serb military there, and driving out tens of thousands of Serb civilians.

Later in August, a busy marketplace in Sarajevo was shelled. Although this was far from being the worst slaughter in the course of the war, the US and international community, still smarting from the humiliations of Srebrenica and Žepa, were by now ready to react. NATO air strikes began against Bosnian Serb positions on 30 August. The first strikes were to break the siege of Sarajevo. Then NATO bombing was expanded to Serb targets elsewhere. As bombing continued, Croat and Muslim forces were rapidly recovering territories that Serb forces had held since the early months of the wars in Bosnia and Hercegovina.

For the first time, defeat and a united effort against them stared Serb nationalists in the eye. They came to the bargaining table in Dayton, Ohio.

The Dayton agreements ended the war in Bosnia and Hercegovina. The US and international community intended that these accords also would create conditions for building a multiethnic, democratic republic of Muslims, Serbs and Croats. In addition to stopping armed hostilities, the accords included the following major elements:

- Bosnia and Hercegovina, Croatia and the Federal Republic of Yugoslavia (i.e., Serbia and Montenegro) agree to respect one another's sovereignty and to settle disputes by peaceful means.

- Bosnia and Hercegovina will continue as a sovereign state within its present internationally recognized borders. It will consist of two entities: the Federation and Republika Srpska. There will be central governing bodies, including a presidency, a two-chamber legislature, a constitutional court and a central bank. (Annex 4)

- The signatories agree to cooperate fully with the UN and other agencies in implementing the peace settlement and in investigating and prosecuting war crimes.

- Bosnia and Hercegovina invite in a multinational military Imple-mentation Force (i.e., "IFOR," later renamed "SFOR" for "Stabilization Force"). IFOR is to be under NATO command and UN authority.

- An Inter-Entity Boundary Line (IEBL) between the Federation and Republika Srpska is agreed.

- Sarajevo is to be reunified within the Federation and open to all people of the country.

- The Muslim enclave of Goražde, although deep in Republika Srpska territory, is to be linked by land corridor to the Federation.

- The status of Brčko is to be determined by arbitration within one year. (Brčko is a key city. Serb forces held it when the hostilities ceased, but Croats and Muslims were adamant that Brčko should be returned to Federation control.)

- Free and fair elections are to be guaranteed, with voters allowed to vote (by absentee ballot, if necessary) in their original places of residence. The Organization of Security and Cooperation in Europe (OSCE) is to supervise elections.[23]

---

[23]Although it rightfully can be criticized for failing to deal effectively with the Yugoslav crisis at (or even before) its outset, the OSCE plays a leading role today in Bosnia and Hercegovina and the Balkans. OSCE objectives include: to enhance

- The Constitution is to protect human rights and free movement of people, goods, capital and services within the country. (Annex 4)
- Persons sentenced or indicted for war crimes by the International War Crimes Tribunal may not run for or hold public office.
- Refugees and displaced persons are entitled to return home safely, and to regain lost property or obtain just compensation. (Annex 7)
- All persons have the right to move freely throughout the country without harassment or discrimination. (Annex 7)
- A High Representative, acting under UN Security Council resolutions, is to coordinate and facilitate civilian aspects of the peace settlement, including those relating to humanitarian aid, reconstruction, protecting human rights and conducting elections. The High Representative has no authority over IFOR. (Annex 10)
- The UN is to create an International Police Task Force. This IPTF will train and advise local law enforcement personnel and monitor law enforcement activities.

---

security in Europe by anticipating and preventing military conflict, to support democracy and respect for human rights, and to encourage cooperation between countries. The OSCE is an offspring of the 1975 Conference on Security and Cooperation in Europe, at which the signatories agreed to 10 points known as the "Helsinki Principles." Among these principles are respect for national sovereignty, respect for human rights, and commitment to settle disputes peacefully. The US, Canada and 51 states in Europe and Central Asia are OSCE members. Yugoslavia was a founding member, but rump Yugoslavia had its membership suspended in 1992. With its substantial role in administering the civilian aspects of the Dayton implementation, OSCE is taking on new and important responsibilities. Disunity and conflicting political agendas among member states sometimes impede OSCE's work in its expanded role, just as politics contributed to its ineffectiveness at the time Yugoslavia was threatening to explode into violence at the start of the 1990s.

Implementing Dayton

"Dayton" and "implementing Dayton" have come to represent much more than a simple peace accord and separation of previously warring parties. Peace cannot be simply declared in Bosnia and Hercegovina. It must be built. Reconstruction and revitalization are critically important, and that was recognized during the Dayton negotiations. Also acknowledged was that the international community of wealthier nations would necessarily pay for much of what needed to be done.

Military and civilian workers implementing Dayton faced—and still face—huge challenges, an enormous amount of work and, of course, never enough money. No matter how much the international community and local people accomplish, far more will need to be done. No matter how well intended, the international effort faces a steep and rocky uphill climb.

Consider the situation facing the international community when it set to work late in 1995 and early-1996. More than half of the 4.4 million people in Bosnia and Hercegovina when the wars began had been uprooted from their homes. Many were moved across the country from their own devastated towns or villages to other ruined communities. Thousands more were refugees in other countries. Perhaps half of Bosnia and Hercegovina's housing was destroyed. Factories and businesses were not operating and were in many cases inoperable. Infrastructure was a mess. Fear, distrust, despair and hatred were the dominant human emotions. War criminals were at large. War profiteers alternately colluded and fought amongst themselves for market share. The police and judicial systems were overloaded and, in any case, deficient in many respects. Local cooperation across the IEBL was rare and difficult to achieve. Local politics and administration were dysfunctional, with corruption rampant and demagoguery the rule in politics. It is not too far from the truth to say that a shaky peace was the sole base upon which to build. Everything else needed to be created.

Repairing physical damage to the likes of houses, bridges, factories, schools and hospitals was only part of the job. International aid workers intended to do much more. They aimed to cultivate democracy in not very fertile political soil. They hoped to help local people to develop an open, objective and informative mass media where existed primarily print and electronic media that were blatantly and malevolently intolerant and nationalist. All of this, too, would take time, effort and money.

Implementing Dayton includes both military and civilian aspects. The military commitment to implementing Dayton initially included more than 60,000 troops. By late-1998, this force has been pared back to near 32,000 troops. International donors committed $5.1 billion to reconstructing Bosnia and Hercegovina over the 1996–1999 period. Foreign troops set up bases around the country. Another army, one of international aid workers, also moved in. Annex 10 of the Dayton agreement assured, though, that the Office of the High Representative would have no power to force coordination between the military and civilian operations.

The unification of Sarajevo, which occurred on schedule in March 1996, demonstrated just how tragic was the poor coordination between the military and civilian implementation efforts. Those areas of Sarajevo which had remained under Serb control through the siege (primarily the quarters known as Grbavica and Ilidža) were to be reunited with the rest of the city. Serbs had continued to live in these neighborhoods throughout the blockade. In the last days leading up to the unification, though, Serb nationalist military forces ordered the Serb residents to leave Sarajevo and to burn their apartments behind them.

Had they been given protection by IFOR, certainly, some of these Serb civilians would have disobeyed the extremists' commands and chosen to stay in their homes. Perhaps many would have remained in Sarajevo. But no protection was given. IFOR just watched. Sarajevo's Serbs burned and left.

Part One:

Among Bosnia and Hercegovina's South Slavs

Getting Started

The drive from my home in Brno (Czech Republic) through Austria and on to Maribor (Slovenia) is scenic but fast. It takes me less than five hours on this picture-postcard September day. I have been down this road before, so I do not dilly-dally to admire the scenery. My car gobbles up the road. Its load is light: just me, my clothes, a laptop computer and a suitcase filled with books.

My spirits are so high that I must remind myself to keep a serious demeanor when I encounter a small complication at the border between Austria and Slovenia. It seems one is supposed to buy a permit before driving on Austria's highways. Well, I suppose I should have known that, particularly in that I have been through Austria a couple times just lately. But, well, gee, I guess I had not read those signs very carefully. The truth is, I had not read them at all.

I am dealing with these two young female border cops. They are rather cute, frankly. I remind myself that these are police officers, that they have a serious job to do, and that I must behave accordingly. They do their best to be really tough on me. Inasmuch as she says I must have known the law, one wants me to pay 1,100 schillings. That is double the price of the full-year decal and a pretty good chunk of change. I put on my best display of meekness, which really is pretty consistent with my normal character. In the end, she makes me buy a full-year decal, gives me a good dressing-down, and makes clear that I am never to be seen motoring stickerless on Austria's highways again.

Driving away, I hope these two will be the most aggressive police that I encounter over the next few weeks and this situation the stickiest.

Germans and Slavs Sort Themselves Out

In the entire area through which I am driving today, German and Slavic cultures have competed and fought, coexisted and blended since the last days of the Roman Empire. More often than not, the Germans have dominated politically. Roman Catholicism is the prevailing religious tradition throughout the region. The West Slavic Czechs and Moravians now hold sway beyond Austria's border, an hour's drive north of Vienna. Just down the Danube River from Vienna, the Slovaks, also West Slavs, now rule. Just beyond Austria's southeastern city of Graz, meanwhile, the South Slavic Slovenes are firmly established.

Slovenia's Maribor and Austria's Graz lie in the region known within the Roman and Habsburg empires as Styria. In Habsburg days, Graz and the Austrians lorded over Maribor (which they call Marburg) and the rest of Styria. These Slavs and Austro-Germans remain well aware of their ethnic distinctions and are mindful of their unequal past relationship, but they have mostly settled their historical differences. It means a great deal that they share a single religious tradition. The stable relations between these Slavs and Austrians are in contrast to those among the South Slavs in neighboring Croatia and in Bosnia and Hercegovina. In these new states that crumbled off from Yugoslavia, with their mixed Orthodox-Catholic-Muslim religious heritage, confessional differences fuel conflict.

Austrians, West Slavs and South Slavs have much more in common than some care to admit. Many Austrians even have Slavic family names and thousands of Slavs have German surnames. Austrian culture is neither homogeneous nor wholly Germanic. In diverse ways and to varying extents, the Slavic, Hungarian, Turkish and Romance cultures that their former empire embraced and encountered influenced the Austrians. In quite a different way, physical geography has contributed to diversity within Austria. Secluded in their mountains and valleys, Austrian communities evolved and preserved local differences over hundreds of years.

These factors of foreign influence and physical isolation operated also in the South Slav lands. There, however, long exposures to the strong and vigorously competing influences of the Byzantine-and-Orthodox, Western-and-Catholic, and Turkish-and-Islamic political and cultural spheres have created a disposition for groups to try and sort themselves out from one another. Should the local people prove insufficiently motivated to separate themselves, then outside forces periodically lend a hand. The world has seen how those differentiating processes can lead to some pretty ugly consequences.

This is not a uniquely Balkan phenomenon, though. In the 20th century, Europe generally has felt a post-imperial urge toward ethnic homogeneity. The urge has played itself out in various ways. Forced assimilation is one way to build uniformity within a given geographic and political domain, but, even when applied rigorously, this is not very reliable. Expulsion and extermination are the more aggressive methods, and these tried-and-true procedures have track records in modern Europe. Genocide and ethnic cleansing were not invented in former Yugoslavia during the 1990s.

In reordering Europe after World War I, and again after World War II, ethnic population transfer was an accepted policy tool. Thousands of families—Germans, Italians, Hungarians and many others—were uprooted. I began my trip today in a zone of one such example.

When I drove the 75 miles from my home in Brno to Vienna, I passed through a region, known as South Moravia ("Morava" in Czech, "Mähren" in German). Today it is ethnically pure Czech. From the Middle Ages until 1945, though, Germans also lived here. Historically, most of the cities and some of the villages in this region have two names. By its Czech name, I live in Brno. To the Austrians, it is Brünn. The border town is Mikulov to the Czechs, but Austrians know it as Nikolsburg. Between Brno/Brünn and Mikulov/Nikolsburg I passed Modřice, Březí, Pohořelice, and Rajhrad. The Germans who once lived here called these towns Mödritz, Bratelsbrunn, Pohrlitz and Raigern.

At the close of World War II, some Czechs turned on their ethnic-German neighbors with a savage vengeance. Eventually, the Potsdam Agreement defining the peace would sanction population transfers, but Czechs did not wait for legal niceties before punishing their German fellow citizens for crimes of the Nazi regime (or for whatever other grievances they felt). There is an eerie familiarity today, in 1998, when I read a report of postwar expulsions occurring between Brno and the Austrian border. The people were being driven on Corpus Christi Day down the very road I traveled:

> These first waves of expulsions were attended by terrible mass-cruelties which caused the death of ten of thousands of Sudeten Germans (*sic*). Among the first victims were chiefly old people, invalids and children. One of the most horrible so-called "Marches of Death" was the march of the expelled Germans of Brünn via Pohrlitz to the Czechoslovak border in the direction of Vienna. In a very short time, sometimes about 10 minutes, the expelled persons had to leave their apartments. They were only allowed to take the most necessary clothes and were deprived of the best of these during the march and on the border. During the march renewed deeds of robbery and violence were perpetrated. Certain measures made to seem those of the local police, but in reality centrally planned and directed, made the situation of the Sudeten Germans intolerable... Their apartments, if they were still in their possession, were open for plundering.[24]

---

[24]Wilhelm K. Turnwald, compiler, *Documents on the Expulsions of the Sudeten Germans*, ed. Association for the Protection of Sudeten German Interests, trans. Gerda Johannsen (Munich: University Press, Dr. C. Wolf & Sohn, 1953), p. xxi. Eye-

That still-recent history certainly does not justify ethnic cleansing today nor excuse genocide. It is, though, part of the context in which the wars of Yugoslav succession occurred.

Peaceful Maribor

Seven-year-old Slovenia is one of Europe's newest and most exquisite little countries. "The green piece of Europe" is the marketing slogan on some of its tourist brochures. Maribor, Slovenia's second city, lies on both sides of the Drava River and at the foot of the Alps. This is my first visit to the sleepy university town of some 100,000 inhabitants, but my decision to overnight here was wholly deliberate. Staying in Maribor, whose environs are known for wine-growing and outdoor recreation, fits into my plan to ease my way toward Bosnia and Hercegovina. Tomorrow's drive to Croatia's Plitvice Lakes also is part of that design.

I find a hotel on the right-bank side, which is to say across the Drava from the old town. It is a 15-minute walk to the center and I stroll at twilight out onto what the locals call "the small bridge." The lights are on, but the hills are still visible in the distance as I look up the Drava. Maribor is quiet, the very definition of peacefulness.

Former Yugoslavia has several renowned bridges and many broken ones. In both those categories, Bosnia and Hercegovina must have the most of all. So far as I know, Maribor's small bridge is not among the famous. The only broken bridges here are those symbolic ones that once existed between Slovenia and the former sister republics that it abandoned in order to become independent.

Slovenia, which has no history of independent statehood prior to 1991, once was an ethnic patch within the Austro-Hungarian Empire. At the end of World War I, Maribor's population had been mixed German and Slovene. The city was joined to the Kingdom of Serbs, Croats and Slovenes. Up the road, Graz was included in the new Republic of Austria that was a closely pruned remnant of the former empire. Also nearby is Klagenfurt, the area around which had come out of World War I populated especially by Slovene speakers who did not regard themselves as ethnically Slovene. They felt a greater affinity for the Austro-Germans than for their linguistic cousins. In a postwar referendum, these Slovene speakers voted to be part of Austria.

---

witness reports in the collection describe in detail stories of robberies, rapes, executions and mass graves.

The "small" bridge opens onto the main square. There stands one of Maribor's most notable landmarks: a monument to victims of the plague designed by Jožef Straub, who was born in Germany but died in Maribor. The "plague pillar" is a ubiquitous feature in central Europe. Even the smallest towns typically have in their central squares such a memorial to those who fell to the medieval Black Death. Maribor's Baroque plague monument is much more elaborate than a mere pillar and consists of several statues.

On this Tuesday evening in September, the well-lit streets and squares are just lightly occupied. Architecturally, the city reflects its long association with the Austrians and western Europe. In no more than a half hour I walk through most of the small old town. The streets are nearly silent, except for one old drunk who is shouting at a group of cigarette-smoking teenagers.

I take a sidewalk table at a small restaurant off to one side of the main square and with a view of Straub's plague monument. I have learned a few words in Slovene, which, in speaking to the waitress, I blend with Serbo-Croatian elements. My hope is that this hybrid will be comprehensible and heard as the friendly display of interest that it is intended to be. The young woman is courteous. If she finds my language comical (and it would be odd if she did not), she shows me only a polite smile and keeps her laughter in check until she gets inside.

Maribor enchants me, just as other parts of Slovenia have previously. Basically Alpine and west European, Slovenia has just enough Balkan influence to make it interesting. Tonight's meal, for example, is absolutely Balkan. Lightly seasoned pieces of ground meat, known as *ćevapčići*, are served with *kajmak* (made from cream and the membranous film that forms on the top of scalded milk) and sheep-milk cheese inside a large and well-oiled pita bread. The pita covers most of the plate, scarcely leaving room for the pile of half-chopped onion to one side.

Noticing that I have not been given a knife and fork, I try to remain nonchalant as I consider how to proceed. I observe what I assume is a local couple eating nearby. They have been served the same thing. She is picking hers up sort of halfway off the plate and bending into it like one might when eating an oversized Sloppy Joe. His approach is different, as he is tearing off pieces with his fingers. I am just starting in—a bit timidly, perhaps—to mimic the gentleman's etiquette, and wishing my small paper napkin were much larger, when the waitress comes by to ask if I might like *pribor*? I recognize the word to mean "silverware."

"Why, yes, please. Thank you very much," I respond, gratefully.

Barbarity through the Ages

Illyrians, Celts, Scythians and Huns

The Slavic and Germanic parts of Europe have an abundance of archaeological, historical and ethnographic museums. Sometimes they are tiny. A really small one might be set up in a little house, exhibit very localized objects, and be open for just a few hours one or two days per week. There is always something interesting in these, but there never are crowds pushing to see the most popular exhibit.

Maribor's Regional Museum is not tiny. It is laid out in a 15th-century castle in the center of town. Still, I never see another visitor during the more than two hours spent exploring its substantial collections. I think I catch sight of other visitors from time to time, but these turn out to be staff. Eventually, I realized that they are turning on the lights in the rooms just ahead of me and switching them off right behind me. This makes me feel watched but special.

The museum has a nice collection of Bronze Age burial urns, plus a good display of grave goods and other archaeological specimens from the Stone Age to the Iron Age. Illyrian and Celtic cultures in Slovenia are particularly well covered. All of history, the exhibits remind me, seems in its basic outline to be military history. Human progress in large measure flows from a dynamic process of cutthroat (all too often literally) competition and opportunistic cooperation between and within societies.

Little is known about these ancient people whose burial urns are on display. It is known, though, that they were overrun in the 8th century BC by foreign tribes. The survivors moved to higher and more remote areas and built fortifications. In the 6th century BC, these strongholds fell to marauding Scythians and would remain abandoned for centuries. Of Iranian stock and springing from the wild steppes of Central Asia, these Scythians were nomads, horsemen and warriors.

The Celts came in the 3rd century BC. Unlike the Scythians, they stayed and settled. The Celts knew how to work iron and had well-developed decorative arts. When the Romans occupied this land in the 1st century AD, they began to absorb these Celts into their own culture. Several more centuries would pass, and the Romans, too, would be overrun before Slavic people would arrive.

Also interesting are exhibits on the founding and history of Maribor and a collection of regional military uniforms from various wars.

Maribor's early days, in about the 10th century, are associated with building a fortress to defend against invading Huns. Among the uniforms on exhibit, that of Marshall Tito merits a specially lit display case. Tito is something of a native son. The future Yugoslav leader was born in the tiny village of Kumrovec, about halfway between here and Zagreb and just on the Croatian side of the border with Slovenia. Born Josip Broz, his mother was a Slovene and his father a Croat.

From Green Maribor to Battered Karlovac

The road from Maribor to Zagreb cuts through agricultural areas. Especially in Slovenia, the small family farms typically include a piece of bottomland and a larger portion of hillside fields. In some areas there are vineyards. Across the border in Croatia, and as the road approaches the Sava River valley near Zagreb, the topography levels off, the fields become larger and the soil richer. This stretch of road follows the river Krapina, on its way to the Sava near Zagreb.

The way passes through a city, also named Krapina, that is known for two of its former residents. The first is *Homo krapiniensis*, a prehistoric man whose remains were found in a cave. There is a museum here dedicated to him. Perhaps better known is Ljudevit Gaj, a 19th-century intellectual who is credited with founding a sort of early Croat national awakening known as the "Illyrian Movement." Born in Krapina in 1809, Gaj, oddly enough for a Croat and South Slav patriot, was the son of a German mother and a Slovak father. Gaj's star may not shine too brightly here these days, for his Croatian nationalism developed strong Yugoslav and pan-Slavic elements. For example, he rejected as a literary language the *Kajkavski* dialect of Serbo-Croatian that is spoken here and around Zagreb. Gaj favored *Štokavski*, the dialect spoken in Serbia and by Croats in Bosnia-Hercegovina and large areas of Croatia. Although he sought common ground upon which the Croat Illyrianists might cooperate with Serb nationalists, Gaj did not get a real positive response from the Serb side.

This is the heart of Croatia, and there was little to fight about here as Yugoslavia disintegrated. When war in Croatia broke out between Serbs and Croats in 1991, this naturally occurred where Serbs were concentrated. That means south from here—in Banija, Kordun and Lika—and on the far east side of the country—in Srijem and Baranja.

Beyond Krapina, the two-lane road turns into a real freeway. The highway forks near Zagreb, and one must decide which shank of this roughly horseshoe-shaped country to follow. Running east and west is

Slavonia, a relatively fertile region that lies between the Sava River (forming the border with Bosnia and Hercegovina) and the Drava River (separating Croatia from Hungary). Continuing south, down the other shank, takes one into rugged, mountainous territory and toward Croatia's beautiful Dalmatian coast. I follow this second route.

Path of Destruction through Kordun and Lika

The highway ends at Karlovac. From here south, there is only a twisting, two-lane road. This is the main route to Split, an ancient city on the coast and a major tourist destination. The narrow road carries a lot of traffic and many trucks. The width of the road is not the only abrupt change. On the far side of Karlovac the idyllic rural setting bluntly gives way to a postwar landscape. Fighting between Serbs and Croats began here in 1991. This was the front line. From here south, I will travel through Croatian territory which, until 1995, had been populated by a Serb majority. Responding to rising Croat nationalism in 1990 and 1991, Serb nationalists in this area first declared Serb autonomy and then a separate republic.

That Serb-Croat war did not start out well for Croatia. By the end of 1991, Serbs had taken nearly one-third of Croatia's territory. Four years later, however, Croat forces swept out the area's Serbs. Today, this territory must be ethnically more Croatian than it has been since the 17th century.

From here to Plitvica, some 50 miles to the south, the evidence of extremely vicious fighting and destruction is everywhere. Along some stretches, every house and building has been destroyed. Some are being rebuilt. It is now fully three years since the Croats drove out the region's Serbs and seven years after those Serbs had initially taken up arms and torches against their Croat neighbors. In that this is an important route for tourists, and that Croatians take their tourism and image seriously, I know that the destruction here must have been ugly beyond description. The signs of destruction get still worse the farther south I drive.

I know from my reading that this wide path of devastation sweeps far beyond Plitvica, the well-known national park where I will spend the night. It must go at least another 100 miles south, beyond Knin. That is the town, previously with a Serb majority, where Serbs in 1990 launched their movement for autonomy within Croatia.

This region south of Karlovac is known as Kordun, so named because it was once a guarded boundary (or "cordon") established to prevent the spread of plague from the Ottoman Empire into the Habsburg Empire. Kordun lies within a broad and oddly shaped zone around Bosnia's western and northern border that had been known as the Military Frontier, or "*Krajina*," when the Ottoman Turks controlled Bosnia, Hercegovina, Serbia and other lands to the south and east. In the 16th and 17th centuries, the Catholic Habsburgs had allowed and encouraged Orthodox Christians fleeing the Turks to settle here in return for their protecting the border area. That is how the ancestors of many (until recently) Croatian Serbs ended up here.

Whatever their ethnic identities, the folks living along this Karlovac-Plitvica-Split road must long have depended upon the tourist trade and the general flow of passing traffic. The land is hilly, rugged and, in a word, poor. There are today numerous restaurants alongside the road, some operating in the open air, several with whole lambs roasting on slowly turning spits. Kordun is here merging into Lika, another region with similar topography but a more ancient name. I begin to see women along the road selling large wheels of a local specialty cheese. Raised on a Wisconsin dairy farm and formerly an agricultural journalist specializing in the dairy business, I have a special weakness for cheese and a fondness for those who produce and sell it. My arteries scream out for cholesterol, and I pull over. An old woman sells me a kilogram of smoked cheese made from sheep's milk. The flavor is mild and less piquant than I would have expected. It is delicious.

The closer I get to Plitvica, the more "*Zimmer/Sobe*" signs I see, announcing (in German and Serbo-Croatian) that one may stop here and rent a room for the night. It is difficult to imagine, though, that the typical European tourist will want to sleep in a home from which one can see several other houses that have been reduced to rubble.

While I am a reasonably tolerant and adventurous traveler, tonight I intend to have a hot bath and to sleep in a real hotel within the Plitvice Lakes National Park. The park features a string of 16 natural lakes interconnected by cascading waters. It was here, in a 1991 battle between local Serbs and Croatian police over control of the park, that the first two deaths in the Serb-Croat war occurred. They were fighting over one of Croatia's many valuable tourist sites.

Tomorrow, I will do some background reading, desperately brush up on my lapsed Serbo-Croatian, and take a walk through the park. I also will psyche myself for the following day's drive to Sarajevo.

Finding Sarajevo

A Foggy Morning with Phantoms

It is a foggy, showery and gray morning at Plitvice Lakes. I do not expect the weather to be any better across the border in Bosnia.

A bad dream woke me early, probably about 5:00. In the vision, I was in the house where I grew up. Some of my family, friends and work associates were there, too. I was sitting in a chair in the living room, when, suddenly and seemingly from out of nowhere, a barrage of tiny but exploding projectiles were coming at me. They were not big enough seriously to injure me, particularly as they rarely hit me directly.

This had happened before, apparently, and most of the others in the room were quite accustomed to it. But it was driving me mad. It seemed I was singled out particularly for this torment. Finally, I could tolerate no more of it and I ran out of the house. Most of the others stayed behind. Outside, there were no more missiles, but that in no way reduced my torment. I was incensed that somebody or something that I could not see would have the impertinence to threaten me so and yet the cowardice to remain hidden.

It is not surprising that I was awakened by such a dream. The last thing I had done last night before turning off the light was to finish reading Zlatko Dizdarević's *Sarajevo: A War Journal.*

So much for the downright giddiness that had infected me during my first day of travel. I must push myself to get on the road. An early start is important, since I did not succeed in reserving a hotel room or making any other advance arrangements in Sarajevo. Nor do I have a good idea how long the drive will take. The distance is only about 250 miles, but it is difficult to factor in road conditions, police checkpoints and other unknowns. I have been reading a lot about the wars in Bosnia and Hercegovina, and it is starting to get to me. I have been doing too much ruminating in a vacuum. I need to get into motion, to confront personally some of the things about which I have been reading.

All Is Better on the Road

My mental state improves dramatically as soon as I am on the road. I backtrack toward Karlovac a couple miles, fill the tank at the small gas station there, then point the car east. I run my recorder to tape my observations, but the story varies little as the kilometers pass: "Many houses destroyed here... In the hills, I see the skeletons of what once were farmsteads... This village seems to have been especially hard hit..."

It is just about 10 miles to the isolated border crossing. The incongruity of my Czech car registration and US passport give the guard on the Bosnian side pause, but he has little to say and soon waves me through.

Through intermittent rain and fog, I begin almost immediately to see the occasional minaret. This is northwestern Bosnia—a sharp elbow jammed into the bent gut of Croatia. Here is one of Bosnia and Hercegovina's highest concentrations of Muslims, although, in light of the fighting that went on here a few years ago, it seems fairly amazing that there are Muslims here at all today. This territory was hotly contested during the recent wars—as it has been at various times across the centuries.

In the first city, Bihać, several white United Nations trucks are on the streets. The UN's High Commission for Refugees has an office here. There must be plenty of work for the UNHCR to do. Although the city's downtown is active and looks entirely functional, there still is almost complete destruction in much of the sprawling eastern suburbs.

Bihać has been a Muslim city since the Ottoman Turks took it from Croatia in 1592. A century later, Austria won the Krajina lands back from the Ottomans, but the Turks kept Bihać and this peninsula-like corner of Bosnia. The point of territory became even more peninsular when, in 1991, Serb nationalist forces captured all the lands surrounding it on the Croatian side of the border. Serbs traditionally have lived in many of the smaller settlements around Bihać, and their relative density had been greater and greater to the south and east. Particularly as Serb forces proceeded to capture and cleanse large expanses of northwestern Bosnia, there was strategic logic to connecting the Serb-held territories in Bosnia with those in Croatia. But driving the Muslims from what became known as the "Bihać pocket" proved impossible.

The Muslim concentration was even greater north of Bihać in the direction of nearby Cazin, the other important city in this area. During the 1992–1995 violence, Cazin and the surrounding territory were run by a powerful local Muslim named Fikret Abdić.

Abdić is today a mortal enemy of Alija Izetbegović, Bosnia and Hercegovina's Muslim president. To Izetbegović, his foe from Cazin is a turncoat and a war criminal. Abdić also is probably the most powerful man in northwestern Bosnia.[25] Some regard him even as a hero.

---

[25]Abdić's power today is wielded *in absentia*. As of this writing he is reportedly in exile in Croatia. In January 1999, Bosnia and Hercegovina authorities

Abdić has quite a history. In the late-1980s, as Yugoslavia was cracking but not yet breaking, he was scandalized when questionable business practices came to light at the agribusiness enterprise that he managed. Abdić went to jail over that. He nonetheless remained popular among area Muslims, no doubt in part because his firm was a major employer. In 1990, when Bosnia-Hercegovina had its first democratic elections, Abdić outpolled Izetbegović. While both were elected to the collective Presidency, Izetbegović was given the larger visible role.

Bihać is far from Sarajevo. Through most of the 1992–1995 wars, this corner of Bosnia and Hercegovina was effectively cut off from the rest of the country. In 1993, Abdić declared the Bihać pocket to be the Autonomous Province of Western Bosnia. That made him a traitor in Izetbegović's eyes. There was a time, also in 1993, when Western forces had wanted to undermine Izetbegović, who, it was felt, was unrealistic in his dogged opposition to partitioning Bosnia and Hercegovina into three ethnic states. Toward that end, they threw support behind Abdić, who consequently was expelled from the Presidency. Eventually, war broke out between rival Muslim groups here and Abdić reached a separate peace of sorts with Bosnian Serb nationalists.

Up through Fog to High Plains

There are mountains beyond Bihać, but these are hidden in fog and clouds. I follow an Italian military convoy up through the fog and mist. After a half hour, the grade levels off, the haze thins, and the road is crossing a desolate high plain. I am reminded of the western US, of driving through New Mexico. There is little evidence of habitation. Even those rare houses that are seemingly dropped in here and there have been destroyed. Occasionally, I see a flock of sheep and their shepherds.

Bosanski Petrovac is the next substantial town. The road skirts past the edge of a settlement by the intersection of the only two major roads for miles around. At that cross in the road stand a shiny police car and a policeman in a uniform that is just about as shiny and new. He is dealing with a truck driver that he has flagged down and does not stop me.

My ethnographic maps show that this general area once had a mixed Muslim-Serb population before the wars. Some three-quarters of the population in this immediate vicinity, though, was Serb. Croats were few. I do not know what the ethnic composition is here now, but

---

in Sarajevo will indict Abdić on war-crimes charges. They are seeking (so far unsuccessfully) his extradition from Croatia.

a couple minarets are visible from the road. I will return another day to Bosanski Petrovac and to Bihać for a closer look. The main objective today is to reach Sarajevo.

I have intentionally picked this route to minimize my travel through Republika Srpska. The US State Department's travel warning creates the impression that the Serb entity might be somewhat less hospitable to Americans in comparison to the Federation. That stands to reason, I guess. I do not know precisely where is the IEBL, but I think that I soon will reach Republika Srpska territory.

Between Bosanski Petrovac and the next major city, named Ključ, signs along the road in several places make it known to local residents and passers-by alike that aid from the EU and other donors is funding projects to reconstruct villages. The Norwegian government, for example, is helping to reconstruct Bravsko, a village apparently of about a dozen houses. It seems a good idea to emphasize to local people that foreigners are paying to help rebuild what the people of former Yugoslavia have destroyed. Perhaps that will help deter them from smashing it again. That is terribly idealistic thinking on my part, I suppose.

Approaching Ključ, I come down off the high plain. This is the most normal looking town I have seen so far. A couple of brand-new driver-education cars move about hesitantly on the streets. The sidewalks downtown teem with people out shopping and strolling. In a fenced-in playground, children and their teachers play outside their school.

Ključ looks like the kind of town Merle Haggard might write a song about. It is nonetheless the main city in its *opština*, which is the Bosnia and Hercegovina equivalent of a county seat.[26] My maps indicate that, as of 1991, this *opština* was sparsely populated by Muslims and Serbs.

A few minutes down the road from Ključ, I begin to see election campaign posters, graffiti and a road sign printed in Cyrillic. Later, when I have better maps and more information, I will recognize that I have just driven into what was referred to in Dayton as "the egg." This oval-shaped extension of Republika Srpska was drawn onto the map at Dayton during a late-night negotiating session. The territory therein was traditionally (but sparsely) populated almost entirely by Serbs. Croat forces had captured the land in 1995, but gave it back late in the peace negotiations to assure that the country was split exactly 51% to 49%

---

[26]The Federation is made up of 10 cantons, each of which is subdivided into several districts known as *opštinas*. The fact that there are cantons should not be taken to mean that the country has been "cantonized" along ethnic lines.

between the Federation and Republika Srpska. "The egg" is drawn almost arbitrarily except for the fact that it leaves the cities of Ključ and Jajce (on either side of the protuberance's stem) within Federation territory.[27]

The sun comes out as I approach Mrkonjić Grad. Well-kept gardens and substantial haystacks from this year's crop give this little stretch of road a feeling of stability and almost prosperity. A Canadian convoy of armored personnel carriers is stopped along the road. Signs around here are in mixed Latin and Cyrillic. I suppose that people here are doing their best to adopt the Cyrillic, which would be the politically correct thing for good Serbs to do. Lying in the valley below the road and about halfway between Ključ and Jajce, Mrkonjić Grad is at the center of the stem that attaches "the egg" to Republika Srpska.

I continue on, passing an International Red Cross vehicle from Geneva and then a British military truck. The road grazes the very edge of Jajce. Political billboards and graffiti clearly indicate that this is a Croatian town. Then, too, a Croatian flag flies over a hilltop castle that is the city center. Even without my looking at a good map, it is clear to me that I am back in Federation territory and coming into central Bosnia. My ethnographic map tells me that from Jajce to Sarajevo I will be passing through territory which, before the wars, had primarily (but not strictly) mixed Croat-Muslim populations. From spring 1993 into 1994, Croats and Muslims here in central Bosnia had been in all out war with one another. This Croat-on-Muslim fighting had been some of the most vicious of all.

What I have seen driving in gives me a sensation that a fiery cyclone from Hell has cut a horrific path all the way from the border to Sarajevo. No city, no village, no farmstead on the 250-odd miles between the border and Sarajevo was spared completely. Of course, that storm did not follow the road as I did. The horror must have been general, sweeping also through even isolated farms and hamlets.

Sarajevo: Scarred but Functional

Sarajevo looks, well, like a city that was under fearsome siege for several years and which has steadily been digging itself out and putting itself right again for several more. Although the scars of war are every-where, Sarajevo clearly is today a fully functioning city. There is much work left to do to the buildings. Some of the tallest office structures still stand blown out and seemingly abandoned. Buildings can be

---

[27]Richard Holbrooke, *To End a War* (New York: Random House, 1998), pp. 284, 299–300.

reconstructed, though, and the most profound long-run changes in the city will have more to do with people than with steel and concrete.

A main street runs up through the valley within which Sarajevo lies. According to my prewar map, this street is called Obala vojvode Stepe Stepanovića. According to the new signs, it is Obala Kulina Bana. Living in central and eastern Europe since 1992, I long ago became accustomed to street names that do not correspond to maps. This is a normal indicator of regime change. Whatever its name, the street is jammed with cars. I creep about the traffic-clogged center for awhile but that does not seem to be bringing me any closer to finding a hotel. Finally, I flee the center for the hills just above town. This turns out to be a very good move.

I quickly find the newly constructed Hotel Saraj. While not inexpensive, it overlooks the old town and offers an easy walk into the center. This will be home for a couple days until I can settle into something more suitable to my preferences and budget.

Joining the *Korzo*

This evening, as I walk down the hill into town, I decide to let Sarajevo initially present itself to me. I will absorb impressions, which I later can examine more closely for their validity or foolishness. I have but few preconceived notions about Sarajevo, although one that I do have falls away of its own weight before I even reach the old town below. I had driven through Sarajevo for the first time a month ago, and when my eyes were not on the road I had turned them to the rim of hills above the city. Sarajevo is a town seemingly designed by Providence to be besieged. It is completely surrounded by hills—hills for artillery, hills for snipers, hills in which to hide. In reading about the siege, my mental image always was of a town lying prostrate and defenseless at the feet of these cruel hills.

In fact, though, Sarajevo is built into its hills and does not just spread out below them. The city does not reach to the valley's rim, but it climbs well up onto the sides. There are lower hills within the city, too, surfaced with houses, churches, workshops, mosques, schools, coffee shops, the restaurants known as *ćevabdžinice*, and cemeteries. Before the winters under siege, there must have been more trees. Among the houses and hills, slender, pointed minarets poke up like petrified white asparagus shoots. Standing below my hotel, at the bottom of the hill, I count five minarets. I am surprised how they remained solidly rooted in Sarajevo's rocky soil through all the bombardment.

As I count minarets, a group of men and children fish in the stream nearby. They ignore me completely. Fishermen must be the same everywhere. During the hours spent focused upon the tackle, the stream, and an ambiguous promise that hungry fish lurk beneath the water's surface, they turn their backs on the world and its goings-on. Here, they are turning away from the veritable alphabet soup of foreign military and aid organizations that crawl all over their country in heavy-duty and expensive vehicles, from campaigns for the elections that are a week away, from the remaining tensions between ethnonational groups. It is not that these things are unimportant, but, sometimes, a man just wants to go fish.

Leaving the fishermen to continue thinking (or avoiding) their own thoughts, I cross the street along with a couple of most un-Islamic stray dogs. We head together toward what turns out to be Baščaršija. The name refers both to the market square and to this small quarter of the old town as a whole. An ancient-looking covered fountain (known as a *sebilj*) stands at the upper end of the gently sloping plaza. Idlers linger in its shade. A woman sells small cups of cracked grain, which children feed to a dense and gray horde of pigeons. In uniform and lightly armed, a trio of Italian soldiers strolls across the square. They seem to attract no more notice from the locals than do the pigeons.

Radiating out from Baščaršija are shop-lined streets. Many of the proprietors are traditional craftsmen. Others offer cheaper souvenirs. There are cafés and restaurants of various sorts. The scene is not so sprawling as a Turkish bazaar, and, this evening, at least, it is without crowds and commotion. It is Eastern, Turkish, but less so. There is an *Arab Lite* feel about the place. Even if many shops are open, this is not prime shopping time. Indeed, it is time for the *korzo*, or evening walk.

I pass an establishment selling *burek*, then turn on my heel and go back. The oily, flaky pastries filled with meat and vegetables look just like those that I sometimes eat back in Brno. That is not too surprising in that the folks selling them in Brno are Yugoslavs. The cheese in my *burek* is more piquant than is the mild sort used in the Czech Republic. The food and I will get along just fine here, I think. Probably too well.

My overture to the local cuisine continues in a *ćevabdžinica*. *Ćevapčići* (or just *ćevapi*, for short) look like a cross between *Tater-tots* and breakfast sausages. They are served by the small plateful, typically with chopped onion and pita bread on the side. Lightly seasoned, *ćevapčići* usually are a mixture of veal, beef and, sometimes, pork. I am pretty sure, though, there will be no pork in those served here on Baščaršija, in sight of several mosques and minarets.

A cup of coffee will complete my alimentary introduction to Sarajevo. The *korzo* is in full swing now, and, while coffee shops in and around Baščaršija are numerous, empty seats are not. I stroll down a narrow street where coppersmiths hammer out the long-handled pots, tiny cups and serving trays for coffee sets. Shaped like tiny electrical-plant cooling towers with handles, the copper and brass pots range from the single-serving size up to those sufficient to serve a small roomful of people. Although I am not a great one for souvenirs, a coffee set of local manufacture seems a near-essential purchase. For those who prefer a souvenir on a different theme, various brass containers fashioned from spent artillery shells are for sale. A few of the artisans are idling this evening in their squat, tiny and ancient shops. The focus at this late hour is more upon coffee, cigarettes and conversation than upon metalwork.

I spot and nab a small open table at a sidewalk café next to a barbershop. This is a popular location. Lots of handshaking and mobile-telephoning are going on at the other tables. My coffee arrives in a small pot of the type I have just been admiring. It contains enough coffee for two small cups. My palate anticipates Turkish-style coffee: unfiltered, boiled and sweet. The coffee is rich and powerful, all right, clearly made from strong-flavored and finely pulverized beans; but it is not sweet and not Turkish. I like it better than Turkish, particularly as I prefer my coffee without sugar. I admit, though, that I am predisposed to acquire a taste for nearly any culture's local means of serving up caffeine (and alcohol). I like to think this is a sign of an open mind and a sympathetic heart.

Friendly to Foreigners (with a Royal Exception)

Reinvigorated by dinner and coffee, I stroll on. Nearby, I am surprised to find a partially scaffolded and graffitied building that is (or at least was) the National Library. Constructed as the City Hall in 1894 during Austro-Hungarian rule, this national landmark was gutted by a barrage of incendiary artillery shells in August 1992. A sign notes that Austria donated roughly $1 million for Phase I of reconstruction, which only has stabilized the wreckage. It remains a shell, completely gutted.

In front of this structure, a campaign billboard promotes the Coalition for a Single and Democratic Bosnia and Hercegovina. The "Coalition," as it is known, is made up of four, mostly Muslim, parties. Among their leaders are President Alija Izetbegović and Haris Silajdžić, who was Prime Minister and a leading negotiator for the Muslim side at Dayton. Izetbegović and Silajdžić are allies sometimes but opponents at other times. They are united now for the sake of election victory. Many regard Silajdžić as more pragmatic than Izetbegović and less of a Bošnjak nationalist. Another group, the Young Social Democrats, apparently does not hold Coalition leaders in very high esteem. Their own poster, tactically posted nearby, parodies the Coalition billboard. It insinuates that the appropriate slogans for the Coalition slate of candidates should be: "Nepotism, Lack of Perspective, Corruption and Unemployment."

Still not quite believing that I had found this landmark by accident, I stop a middle-aged woman on the street and ask her if this is truly the National Library. "Yes," she assures me, and then proudly carries on with a lengthy explanation of when the City Hall was built, its importance as the National Library, and how it was destroyed. I understand no more than 10% of what she animatedly tells me, but I am impressed with her interest (and with my need to improve my local language skills).

It is not too surprising that Austria would target the Old City Hall for reconstruction assistance. If anybody understands the historical significance of this building, the Austrians should. It was in the City Hall, in 1914, that Archduke Franz Ferdinand, heir to the Habsburg throne, had his last reception. A few minutes later, and just down the street from here, Gavrilo Princip, a Bosnian Serb revolutionary, assassinated the Archduke and his Czech wife, Sophie.

If I can stumble onto the City Hall, perhaps I also can find Princip's bridge. That is the bridge near which Princip had fired at the Archduke. There are about a dozen bridges across this river running the length of Sarajevo. I walk out onto the nearest one, which is being repaired and is closed to vehicular traffic.

"Is this Princip's Bridge?" I ask an old man coming my way.

"No," he responds, "Princip's is the next one."

"And what is the name of this river?"

"This is the Miljacka. By the way, are you German?"

"No, American. I just arrived here today. I'm just getting to know your city. It is interesting, and pretty."

I am rather pleased with myself. This is almost like having a real conversation. I think I used all Serbo-Croatian words, too. Had I tried to say anything more complex, of course, an odd mixture of Czech, Serbo-Croatian and Russian words would undoubtedly have come out. It must be something terrible for the local ears when I speak that way, but it gets me pretty far sometimes (and only occasionally in trouble).

The old man wants to talk more. As the sunset calls to prayer begin to wail from a nearby minaret and to float across the city from others, he is telling me about how, before the wars, he had gone to live and work in Germany in order to support his family. As in my encounter with the woman near the National Library, I listen closely but do not understand everything. To have a local person speak to me in an interested manner, though, makes me feel comfortable and welcome.

Across the bridge and a few yards up the river is a small mosque. A low wall encloses the mosque and a small yard filled with mostly ancient-looking grave markers. This is the 16th-century Emperor's Mosque. A pair of young women, conversing softly, wait in the twilit cemetery for their husbands (presumably) to finish their prayers inside. The women's heads are covered loosely, one might say casually, by sheer and colorful scarves that flow down over their shoulders. Few of the young women on Sarajevo's streets cover their heads, and none really hide their faces. Those who dress in a moderately Middle-Eastern style do so colorfully and tastefully. Stepping through the gate into the yard, I attempt to maintain an air of indifference while straining a little to see these women's faces. They are quite beautiful. The head coverings, in fact, focus a man's attention upon their facial features. When I realize that one of the women has noticed me, I shyly retreat.

A Calm and Pleasant Place

My inaugural stroll through Sarajevo's old town ends in the riverside garden of the *Restoran Bazeni*, at the bottom of the hill below my hotel. This restaurant is named for its location near a public swimming pool that is apparently now closed. The garden looks out across a bend in the wide but shallow river and up to a Muslim cemetery clinging to the hill that is the far embankment. Across the way, a stone stairway leads up into the hills and to the graveyard. It is a peaceful place and time. I order a beer and watch the city lights come on. The shadowy figures of young couples stroll and sometimes sit on the opposite bank.

The beer is cold and good, and Slovenian. A Christian by upbringing and a beer drinker by choice, I find this Slavic version of Islam, with its toleration for the likes of me, to be quite agreeable. My first impressions of Sarajevo are sinking in, and these are pushing aside the less positive sensations from today's drive.

"You are a lucky man," I tell the waiter, as I settle the bill. "You have a beautiful city, a beautiful town." He shrugs and thanks me politely, probably thinking that I am at least a little bit nuts. Perhaps, though, in spite of everything that has happened, he still sees Sarajevo's beauty.

Through Old Sarajevo with a Drowsy Poet

The map of Sarajevo's old town set up across the street from the Hotel Evropa is a metaphor for tourism in this beautiful but beleaguered city. It is tattered but functional. The display's glass was blown out several years ago when five bullets or shrapnel fragments ripped through it. Just around the corner, on Zelenih Beretki ("Green Berets") Street, there is a small staff at the Tourist Information Center.[28] Sirija, the older woman behind the counter, offers me a detailed city map. The map is prewar and out-of-print, but it includes a supplement listing the names of the many streets that have been changed. Sirija will not direct visitors across the street to the Hotel Evropa or down the road to the high-rise Hotel Bristol, as these were damaged beyond habitation during the siege and are not yet reconstructed.

Tourists coming to visit Sarajevo should bring along their own guidebooks. Second-hand bookstores are the places to find these, since virtually no up-to-date ones are now available. Information in prewar guidebooks regarding accommodations, prices and restaurants will no longer be relevant, but the historical, cultural and geographic background remains interesting. Tourists may be surprised to see just what that is described in an old travel guide has survived (e.g., most of Sarajevo's mosques and churches), what has not survived (e.g., nearly all mosques and other monuments of Islamic culture in what is now Republika Srpska), and what has changed (e.g., street names and museum exhibits, for reasons of nationalist politics).

New Leaders Mean New History

Zijo had just gotten home from doing an all-night radio show when Sirija had called him from the Tourist Information Center. The prospect of leading around some American demanding a private city tour at short notice on Saturday morning probably did not have much appeal today. But, hey, a job is a job, so this bleary-eyed Zijo found his way to meet me. In that I am a writer, Sirija remarks in introducing us

---

[28]Green Berets here is not a reference to the US military's elite special forces. These Green Berets were Sarajevans who were hastily organized and armed to defend the city as Serb forces were surrounding it in 1992. The Green Berets ranged from former Yugoslav army soldiers to shadowy underworld types to regular citizens with only the vaguest idea how to use the weapons suddenly thrust upon them.

to one another, and that Zijo, in addition to being a tour guide and amateur radio host, is a poet, perhaps we will get along well.

We have no more than stepped out onto Green Beret Street when Zijo runs into an old acquaintance. I think nothing special of it just then. But in Sarajevo, and in Bosnia and Hercegovina, running into an old classmate, neighbor, friend, co-worker, lover or enemy is likely to arouse a complex amalgam of sentiments, questions and issues. The man is Zijo's former history teacher. The two have not seen one another in perhaps a decade. They seem genuinely pleased to meet. The teacher is a Serb who left Sarajevo during the siege. He has just returned. The former student is a Muslim who stayed in Sarajevo through the blockade and bombardment. They agree to look one another up sometime soon. Probably, though, I realize only later, they will not do so.

Zijo speaks highly of this teacher. The man was a walking, talking history book. The problem with history, he says, however, is that now much of what he was taught has changed. With new people in power, there are new laws, new ways to behave, and new history. Zijo illustrates his point by taking me to the corner of Zelenih Beretki and Obala Kulina Bana streets.

This is perhaps the most historic street corner in all of Europe. Across Obala Kulina Bana is the Latin Bridge. Until recently, this was named Princip's Bridge. In the concrete of the sidewalk here once had been cast a set of footprints to mark the position in which Gavrilo Princip stood when he fired the shots that killed the heir to the Habsburg throne. Those marks are gone. To our backs is the building that the old guidebooks call the Young Bosnia Museum, named for the revolutionary movement, made up especially of Serbs (including Princip) who opposed Austria's annexing Bosnia and Hercegovina. Today it is renamed the Museum of the 1914 Assassination in Sarajevo, and it is closed. A plaque commemorating the event also is gone.

In communist days, Princip was regarded as a hero—not for being a Serb and an assassin, but because he was a revolutionary who had opposed imperialism and fought against a Germanic occupier. Today, few important Serbs from Sarajevo's history will be memorialized here. The attitude toward Austria's place in local history has changed, too. Muslims can regard both of the old empires as having protected them from real or potential Serb aggression. From occupying Bosnia and Hercegovina in 1878, through its annexation into the Empire in 1908, and up to the 1914 assassination and war, the Austrians invested much to develop Sarajevo.

Prayer and Pain in Baščaršija

Built nearly 470 years ago, the Gazi-Husrevbeg Mosque is Sarajevo's most important Muslim house of prayer. The structure sustained minor damage during the bombardment, but that has been repaired. Devout Muslims pray five times daily, but they need not go to one of Sarajevo's more than 70 mosques to do so. On Fridays, though, Zijo says, they are supposed to come to this mosque. Several hundred do. Tens of thousands do not. Islam is more secular than fundamentalist in Sarajevo. Muslims here share a self-identify that is Muslim, but, for most, that does not include a strong feeling of religious obligation.

One might think that a grand mosque like Gazi-Husrevbeg would have been a favorite target of the Serb besiegers in the hills above Sarajevo. Not so. The artillerymen did not waste their shells on such things. First of all, Zijo explains, it is impossible to burn such a structure. Second, the main objective of the shelling was not to destroy buildings, but to kill people. Preferred targets were places where people queued up or otherwise congregated—for example, public wells, breadlines, public transport, food markets and apartment and office buildings. They did point their weapons, however, toward the National Library, the Presidency Building, and the building of *Oslobodjenje*. The latter is a daily newspaper that continued to be published and distributed in Sarajevo throughout the siege. *Oslobodjenje* (whose name means "Liberation") has been an independent albeit somewhat anti-nationalist voice.

Gazi-Husrevbeg Mosque is one of the prominent buildings in Baščaršija, the old town and market district in which I strolled yesterday evening. The stone streets and small shops are active now, but not overcrowded. Cafés are mostly full, and young men carrying trays move through the streets to deliver small pots of coffee to store proprietors.

Coffee is important here. Everywhere there are rituals associated with coffee, with its preparation and consumption. In America, coffee is a fad item and so the ceremony changes with fashion. In western Europe, the rites are more established but there are myriad ways to take one's coffee. But in Baščaršija, the ritual varies little. Coffee drinking is something too important, too serious for experimentation.

During the 1992–1995 siege, the traditional stimulants became scarce and expensive. Prices for coffee beans rose to between $35 and $45 per pound. Cigarettes were generally less than $5 per pack for the local *Drina* brand, recalls Zijo, who is a heavy smoker, but *Marlboros* were about twice that. Nevertheless, he says, many people began smoking under the stress of the bombardment. In those terrible days, sugar sometimes cost $18 per pound and cooking oil about that much for a liter. A 350-gram tin of meat could cost about $10. Gasoline was priced at $17 to as much as $60 per gallon.

And why did people need gasoline? Could they actually drive about during the siege? Actually, Zijo explains, a car and gasoline could be a very handy combination to come upon. If one needed to go across the city or to transport something, blasting down the street in a speeding automobile was a way to dodge sniper fire. There were, he recalls, abandoned cars about the city and, if one got hold of gasoline, a driver might hot-wire the car and use it until one's gasoline ran out.

I understand high prices. That is just supply and demand. What I have a hard time comprehending, though, is how people in fact were able to pay those prices. "I ask myself that question sometimes," Zijo relates, "but we had to pay it. For example, I had good clothes. I traded my clothes to somebody who needed clothes. I sell to him this jacket, he gives me 50 deutschemarks, and I buy one kilo of sugar. If I have a TV set, I sell it for 200 or 300 marks, and I buy one kilo of coffee, one kilo of sugar, five tins of food, a box of cigarettes."

In addition to selling one's own possessions, desperate Sarajevans could deal in those they bought or stole from others. If a neighbor had fled his house and city, then his abandoned possessions might be seen as fair game for those who remained behind. Sarajevo's middlemen also could deal with people in surrounding villages who did not know the prices in the city or were unable to transport into Sarajevo the possessions they had for sale.

Among the luckiest in Sarajevo through the siege were those with relatives abroad who were able to channel a portion of their foreign earnings to their stranded loved ones. A connection with one or another of the international organizations was another advantage. Inevitably, some foreign aid ended up on the black market through such connections.

Austrians, Politics and Islam

We stroll toward the fire-gutted Old City Hall. My guide tells me about some of the Habsburg achievements here, one of the first and finest of which was the City Hall. The Austrians also built the National Theater, the Main Post Office, the Roman Catholic Cathedral and retaining walls reinforcing the banks of the Miljacka.

The relationship got off to a shaky start, though. Historians tell us that Sarajevans put up a stiff but futile resistance to the Austrians when the imperial army arrived in 1878. The Austrians, who had hoped their occupation would be welcomed with open arms, were greeted instead by blazing firearms. Even so, that battle for Sarajevo lasted only half a day. Bosnia, Hercegovina and the Sandžak were occupied in less than three months. Serbia also had designs on Bosnia and Hercegovina. The Austrian occupation and annexation added to the bad blood between the Orthodox Serbs and Catholic Austrians.

In any case, Sarajevans were in recent decades proud of the Austrians' architectural legacy in their city. As I look again at the humbled but formerly pretentious, Moorish-style Old City Hall, Zijo recounts how, for several days as the building was bombarded and incinerated from within, the citizenry worked to rescue books and documents. Nevertheless, most of the library's collections were lost.

We stop at the Coalition billboard that I had seen last night. My guide says he does not like politics very much, but that he is a member of the SDP (Social Democratic Party). He is being cautious or modest with me in saying so, because he is in fact quite well informed. Zijo tells me about some of the major political figures, parties and coalitions about which the public will be deciding one week from today.

He is concerned particularly about the election for the assembly in his Sarajevo Canton. More momentous for the country as a whole, though, are the elections to parliaments in both the Federation and Republika Srpska, to the joint parliament, for the three members (one Muslim, one Serb and one Croat) of the joint Presidency, and for President of Republika Srpska.

In Sarajevo Canton, Zijo predicts the four parties in the Coalition for a Single and Democratic Bosnia and Hercegovina will win at least 50% of the vote. He expects (or hopes) that his SDP will draw as much as 28%. Several Croatian parties together should garner most of the remaining votes. Sarajevo Canton apparently has no important Serb parties.

Although Zijo feels that he is a Muslim, he is no nationalist. His SDP shuns nationalism. He tells me about the Islamic parties, the most powerful of which are in the Coalition. There are, he says, two factions within the Coalition. One takes a fundamentalist view. The other is made up of secular Muslims. The first faction wants to build a society like that of Iran; the second wants a secular society more like that in Turkey. He says he does not know which will come out on top.

In any case, Zijo remarks, "Muslims can control only 22% of Bosnia and Hercegovina. If you want fundamentalism in your country, you will get 22%. After five years you will be in isolation and you will be finished. Normal people understand that situation." Why 22%? While the Muslim-Croat Federation got 51% of Bosnia and Hercegovina at Dayton, the larger share of that was (and remains) controlled by Croat political forces. There is, Zijo allows, also a practical consideration motivating fundamentalists within the Coalition: Eastern Islamic countries (some of which are oil-rich) have shown willingness to help the Bošnjaks. Less secularism might mean more financial assistance from those sources.

Four Faiths, One Neighborhood

For hundreds of years, no fewer than four religious faiths competed for souls within Sarajevo. In contrast to many other cities in Bosnia and Hercegovina, most of Sarajevo's houses of worship survived the 1990s violence. Orthodox, Catholic, Muslim and Jewish religious buildings stand in close proximity to one another in the old town. Gazi-Husrevbeg Mosque, a Serbian Orthodox church and a synagogue all date to the 16th century. The Roman Catholic Cathedral, built late in the 19th century on the site of a 12th-century church, is in the same neighborhood. Within sight of the Catholic Cathedral is the New Serbian Orthodox Church, also built in the 19th century.

We go first to the Old Orthodox Church, which had remained open and active under the Ottoman Turks. They had insisted, though, that a tall wall be put up around it to screen this infidel place of worship from the Muslim faithful. The Old Orthodox Church was just lightly damaged in the 1992–1995 bombardment. It did take one direct mortar hit, and the irony in a Serb shell's landing on an Orthodox church is not lost on the locals. A brochure from the small and sparsely stocked souvenir shop explains that the small church has been ravaged by fire at least four times in its long life. By comparison, one little artillery shell is not such a big deal.

The church is small and dim inside, the air cool and close. Somehow, this space seems unfrequented. More people are coming here to pray day by day, Zijo says, but they still are very few. As we look about the small sanctuary, we discuss the situation of Sarajevo's Serbs. According to 1991 census data, Sarajevo's population of 416,000 included some 108,000 Serbs, or 26% of the total. Estimates of the Serb population here vary, but the number today may be less than 30,000. Zijo says Serbs no longer need be afraid to come here, but he also understands their fears. "If you are a Serb and you lived in Sarajevo during the war," Zijo explains, "you had two enemies: Other Serbs were an enemy for you because you were a traitor. And Muslims didn't trust you. It was very difficult for Serbs in Sarajevo during the war."

Before the siege and wars, Sarajevo's population included some 208,000 Muslims (50% of the total population), 31,000 Croats (7% of the total), and about 68,000 people of "Yugoslav" or other nationalities. Today, the city's population is smaller, but so is the extent of its available housing. It is difficult to say what is the real population now.

As is the case in other parts of Bosnia and Hercegovina, many of Sarajevo's residents have emigrated. Zijo believes a high proportion of the city's best-educated and most-skilled residents have left. Sarajevo's population is nonetheless growing by in-migration (even as its natural population growth rate is negative), and the bulk of those arriving daily are Muslims. Another demographic phenomenon is that the number of formerly married women is rising. Many of these are young and their husbands were killed during the wars. An imbalance of youthful and eligible women, Zijo says, strains some of the existing marriages.

Several thousand of those counted as "others" in the 1991 census were Jews. All but a handful of them left during the siege. There remain, though, two synagogues in Sarajevo. The "old" synagogue is just down the street from the Old Orthodox Church. It is now a museum but, like most of Sarajevo's museums, as of this visit, it has not yet been reopened since the siege. (The last stop on today's introductory city tour will be the Jewish Community Center, near the New Synagogue that was built in 1902. The tiny Jewish community operates a feeding center there. It is open to whomever is in need, without regard to nationality or creed. It was in operation also during the siege. The center now feeds about 250 people daily.)

Bloody Markets in the Steeple's Shadow

With its tall twin spires, clean stone construction and setting in a substantial and open square, the neo-Gothic Catholic Cathedral stands out proudly in Sarajevo's center. Completed in 1889, this is one of the most Austrian-looking among the major buildings here in the old part of Sarajevo. The church was damaged only slightly during the bombardment, which fact borders on the miraculous. The Cathedral, after all, stands in Sarajevo's main shopping district. The area was a favorite zone into which to lob artillery shells during the siege.

Noticing a splattering of pockmarks on a building at the edge of the square, I ask my guide if that damage would have been made by machine-gun fire or by artillery. Surely, he explains, fragments of metal and stone thrown up by an exploding artillery shell have scarred the building. There were no enemy soldiers firing their guns here in the center of Sarajevo. If Serb snipers and artillerymen ever sneaked into town during the siege—and sometimes they did, paying bribes to pass the soldiers guarding the city—they came as black marketeers. Some of the same soldiers who were sniping or firing artillery at Sarajevans one day were providing them with cigarettes, fuel and food the next.

Just west and northwest of the Catholic Cathedral are sites of three particularly bloody artillery attacks. These generally are known as the "marketplace massacres," and each gave rise to controversy and drew international attention. The last two even spurred the international community to take vigorous actions. Various sources give different figures for the numbers of dead and wounded. It depends, I suppose, upon how one counts, as some of the wounded lingered before their names moved from the wounded list to the fatalities column.

In May 1992, a mortar blast killed 22 people standing in a breadline just down the street from the cathedral. General Lewis MacKenzie, a frustrated Canadian then in command of UN troops in Sarajevo, made remarks at the time which implicitly supported Serb nationalists' charges that the Muslim army had bombed its own people in order to draw international sympathy and military aide. MacKenzie made his remarks on the basis of little or no supporting facts. Nevertheless, informed observers generally agree that MacKenzie was correct in his more general assertion that Izetbegović and his mainly Muslim government were waging a publicity offensive. Considering that the Muslims were desperately outgunned and that they faced an international arms embargo, it is only to be expected that Izetbegović would play up the very real tragedies his people were facing.

We walk to Sarajevo's main outdoor food market. It is not large, but it is active and full. People offer chocolate, cigarettes and other small wares even in the aisles between the stalls. Within this bazaar, the grip of government regulators is weak, but that of cartel regulators is strong. There are no taxes or consumer-protection regulations, but every vendor knows the single price implicitly agreed upon for every good he or she has on offer. To undermine that price is not allowed, Zijo assures.

The outdoor market must have been busy, too, on the day in February 1994 when a shell exploded here and killed 69 people. It was Sarajevo's largest single massacre of the siege. That disaster was the impetus for the US, with the support of France, to force NATO into issuing an ultimatum to the Bosnian Serb Army. The Serbs were told to end the bombardment or face aerial bombing of their own positions. Britain actively opposed the ultimatum tactic, and Russia's pride was wounded because Moscow had not been consulted. Subsequently, in a move saving face for both Russians and Serbs, the latter ended their bombardment but insisted they had done so only as a favor to Russia. In any case, the shelling stopped for a year. The blockade continued.

Sarajevo also has an important indoor food market. Solidly constructed in 1894 of brick and stone, this Markale Market looks more like a civic or cultural building than a place to buy meat, dairy products and vegetables. It stands near the Catholic Cathedral. Besieged Sarajevans must have felt less vulnerable when shopping here; in addition to its being strongly constructed, the indoor market building stands diagonally across a public square from the New Serbian Orthodox Church.

It was behind the Markale and also near the open-air market that the third momentous massacre occurred in August 1995. Forty-one people died from that blast. At that time, the UN and western diplomatic community were smarting under the disgrace that, one month earlier, they had allowed Serb nationalist forces to overrun the so-called "safe areas" for Bosnian Muslims in eastern Bosnia. Thousands of Muslims had been massacred there. Relative to the Srebrenica killings, this latest slaughter in Sarajevo was a crimson drop in a bloody bucket. But it was the catalyst that provoked massive NATO bombings of Serb targets. Sustained bombing, complemented by an intensified Croat and Muslim offensive on the ground, forced a cease-fire and brought the warring sides to Dayton.

Alphabet Soup with a Grain of Salt

In downtown Sarajevo there is a large presence of foreign military personnel, on foot and in military vehicles. There are, as well, various offices and vehicles of foreign aid and security organizations. The locals regard this presence with mixed—and changeable—feelings. That is the way it has been for the past six years. In the early days, when UNPROFOR first showed up, the people of Sarajevo welcomed these forces with joy. It did not take long, though, before cynicism set in and local attitudes began to change.

This first wave of UNPROFOR soldiers, as Zijo recalls, was made up of French Legionnaires. These swashbuckling adventurers soon gained a reputation for drinking, womanizing and dealing on the black market. This did not set well with the locals.[29] Later, when the British, German, American and other soldiers came, people were skeptical. Their opinions of the various groups changed like the wind. Some of those working in humanitarian organizations also have engaged in dubious activities. Although much good is being done, unsavory tales still swirl about. In Sarajevo, at least, public opinion about the foreign alphabet soup is probably more favorable than negative, but it is fickle.

Undoubtedly, some goods intended as humanitarian aid were sold on the black market during the siege. That still is true, although probably to a lesser extent. Not all such sales were, or are, exactly illegitimate. Sometimes, for example, a family might receive more cooking oil or flour than it needs but lack sources of protein or vegetables. Trading helps to resolve such imbalances.

Food supply during the siege has given rise to a multitude of controversies. It is important, my guide insists, that I understand this situation. Taking my pen and a scrap of paper, he illustrates it. Zijo draws an oblong loop representing the line of blockade around Sarajevo. From the boxed-in east-and-northeast end of the valley in which it lies, Sarajevo stretches seven to eight miles down on both sides of the Miljacka River. At the wider and flatter southwestern end of the valley lies the suburb of Ilidža. During the siege, Serb forces had controlled Ilidža. Southeast of this suburb is a gap at the lower-valley end of the loop. Sarajevo's airport and its landing strip span that breach. Ilidža is at one end of the runway and gap. Serb forces also had controlled the territory at the other end of the landing strip.

The runway was officially (if not always practically) controlled by UNPROFOR. It was the only break in Sarajevo's encirclement. Beyond the landing strip was a swath of Muslim-held territory. This strip, in

---

[29]This view is in accord with that expressed by Zlatko Dizdarević in *Sarajevo: A War Journal.* For example, in his journal entry for 18 June 1992, entitled "The Un-Protection Force," Dizdarević remarks: "In a few months, the Blue Helmets, once the darlings of Sarajevo, have become targets of resentment and scorn. They have also come to symbolize international hypocrisy and political dirty dealing. In the beginning, people would approach these boys in the street and shake their hands. They were welcomed with applause in the cafés, people treated them with sympathy, even love. Now those feelings have turned, in some cases one hundred eighty degrees." In his entry for 2 July 1992, called "Canned Goods," he writes: "The French and the Canadians arrived at Sarajevo airport today to ensure the safe delivery of canned goods to black marketeers. Whatever they don't want is then distributed to honest folk." In fairness, one should recognize that UNPROFOR was stationed in Sarajevo to guard aid convoys and workers, not to protect civilians.

turn, connected to the central part of Bosnia that Serb forces had not overrun. Whether in the form of humanitarian aid flown in, goods trafficked in by black marketeers, or provisions run in across the runway by desperate citizens, Sarajevo's food by and large came from the airport at the southwest extremity of the city.

Successfully to cross the width of the runway was to reach food. In a straight line beyond the landing strip were the free villages and suburbs of Butmir, Sokolovići and, at the foot of Mount Igman, Hrasnica.

"There is a lot of food in Hrasnica," Zijo explains, pointing with the pen. "But in Sarajevo, almost nothing. The French soldiers are patrolling, and they don't allow during the night our trucks to bring food. It's only, let's say, 500 meters. They don't allow it. Therefore, to solve the problem, they (Sarajevans) decided to dig a tunnel. Five months, without stop, they dig the tunnel under the airport."

The military controlled this tunnel and rented it out to middlemen supplying food to Sarajevo. Everybody refers to these merchants as black marketeers. The fact that a few people became very rich on the misery of all the others is a thought that bothers Sarajevans. Still, most agree that the tunnel saved Sarajevo.

In retrospect, some question whether fighting to break a hole through the Serb encirclement might not have saved more lives. During the siege and bombardment, Zijo points out, more than 10,600 people were killed within the city. Sarajevo and the government lobbied, pleaded, hoped and waited for NATO attacks that would break the siege. Had there been no tunnel, the Muslim military would have been forced to take Ilidža in order to open the city and save starving Sarajevo. To do so would have cost many soldiers' lives, but perhaps it would have saved civilian lives. Hindsight is in this case relevant only to historians, but the local people remember who among them the tunnel made rich.

Tins, Tins, Tins, Tins

We pass several booksellers as we walk toward the National Theater. Zijo remarks upon how cheaply the books are offered. "Nobody respects books—not even me. Nobody buys books," he says. "People are afraid of hunger. People are looking around, trying to find some job. People are disillusioned. People are tired. They don't like to read."

Built by the Austrians in 1899, the neorenaissance National Theater stands in a zone subject during the siege to regular shelling and sniping. One source that I have read recalls that plays staged here during the siege sometimes filled the house. Zijo's memories are less upbeat. The

hall, he says, can seat some 2,000 people. There are regular perform-
ances here, but the audiences tend to be small. That does not reflect on
the talents of the theatrical companies but upon the potential audience.
The situation is like that in regard to reading books, but he figures there
is even more to it than that. Interest in artistic culture is greater where
ethnic culture is more diverse. Sarajevo used to be much more a
multicultural city. Today, the Serbs and Croats are mostly gone. Those
remaining are fearful about coming to the theater. This has become more
a Muslim city than at any time in living memory. Tourist traffic is sparse.

Then, too, culture—like so much in former Yugoslavia—has become
politicized. To use a Western term, it would not be "politically correct"
for Muslims to show a strong interest in musical or theatrical offerings
from the West, say, or especially from Russia or another traditionally
Orthodox country. If a good show were scheduled from Turkey or
another Islamic country, Zijo remarks, then the house might be full.

Baščaršija and the main parts of the downtown all are on the right-
bank side of the Miljacka and here at the upper end of the valley. From
the theater we cross over to the left bank. We are walking downriver to
the building of the Academy of Fine Arts, which was once the
Evangelical Church. Back across the river and down from the National
Theater are more buildings, civic and commercial, from Sarajevo's
Austrian era. Prominent among these are the empty shell of the Main
Post Office and the battered but functional Law Faculty.

The Post Office is in a similar state of destruction as is the Old City
Hall of its same era. On 2 May 1992, the Post Office was rocked by
dynamite planted inside. Sarajevans believe hostile postal employees
placed the explosives. Incendiary shelling from the hills followed that
blast. As this was also the main telephone center, all but some 2,000 of
Sarajevo's phone lines were thereby taken out for the duration of the
siege. The Law Faculty was shelled, too, but remained open through
the siege. It in fact functioned then as the main university building. The
EU now is providing funds to assist in its reconstruction.

As we walk, I am putting to my guide a rambling question about
local attitudes toward the international organizations. He interrupts me:
"Do you see this building? It is the most protected in all of Sarajevo.
Two police officers are watching us now. Why? Because it is the Iranian
Embassy." The building is not large but its architecture is exquisite and
has been handsomely reconditioned. There are many mortar scars on
the pavement in front of the embassy. These starbursts are there
somewhat coincidentally, as this was not Iran's embassy until after the

wars. Zijo does not comment further upon the embassy building. He had heard my question, which is not to say, of course, that he completely understood it. His answer is even more indirect and discursive than was the query put to him:

"The answer for your question is that every day I learned something new—during the war especially. Every day I changed my mind. Every day I don't know what to think, but only my thoughts are how to survive. And now, imagine: no electric energy, no water, no food of good quality. Imagine that you eat only tins. Only tins, tins, tins, tins! Old bread. Bread without salt, for example.

"And what to think? How to learn? How to read books? How to think about the future? How to think about to be married? He who is married, he produces children. But now, the (birthrate) is low... Everybody is afraid, because... What kind of future can there be for my child? School is very important. What kind of school will there be? For three months I heard the discussion how to establish in the school special classes for Croat children, special classes for Muslim children, special classes for Serbian children. And parents were against it. Parents! I was surprised. Parents of all children said, 'We don't want you to separate our children. We don't want it. We refuse.' And the Minister of Culture, a member of SDA, the Muslim party, he said to them: 'You can continue as you like, but the program you will learn will be our program.'"

Perhaps this digression would have found its way around to the subject of my question, but we have arrived at the Academy of Fine Arts. A young woman outside tells us in fluent but accented English that the former church building was renovated for the 1984 Olympic Games. It was then donated to the University of Sarajevo's Art Academy. The building was damaged in the bombardment but took few direct hits.

Across the river, meanwhile, a noisy and flashy cavalcade of cars is rolling up Obala Kulina Bana. It is a wedding procession, but political banners and logos decorating the cars suggest, too, that it is part campaign parade. An important SDA official is on his way to the mosque to be married, Zijo explains over the rising din of horns and blaring music. "You see, there are a lot of cars. Many, many cars. That means that guy is very rich—and very popular."

Gorky Is Out, Humo In

Sarajevo is famous for three events: The 1914 assassination of Franz Ferdinand, hosting the 1984 Winter Olympics, and the 1992–1995 siege. Ultimately, this latest historical episode will, as have the others, become part of what attracts visitors to Sarajevo. Wars create their own tourist attractions. They destroy others. In Bosnia and Hercegovina, each of the constituent nations has demolished some cultural artifacts of the others. The Serb nation has obliterated the most, and probably more than have Croats and Muslims combined.

I am pleasantly surprised, however, by how much of the Sarajevo described in my 1989 guidebook still exists today. My walking tour has taken me through much of the old town and to the edge of what is named New Sarajevo. None of the tourist sites cited in the book have disappeared. Some have not yet reopened. A few sites have been damaged and not yet fully repaired. Some of the names have changed.

Throughout former Yugoslavia, hundreds of streets have new names. Sometimes, historians have had to dig deep to find enough historical figures of note such that every street can have a patriotic appellation. This is serious business, and it is a small but important part of the nation-building processes that are going on.

When I approached the Old Orthodox Church today, I was walking along one of Sarajevo's busy main streets. It formerly was named for Marshal Tito. Part of it still is. The particular stretch by the church, though, has been renamed for Mula Mustafa Ševki Bašeskija, a Muslim and 18th-century chronicler of life in Sarajevo.

Mula Mustafa Bašeskija Street is part of a loop of streets that are connected by a streetcar line serving Sarajevo's downtown. It is illustrative to see what has been done with those street names. Tito has done well, all things considered, in that he has kept part of the street bearing his name. That is appropriate. After all, if ever there had been a part of Yugoslavia that benefited from Tito's schemes and determination to keep South Slav nationalisms in check, it was Bosnia and Hercegovina. Then, too, Tito had brought prestige to Yugoslavia's Muslim community through his leadership in the global Nonaligned Movement. That Movement had attached great importance to the Islamic element within Yugoslavia.

After Tito on the loop is a street named for Hamza Humo, a Bošnjak singer and poet popular early in the 20th century. Formerly, Humo's street had been named for Maxim Gorky, the Russian author who would have been Humo's contemporary. The last (and longest) part of the loop formerly was named for Stepa Stepanović, commander of the Second Serb Army in World War I. That important street now is named for Kulin Ban, the medieval ruler who asserted Bosnia's independence against foreign hegemony.

Searching for Liberation

As there is still a chill in the air, the waiter does not encourage me in my notion to take Sunday breakfast on the restaurant's terrace. He nevertheless yields to my preference without a struggle. There is a southern exposure, the sun has risen over the mountaintop, and the haze is burning off. Sarajevo is still quiet. Like me, the city is waking up gradually. Sipping my first cup of strong coffee, I speculate to myself as to the business connections and commercial acumen of whomever built and operates the new Hotel Saraj. He (or perhaps she), I think, is strong on both measures.

The location and name both are near ideal. Hotel Saraj is built into the hill forming Sarajevo's back wall, the natural limit of the city. On top of the hill, above the hotel, is Sarajevo's fortress. Below is the bend in the Miljacka where the river enters the valley that is Sarajevo. The Old City Hall stands below, on the right bank. Beyond that is Baščaršija. Across the river bend, Muslim grave markers crowd the hillside. The ancient-looking cemetery appears recently to have spread and filled.

Until the Ottoman Turks had conquered it in 1451, this town had been known by the purely Slavic name of Vrhbosna. That medieval name means "Above the Bosna," referring to the river after which Bosnia is named. The headwaters of the Bosna (and a popular public park known as Vrelo Bosne) are located at the far end of the valley and just outside the city. The name Sarajevo derives from the Persian word *saraj*, referring to an inn at which caravans stop. The term came to be used for the Ottoman governor's residence here. By late in the 15th century, the term had been given a Slavic-language ending, to become Sarajevo, and was used to denote the growing town. The name of my hotel, then, evokes both senses of long history and of exotic luxury.

Down along the Miljacka

When I consider the layout of a medium-sized city like Sarajevo, I think in terms of three broadly defined sections, corresponding to three general stages of development. A town was founded, usually starting out as a village. That portion now should be the old town. In time, the town gains popularity, as, for one reason or another, people decide that this is a favorable place to live. This early-expansion stage corresponds to the so-called "new town." In European cities, new towns generally are several hundred years old. Finally, there is the late-expansion section made up of the modern residential and commercial suburbs.

The physical pattern may differ. If a city is built on an open plain, the latter two sections may be concentric circles around the foundation village. Should the original settlement have sprung up on a river, and if that river is not too large, the new town sometimes is on the opposite bank from the old town. If hills, a lake, cliffs or other natural barriers are present, the city develops a shape that reflects the local conditions.

Sarajevo exemplifies the way many towns take shape here. Bosnia and Hercegovina is a land defined by mountains and hills, rivers and streams. The mountains and hills form valleys; the rivers and streams cut those valleys deeper. Towns and cities grow up in these valleys and along these streams. Typically, a town is confined to one valley cut through by a single main stream, and it grows linearly down its valley.

Sarajevo was founded at the upper end of the lower Miljacka River valley. The old town begins beyond the bend in the river—below Hotel Saraj—where the Miljacka enters the city. The Miljacka is not a long river. It runs not much more than 25 miles altogether. The river originates east of Sarajevo, in the watershed of a mountain known as Romanija, then flows through the town of Pale (known abroad as the political center of the Bosnian Serb nationalists). Once the Miljacka winds its way to Sarajevo, it runs a straight shot through the city. Beyond where Sarajevo and its suburbs peter out, the Miljacka flows into the Bosna.

Somewhere down the valley stands the largely demolished headquarters of the independent newspaper *Oslobodjenje*. The newspaper is known at home and abroad for its collective effort to maintain professional objectivity under the extreme circumstances which led up to, accompanied and followed the wars in Bosnia and Hercegovina and the siege of Sarajevo. During and since the siege, several books have been written about *Oslobodjenje* and by members of its staff. One of my objectives today is to find the Oslobodjenje building.

May Bosno-Serbo-Croatian Peace Prevail

I walk down the right bank to Princip's Bridge. Calling it "Latin Bridge" just does not sound right to me. The new name actually is a reversion to an earlier one, originating in the fact that the bridge led to what once was the Catholic (or "Latin") quarter on the left bank.

At the access to the bridge, a simple four-sided pole has been erected. Printed vertically down one side are the words, in English, "May Peace Prevail on Earth." The same message is presented on the other three sides in what I guess are supposed to be the Bosnian, Croatian and Serbian languages. That means that on one side the plea for peace is in the Cyrillic alphabet. That is supposed to make it "Serbian." On the two remaining sides, the same words are written twice in the Latin alphabet— presumably, once in "Croatian" and once in "Bosnian."

I find it ironic that people here cannot erect a simple monument to peace without displaying their attempts to divide themselves from one another. Serbs, Croats and Bosnian Muslims all speak the single language that at university I learned to call "Serbo-Croatian." While I am in this country, I refer to it as "Bosno-Serbo-Croatian." In coming days, in order not to cause offense, I increasingly will call it "Bosnian" when speaking with Bošnjaks. I nevertheless refuse to regard this as two or three languages. This whole notion is an artificial expression of nationalism by people looking for reasons to separate themselves from one another and to not get along.[30] And please do not insult me by trying to convince me it has something to do with "celebrating diversity."

I cross the bridge to the left bank and pass a small, green park. Rebecca West had written of visiting this very park with her husband in 1937.[31] She had enjoyed looking at the flowers "and the people, who were almost as decorative as flowers." While drinking coffee in the park's café, she had observed at the next table a veiled Muslim woman who was "wearing a silk overall striped in lilac and purple and dull blue."

People have changed since West's day. Women no longer hide their faces behind veils and men long ago shed their conical fezzes. A minority of Sarajevo's women do still cover their heads and shoulders with scarves and some of the Muslim men, especially the older ones, wear berets. I have noticed in driving through smaller cities and villages that the more traditional, concealing yet colorful costumes are more common there. I have yet to see a veil. Croat and Serb women also wear scarves.

West had been impressed by the fact that two Muslim men sitting near her and arguing politics over a newspaper had had the height,

---

[30]In *To End a War*, Richard Holbrooke gives an example of this absurdity. Negotiators at Dayton had headsets for simultaneous translation into six languages: English, French, Russian, Bosnian, Croatian and Serbian. The last three were on channels 4, 5 and 6, respectively. The Balkan participants all insisted that they listen to the negotiations in their "own" languages. In fact, a single interpreter's voice came across all of channels 4 through 6. The translators' booths, Holbrooke writes, "came to symbolize for me the stupidity of the war... Language, which had once helped unify Yugoslavia, was now another vehicle through which people were being driven apart."

[31]Rebecca West, *Black Lamb and Grey Falcon: A Journey through Yugoslavia, reprint, paperback* (London: Macmillan London Limited, 1940, 1941; Edinburgh: Canongate Classics, 1997), p. 297.

bronze hair and blue eyes of Danish sea captains. Had they not been wearing fezzes, she would not have known they were Muslims. As in West's day, foreigners still expect Bosnia and Hercegovina's Muslims to be dark complexioned and somehow Asian looking. Some are dark, but so also are some of the Croats and Serbs.

SPLAT! on Olympic Sarajevo

I wander along down the river. As it is midday and the weather warm, I am surprised by how few Sarajevans are out and about to enjoy the sunshine. There is less natural shade these days under which Sarajevans may stroll and sit than in prewar days. Craters where once were trees now mark some formerly shady streets and promenades. During the siege, many of Sarajevo's trees were sacrificed to provide heat and cooking fuel. Here and there, splatter scars from impacting artillery shells blemish the pavement. These are especially numerous at major and open intersections. Most of the circular imprints are just about a foot in diameter and shallowly cut into the pavement. These are from grenade-type shells, which are designed not to do structural damage but to kill and maim with scattering shrapnel. At the sight of these violently hewn rosettes, I involuntarily cringe and hear in my mind's ears the piercing blast from the shell bursting in front of me.

Walking about, I frequently find myself gazing up at the rim of hills around Sarajevo. When I see the SPLAT! mark of an artillery shell in a street intersection, at a bus stop or in front of a high-rise building, I instinctively look up and begin to reckon from where that shell might have come. I observe the general direction of the splatter, then try to approximate where the gun had been positioned.

Farther on, beyond the turn-of-the-century "new" synagogue and the former Protestant church that is now the Art Academy is the Skenderija complex. This once had been primarily a sports facility, was occupied by UNPROFOR during the siege, and now hosts trade fairs and other events. An international fashion trade show was here last week. International medical products and auto exhibitions are scheduled for later this month. Business, while not yet booming in Sarajevo, is at least reemerging.

Across the river, set well back from the right bank, several tall buildings tower over the city. They stand brutally bruised and battered like idiot boxers with their feet set in concrete. Dumbly unwavering, these chumps had absorbed blows and piercing blasts throughout the siege. Perhaps, I think, one of these is the Oslobodjenje building. Before walking over to find out, though, I take a closer look at something somehow even more jarring. On the left bank, and rising up across the river from what once was a cheerful promenade, are four identical, burned-out apartment buildings.

Other structures in this neighborhood are damaged—some of them severely—but these four are gutted completely, and they cut a particularly horrific profile. They stand shoulder to shoulder like sentinels—or a firing squad. It is frightening to look at the gutted, blackened towers. In stony silence they stare menacingly across the Miljacka at the distant chump boxers. Dozens of eyes that are their row upon row of smashed and darkened windows cast sideways glances up and down the valley.

Eventually, I realize that this is the front line of the siege. I am standing, too, in the path along which, in April 1992, Serb forces had made their first assault on Sarajevo, as well as along which (in the opposite direction) peace demonstrators had marched to show multiethnic solidarity. Behind me is Vrbania Bridge. Suada Dilberović, a medical student and one of those demonstrators, had been the first to die in Sarajevo as she and others had marched across this bridge.[32]

Behind the four demonic sentries is Grbavica, a quarter that was taken by Serb forces in the first drive and was held throughout the siege. Grbavica was a notch cut into the valley's left flank, the farthest the front line had penetrated into central Sarajevo. The invaders had intended to cut Sarajevo in two at this, one of its narrowest, points. That assault failed to cross the river. For the better part of four years, Serb snipers must have perched in these four towers and fired into Sarajevo's downtown. Many of Sarajevo's Serbs remained here, among the Serb military personnel, until March 1996. In that month, Sarajevo was officially opened under terms of the Dayton accord. Those Serb civilians remaining were ordered by the Bosnian Serb Army to torch their own apartments and to abandon the city.

The very name "Grbavica" sounds wicked and frightful as I whisper it to myself. Grbavica must be related to the word *grbavac*, meaning "hunchback." But it brings to my mind words like *grub* (meaning "vulgar" or "crude") and *grob* (meaning "grave" in Serbo-Croatian and "coffin" in Russian).

One of the tall buildings beyond the right bank that I had thought might be home of the independent newspaper *Oslobodjenje* is the Parliament and Government Building. This complex centers on a wafer-

---

[32]Laura Silber and Allan Little, *Yugoslavia: Death of a Nation*, 2nd revision, paperback (London and New York: Penguin Books, 1997), pp. 227–228.

like office tower of about 20 stories. The tower stands tall, empty, dead and unsightly. Its slender body has been slashed and pierced through by dozens of rockets and shells. Scars mark one end wall where two particularly massive missiles had plunged into the structure. Smoke-darkened curtains and blinds flutter out into the breeze from glassless windows as wind blows clear through the building.

Across the street is the brightly painted Holiday Inn, which looks none the worse today for its war experiences. Although the Holiday Inn stood in the thick of the bombardment, it operated throughout the siege. With its yellow and chocolate-brown paint, modern architecture and location on the main street through Sarajevo, the Holiday Inn is impossible to miss. Sarajevans love the gaily colored hotel. It was built for the 1984 Winter Olympics and is one of the most visible reminders of that proudest event in their city's recent history. That the Olympics remain a powerful symbol for Sarajevans is suggested even by the campaign message on a nearby billboard. "For Olympic Sarajevo," reads a slogan for the New Croat Initiative (NHI). Pictured on the billboard is Krešimir Zubak, the Croat member of Bosnia's three-man presidency. Zubak promotes his new party as a moderate alternative to Franjo Tudjman's Croatian Democratic Union (HDZ).

Sarajevans' memories are made bittersweet by the fact that in April 1992 some of the first shooting from Serb snipers came from the upper floors and roof of the Holiday Inn. Radovan Karadžić, leader of the nationalist Serb Democratic Party (SDS), had had up to that time his headquarters in the hotel. His bodyguards were firing upon peace demonstrators assembled across the street at the Parliament Building.

A sign out front of the Parliament announces an EU-sponsored reconstruction plan, but there is nothing to suggest that any project actually is in process. There, too, is an indifferent-looking military guard. I ask him where is the Oslobodjenje building. The look on his face alone tells me that it is not close. Gesturing with a vertical sweep of my arm, I ask if it is farther down the valley. Yes, he indicates, very far. At least 30 minutes on foot. I am not sure that I believe him (or that he had understood correctly what I was trying to communicate). A blister is rising on one foot, but I decide to venture on a bit.

Across the way, next to the Parliament Building, is a neorenaissance building marked, simply, "Museum." This actually is a small complex around a central courtyard. Upon closer investigation, I learn that it is the State Museum. The museum had been backed up to the front line of the siege. Separated by the shallow Miljacka from Grbavica, the State

Museum was in wading distance of the besiegers and their guns. The museum buildings absorbed more than 400 artillery rounds. Fortunately, none of the most valuable exhibits took direct hits. Compared to, say, the National Library, this museum came through in quite good condition. Founded in 1888, the State Museum houses departments of archaeology, ethnography and natural history. It is considered to be the oldest cultural and scientific institution of its kind in Bosnia and Hercegovina.[33]

A sign on the front door reads: "Museum is open only for announced events." I cannot see much by peering in through the windows, but I sense that things are being put back in order. Hopefully, the next time I visit Sarajevo, the museum will be open.[34] I can imagine that, meanwhile, the museum's curators and administrators, along with academic specialists in archaeology, ethnography and history, will debate long and hard on how—in consideration of present political realities—to use artifact materials to present the history of Bosnia and Hercegovina.

History is sculpted from pretty malleable material, after all. In modern times, basic historical facts are fairly well established. These can be structured, though, into any number of basic story lines. The details, then, may be filled in and interpreted according to the historian's tastes, opinions and external guidelines. I do not mean to say that historians do not tell the truth. But their renderings of the past do tend to reflect the writers' own epoch and are subject to later revision. Still, the history written and endorsed here today and tomorrow will be that which the present and next generation of this country's youth will learn. Once transformed into the published word and sanctioned in the schools, standard-textbook versions of the past and its meaning will become regarded as something like gospel truth. Historical truth for the next several decades will be colored by emotions aroused during the wars of Yugoslav succession.

In recent months and years, I have visited many museums in former Yugoslavia and in former communist countries. It is interesting to observe how their depictions of history have been modified to reflect new politics. Typically, and in that the communist world has broken up into nation-states, a new accent on nationalism replaces the previously emphasized socialist internationalism. The new history may be more or

---

[33]FAMA, *Sarajevo 1992–1995* (Sarajevo: FAMA, 1996).

[34]Indeed, when I return in March 1999 I learn that the Museum is open to the public for several hours two days weekly.

less accurate than what was presented under the former regimes. In any case, it is being used for somewhat different purposes now.

In front of the museum is a bus stop, and across the street is a technical school. At the bus stop, the pavement is terribly scarred from artillery shell explosions. The school, too, has been repeatedly and severely blasted. This spot is very open and exposed, and I will later read that many people died here. Even after the Dayton agreement was signed, a murderous artillery shell smashed into a streetcar here.

I wander on. There is the Bristol Hotel, a high-rise that was one of Sarajevo's finest hotels. Also on the front line, it fared less well than did the Holiday Inn. The Bristol stands shot-up and empty. Nearby is the Elektroprivreda building. A large structure, also on the receiving end of many artillery shells, this is the main office for Sarajevo's electric utility.

"Merhaba Uzeir Aga!"

At this point in the length of Sarajevo's valley, the new town is transitioning into the sprawling and amorphous outer reaches that are the modern residential and commercial suburbs. These go on for several miles. My blistering feet strongly advise against my going farther in that direction and to suspend for today my search for the Oslobodjenje building. Minding my feet, I turn back up the valley.

A large office tower is nearby. It is the headquarters of Energoinvest and, like Sarajevo's other skyscrapers, is very messed up from heavy shelling. Energoinvest once was a major employer. I will meet several people in coming days who formerly worked for this company—but none who do so now. Energoinvest has been involved in all sorts of manufacturing and engineering work related to high-voltage electricity, from transformers and power lines to turn-key electricity plants.

Energoinvest had plants in numerous cities. Some of these lie now in Republika Srpska while the others are in the Federation. There must be some untidy details to work out there over such issues as enterprise ownership, trademarks, and responsibility for outstanding debts. Many industrial enterprises face such situations, and they are unlikely to begin really producing again until major issues are resolved.

Business experience in former Czechoslovakia has shown me first-hand how privatization and splitting a country can hamstring enterprises. The problems must be even much worse here where the split—first from Yugoslavia and then into the Federation and Republika Srpska— is much uglier than was the "velvet divorce" that separated the Czech Republic and Slovakia. Five years after the Czechs and Slovaks went their own ways, there still are unresolved economic issues between their countries. Settling such disputes here will drag well into the next century.

Just back up past the Holiday Inn and the Parliament, I get a strange feeling in the open area around Tršćanska Street. St. Joseph's, a small Catholic church stands there in a sunny plaza. It was scarcely damaged in the bombardment, by all appearances, although a sign announces a project to make some repairs to the bell tower. Beyond the church and square is Sarajevo's largest skyscraper, the twin-towered UNIS Building. These UNIS towers are the feature-event chump boxers. Stretching tall over the undefiled St. Joseph's, they had been favorite artillery targets. The twin towers' proudly shining blue-glass hides had been punctured hundreds of times. Flames have gutted their upper floors. Only some offices near street level are being used now.

I will read tomorrow, when I research further, that Sarajevans call the twin towers Momo and Uzeir after two famous characters from Sarajevo jokes. Momo is a Serbian name and Uzeir is of Muslim origin, "and since the buildings were of equal height they symbolized the Sarajevo Brotherhood and Unity. Nobody knew which one was Momo and which one was Uzeir, so the aggressors destroyed both."[35] In communist times, when people wished to ridicule foolish politicians without mentioning their names, they would make jokes substituting Momo and Uzeir for the real target objects of derision. Often, the story would begin with Momo using an old Turkish expression to address Uzeir: "*Merhaba Uzeir Aga!*" (Good morning, Your Highness Uzeir!)

It must be the contrast between the small and scarcely blemished St. Joseph's and the enormous but ravished UNIS towers giving me the queer sensation at this corner. I will read later that the highest incidence of casualties by sniper fire was in the vicinity of Tršćanska Street. Beyond the battered towers is the Red Cross building and one of Sarajevo's major hospitals. The hospital remained open and was shelled during the siege. The Red Cross building was completely gutted.

"With Us, Bosnia and Hercegovina Can Be Better," reads a nearby election billboard for SDP. That party is the direct heir of the Communist League that once ran Yugoslavia. Now, as then, the SDP opposes nationalism in all its destructive forms. Here in the shadows of Momo and Uzeir, the poster is well placed to maximize the impact of its message.

---

[35]FAMA, *Sarajevo 1992–1995.*

Down at the End of Sniper Alley

I meet a fellow at breakfast who is from the US Embassy. He is out here from Washington to help with monitoring next weekend's elections. His job is to help keep track of the volunteer monitors, a pretty big crew of which is here or en route to here. America, he explains, has a corps of election junkies who get a kick out of flying around the world to watch over the freeness and fairness of budding and fragile democratic processes.

There should be some diplomatic bigwigs coming in for the vote. I notice as I walk into town this morning that the upper end of Obala Kulina Bana, the main street through Sarajevo, is guarded by heavily armed SFOR troops. They even have a couple of armored personnel carriers. As I approach Princip's Bridge, a caravan of SFOR vehicles rolls up across the way on the left bank of the Miljacka with lights flashing and a voice through a megaphone warning passers-by to stand clear. The convoy scoots across the river by the bridge farthest upstream and continues on in the direction of the Presidency Building.

I stop at a newsstand and pick up today's *Oslobodjenje.* Standing on a bridge over the Miljacka, I page through the paper. I see that Slovenian President Milan Kučan is to be in town today for a meeting with President Izetbegović and other officials. Perhaps that was his retinue that just went past. Kučan also is to participate in the opening of a pharmaceuticals production line, which was modernized in a joint project between a local firm and a Slovenian one.

Fear Mongers and the Displaced

On today's front page, the banner headline points out that the government owes the average pensioner some 2,750 deutschemarks (about $1,800) in back payments. Also on the front page, Ante Jelavić, presidential candidate from the HDZ, is pictured. The article is about the fact that Jelavić refused to participate in an OSCE-sponsored television debate. Izetbegović also had declined to join the debate. Both Jelavić and Izetbegović are "fear mongers," had remarked Senka Nožica, a minor-party candidate for the Croat seat in the Presidency and who did take part. Robert Barry, head of the OSCE mission in Bosnia and Hercegovina, stated during the debate that he thinks the country's voters are tired of nationalist slogans. Barry said he hopes they will reject nationalist parties in favor of political leaders working to build a multiethnic society. The forum's participants did not seem to share Barry's view that the voters were about to turn away from nationalist politics.

Relations between OSCE and the HDZ are not warm, to say the least. An article explains that Croatian President Tudjman is calling upon the OSCE to reinstate 15 HDZ candidates that OSCE had stricken from the official list of candidates due to campaign irregularities. HDZ is threatening to boycott the election. A front-page editorial criticizes the OSCE and High Representative Carlos Westendorp for striking the candidates from the list, saying that its action indirectly supports the Muslim SDA party.

Westendorp, a former Spanish foreign minister, is arguably the most powerful man in Bosnia and Hercegovina today. He took over as High Representative in July 1997 from Carl Bildt, a former Swedish prime minister.[36] Westendorp, who has a two-year mandate to oversee civilian aspects of Bosnia's peace process, at times is able to overrule local, elected political leaders and, effectively, to govern by decree. Westendorp is generally perceived as strong and to have done a good job in an extremely difficult situation. Some would argue that in order to achieve real democracy in the long term, the High Representative should have even greater powers. Because the Dayton agreement specifically separates the authority of the High Representative (a UN appointee) from that of SFOR (which is under NATO command), Westendorp's decrees do not carry the implication of enforceability by military force.

Another prominent theme in today's newspaper relates to the difficulties of returning refugees. Under the terms of what is known as the "Sarajevo Declaration," local officials committed themselves to work toward returning former residents of the city to their homes. Sarajevo is today a predominantly Muslim city, but an official responsible to direct the Declaration's implementation has informed Westendorp that between 7,000 and 8,000 Croats and Serbs have been resettled back into Sarajevo Canton. That is not many. The local official emphasized, though, that resettling refugees into Sarajevo depends upon reconstructing damaged housing within Sarajevo. It also depends upon moving refugees now within Sarajevo but originally from other areas out of the city to make room for those who would return.

---

[36]Bildt, the first High Representative, had been appointed in June 1995 to replace David Owen as the EU mediator responsible for the former Yugoslavia.

Indications are, though, that not all of Sarajevo's newest residents wish to return to their former hometowns and villages. Another news story tells of a group of Muslim refugees who traveled recently from Sarajevo to their former homes in Rudo, which is in far eastern Bosnia and virtually on the border with Serbia. They found Serbs living in their homes, many of whom are themselves refugees from Sarajevo. There are no empty houses in Rudo. The article concludes that few of either the Muslim or Serb refugees really wish to return to their former homes.

Oslobodjenje features today an interview with Germany's ambassador to Bosnia and Hercegovina. Some 200,000 refugees have returned here from Germany since 1997, he said, noting that only about 1% of those were forcefully ejected. The rest left of their own free will. Some 150,000 to 160,000 refugees from Bosnia and Hercegovina remain in Germany. The ambassador said they will leave in due time. He expressed optimism that a result of this weekend's elections will be improved conditions in this country for the return of refugees now residing abroad. The international community hopes for and expects a great deal of this vote and its aftermath.

Sarajevo's Muslims will soon have another mosque and *mekteb* (an Islamic elementary school), according to the paper. There was a dedication yesterday. Donations have been secured to cover the construction costs. The mosque is to have a minaret some 130 feet high and is expected to serve 500 worshipers daily. Sarajevo is to have many new mosques to serve its Muslims. No matter how many are built here, though, it is unlikely they ever will outnumber those that have been razed to the ground in Republika Srpska.

Somebody's Uncle in Nedjarići

Living in a hotel room is no way to maximize my absorption of local life and culture. My game plan calls for me to live with a family. It is high time to put that plan into operation. I have contact information in my briefcase for one such potential household. Also, I have put out feelers with the people at the hotel's front desk and at the Tourist Information Center. The second, indirect approach does not look as though it is going to pan out very quickly. As to the first option, I know a name, a telephone number, that the person is the uncle of somebody I met in Croatia during the summer, and that he does not speak English. It seems that there is a daughter there who does know English.

After lunch, I spend a few minutes rehearsing in my head the upcoming conversation in Bosno-Serbo-Croatian. Even though I want to live in a situation that will force me to use this language, I will not be disappointed if the English-speaking daughter answers the phone. She does not. In fact, I find out pretty quickly, the daughter does not live with her parents, and, in any case, she is out of town for a few days. The older gentleman who answers the phone is the Mr. Babić who I seek, and he is quite surprised to hear from me. His niece has not informed him that he might get a call from a foreigner looking to put a roof over his head. He is friendly and curious. We agree that I will come out and visit him and his wife in a couple hours.

That went pretty well, I tell myself as I hang up the phone. It was my longest conversation thus far in the local tongue. I am sure that it was not pretty to listen to, but it basically worked. And I am just starting out after all. Encouraged by my latest successful attempt to communicate, I strike up a conversation with the cab driver taking me out to visit my prospective landlord. We are going to the quarter known as Nedjarići, in the lower end of the valley. The driver takes the back way, up across the hills and past residential neighborhoods that are above the Miljacka's left bank.

The cabby wants to be sure I understand that he is not taking the back way in order to cheat me. Because of the Slovene president's visit, he explains, the main street down through the center of the city and valley is partially blocked off. We pass near a Jewish cemetery, which is on the outside edge of the Grbavica quarter that Serb forces had occupied throughout the siege. The driver makes a couple unkind remarks about *Četniks*, then quickly remarks that all of that is over now.

Snajperi! Snajperi!

Mr. and Mrs. Babić, the uncle and aunt of my passing acquaintance from earlier in the summer, are looking and waiting for me on the balcony of their high-rise apartment building. They wave when I step out of the taxi. Even from below, I can see that they are pleased and relieved to see that I have arrived. The husband has put on a suit for the occasion. They are taking my visit very seriously, but their hospitality and curiosity quickly generate a charming warmth. An English-speaking neighbor girl is kindly helping to sort out the situation.

I quickly sense that it would be delightful to stay with this pair of pensioners. I also realize, though, that it might be quite an imposition for me to move into their small apartment with them. Everything can be worked out, they insist, though, and it will be no imposition. They will set up a place for me to work. Coffee, breakfast, hot water, laundry—they can take care of it all. In the end, we agree that I will move in tomorrow after lunch.

Mr. Babić insists upon walking me to the streetcar that will take me back up to the other end of the valley and to my hotel. As we walk together, I notice that a couple hundred yards from their group of apartments are the remains of a building that looks to have been damaged particularly badly. This once had been a large building, it seems, but it is difficult to imagine what it would have looked like before it was blown up. That, Mr. Babić tells me, is (or was) the office building of a newspaper by the name of *Oslobodjenje*. (Ah-ha!)

He then points to a small building, behind their row of apartment buildings but even much closer than the long-sought Oslobodjenje wreckage. A man with a good arm could just about hit that building with a stone thrown from this courtyard teeming with children at play. "*Snajperi! Snajperi!*" Mr. Babić hisses, gesturing toward the small building and then imitating with his hands and squinting eyes the aiming and firing of a rifle. Throughout much of the siege, it seems, people in this complex had known that one of "their" snipers was nested in that building. They all were the targets. I do not feel the time is right to ask my host how many of his neighbors had been gunned down by the *snajperi*.

It is about a 20-minute ride by streetcar—straight up the valley—to the National Library and my hotel above the bend in the Miljacka. I am pleased finally—albeit accidentally—to have found the Oslobodjenje building. When walking yesterday, I had not even come close. The soldier guarding the Parliament and Government Building, I now realize, had understood me perfectly and had answered me appropriately when he had told me it was far away.

During the siege, this main street into the center had been known as "Sniper Alley." Oslobodjenje staff daily blasted up and down this street in cars: First, to get the news from the downtown office to the printing plant that continued to operate in the basement beneath the rubble in Nedjarići; second, to deliver the newspapers into the city. That was war; this is peace. Tonight there are SFOR troops at nearly every intersection, as President Kučan must come out this main street to reach the airport.

Sarajevo Hospitality

Election monitors are moving into Hotel Saraj, and I am moving out. That is a little unfortunate in that I suspect these monitoring folks will have some interesting stories to tell. First, though, I am going this morning to the US Embassy. The State Department recommends that I register there. I find the US Embassy in the same fortified compound that serves as SFOR headquarters. Security is tight, but the people are very friendly.

Properly registered, I pick up a newspaper and sit down at a café a few blocks from the Embassy and near the Presidency Building to read over the headlines. Across the way is a city park, green and pleasant, with ancient-looking Muslim headstones scattered about. Some, with turban-shaped tops, look like mushrooms that have popped up during the night. I recall reading somewhere that several of Sarajevo's parks are in fact old cemeteries.

Nuances in Cross-Border Campaigning

Izetbegović and Kučan are pictured on the front page of today's *Oslobodjenje* cutting a ceremonial ribbon to open the new *Bosnalijeka* ("Bosnia Medicine") production line in Sarajevo. Kučan used the occasion to emphasize that there is great scope for economic and political cooperation between their two countries. This makes for a nice campaign appearance for Izetbegović (although the probability of his not being reelected to the Presidency is very close to zero).

Electioneering continues on all fronts, and the international community is showing its own interest. The President of the European Parliament, Jose-Maria Delgado was in town this week for a two-day visit. He expressed hopes that the upcoming elections will create conditions for a more civil and multiethnic country and that, after the vote, more refugees will return to Bosnia and Hercegovina from other European countries. Delgado offered his view that the non-nationalist parties may improve their positions in the weekend elections and that that would be a fine thing indeed.

Delgado met with Izetbegović, who is regarded as a Bošnjak nationalist. He met also with Krešimir Zubak, the Croat member of the Bosnia and Hercegovina Presidency. Zubak is running this time under the banner of his New Croat Initiative (NHI), which presents itself as a more democratic spin-off of the HDZ and which supports full equality for all nations in a unified Bosnia and Hercegovina. Asked why he did not meet also with Momčilo Krajišnik, who is the Serb member of the Presidency and a member of Karadžić's Serb Democratic Party (SDS), Delgado said he could not sit down with one who is clearly opposed to democracy.

Last week was a good one for Zubak. He was invited for a meeting at the Vatican just days before the election. Among Croat political forces, not only the Holy See clearly favors him and his NHI but so, too, does the international community at large. Croats in Bosnia and Hercegovina can vote along their ethnic line and still have something like a clear choice. The HDZ's Jelavić, supported by Tudjman and Croatia, is a hard-line nationalist who will irritate the international community. Zubak is a moderate nationalist with whom the international community knows it can work. Nobody realistically expects, though, for Zubak to win.

Tudjman, Jelavić and their HDZ, meanwhile, continue under pressure. The OSCE's electoral commission has refused to reconsider its decision to take the names of 15 HDZ candidates off the electoral lists. If there ever was any question as to whether or not the HDZ in Bosnia and Hercegovina was really under Tudjman's thumb, all doubt now has been removed. He has demonstrated a strong, personal interest in this election and the tribulations of his party's branch in Bosnia and Hercegovina. The US State Department, meanwhile, is suggesting that HDZ actions and statements coming out of Zagreb demonstrate that the Croatian powers-that-be do not sincerely support the concept (declared and established in the Dayton agreement) of a Bosnia and Hercegovina unified within the existing and internationally recognized borders. The international community is warning Croatia not to allow its military and its television and radio stations to interfere with the Bosnia and Hercegovina elections.

Oslobodjenje reports, too, today that OSCE's chief in Bosnia and Hercegovina, Robert Barry, also is warning Vojislav Šešelj, leader of the Serb Radical Party (SRS) in Yugoslavia, to keep his fingers out of the election campaign. Šešelj is Serbian Deputy Prime Minister, an open and staunch opponent of the Dayton peace accord, and an unrelenting proponent of expanding Serbia's borders into Bosnia and Hercegovina, Croatia, Macedonia and Montenegro (in the latter case, by annexation). Šešelj has a long history of nationalist activities, for which he was jailed in the 1980s. In 1991, Šešelj was one of the first Serb nationalists to organize a paramilitary group to fight in Croatia and in Bosnia and Hercegovina. He proudly named his army the *Četniks*. According to

Barry, Šešelj has been "ridiculing principles of the Dayton accord" and using nationalist and derogatory language in radio programs broadcast in Bosnia and Hercegovina. He is no longer allowed to send campaign-related messages through this country's electronic media.

Good Grapes, Great Water

I say goodbye to the Hotel Saraj and drive out to my new accommodations. Mrs. Babić makes coffee and her husband asks if I would not like to join him in having a glass of *rakija*, a clear and strong brandy made from grapes. This *rakija*, he explains, comes from the region near Mostar in Hercegovina, which has lots of sun and good conditions for growing grapes. I have to agree that this is a very nice *rakija* indeed. I nevertheless decline a second glass, as I want to settle in and do some work.

Mrs. Babić brings a tray with coffee. A rich head of foamy particulate tops the pot. As a prelude to pouring, she begins to spoon off the froth into the tiny porcelain cups. Her husband gently gestures her away from doing so into my cup. Seeing this, I quickly insist that she should proceed per usual. When in Bosnia, I explain, I prefer to do as the Bosnians do. If the hosts get scum in their coffee, then I want it in mine too.

After coffee and a bit of work on my part, my hosts invite me to join them for dinner. This is not part of the deal we agreed to, but they insist. We have a simple and hearty meal of meat, potatoes, pickled white peppers, bread and beer. People in the Balkans really like their peppers. These are the spicy sort and delightfully complement the local beer, named *Sarajevsko pivo*. Although I always expect to enjoy any food or beverage served to me in hospitality, I am particularly surprised as to how much I like this local "Sarajevo Beer." Living in the Czech Republic, I have become rather spoiled on good brew. I guess I did not expect to find exceptionally good beer in this partially Islamic country.

I will learn later that Sarajevo's brewery was built in 1881, just a couple years after the Austrians occupied the city and country. This, it seems to me, is one of the Austrians' finest gifts to Sarajevo, although I suppose the local Islamic leaders would have to disagree (at least in public). Good beer can be brewed only where there is great water, and Sarajevo is blessed with an exceptional underground aquifer.

During the siege, the brewery had been an important water source for the people of Sarajevo. It had been able to draw from its aquifer even when the city's central system was down. The Serb besiegers therefore regarded the brewery as an important target. People would sometimes walk for miles and then wait long in line to draw water there. Quite a few were killed while coming, going or standing in line.

After dinner Mr. Babić and I get to talking about a still-continuing struggle over a key city, named Brčko, in northern Bosnia. The struggle now is waged by way of heated argument rather than force of arms. As agreed in Dayton, control over this city on the Sava River is to be settled by binding arbitration. The subject of Brčko comes up as I am noting to my hosts some of the places around the country that I plan to visit in coming days.

I had tried to make the point that Brčko is very important to the Serb nationalists and that, it seems to me, they might even go back to war in order to keep it. Brčko is the key connection between the two lobes that constitute Republika Srpska. What I had meant to communicate is that the city is very important to them in strategic terms. I did not intend in any way to suggest that Serbs and Republika Srpska have more right to it than do the Federation, Croats and Muslims.

"It is important to us, too!" exclaims my host, going on to explain that Brčko is more a Muslim than a Serb city. Pretty soon he is rummaging about in a cabinet for what turns out to be an ethnographic map of Bosnia and Hercegovina. It is more detailed than my own ethnographic map. We look at other cities and regions, too, including the city and *opština* of Višegrad, which I also intend to visit. Located just 15 miles from the border of Serbia proper, Višegrad now is buried deep in Republika Srpska. The prewar population of the *opština* was two-thirds Muslim and one-third Serb. I do not expect to find any Muslims when I visit Višegrad.

High-Rises on the Front Line

I decide to take a walk around the neighborhood before dark. My host insists upon showing me about, and I happily accept his offer. This newish settlement of high-rise apartments, he relates, is known as *Sarajeva Polja* (or "Sarajevo Fields"). As we walk about, it becomes clear that the neighborhood was a lot harder hit in the bombardment than I initially had thought. The backside of these apartment buildings had faced directly into the front-line shelling. The apartments on that side were blasted hundreds of times. Some still are completely uninhabitable.

My hosts are fortunate to have had an apartment on the side of the building that faced away from the artillery and out into the central courtyard formed by a double line of residential towers. Mr. Babić explains to me, though, that on at least one occasion (and perhaps several times, although this is not quite clear to me) tanks drove down through that yard and fired upon the apartments on both sides. He tells me of having been ready with a homemade gasoline bomb that he could have thrown from his balcony.

The Sarajevo Fields apartments had been built about the time of the 1984 Olympics. In the same neighborhood are: Children's Village (a little community of houses built for orphans), the Olympic Village (colorful residential towers that had been built especially to house participants in the Winter Olympics), a specialized medical clinic (which was badly damaged and has been only partly rebuilt), and two modern dormitories (which are gutted and just now beginning to be reconstructed) that had been used for university students.

We walk by, too, the original village on the edge of which the *Sarajeva Polja* apartments had been built. This must be Nedjarići, for which this part of town is named. The small family homes all are badly smashed up. My host assures me that the people who lived in those houses will not return. Most of them, it seems, were Serbs.

Politics

You Get What You Vote For

Make no mistake about it: A great deal hangs on this weekend's election outcome. Donors among the world's democratic and developed countries will condition continuing aid to Bosnia and Hercegovina upon indications of progress toward building democracy and controlling nationalistic excesses. "Help Depends Upon Election Results," reads a headline in today's *Oslobodjenje*. The article points out that the EU is watching this election very closely and is considering how much to invest in this problematic country. The implication is that new programs and funds will be available if the right candidates are elected and if standards of democracy and human rights are accepted. Nor is this just a matter of handouts. Solid evidence of political and economic stability will be critical to encourage the private sector to lend and invest in this country.

Republika Srpska is the part of Bosnia and Hercegovina that the international community of aid donors and peace enforcement finds most perplexing and frustrating. It is the entity that stands economically to lose the most if these elections, from the donors' viewpoint, go the wrong way. On the Serb side, this is shaping up to be a close vote between the forces of extreme nationalism that could snuff out prospects for continuing foreign aid and the forces of also-extreme nationalism but which have a proven track record in attracting foreign aid. In any case, Serbs will elect nationalists.

In the relevant realm of Serb politics, there are essentially two opposing coalitions: *Koalicija Sloga* (i.e., "Coalition Unity") and the SDS-SRS coalition. The international community prefers Sloga (as Coalition Unity is generally known) over SDS-SRS. Sloga leaders at least pay lip service to honoring commitments made in the Dayton peace accords. SDS-SRS leaders are more inclined to talk and act as though the Dayton agreement is just another cease-fire.

SDS is the party of Radovan Karadžić, and SRS is that of Vojislav Šešelj. Because Karadžić has been indicted for genocide and other war crimes by the International War Crimes Tribunal in The Hague, he technically is not allowed to participate in politics within Bosnia and Hercegovina. *Oslobodjenje* reports today, though, that Karadžić's picture has been showing up in Republika Srpska on small-format posters carrying the caption: "He meant peace." Šešelj, meanwhile, is reported today to be protesting OSCE Chief Robert Barry's banning him from participating in the SRS campaign in Republika Srpska. Šešelj, who says OSCE is threatening that some of his SRS candidates could have their names stricken from the electoral lists, has stated in a radio broadcast that he will no longer campaign.

Sloga, meanwhile, is a coalition of three Serb parties, which are assembled around three personalities. Biljana Plavšić is, until the election, at least, President of Republika Srpska. Milorad Dodik is Prime Minister of Republika Srpska. Plavšić and Dodik each have their own parties, made up of people who broke away from Karadžić's SDS.[37] Plavšić's and Dodik's parties stand for cooperating with the international community and working to build a market economy. In words more than deeds, they support full implementation of the Dayton accord.

Plavšić is a former Karadžić crony who became President of Republika Srpska in 1996 (initially as acting president) after Karadžić was indicted for alleged war crimes. Some regard her to be, at heart, as vicious in her ultranationalism as any other Serb leader. Portraying herself as a model of reasonableness, toleration, and even democratic values, Plavšić won over the international community. Partially in return for opposing Karadžić and his crew in Pale, Plavšić (and especially her western piece of Republika Srpska) were rewarded with international aid and a cloak of respectability.

Rounding out Sloga is the Socialist Party of Republika Srpska and its leader, Živko Radišić. The party shares the name and similarities in outlook with Slobodan Milošević's party in Serbia and rump Yugoslavia.

Many Nationalists from Which to Choose

Typical of an underdeveloped democracy, there are dozens of political organizations participating in this election. These include 58 parties, 10 coalitions, 5 alliances and 10 independent candidates. Many of these, though, are practically irrelevant. All over Sarajevo and throughout Bosnia and Hercegovina candidates' countenances beam out at voters from billboards and posters. In many ways this campaign is similar to electoral campaigns anywhere. Exceptions, though, include the facts that television and radio advertising are not allowed and that

---

[37]For the record, Plavšić's party is called the Serb People's Alliance Biljana Plavšić. Dodik's party is the Party of Independent Social Democrats.

an outside force—the OSCE—is closely supervising the candidate-selection process, the campaigns, and the voting itself.

All parties and candidates must publicly declare their positions on several specific issues, such as the return of refugees and displaced persons to their homes, minority rights, and matters of education and social affairs.[38] In short, each party must state its view in regard to implementing the basic elements of the Dayton agreements. Of course, politicians most always and everywhere take considerable liberty with the truth, and, in former Yugoslavia, where byzantine duplicity is normal practice in diplomatic and political matters, one cannot have very high expectations for truth in election campaigning. Radio and television advertising would only accentuate the demagoguery, so it probably is a good thing that electronic-media advertising is forbidden.

Indications are that the OSCE, through its Provisional Elections Commission (PEC), is running things pretty strictly. It was a PEC subcommission that struck some of HDZ's candidates from the electoral list. The PEC is sticking to its guns. Election regulations were violated, the PEC says, and the disqualifications represent the cost of breaking the rules. Tudjman calls this "elections engineering." This has a hollow ring coming from the Croatian president, who arranged—with the clear intent to boost his own party's results—for Croats from the adjoining sovereign country of Bosnia and Hercegovina to vote in Croatia's 1995 elections.

The most important races in this weekend's voting are for:

- Presidency of Bosnia and Hercegovina,
- President and Vice-President of Republika Srpska,
- House of Representatives of Bosnia and Hercegovina,
- National Assembly of Republika Srpska,
- House of Representatives of the Federation, and
- Assemblies for each of the 10 cantons of the Federation.

The Presidency of Bosnia and Hercegovina is made up of three members: One Croat, one Muslim and one Serb. Under new rules, the Muslim member will not automatically become President of the Presidency just because he receives more votes than do his Serb and Croat colleagues. In fact, the member of the Presidency who wins the second-largest number of votes (which demographics assure will be the

---

[38]Media Plan, *Guide for Journalists in Bosnia & Hercegovina: Elections '98* (Sarajevo: Media Plan, 1998).

Serb winner) will serve first as head of state. The term will be for eight months. The number-three vote-getter among the Presidency members (which will be the Croat winner) will serve as President for the next eight months. Only after 16 months, then will the Bošnjak member rotate into the top spot.

There is no question that Izetbegović, the Coalition's presidential candidate, will win the most votes. Despite the professed expectations and idealistic wishes expressed by representatives of the international community, most voters will cast their ballots along their prospective ethnonational lines. That means the majority of Muslims will vote for the Coalition for a Single and Democratic Bosnia and Hercegovina. Although the Coalition consists of four parties, it effectively is led by Izetbegović's SDA. SDA is the largest, strongest and best-organized of the coalition partners. Its leaders like to regard SDA as the absolute leader of the Bošnjaks. SDA presents itself as a centrist party that wants to rebuild a multiethnic Bosnia and Hercegovina. In fact, though, good Bošnjaks regard SDA as "their" national party. SDA is based in the Federation and has no contacts with any party in Republika Srpska.

Izetbegović has been SDA's leader from its founding and President of Bosnia and Hercegovina since 1990. A lawyer and writer by profession, Izetbegović was twice jailed by the communists for Islamic nationalist activities (in the 1940s and again in the 1980s). There is wide difference of opinion as to just how dedicated he is to building an Islamic and Bošnjak state versus a secular and multiethnic one.

Although he is not really serious competition these days, Izetbegović's archenemy, Fikret Abdić also is running for the Muslim seat in the Presidency. Abdić's party is the Democratic People's Union (NDZ) and can be expected to make its best showing in the Bihać and Cazin area of northwest Bosnia. Abdić has a different conception than does Izetbegović as to how Bosnia and Hercegovina should be organized and run. He favors dividing Bosnia and Hercegovina along ethnic lines into cantons. Predominantly Serb and Croat cantons, then, could have close ties with Serbia and Croatia.

The current Croat member of the joint Presidency, Krešimir Zubak, is running as an underdog. He was earlier elected as a HDZ member, but broke away from that extreme nationalist party only in late-July 1998 to start his more moderate nationalist party. Compared to the HDZ, Zubak's NHI stands for more democracy and normalized relations between peoples. The man most favored to win the Croat seat in the Presidency is Ante Jelavić, the HDZ candidate. SDP, the strongest party not of the nationalist persuasion, has chosen as its presidential candidate, Gradimir Gojer, who is running for the Croat seat.

Voters in Republika Srpska will elect the third member of the joint presidency. Momčilo Krajišnik (SDS) is the reigning Serb member in the Presidency of Bosnia and Hercegovina. He is of course running on the SDS-SRS ticket. The general view seems to be that a vote for Krajišnik is the same as a vote for Karadžić. Sloga is putting forward Živko Radišić, the Socialist Party head, as its candidate for the joint Presidency. The international community—holding its collective nose—prefers Radišić over Krajišnik.

In Republika Srpska, the big race to watch is that for president of that Serb entity. Sloga is fronting the Serbian Iron Lady, Biljana Plavšić. The SDS-SRS coalition offers Nikola Poplašen, a black-bearded ultranationalist from Šešelj's party of Radicals.

Public Enemy Number One

Zijo is joining me for lunch today. Although my invitation had been stated in terms of this being a social occasion, I am not too surprised to learn that he has arranged a meeting with some local leaders of the SDP. First things first, though, and so we have pizzas at the Pizzeria Princess, which is out at the edge of town and just down the hill from where I am staying. Zijo tells me I am lucky to live near one of the better pizzerias in town. There are several SFOR and UN vehicles out front, so I guess word about the food has gotten around.

SDP is the direct descendant of Bosnia and Hercegovina's former League of Communists. It is now regarded as the largest, best-organized and strongest opposition (i.e., non-nationalist) party. That is in spite of the fact that the SDP performed poorly in 1990, when the first multiparty elections were staged all around what was then Yugoslavia. Nationality was the major issue in the 1990 vote, and SDA, SDS and HDZ (elected by Muslims, Serbs and Croats, respectively) had come out on top in that vote. It has taken a few years for the SDP to rebuild market share in the political environment defined by nationalisms.[39]

---

[39]There is a second, and competing, party of social democrats. Known as the Social Democrats of Bosnia and Hercegovina (to distinguish it from the Social Democratic Party of Bosnia and Hercegovina, or SDP), this party is ideologically almost identical to the SDP. Issues of personality and control over assets of the former League of Communists have stymied efforts to merge the two parties. This second social democratic party is associated with the name of Ante Marković, a strongly reformist prime minister of Yugoslavia who was attempting to keep his

The SDP has its headquarters for the municipality of Sarajevo's Novi Grad ("New Town") conveniently located in the Novi Grad municipality building. Across the street is the television building, which does not appear too badly today considering that it had been a favorite and frequent target for the gunners in the hills during the siege. There is nothing ceremonial, and certainly nothing luxurious, about this local SDP office. There are two rooms, several desks that look like they get little use, and a round conference table for six or eight people. The conference table is the heart of the office. There is a telephone on the table. A fax machine in the corner is getting more use as a telephone than as a fax. Ashtrays are ample in number. A jumble of books partially fills one shelf of a bookcase in a corner. Two of the books are by Edvard Kardelj, who had been Tito's chief ideologist. One of Kardelj's tasks had been to develop a constitutional formula to encourage—or force—the various ethnonational groups to live together in peace. The Kardelj books are at the end of the row and look like they actually have been consulted from time to time. My feeling is that most of the Novi Grad SDP's work is done not in this office but rather out in the campaign trenches.

Four people are at the table when we arrive. Each is introduced by name and ethnic identity. At least one person from each of the three major ethnic groups is present. The hospitality borders upon the overgenerous. Before I know it, in front of me are a shot of brandy, a cup of coffee and a glass of *Fanta*. The municipal SDP president, a Mr. Mahmutović, has been delayed in another meeting, but we start talking without him and continue adding to the room's already dense cigarette smoke.

A Mrs. Lukić, sitting to my right, finishes her phone conversation, then introduces herself and her party. She is a Serb and a member of the SDP's ruling council for Bosnia and Hercegovina. Friendly, confident and strong, Lukić has the demeanor of one who is not at all new to politics. SDP, she makes clear, regards nationalism as public enemy number one in Bosnia and Hercegovina. SDP is the only major party that is active throughout Bosnia and Hercegovina—both in the Federation and in Republika Srpska.

---

country together during the last couple years before it disintegrated altogether. A Croat from Bosnia and Hercegovina, Marković had won weak support from the US as Yugoslav Prime Minister and even was popular among his countrymen, but he and his government increasingly were frustrated in their efforts by powerful and increasingly nationalistic politicians in the individual republics.

Lukić and SDP regard religion, education and the role of women in society as key issues. Religious freedom is important, but, in this country, as religion is the main defining element of national identity, and nationalism is divisive, so religion should be a purely private matter. Lukić criticizes specifically the assertion that parliamentary proceedings should be interrupted for prayer.

Education and women are related issues. Many Muslims want to send only their boys to school. Lukić says she is especially concerned that a self-perpetuating underclass could be created on the basis of the many Muslim families who were left fatherless by the war. There is a danger that today's poorly educated and widows will raise undereducated daughters and may have no one to support them in their old age.

A smiling and apologetic Mr. Mahmutović, looking like he has just stepped off a campaign poster, comes through the door. He is the glad-handing public-face politician in contrast to the diligent and capable functionary that is the Lukić character. Mahmutović asserts that, after this election, the leading coalition will need to consult SDP on every issue. His party will be a strong and active opposition. SDP will assure those steps needing to be taken to build a civil society and strong economy will not be ignored for the sake of purely national issues. SDP, he emphasizes, aims to be a classical left-wing party in the European sense. Few of its members yearn for the communist past.

Integrity Is One Thing, Politics Another

Will this be a free and fair election, I asked Zijo as we leave the municipal building. "Never fair," he responds matter-of-factly. And why not? Will there not be election monitors, for example, to assure fairness? Indeed there will be, he assures, noting that both foreign observers and the political parties' own monitors will be at the polling places. But there are ways to influence the outcome, and most of these will benefit the Muslim coalition. For instance, he says, some people are blind or very old and need help to vote. There will be one person at each polling place authorized to provide assistance in the voting booth. That person, in addition to all the other polling-place personnel will be chosen by SDA.

Zijo is quick to note that Izetbegović almost certainly is a basically good man. But he is old and tired and maybe not entirely so sharp mentally as he once was. It takes many people to build and to run a political organization, and human integrity may not always be the strongest character trait of those who are able to get the work done.

Several authors writing about the decline of Yugoslavia and Bosnia and Hercegovina's war-time tribulations remark upon Izetbegović, even in the early-1990s, as an apparently exhausted man and reluctant politician. Izetbegović, who is now 74, entered electoral politics only in 1990, but he was an anticommunist dissident and Islamic activist from his very youth. In 1970 he wrote and distributed a religious and political tract called the *Islamic Declaration*. Serb nationalists find in this work an intention to build a fundamentalist Islamic state. They exaggerate. Certainly, though, *Islamic Declaration* promotes strengthening Islamic values in society and among secularized Muslims. Today, Izetbegović is criticized by some for being overly fundamentalist and by others for being too moderate. From all that I have read about the man, I get a sense that Izetbegović truly would prefer a Bosnia and Hercegovina in which Serbs, Croats, Muslims and others can live together. But he must be a practical politician now; if this society is to be divided along ethnonational lines, he wants the Bošnjaks to be united, organized and strong.

Feeling Freedom Yet?

It is a long walk from the center of Sarajevo to Žuć, a hill north of the city that once was forested but is today nearly treeless. Žuć was stripped bare as the besieged city's residents gathered wood there. This was a hazardous but necessary wartime activity. Žuć is also the site of one of the bloodiest battles in the struggle for Sarajevo. The fight was over much more than wood-cutting rights.

At 850 meters above sea level, Žuć is small relative to other high points overlooking Sarajevo. The mountains Trebević and Igman, by comparison, stand 1,502 and 1,629 meters, respectively. But Žuć is situated in a strategically very advantageous place. A line drawn south from its peak would bisect widthwise the Miljacka valley basin that is filled by Sarajevo and its adjoining suburbs. From its top, one may peer down into virtually all parts of the city. The Bosnian Serb forces dearly wanted that hill; the Bosnian Muslim army knew that to lose Žuć might well mean to lose everything.

Only a few burned-out houses dot the lower side of Žuć as seen, across a small valley, from where I stand in the little community known as Sokoje. Sokoje is on another, lower hill which stands between Žuć and Sarajevo. Although I am in one small segment of a front line that was a tight ring around and above Sarajevo during the siege, people here sometimes feel as if they were 100 miles from the capital city.

"Nobody ever comes up here—no foreign aid workers, no journalists," remarks Zijo, who himself lives nearby. "They are afraid to come here. I don't know why." While Sarajevo proper teems with the staff and vehicles and activities of foreign assistance organizations, the poor communities standing between Žuć and the city center are very, very quiet. Of course, Sarajevo is no Shangri-La. There is not sufficient housing there, either, for all who wish to live in the city. Today I will encounter several people in this community who officially should be living in Sarajevo proper but are staying up here in the hills with family or friends until their houses or apartments in town can be reconstructed.

If Sokoje feels abandoned, and if nearby Briješće, which I also will visit today, believes it is being ignored, then how many other communities are there, much farther from Sarajevo, where people feel forsaken? I will begin next week to visit villages and cities throughout Bosnia and Hercegovina. Then I will see. Perhaps all is relative, and people feel more ignored here in their hillside villages because they see so much going on in town.

In a (Not Very) Mixed Neighborhood

We stop in to visit Jozo. He and his family are the only Catholics in the sea of Muslims that is his village. Jozo stayed in his home throughout the war. Serb fighters were all around, he says, and he, like most of his neighbors, needed to stay to protect his house. Perhaps I should say that Jozo stayed "near" to his home. He takes me around to one side of his house and shows me the underground bomb shelter hidden there and in which he and his wife slept most nights for nearly four years. The shelter is dug well down into the ground, and more soil is mounded on top. A ventilation tube pokes out horizontally from the mound and elsewhere a small pipe for a chimney. Jozo says it was cold and uncomfortable sleeping in that hole in the ground. During the conflict, several shells did fall into his yard and damaged his house.

Jozo is a respected member of his community, and war did not change that. He points out that he always has gotten on well with his Muslim neighbors. Some Muslims even helped to build the Catholic church that he and his family attend, Jozo says. There were only a handful of Serb families in his neighborhood, and they are mostly gone now. Jozo assures that he never had any trouble with them, either.

Our threesome in Jozo's yard begins to grow. A young man from the electric company comes by to read the meter. He can look at the meter, of course, Jozo teases this clean-cut and affable Muslim, but Jozo says he has no money to pay the bill. The meter-reader is a former policeman. Many people would count themselves lucky to have such a job. Somehow, though, this young man apparently lost his taste for police work. The next-door neighbor, also a Muslim, drops in to return Jozo's car, which he had borrowed to go into town. All are sitting at his table, and Jozo still speaks openly.

The neighbor has on his house a new roof that was paid for by a German relief organization. He is thankful for the assistance but notes, too, that more money is needed for materials to finish the work. Additional money was committed for that purpose, but somehow that money got lost in the bureaucracy. Apparently, that happens a lot.

Whether or not the current peace will last, Jozo believes, depends upon politics and the politicians. The common people are full up with war, he says, but, from where he sits, it looks like the last war was created by only about 15 people. Jozo is afraid that the major political parties (without regard to their ethnic makeup) are filling up with criminals, and he points out, too, that some of those politicians would just as well go to war again.

I ask Jozo how long he thinks the SFOR troops will need to stay. Completely serious, he says the foreign forces might need to remain as long as 50 years. Within 24 hours after SFOR would leave, war would start again. Only this time, Jozo insists, it would be worse: Muslims would fight Muslims, Serbs would murder Serbs, and even Croats would join in killing other Croats. After the last war, people have histories, and their past doings are known to others. Some people even got rich out of the war, and that has built up a lot of anger and resentment.

•   •   •   •

As we stroll down the scarcely paved road, I ask Zijo about the foreign aid programs for house rebuilding and, in particular, about the "lost" money that was referred to in regard to the neighbor's house. Out of politeness, I had been reluctant to press the man for details. This is an altogether sensitive subject. After all, if one is getting aid, who wants to complain about how much it is or how it is being administered? People here have their pride, but many also have great need. At the same time, there is no small amount of fear and distrust.

In this neighborhood, Zijo remarks, if a house has a completely new roof, it most probably was paid for with foreign aid. Oftentimes, such a program will provide for little more than to put a new roof on a home. With that much done, the house may be regarded as minimally inhabitable and the homeowners may be left to their own resources and resourcefulness. In some cases, though, additional money may in fact be budgeted in order to make a home truly inhabitable. If some of that money disappears, there also may no longer be any officially responsible person around to whom one could go and inquire about it.

Thousands of new roofs are going on in Bosnia and Hercegovina. I see them every day as I drive about. Indeed, there is a great deal of construction in general. (In Bosnia and Hercegovina and Europe, as this country is rebuilt, somebody is making lots of money in the building materials business.) Still, there is much more work to be done than has been completed (or even yet begun) to date. This must create a logistics nightmare, and the potential for graft and corruption is huge. There also are cases where roofs have been stolen when the owner of a house under reconstruction was not around for a few days to guard it.

As we walk, we approach a small but beautiful new mosque, its pearly white minaret rising toward heaven. An uninhabitable, blown-out house stands almost next to it. Many inhabited homes in the neighborhood do not look much better. Without wishing to appear antireligious, it strikes me that somebody's priorities are a bit out of kilter. Yes, Zijo says, many new mosques are being built. He, too, sees the irony in providing people fine places to pray when they do not yet have decent homes in which to live and when the factories in which they once worked need investments in order to operate again. Officially, though, Zijo relates, donors in Islamic countries fund this construction, and they require that their money go specifically to building mosques.

We stop in to see an official for one of these hillside communes. I ask the kind of long-view question that a politician usually would relish. What does he envision his community will be like 10 years from today, not only in regard to housing and infrastructure but also in terms of a sense of community. I am surprised to hear his reply, which basically translates as "Your guess is as good as mine."

Formerly with a mixed population, this commune is today more than 90% Muslim. Roughly one-quarter of the people living here now are classified as displaced (generally because their own homes in the commune were destroyed) or are refugees from other parts of Bosnia and Hercegovina. Most of the commune's Serbs and Croats left before, during or after the wars. A few are now returning. They are finding, though, that their homes either are destroyed or are occupied by other people, generally Muslims. The people who remained here through the wars were especially ruthless in their loathing for those Serbs who fled their homes. These Serbs were labeled *Četniks*, and their houses generally were looted and burned.

The attitude was different, though, toward those few Serbs who did not abandon their homes and community. We stop in to visit one such Serb family. During the conflict, the family had been subjected to some verbal attacks but no physical violence. They stuck it out. The son, who had served in the army and fought on the Federation side, declares that he and his family are as much a part of this community and country as are any of his Muslim neighbors. There was not hate before the war, he recalls, and people need now to learn how to respect one another again. The former soldier remarks that the nationalist political parties are working to slow the healing. "The people here don't feel freedom yet," he says, and they will not until the nationalist parties change dramatically or disappear entirely.

Good Fun and a Show of Strength

Today is the last day of the election campaign. It is ending, at least here in Sarajevo, with considerable fanfare. Those who are particularly engrossed in politics are pretty worked up about it. I am watching this evening from a garden seat at Pizzeria Princess, which faces out onto the main road coming into town.

An SDA caravan goes by as I am putting in my order for a *Sarajevsko* beer and a Princess pizza. The caravan is made up mostly of taxis. I have been told that taxis are carrying passengers for free today to show their support for SDA (and that they, in return, will likely get a future tax break). The taxis fly SDA's green and white banner. Trucks, too, have been mobilized for the event. There is a large open truck filled with teenagers and banners. Fast behind is a *Coca-Cola* truck and a livestock truck (but with no animals inside). The *Coke* truck has kids clinging to its roof, but nobody has yet clambered on to the cattle truck, which only carries a banner.

Several military helicopters sweep diagonally across Sarajevo's valley. Another chopper hovers long over a hill to the north side of town, above where I had been this afternoon. Here in the valley, armored personnel carriers and jeeps are at nearly every intersection of the main road through town. Armed soldiers are spread about the major thoroughfares. Motorcycle cops and local police cars are zipping about, sometimes with their blue lights flashing. White vehicles labeled "UN" and "OSCE" are out in abundance, but that seems not too extraordinary. A television crew sets up on the boulevard for a few minutes to capture some footage for the nightly news.

Two very comfortable looking motor coaches roll toward town with SDP banners. Presumably, the party faithful are being bused in to attend the Social Democrats' final rally to be held this evening in front of the National Theater.

In short, there is a good show of military and police strength and people seem to be having fun. Tomorrow will be much quieter. That is the law, as today officially is the last day of the campaign. The day prior to the election is to be orderly and, one presumes, people are expected to be giving final contemplation to how they will cast their votes.

In Ali Pasha's Field

As I write this evening, I hear a party going on nearby. It sounds like a pretty big one. Curiosity finally gets the best of me, and I wander out to find the excitement. A Coalition rally, it is just a couple blocks away in another high-rise housing development, called *Alipašino Polje* (Ali Pasha's Field). The focus seems more on music than rhetoric.

A four-piece band is playing when I arrive and accompanies a blonde female singer in a long and slinky black-velvet dress. Although the words she sings are in the language locals like to call Bosnian, the undulating rhythm and intonation are more Eastern than European. Her voice bounces from high-rise to residential high-rise within the large quadrant at one end of which the stage is set.

Several thousand people of all ages are in and around the courtyard. Thousands more, no doubt, are listening, both voluntarily and involuntarily, from their apartments. For most of these people, this has got to be more entertaining than to watch the television debate that presently is going on and that features three Serb political candidates.

The rally is good, clean fun. Soft drinks are being sold, and if there is any alcohol on offer I do not see it. Some young people are dancing in a folksy, Eastern style. About the only mischief I see is the occasional group of boys who really ought not to be smoking those cigarettes they have managed to obtain. Then, too, a bevy of preteen girls have positioned themselves on top of a concrete bus shelter and are taunting a group of preteen boys by chanting the initials of a non-Coalition party.

The only military presence I see consists of three tired-looking soldiers sitting on a step and listening to the music. The military, I figure, must be on the periphery. I walk all around the area, though, and see not a single armored vehicle or even another soldier. In light of the general military presence in and around the city, the military is conspicuous here by its absence. Several Sarajevo Canton motorcycle police are patrolling the area slowly and continually, their blue lights flashing. It seems to me a virtual certainty that Coalition officials have cut a deal with the international military that allows them to use local police to protect the peace and requires SFOR to stay away. Dozens of Sarajevo Canton buses have also been hired to bus attendees in and out. Thousands of Coalition supporters (along with those who just like a good party) will get a free ride home tonight and be reminded that this has been brought to them by the ruling Bošnjak parties.

I walk back and then listen even from my bedroom as several more singers perform to a pleased crowd. A short volley of fireworks is set off at 11:45. It seems merciful to me that the pyrotechnics show is brief. In a housing development still pockmarked by hundreds of shallow shell craters, missile damage to every building, and skeletons of blown-out buildings on the periphery, it is hard for me to imagine that everyone here can really enjoy a good fireworks display the way they once did.

A Quiet Day

My relationship with my hosts, Ramiz and Vahida, has been on a first-name basis for some time now. We have fallen, too, into a routine. The three of us drink coffee together every morning at 7:30 and I talk about what I plan to do during the day. We call the strong coffee my *jutarnji lijek*, which means "morning medicine." I rarely have trouble to get out of bed at the start of the day, but I do need a little stimulant to get all systems operating properly. The radio or television is on, and Ramiz is almost always cheerful in the morning. Sometimes he sings a little and, as best we can, we discuss politics and current events. Each day Ramiz and I communicate a bit better than we did the day earlier.

I am learning more about my hosts. Although they have spent their adult lives in Sarajevo and raised their children here, both were born in eastern Hercegovina. Their hometown, which is almost on the border with Montenegro, now lies within Republika Srpska. Before the wars, the population there was about two-thirds Serb and one-third Muslim. Ethnic cleansing in that area apparently was thorough, and there are virtually no Muslims there now. I have not asked about their families and friends there. It seems, though, that quite a few friends and family of their generation moved away from their hometown already long before the violence of the 1990s. Quite a social circle from that town is here in Sarajevo. Several, too, now live in other European countries. Until the 1981 census allowed them to declare themselves Muslims, my hosts actually had identified themselves, for official purposes, as Serbs.

In the late afternoon or evenings, the three of us have coffee and discuss the adventures I have had that day. Sometimes we watch the evening news together, and Ramiz and I drink a little beer or *šljivovica* (a strong and clear plum brandy). In anticipation of the elections, there are advertisements every evening on television that are sponsored by SFOR and the local police. In the ads, an SFOR official explains that he believes the elections can be run quietly and fairly; then the local police from each the Federation and Republika Srpska tell about their commitment and ability to protect the voters and the voting process.

All Camps Had Their Parties

Today, Friday, seems exceptionally quiet in Sarajevo. On the 20-minute streetcar ride into the center, I notice that the SFOR military presence is much reduced relative to yesterday. The idea, it seems, is to demonstrate today that the local police can do the job, as advertised.

Sarajevo's finest, with their shiny Italian motorcycles and new police cars, are out in full force and active.

The elections tomorrow and Sunday are an opportunity for the proponents of peace and order to illustrate that Bosnia and Hercegovina is a civilized country. It is only realistic, I suppose, to expect that some others might use the event as an opportunity to demonstrate that all is not yet well in this country. Along with the vote tallies, another barometer of progress toward peace and harmony here will be to gauge how smoothly the polling process operates.

Oslobodjenje reports today that there will be 2,650 polling places and that 2,700 foreign observers from 37 countries will supervise them. The EU has donated about $6 million to finance the election. Some 2.75 million voters have been registered, but only 2.0 million of those will be present in Bosnia and Hercegovina to vote. The remaining 750,000 may vote at polling places in other countries or by mail.

The Coalition probably had Sarajevo's biggest preelection rally last night, but it was not the only one. *Oslobodjenje* has coverage today from several of these. Addressing the Coalition rally, Izetbegović said that "our goal" is neither victory for individual parties nor for the Coalition as a whole. Rather, the goal is to have a (unified) state of Bosnia and Hercegovina. After the election is over, he stated, "there will exist only two parties: the one in favor of Bosnia and Hercegovina and the one that is against it." Izetbegović called upon those not voting for the Coalition at least to vote for "moderate" parties.

Ejup Ganić, SDA vice-president, also addressed the crowd. His remarks, in my opinion and as I read them, demonstrate a sort of schizophrenia existing among some Muslims and moderates: "Because of us, Europe lives here," Ganić claimed. "In Sarajevo are heard both the sounds of bells tolling and of the calls to prayer.[40] In Sarajevo are spoken Bosnian, Croatian, Serbian, German and English. In this city one may watch all on television and read all in the press." In his words, I see again the fanciful notion of separate Bosnian, Croatian and Serbian languages. Language once was a unifying factor in Bosnia and Hercegovina. It transcended religious differences and other divisive elements of nationalism. Now, even some, like Ganić, who speak of

---

[40]Islamic practice does not use bells as a signal of celebration or to call their faithful to worship. Muslims are reminded to pray five times daily by calls to prayer that are cried out from minarets.

building a unified and pluralistic country seem bent upon contriving from language an instrument to divide people from one another.

At the Social Democrats' rally last night, their party president emphasized that SDP stands for tearing down all internal divisions within the country and for creating a single Bosnia and Hercegovina.

"Bosnia and Hercegovina is sick and tired of nationalism," SDP's Croat presidential candidate, Gradimir Gojer, told the SDP faithful. "I decided that I will fight against the (Croat) nationalism of Jelavić and Zubak. The largest multiethnic force in the state of Bosnia and Hercegovina nominated me. We must build up our country. We must assure that this no longer will be a devastated country. I am asking for the votes of Izetbegović's Bošnjaks, for the votes of Zubak's and Jelavić's Croats, and for all of Bosnia and Hercegovina to vote for me."

Although SDP's presidential candidate is a long shot, Gojer will benefit from Muslim crossover voting. A vote for Gojer, after all, is a vote against the Croat nationalist candidates. Izetbegović is a shoo-in for the Bošnjak presidential spot, after all, and he does not need all the votes he will receive. Also, some of the few Serbs living and voting within the Federation will vote for the Social Democrat. Gojer will benefit, too, from the fact that Zubak, with his breakaway NHI is splitting the Croat nationalists' votes.

At the restaurant on the bend in the Miljacka where a few days ago I contemplated the beauty of Sarajevo, there were meeting last night the sort of non-nationalist political forces that the international community favors.

"We are a coalition which does not want to go either to the left or to the right. *Koalicija Centra* ("Coalition of the Center") is not fighting for power but for the survival of the nation and state of Bosnia and Hercegovina," declared Salih Fočo, a *Koalicija Centra* leader.

This coalition consists of just two parties, the Republicans and the Liberal Bošnjak Organization. Stjepan Klujić, a former president of HDZ in Bosnia and Hercegovina, leads the Republicans. Klujić had been elected into the Bosnia and Hercegovina Presidency in the 1990 elections, but he was run out of the HDZ for being insufficiently Croat-nationalist and too willing to cooperate with other groups. The Liberal Bošnjaks, too, are a spin-off from a more nationalistic party. As a practical matter, *Koalicija Centra*, which has no ethnonational identity, will have done very well if it wins a single parliamentary seat in this election.

Nationalism's practical importance is demonstrated by the fact that to be regarded as insufficiently nationalist is the greatest political danger to any Serb party. Plavšić and Dodik have been defending their nationalist credentials in the final days of the campaign. *Oslobodjenje* today summarizes an interview that Dodik gave to a Belgrade newspaper. He rejected critics' accusations that his Republika Srpska government is moving in a direction that would cause the Serb entity to be merged into an undivided Bosnia and Hercegovina.

The State Department Warned Me, After All

My main objective for today is to obtain deutschemarks. That is the de facto currency here, although the official currency is the so-called "convertible mark." Convertible-mark banknotes circulate alongside deutschemarks and the two types of bills are completely interchangeable. The US State Department's travel advisory had warned me in advance to bring plenty of deutschemarks. It also advised that "almost all of Bosnia and Hercegovina is a cash economy" and that things here are expensive.

Good advice. Be that as it may, what I had thought would be plenty of deutschemarks is not going to be enough for my entire stay. I spend a good part of the afternoon going from bank to bank and travel agency to travel agency trying to draw money on my *Visa* or *MasterCard.* I now accept that it is not possible to do so in Sarajevo. This is a *Diners Club* town. To use a *Visa* or *MasterCard* for cash, I must go to a Croat bank in either Vitez or Mostar. I plan to visit both those cities next week anyway, so I will see.

To my way of thinking, time is rarely wasted by wandering (be that aimlessly or purposefully but in vain) in a city that is new to me. That is how I learn my way around, and I am always finding something interesting or useful. And so it is today. In my roaming about, I come upon a bookstore selling English-language newspapers. I also find there Richard Holbrooke's new book, *To End A War.* This had been released in the US just prior to my departure, but I had not had an opportunity yet to buy it in Europe. Holbrooke is the US diplomat responsible for managing the Dayton peace negotiations.

●　　　●　　　●　　　●

Following the evening news and coffee with my hosts, I sit down this evening to start in on Holbrooke's memoir. I manage to knock off the first 152 pages before falling asleep. That gets me so far in the diplomatic chronology as 2:15 a.m. on 14 September 1995, that is, to a point almost exactly three years ago. In an unscheduled negotiating session with Bosnian Serb leaders at Milošević's villa outside Belgrade, the US team had just hammered out an agreement to end the siege of Sarajevo in return for a cessation of NATO bombing.

A few days earlier, the US effort, supported by that NATO bombing, had brought Bosnian Muslims, Serbs and Croats to the bargaining table in Geneva. There, the three sides' foreign ministers had agreed for the first time that Bosnia and Hercegovina would "continue its legal existence with its present borders and continuing international recognition." Further negotiations were to go forward, however, on the basis that the country would be internally divided between a Republika Srpska and a Federation of Muslims and Croats.

Tomorrow morning, elections will begin in the internally divided country that eventually emerged from those negotiations.

Supervised Democracy in Action

Quiet Day at the Polls

Zijo is monitoring for SDP today at his neighborhood polling place. I drop in to see what there is to see. Nothing too exciting is going on there, which, of course, is exactly as it should be. The setting is not much different from what one would expect to see in any small-precinct voting site in the US, with the possible exception that there are three or four bored policemen milling around outside and several election monitors sit on each side of the room. A big ballot box that is sealed with security tape stands ceremoniously on a table in the middle of the room.

On one end of the room, election workers check voters' identification against the registration list, examine their fingers with an ultraviolet light to make sure they have not voted before, hand out ballots, then daub the voters' fingers with an invisible and indelible dye. The voters mark their ballots in a private booth at the other end and drop their ballots into the box on the way out.

Zijo has told me in the past, as he will again in the future, that Bosnians are always finding some reasons to be jealous of one another. Today, he is jealous that the Coalition has provided its monitors with plentiful food and drinks. SDP is not feeding its monitors, at least not those up in the hills above Sarajevo.

While he had feared there might be indirect pressure on some to vote for the ruling Coalition, Zijo says he has seen no evidence of that yet. Overall, he thinks things are going better than was the case in 1996, when was the last general election. There were then quite a few difficulties. If there is any controversy this time, he says, it is likely to come at the end when the numbers of votes and ballots must be reconciled against the number of voters recorded to have passed through.

This voting station is well-provided with international monitors: three Japanese and one Italian. I speak with Yoshi, a Japanese monitor who is watching with the aid of a local interpreter. Yoshi says he has seen no direct pressure to influence anybody's vote.

Five Quarters of Hell and a Poor Example

So long as I am out and about with the car, I decide to take a drive past the airport and a quarter of the city known as Dobrinja. Early in the war, when Zlatko Dizdarević wrote his *Sarajevo: A War Journal*, his journal entry for 19 November 1992 was entitled "Songs in Dobrinja."

Sarajevo's bombardment and blockade had been going on for a few months at that time. The population already was desperate, but the siege still had three years to run. Dizdarević wrote of the exceptional inner strength, cooperation and humanity of Dobrinja's residents. Yesterday, I was reminded of Dobrinja by an editorial in *Oslobodjenje* under the headline "On the Edge: Dobrinja's Bitterness."

As I drive eastward out of Sarajevo at the lower end of the valley, the terminal and runway of Sarajevo International Airport are on my right, with the landing strip running parallel to the road. On my left is the outer edge of Dobrinja. It is a hellish mess.

Dobrinja is a substantial suburb on the very edge of Sarajevo, just over a low hill from where I stay in Nedjarići. It is made up of mostly low-rise apartment buildings and semidetached houses. These are solidly constructed of concrete and generally less than 20 years old. Early in the war, Serb nationalist forces had taken control of the airport across the road. They had surrounded the isolated suburb on three sides and had placed big guns in the nearby hills. Dobrinja's residents were commanded to surrender, so that the ethnically mixed residential quarter could be made a Serbs-only community. The residents refused, and they defended Dobrinja as best they could. Dobrinja never submitted and never was taken. It was, though, cut off from the rest of Sarajevo and pounded by thousands upon thousands of artillery shells.

Dobrinja is divided into five quarters, known as Dobrinja 1 to Dobrinja 5. When the dust of the war settled and the peacemakers had drawn their lines, Dobrinja 5 lay within Republika Srpska while Dobrinjas 1 through 4 were in the Federation. Yesterday's editorial decries the plight of families caught on the wrong side of the line and who are temporarily living in housing that is owned by others. The return of displaced people to their homes has become a contentious issue between local officials and international donors, and aid to Sarajevo for refugee programs has been frozen.

Under terms of the December 1997 Sarajevo Declaration, Sarajevo was to be "a model of coexistence and tolerance for the rest of the country." Representatives of Bosnia and Hercegovina, the Federation, Sarajevo Canton and the international community adopted this Declaration. It set a target of returning at least 20,000 non-Muslims to Sarajevo Canton during 1998. Aid to Sarajevo from the international community was conditioned on fulfilling that goal.

"Seven months on," concludes a recent report, "the Sarajevo authorities have failed to meet most of the Declaration's main benchmarks or take adequate, concrete steps to enable the return of anywhere close to 20,000 minorities this year. Indeed, as of early-August, only 1,300 minorities—7 percent of the target number—had actually returned. These failures are, in large part, due to stalling, incompetence and general lack of will on the part of Sarajevo authorities and officials of the ruling SDA."[41]

The difficulties of displaced people go far beyond Dobrinja and Sarajevo. As noted in the editorial, some of the homes, for example in Dobrinja, to which Serbs might return are occupied by Muslims who were forced out of their houses in what is now Republika Srpska. These Muslims may have an abstract right to return and to live among Serbs, but that does not mean that, as a practical matter, they can or wish to do so.

An enormous number of terribly difficult problems must be sorted out in this devastated country. Foreign aid can help—and is helping. But there are barriers to resolving many of these difficulties that local people and their leaders must get over on their own. That will require the kind of inner strength, cooperation and humanity that helped Dobrinja's residents to survive their terrible siege.

Electioneering Spin

At the end of day one, the elections process is getting decidedly mixed reviews. There have been some problems today, according to news reported this evening on an OSCE-sponsored Elections '98 television program. At least several dozen polling places did not open according to schedule, usually because they did not receive on time their official rosters of registered voters. In volatile Mostar, a town and district shakily divided between Croats and Muslims, there was an incident as one polling place was opening. According to an OSCE spokesman, a man entered the polling place and began hurling abuse on the workers and observers while sweeping documents and materials from the tables.

On the other hand, many smiling voters were interviewed as they left their voting sites. Shown on television were people who used glowing terms to describe the organization of the voting process. Another, though, noting that millions of deutschemarks had been spent to run the vote wondered aloud why it was such a shambles.

---

[41]International Crisis Group, *Too Little Too Late: Implementation of the Sarajevo Declaration* (Brussels and Washington: International Crisis Group, September 1998).

A Bošnjak and His *Vikendica*

Ramiz and I are driving this Sunday morning out to the *vikendica*, which he has been describing to me (only half in jest) as his "ranch." This weekend cottage is just a few miles out of town on the road to Mostar. Ramiz is eager to get going.

On our way out of town, while we are stopped at a traffic light, I notice a dark man on the center island. He is often there, and so sometimes are other members of his family. He limps up and I pass a deutschemark through the window. "He is a Gypsy," flatly remarks Ramiz, conveying information but neither surprise, approval nor disapproval.

Beyond Ilidža, an old spa town at the end of the Miljacka valley, the countryside is rugged, green and beautiful. It is all hills and mountains and valleys, with a few farms, cottages and villages thrown in. I surely drove this road into Sarajevo when I had come up from Mostar earlier in the summer. But I do not recognize it now. The first time I had traveled this road, the very fact that I actually was driving from Mostar to Sarajevo made it a big adventure and I had been primarily concerned about getting to my destination. This time, it is not an adventure but merely an excursion, and I am now comfortable with being in Bosnia and Hercegovina.

The villages in this direction show very little war damage, which is quite in contrast with what I had seen in villages just a few miles away. This is traditionally a predominantly Muslim area, although with some Serbs and a very small proportion of Croats. When I remark on this, Ramiz tells me that "the *Četniks*" had not been in these villages. Be that as it may, he points out several factories along the way that he says Serbs had stripped of their machinery and equipment. The production lines had been taken off to Serbia. These include a furniture factory, a wood-products plant, and a drinks-bottling plant.

Much of the black-market traffic to supply Sarajevo during the siege had been conducted through this area. We pass the road to Mount Igman, which in American military and diplomatic history always will be associated with the accidental deaths of three American diplomats. The first chapter in Holbrooke's *To End a War* details why and how Robert C. Frasure, Joseph Kruzel and S. Nelson Drew died in August 1995 trying to reach Sarajevo on that dangerous road.

●　　　●　　　●　　　●

The *vikendica* is a sturdy, two-story, wooden cottage with a steep-pitched roof. It stands back on a level break above a long and steep slope that drops down through a pasture and forest to the valley bottom and a mostly hidden village below. Behind the cottage, the slope rises gently across Ramiz and Vahida's small vegetable garden, now depleted for the season, through an orchard and up to a hilltop pasture. A small shed for firewood and tools and an outhouse complete the "ranch" estate.

Inside the *vikendica*, the single room on the ground floor is dominated by a large table with benches and chairs all around. The benches are built into the walls and double as beds. In the back corner is a kitchen with a wood stove. We climb the stairs to the loft. There is plenty of space for an entire family to sleep.

Ramiz leads me to the front of the loft and pulls open a big double window. We stand and admire the panorama. The dimensions of a Bosnian vista are determined primarily by the height of one's vantage point relative to the surrounding hills and one's position vis-á-vis the valley or valleys. Everywhere there are hills, and one generally is either looking up, down, or across one or more valleys.

Here, beneath the roof's peak, are a table and two stools. A bottle of Croatian brandy appears, and two glasses. It is very good brandy, Ramiz assures me, and, fortunately, it is available again now that the wars are over. We sit before the wide window and the even wider panorama. The brandy, I confirm is very fine. A cow lows somewhere below us, but I do not see her. What I do see are several small, cone-shaped haystacks, each constructed around a vertical pole. These are common in this part of the world, where small-scale farmers have but few animals to feed. Beyond the village below and across the valley, pale yellow splotches are beginning to dapple the tree-covered hills and mountains beyond. Autumn will arrive just about the time that I leave Bosnia and Hercegovina to return to Brno.

Perhaps, Ramiz queries hopefully, we can come out to the *vikendica* another time and stay overnight? We will roast meat, and he describes two different ways that he would like to do so, walk in the forest, search for mushrooms, and sleep where the air is fresh. As we gather some plums and apples to take with us back to town, Ramiz contemplates all that we will do when we come back the next time.

On the road back to Sarajevo, we pull into a roadside restaurant for roast lamb. As we drink *Sarajevsko* beers and wait for our food, I gently tease Ramiz about not being a good Muslim. He remarks that he is not a fundamentalist, but that he knows the *Koran*, goes without alcohol for 30 days each year during Ramadan and fasts during that period from morning until night. The *Koran*, he notes, is a good book of philosophy.

After our meal, we stop up the road to visit Ramiz's brother-in-law. There is much talk of politics, and, while not all is clear to me, it is obvious that there are different views represented. Ramiz, the brother-in-law and the latter's wife all talk as though each voted today for different parties. The brother-in-law teases Ramiz about supporting SDA and the Coalition: These, after all, are parties for Muslims. What kind of Muslim is Ramiz? He is fond of alcohol, does not go to the mosque, does not cover his head.

Ramiz is a pretty typical Sarajevo Muslim, in fact.

Welcome to Vitez

Keeping Sarajevo under siege from 1992 through 1995, but while not starving it completely, had excellent strategic value for the Serb side. While journalists and world attention were focused on the capital city, Serb forces were steadily going about their bloody business to clear Muslims and Croats from large portions of northern and eastern Bosnia and Hercegovina. Croat forces, too, were engaging in this brutal activity, as were some Muslims.

As terrible as was the siege of Sarajevo, then, that city and its citizens were lucky in comparison to many, smaller communities in which people were brutally tortured and slaughtered, sometimes by the dozens or hundreds. Beyond Sarajevo, people were driven from their homes, had their houses burned and their other belongings stolen, and, in many cases, saw their beloved mosques and churches leveled.

Central Bosnia is where some of the most hideous violence between Croats and Muslims occurred. That was especially in 1993–1994. Muslims and Croats must share that territory still today, because neither group was able to drive the other out. They did manage together to chase away most of the Serbs. I drove through that territory 10 days ago on the way in to Sarajevo. Now I will begin to take a closer look.

The world has seen time and again, as former Yugoslavia tears itself savagely apart, that sometimes the very efforts to find a way to peace arouse ever more violence. Such was the case in central Bosnia in response to the January 1993 Vance-Owen plan for cantonizing Bosnia and Hercegovina. The well-intended plan added fuel to a Croat-Muslim conflict already smoldering and flickering in central Bosnia. Even though Vance-Owen would die on the vine, by April 1993 there was vicious Croat-Muslim fighting in the Lašva River valley that runs from Travnik to Vitez and to Zenica.

Your Vote Counts (But Your Party Affiliation More So)

The calendar may disagree, but autumn has come to Bosnia. With Sarajevo to our backs, we head up the Bosna valley. Flecks of yellow already are splattered onto the landscape. It looks like intermittent rain and sunshine will be the order for at least the first part of the day. South of Zenica, the road forks. The Bosna continues north and the road with it. We turn west near the village of Lašva, and follow the river valley that is also named Lašva.

Along the way, Zijo tells me a bit about the counting of the ballots and why that may slow the release of results from the weekend's voting. When the ballot box was opened and the votes counted at the polling station he was monitoring, perhaps 15% or more of the ballots had simply been voided. Typically, a disgruntled voter would draw a giant X across the ballot and not select any candidates. Some wrote pointed messages on their ballots.

Why, one might well ask, had these individuals bothered to come to the voting place at all? The answer is simple, really: pressure. The monitors cannot tell who casts what vote, but they can keep track of who has been to the polling place and who has not. After a light turnout on the first of the two days of voting, it is probable that party activists had gone out to the villages and beaten the bushes, as it were, looking for votes. The message, subtle or otherwise, could have been that humanitarian aid, city services and employment might not get through to those who do not vote.

Politics is important in Bosnia and Hercegovina, and much more crucial to one's daily life than is true in some other countries. The choice of political party affiliation, for example, can be an important personal decision, both in terms of professional development and defining one's prospective social circle. Depending upon the town or area in which I visit, for example, I will be told by some people in coming days that only card-carrying members of the locally dominant nationalist party (be it Bošnjak, Serb or Croat) are able to start businesses. That might be a bit exaggerated, but I am sure there is more than a little truth in it.

In some cases, two or more parties may have to cut a deal locally to divide the available jobs and the other fruits of public service. That is the Bosnian version of equal opportunity. But it is not always just about jobs. Some people have strong political sentiments and prefer to associate only with those people who they know to share their views. Others feel pressure to behave in that way.

All Need Not Love One Another

A couple signs reading *Dobro došli u Vitez!* ("Welcome to Vitez!") show up along the road well before the city itself does. We drive on and nearly overshoot the town. There is some new construction out along the highway, but the main city lies a bit south of the main road. Getting our bearings, we come in on the west side of town. This turns out to be what is known as Old Vitez and is the Muslim part of the city.

It indeed looks old, but this is no picturesque old town. In fact, Old Vitez appears poor and crowded. New Vitez, we will be told, has a population of about 20,000 Croats and perhaps 20 Muslims. Old Vitez is home (at least for now) to some 1,500 Muslims and about 30 non-Muslims.

Using Zijo's party affiliation to get us started, we find and introduce ourselves to a local municipality official who also is an SDP leader. He and other municipal officials are a bit on edge today. Official results are not out yet, but, after the weekend's elections, a reshuffling of jobs can be expected. The official fills us in on what the resettlement situation looks like in his city.

Some Muslims now are returning to live on what is unofficially the Croat side of Vitez, and vice versa. But such cases are exceptional. There were a few Serbs who did not flee Vitez before, during or after the wars. Again, though, these are the rare cases, and no Serbs who had fled have yet returned. A few weeks ago, a group of Muslims who had run away from Vitez earlier attempted to return. The local Croats would not allow them peacefully to move back into their homes. According to the official, Ante Jelavić, the HDZ chief and Croat presidential candidate, is credited with stepping in personally to assure that the Muslims would be allowed to return to their homes. If the story is true, this seems an odd move for a nationalist Croat politician during an election campaign. Perhaps he needed to gain some brownie points with the international community.

We speak briefly about the local public administration and especially about the organization of the police force. In addition to the power-sharing dynamics created by political parties, there must be sharing between Croats and Muslims. The 1991 census showed the population in Vitez *opština* to be almost evenly divided between Muslims and Croats. The *opština* and the Central Bosnian Canton of which it is a part have a combined police force. The police commander is a Bošnjak, but the police officers are a mix of Muslims and Croats. The International Police Task Force (IPTF) demands that the police of the two ethnic groups work together.

The UN created the IPTF under terms of the Dayton accord. Its responsibilities include to train and advise local law enforcement personnel, as well as to monitor the activities and performance of the local police. Although it has plenty of difficulties, too, the IPTF garners considerable respect in Bosnia and Hercegovina. It greatly emphasizes protecting human rights. New, IPTF-trained policemen are everywhere around the country. Especially in the Federation, they typically drive new cars or motorcycles, have snappy uniforms and, by local measures, are quite well paid. I also see them on foot and, in Sarajevo, even on bicycle patrol. In light of the advantages and status these men and women in uniform enjoy, I am told that they are quite careful about keeping their jobs. That means they must follow the rules that IPTF lays down.

Our next stop is the local office of the Red Cross and Red Crescent, which occupy a small space barely large enough for two desks and a few chairs.[42] There, we meet a pretty young woman who is minding the shop. Shortly, an older woman walks into the small office and takes a seat. It is not quite clear whether she is an employee, some sort of local official or just what. She basically seems to belong there, though, and is interesting to speak with.

The young lady explains that her chief, Osman Smajić, is responsible for Red Cross operations throughout the Central Bosnian Canton, which includes eight *opštinas*. There is not enough money to do very much for the refugees, she says. Primarily, this office is distributing basic-food packages to roughly 500 people over the age of 65. Each monthly package includes 7 kilograms (about 15 pounds) of flour, 1 kg of beans or peas, 1 kg of rice and 1 liter of oil. That is not nearly enough to survive on, of course, but it is just enough to be worth coming after (if the distance to get here is not great). Most of the program participants are Muslims. A few Croats come for food but no Serbs. There seems to be some question as to how long there will be sufficient funding to continue this program.

All the Muslims in Vitez were pushed out on 15 April 1993, the older woman recalls. Many of them are now returning. The women agree that they would prefer to see Vitez return to the mixed-ethnic complexion that it had before the wars. The younger woman says, though, that Vitez never again will be as it was earlier. The elder is more optimistic, sensing that there is now some change for the better taking place. It is not necessary, she says, for all to love one another in order to live together. The older woman suggests, though, that we ask the people on the other side of town (meaning Croats) what they want. She has a skeptical tone in her voice.

Mr. Smajić arrives, and I ask him how he sees this now-divided community five to 10 years into the future. He asserts that life here will be just as it was before, no buts about it. That sounds to me more like

---

[42]Red Crescent is a humanitarian organization similar to Red Cross but which operates in, and is supported by, Islamic countries.

an official position than a realistic one. But he is insistent. Maintain peace and create jobs, the Red Cross coordinator says, and the people in their communities will take care of the rest.

Keeping the peace and creating jobs are top priorities in the minds of most people with whom I will speak during my travels here. Maintaining a virtual military occupation of the country may be enough to prevent new war, but creating sufficient jobs could be even more difficult. For the most part, that means opening and reopening factories. But a precondition for starting production is investment. Smart investors want to know how risky will it be to put their capital into projects here and what kind of returns can they get for exposing their money to those risks. For foreign investors, the risks here look very great indeed.

The main factory in Vitez, today as before the war, is a chemicals plant that is largely oriented to military production. Smajić formerly was responsible for nitroglycerin production at the factory. Before the wars, he had worked there for 30 years. The plant once had a mixed labor force, but Muslims all were dismissed from their jobs on 16 April 1993. The chemicals factory is said now to employ only Croats and to be virtually under the control of the Croat Council of Defense (HVO). The HVO is an army of HDZ.

We speak briefly about Ahmići, a Muslim village on the edge of Vitez which was destroyed, beginning at dawn on 16 April 1993, and which I will visit this afternoon. About 200 people were killed at Ahmići, Smajić says, noting that he himself helped to bury some of them. Many were children. Some entire families were killed, including 17 members of one family. Roughly 100 Muslims have returned to Ahmići, he notes, and they are beginning to settle in.

"Muslims want peace, and we want to live together (with the Croats)," Smajić declares. "We can forgive, even if we cannot forget."

Disarming the Media

Diplomacy, it has been said, is the continuation of war by other means. In Bosnia and Hercegovina, peace is yet another means to pursue the objectives of war. So long as they are not openly killing one another's populations, the national groups and their leaders are able to get away with more subtle offensives. In battles without guns, the print and electronic media are among the mightiest weapons.

Prior to and during the wars here, ultranationalists used the media effectively to incite war and to persuade people to abandon their homes and villages. Terror is the most powerful tool for ethnic cleansing, and fear is the strongest obstacle to throw before those who would undo ethnic cleansing. Nothing generates fear like hate-inspired rhetoric and nationalist demagoguery that is spread through the mass media. Media hate terrorizes all. It is a peacetime version of the randomly planted land mine or artillery shell lobbed into a crowded marketplace.

In a combined carrot-and-stick effort, the international community here has made some progress in moderating chauvinistic and bellicose media and in cultivating diversity. But it is an uphill battle, to say the least. During and after the wars, the leading nationalist political parties grabbed up television and radio production and broadcasting facilities and equipment. HDZ, SDS and SDA control the bulk of the most influential television and radio stations. Especially in Republika Srpska and HDZ/HVO-controlled areas of the Federation, other ultranationalist Serb and Croat voices have set up stations. These relay to their listeners news and editorial content that is wired in from Tudjman's Croatia and from Šešelj and Milošević's Serbia. Inflammatory language, misinformation, unbalanced coverage and even anti-Dayton and anti-SFOR rhetoric are commonplace.

Radio for the Nations

Vitez has two radio stations—one on each side of town. Independent Radio Vitez broadcasts from what is effectively the Muslim side of Vitez. It presents itself, though, as a radio station for all Bosnians. Independent radio has few resources and a shaky existence. There is a good chance that it no longer will exist by the time you are reading this. Croatian Radio Vitez broadcasts from the other side of town. Its name makes clear what are its local target audience and foreign source of support. The station has resources enough. So long as Croatian Radio Vitez stays out of trouble with media regulators, its existence is not greatly at risk.

I ask Muris Sulkić, Independent Radio's very young director, to join us for coffee. Sulkić and several of his similarly youthful broadcasting associates tell us about radio and about the youth of Vitez.

"For our generation, there is no future here," remarks one of Sulkić's colleagues. All agree that the majority of young people are trying to get out, and a good many of the adults wish to leave, as well. Invariably, America is the first choice of destination, but, as these are easier to enter, Canada and Australia are seen as more likely places to go. Independent Radio recently did a call-in show on this topic. There was a near consensus among the callers that people would like to remain in their native country, but conditions are not suitable for them to stay. Muslims who had previously lived in rural villages might find life in Bosnia and Hercegovina's reconstructing cities to be an improvement over their previous habitats, but the young people who grew up in the cities are in the vanguard of the out-migration.

Independent Radio Vitez was founded in May 1995. The United States Agency for International Development (USAID) and the Danish Refugee Council helped to start and to sustain the station, but that assistance will soon end. There are a few minutes of advertising each day, and the staff is made up mostly of volunteers. Muslims and people from ethnically mixed marriages operate Independent Radio. There is an obvious and understandable rivalry with Croatian Radio Vitez, which bills itself "The Voice of Central Bosnia."

The Croat station plays only Croatian or foreign music, points out one young man. Artists who are Muslim or of other South Slav nationality get no airtime there. Whereas Croatian Radio Vitez is very politicized, he adds, Independent Radio is more oriented toward entertainment, culture, and the nonpolitical aspects of people's daily lives.

I decide also to visit Croatian Radio Vitez. It is only a few blocks to the Croat side of town. Everything is relative, of course, but life looks much more prosperous just a few hundred feet down the road. New Vitez is not new in the sense of brand-new. It is just the real center of what used to be a less divided Vitez. It is where one finds the nicest shops and the choicest public buildings.

Our first task over here, though, is to find the Vitez branch of a Croatian bank which is one of the few places in Bosnia and Hercegovina where one can draw cash on a *Visa* card. Having accomplished that, we have lunch at a perfectly agreeable pizzeria. I notice all the other customers are paying in Croatian kunas, but the waiter kindly accepts my convertible marks.

Croatian Radio Vitez is located in a municipal building called *Hrvatska Dom* (Croatia House). There we meet Mario Mlakić, the station director. Mlakić's last name would appear to derive from the Serbo-Croatian root meaning "weak-willed" or "lukewarm." But there is nothing irresolute about the black-bearded head of Croatian Radio Vitez.

A good politician and public-relations man, Mlakić asserts that theirs is an independent radio station. In the campaign running up to this past weekend's election, he points out, the station offered airtime for all political parties wishing to present their programs. In addition to Croatian parties, the Coalition and SDP took advantage of that opportunity. The Serb parties did not, but, then, I realize that there are few Serbs left in this area who could hear such messages.

Vitez, Mlakić asserts, is not a divided town. The fact that Muslims live mostly on one side of the city does not amount to a division, he says, insisting that there is perfect freedom for people to move about Vitez. I remind myself, that in Yugoslav days, too, the people of ethnic groups had a tendency, especially in rural areas, to live in their own separate communities. That is not to say, though, that life here is not different from what it once was.

"Bosnia will never be the same as it was before," Mlakić says, his words an echo in my ears, as I have heard this said several times before (and will hear it many times again). In many respects, he adds, the situation was certainly much better in Tito's days than it is in today's war-ravaged remnants of Yugoslavia. The Communists, though, missed their opportunity to improve Yugoslavia. Tito, remarks Mlakić, created "a big circus with a lot of clowns." Surprising me, he comments that Tudjman and Izetbegović have not done better.

What people need now are jobs. If the people have work, he suggests, politics will take care of itself. But he implies that nation-building is not going to go away. There is a freedom and an interest to look at the past that did not exist in Yugoslav days. All the nations, Mlakić remarks, are now examining their own histories and looking out for their own interests.

The station director points out that in the 1992 referendum on independence for Bosnia and Hercegovina, Croats as well as Muslims overwhelmingly voted for independence. But Izetbegović wanted a political structure of one-man, one-vote, Mlakić protests. That would have meant that the Muslims would always win. "The Serbs' answer to that," he notes, "was war."

Croat soldiers in Croatia got their first experience fighting against Serbs in Croatia, Mlakić recalls. Some Croats from Bosnia and Hercegovina went there to fight, too. By the time Croats in Bosnia and Hercegovina began organizing against both Serbs and Muslims, they already had a core of seasoned soldiers. When Serb ethnic cleansing drove more and more Muslims into central Bosnia, the Croats, already a minority, felt encircled. That is when Croats began truly to hate, Mlakić relates, adding that such sentiment might never end.

In some political sense, Bosnia and Hercegovina's Croats recognize that they are citizens here, but, in a stronger way, he asserts, they feel a part of the larger Croatian nation. Mlakić, in short, is a solid HDZ man, whatever may be his real views on Tudjman. Arguably, I guess that puts him in what might loosely be called the "center" of the Croat nationalists.

On the one hand, he derogatorily labels as "*Ustaše*" the extreme Croatian Party of Rights (HSP). Founded in Zagreb in 1990 by Dobroslav Paraga, a longtime dissident and extreme Croat nationalist, the HSP is strongest in and around Mostar. That is where HSP has its headquarters for Bosnia and Hercegovina. The HSP's name is taken from a 19th-century nationalist party whose founder advocated overthrow of the Habsburgs and Croatianizing all South Slavs (thus including Slovenes, Serbs, Muslims and Macedonians) with the exception of Bulgarians. Even Tudjman (who certainly is neither really moderate nor a democrat) found Paraga and his HSP to be too extreme, and he once had the party leader jailed without trial.

At the same time, Mlakić is critical of the more moderate New Croat Initiative. This upstart NHI and its leader Krešimir Zubak declare themselves in favor of democracy and for full and equal rights for all people in the country. Croats in Bosnia and Hercegovina, Mlakić insists, do not want to be known as "Bosnian" Croats. They want to be recognized as Croats, period.

As we are leaving the station, Mlakić shows us the well-equipped studio. The music selection is, indeed, long on Croatian music and without offerings from other South Slavic artists. At the door, the director remarks that, in just a few weeks, the Independent Media Commission (IMC) will be ruling as to which radio stations may continue to broadcast and which may not.[43] That Commission might also choose to limit the reach of radio stations it does not feel meet standards appropriate for responsible broadcasters. Today, Croatian Radio Vitez has a rather wide broadcast radius of about 60 miles.

---

[43]High Representative Carlos Westendorp announced creation of the Independent Media Commission in June 1998. The IMC has broad powers to establish a regulatory regime for broadcasting and other media. It will license broadcasters and enforce license conditions and an established code of practice for the media. The IMC is not to be a censorship committee, but it will be able to prohibit the use of hate language in the broadcast and print media. It is to create rules requiring the media to follow such professional standards and principles of journalism as objectivity and providing proportional media access to competing views. The IMC may issue warnings, require that apologies and corrections be issued, impose penalties and even close down violating media operations. The IMC is to carry on the work of the OSCE's Media Experts Commission (MEC), whose mandate expires on 31 October 1998. IMC has a broader mandate than the Commission has had.

Mlakić says he believes that, once the Commission's review is complete, his station will remain on the air.

This Was Ahmići

Zijo already has found somebody with whom to speak while I am still out by the massive sign detailing the major donor organizations helping to rebuild Ahmići. "Just a minute!" I call to him and quickly jot down the names: USAID, UNHCR, UMCOR, Government of Japan and World Bank. UMCOR is a new one for me. The acronym stands for United Methodist Committee on Relief. Seeing as I am Methodist, I suppose I should have known that. I have no idea whether or not some small part of my occasional contributions to the church of my up-bringing go to UMCOR or not, but it makes me feel good all the same.

I walk over to meet Mirsada, a former and future resident of this village who hopes to bring her displaced family back to Ahmići before winter sets in. Where once was a home, there has now been rebuilt a roof and four strong walls. Some of the workmanship is not very good. It is a start, though, and much more than what thousands of other displaced families will have to call their own this winter. But the work is only just begun.

"Mir sada" literally means "peace now." After Mirsada shakes my hand and tells me her name, I think to myself *"Nadajmo se!"* ("Let's hope so!"). Hers is a beautiful name and, it seems to me, a sad plea. It is just as well that my mind is not so quick that I responded out loud to Mirsada's introduction. Ahmići is not really a place to be so clever.

According to indictments against accused war criminals, some of whom are Croats from Ahmići and adjoining Vitez, more than 100 people were killed in the village on a spring morning now more than five years ago. But local people say the figure was near to 200. British UNPROFOR soldiers assigned to the area reported recovering 96 bodies just among those whose charred remains were removed from burned homes after the flames had subsided.

Testifying at war crimes trials in The Hague, Ahmići survivors have given evidence that Croats from within the village directed the attackers. In testimony before the war crimes tribunal in the case of a Croat general indicted for the destruction of Ahmići and several additional villages in the Lašva River valley, a UNPROFOR platoon commander described the scene he and his men found that morning when they arrived in Ahmići:

As we approached, we saw a lot of smoke rising...(W)e saw lots of houses on fire or smoldering and to the left lots of bodies (of) women and children in the fields (killed) as they were fleeing...We continued to the Catholic cemetery and we saw (a) man and a child...(T)he man had (his) left arm around the child, both were dead, and a dog was licking the blood up...(W)e noticed some movement on the left and there was a woman crying and asking for help...(I) saw a large number of (Croatian) soldiers in dark uniforms...They all had new weapons and were drinking beer from cans, they were jeering and were very happy.[44]

"All of them were good."

Mirsada calmly invites us into the one closed-off room of her partially reconstructed home where she has a wood stove, a bed and a few pieces of furniture. The rest of the rooms are completely empty. Her husband, 20-year-old daughter and 18-year-old son temporarily live a few miles away in Zenica. Mirsada stays here because otherwise the workmen reconstructing the house might not get the job done. She offers us coffee and we look at pictures of the comfortable home her family had prior to 16 April 1993.

There had been about 220 houses in Ahmići before that day of carnage. Just two houses across the highway from the main village and a couple more on the uphill edge of Ahmići were to remain whole. These are (and were also then) inhabited by Croats.

The beer-swilling soldiers celebrating a massacre well done sound nothing like the people who Mirsada wishes to remember as her neighbors. Until five years ago or so, Mirsada says she had scarcely even known who were the Croats in the village. "All of them were good," she remembers. "You didn't think about it."

Even today, Mirsada notes, she has faced no difficulties in returning to Ahmići. No one has tried to intimidate her. She says her family always had had good relations with others in the village, and she is hopeful that soon that situation will exist again. Ivo Papić, a local businessman whose son, Dragan, is on trial in The Hague for alleged participation in the massacre, has offered assistance to Mirsada and to others returning to the village.

---

[44]The Institute for War and Peace Reporting, *Tribunal Update No. 51* (London: The Institute for War and Peace Reporting, 1997).

Virtually all of Ahmići's survivors intend to come back once their houses are in order, she reports. Many houses are in various stages of reconstruction, but others are not yet begun. By appearances, almost no families have settled in fully and permanently. I expect Ahmići will look much different one year from now. Where some houses once stood, of course, there will be no families to come back.

Mirsada, who formerly worked in Vitez at the explosives factory that today seems to have jobs only for Croats, says that now, finally, five years after the massacre, she sees some future. Her children are alive, their house will be completed, and she or her husband eventually will find a job.

Ahmići's territory gently slopes up and away from the north side of the highway just where one comes into Vitez from the east. The village must have been virtually abandoned for the first few years after 1993, as it has not yet again taken on a definite shape. Ahmići is reemerging bit by bit from weeds and rubble. We drive up the slope a ways, looking for the rest of the village.

A few hundred feet up the road, there is a toppled minaret and the remains of a mosque. Ahmići once had two mosques. Both were destroyed while the citizens were being massacred. At least the rubble has been left here so that Muslims can see where their mosques once were. In some areas, and particularly in Republika Srpska, ethnic cleansing went so far as to erase all traces of mosques.

Driving on, straight up the slope to the end of the road, we find a pair of undestroyed houses. We park and get out. A couple of young men are poking about under the hood of a car. Zijo tries to start up some small talk, but these fellows are not much interested in light conversation (or any other kind of discussions, for that matter) with strangers.

"Who," one asks, without straightening up, "are you?" Zijo explains who we are and what we are up to. "You are a Muslim?" Yes, Zijo answers, and tells that he is from Sarajevo. "You are looking for Ahmići? This is not Ahmići. Ahmići is over that way," this talkative one says, waving with his arm to the east. Conversation over. These, obviously, are some of Ahmići's Croats—the ones living on the edge of the village.

I take the other fork in the road. Driving up and across the slope, we pass what we think are the remains of the second mosque. It is hard to know for sure, as, whatever the structure may have been, it was terribly damaged. We pass a small kiosk offering a few grocery items and personal needs. Now closed for the evening, the sales kiosk seems out of place. There does not appear to be much of a market here for the likes of chewing gum and toiletries. Ahmići is quiet now, but there probably are more people and greater activity during the day. The kiosk somehow is a good sign, I feel.

Near the end of this road that cuts across the top of the weakly reemerging village, we come upon an old man and woman working in the front yard of their partially reconstructed home. A dozen plump, reddish-brown chickens scavenge about. After Ahmići was destroyed, this Muslim couple had lived in Zenica for a time, then in a Norwegian camp for refugees, then returned to Zenica and a temporary job for the husband.

Now, they are back in Ahmići and live in a little hut alongside what hopefully will one day again be their house. The nights already are chilly, the shanty in which they live looks barely habitable, and the old woman is sniffling. She acknowledges that it is not really warm enough where they are sleeping.

The old couple have substantial needs of their own, but they also are concerned about the needs of the community. New leaders are needed most badly, they make clear. "The leaders promise everything and then build nice houses for themselves and give nothing to the others. They want war again," the old woman says, and she begins to cry. "People can live together, but the authorities don't want to do what is best for the people."

People need to learn to trust one another again. Until that happens, the old man says, there is no future here. It seems that political leaders and administrators at all levels, including some of those responsible for dispensing international aid, are far from earning the respect of the people they are supposed to serve. The husband points, for example, to several instances in which construction materials and food aid have disappeared. Presumably, this was stolen.

This sad refrain I will hear time and again in the days to come. Most probably, some of these stories grow as they make the rounds, and the amount of cement or flour or roofing materials inexplicably "lost" gets bigger and bigger until perhaps it exceeds the truth. Be that as it may, I am convinced that corruption and theft are substantial and that many people completely have lost confidence in their leaders. If they cannot put good leaders in place, and if democracy is not working now, then people may never believe that democracy can function here.

"Without young people, there is no life here," the woman says. "But young people need to go to school." Ahmići's children attend school in Zenica, and she feels that they should be learning in their own community. But there are no teachers and no school building here. With a pitchfork, she scratches in the dirt a diagram of where stood the school that Ahmići's children formerly attended. Croats, she says and draws, put up other buildings which encroach on that space. Now, aid workers object to putting a school there again.

Driving slowly back through the village, I wonder to myself how the old couple will get by on the husband's pension of some $80 per month. There are thousands of others no better off than they are, and I suppose thousands more whose situations are still worse. At least the killing has stopped. Somehow, people survive.

"*Mir sada,*" I think to myself, as we leave Ahmići. "*Nadajmo se!*"

Immensity and Wickedness

I am pensive on the drive home. Normally, after a day of gathering material, I begin on the drive home to sort through my thoughts, to solidify my impressions, and to formulate how I will relate to others what I have heard and experienced. Having ended my day of research at Ahmići, I especially have a lot to ponder.

"What's the matter, Kirk?" Zijo asks me after a few minutes of silence. (He has gotten into the habit of calling me "Kirk," or sometimes "Mr. Kirk.")

"Nothing," I respond. "I'm just tired and I'm thinking."

"Don't think too much that you will forget about your driving?"

"Ah-huh. No, I won't. Okay."

Zijo wants to talk, and so he talks. My mind slips back into a swirling overabundance of observations and impressions, ruminates upon partially processed thoughts, sorts through a deluge of contradictions. My head hurts, and I am struggling to make sense of it all. I am brooding about regular folks drifting through lives that have been sucked through something hysterical and immense and wicked beyond their comprehension.

Same People in New Clothes

On the nightly news and in the newspaper, I see OSCE reports that the elections were satisfactorily completed during the weekend. The official spin from the international community is that the elections came off with few difficulties. The voting was declared "free and fair." The turnout exceeded 70% of registered voters. Carlos Westendorp is quoted as saying the elections atmosphere here was "similar to that in all normal European countries."

Westendorp probably is being overly generous in his assessment of the local situation (or is perhaps slighting several western countries), but all seem to agree that this election went much better by far than did the 1996 general election or the 1997 municipal elections. Closer examination will reveal more tarnish and thin spots in the gilding of this glistening episode than are first represented. There are reports of various irregularities, ranging from improper campaigning (which was not allowed under the rules at all during the voting) to mismatches between the numbers of marked ballots and the numbers of people passing through the polling places to mark those ballots. Although the polls closed 24 hours ago, preliminary results will not be released sooner than tomorrow.

Oslobodjenje carries today several interesting stories about voting in Republika Srpska and what it may (or may not) mean. "Compromise at a Standstill" reads the headline on a story about voting in (or near) Srebrenica, a city once designated by the UN as a "safe area" for Muslims. Serb forces slaughtered several thousand of those "safe" Muslims in 1995, and now only Serbs inhabit the city. Nevertheless, Muslims from Srebrenica had the right to vote in Srebrenica.

The voting in Srebrenica was peaceful, *Oslobodjenje* reports. Srebrenica's election-period calm was due in part to the fact that Muslims marked their ballots some 20 miles distant from the city. Most of the 15,000 to 17,000 Serbs living in that east Bosnian city are refugees and many of them are from Sarajevo. Westendorp's representative, Hans Schumacher, recently visited local authorities in Srebrenica. He then stated his dissatisfaction with the efforts of Republika Srpska officials to facilitate the return of Muslims displaced from their homes. Schumacher promised that financial aid will come once the return of Muslim refugees commences. Of course, it would help a lot, too, if Sarajevan Serbs now in Srebrenica could, or would, return to their homes.

In the western part of Republika Srpska, meanwhile, *Oslobodjenje's* Banja Luka correspondent conducted an informal poll on the second day of voting. Her article is headlined: "Same People, New Clothes." Those polled generally indicated they expect little to change for the better—or at all—because of this election.

Where Dinosaurs Roam

I was dog-tired last night. That was a good thing, because there was a lot of singing and general merrymaking going on somewhere in the neighborhood. The party noise bounced back and forth between the two facing rows of apartment towers that constitute the immediate neighborhood. For those not attending the party and who were less exhausted than I, this must have been rather annoying. But none of it kept me awake. It only took a couple chapters of Rebecca West's *Black Lamb and Grey Falcon* to knock me out. I am sure that West's book is indeed the literary masterpiece that it is reputed to be, as it has the same sedative effect upon me as does *Moby Dick* or *War and Peace*.

Toward Military Balance

Over morning coffee, I find out that my hosts had been participants in last night's revelry and that it had been going on in the apartment immediately below. The neighbor's son, along with another young man living in this complex, will go off to the army today. Last night, they were getting a proper send-off from their friends and neighbors. Ramiz and Vahida ask if I heard the singing and whether or not it had kept me awake. Vahida teases her husband about his own contribution to the rowdy singing. Ramiz indeed loves to sing, as he has demonstrated to me numerous times. He knows all sorts of South Slavic folk songs, as well as some in Hungarian, Italian and German.

As I am writing this and waiting for the call to breakfast, I again hear a boisterous chorus outside in the courtyard. Below, I see two white cars standing together end to end and looking like they are about to go somewhere of significance. That both cars are white I assume is a coincidence and has no symbolic importance. A company of young men surround the cars and are the core of the choir. One young woman also is among them, who I am going to assume is an unhappy sweetheart. Assembled off to one side is an older, parental-looking group. The send-off is reaching its climax.

Coincidentally, and appropriately, in one of the chapters I read last evening, West, writing in 1937 while visiting the Croatian island of Korčula, describes a scene reflecting a theme similar to that I am witnessing. It seems that Dame West had been awakened one fine morning

> ...by the sound of singing a little rough and wolfish for
> mere gaiety. When I went to the window there was a

crowd of young men standing on the quay, each carrying a bundle...

As we came out of the front door of the hotel, our cups of coffee in our hands, a white steamer came round the peninsula, lovely as a lady and drunk as a lord. She listed deeply landwards, because she already carried a freight of young men, and they had all run to the side to have a look at Korčula. "It is the steamer come to take the conscripts away," said a man standing beside us... "They go now to do their military service for Yugoslavia...but they are good Dalmatians, they are good Croats. Those songs you have heard them singing are all against the government."

...As the ship drew nearer we heard that these young man leaning over the rail were singing just those same angrily hopeful songs as the young men on the quay, and by the time she came alongside the quay they were joined in one song.[45]

I suspect (but do not know) that the songs sung by these Bošnjak Muslims are not against the government. It does strike me, though, that the shaky situation in Bosnia and Hercegovina as of autumn 1998 bears a disconcerting resemblance to that in the Yugoslavia of 1937.

In the Yugoslavia that West visited, nationalist Serb and Croat political leaders were gaining power and growing provocative. Croat nationalists hated the very idea of a unified Kingdom of Yugoslavia, and they soon cut a deal with the Serbs to divide Bosnia and Hercegovina between their two nations. Muslims, meanwhile, had been suggesting at the time that a multiethnic Bosnia-Hercegovina might be a good model for all of Yugoslavia. With the help of the Germans, Serb and Croat nationalists destroyed that first Yugoslavia.

In today's Bosnia and Hercegovina, Croats, Bošnjaks and Serbs each have their own armies. The US is pressuring Croat nationalists to put their HVO under unified command with the Army of the Republic of Bosnia and Hercegovina. The latter, referred to as (the) *Armija*, is effectively a Muslim force. Post-Dayton, the US has provided arms and training to *Armija*. The US wants to see a unified Muslim-Croat Federation army and is conditioning military aid upon cooperation toward that end. So far, though, Croat chauvinism is more important

---

[45]West, pp. 219–220.

to the HDZ/HVO than is the prospect of foreign military aid. The Republika Srpska army is of course completely separate.

The military imbalances that existed during the Bosnian wars are today much altered. Where the Serb, Croat and Muslim armies had stood in that order of strength and effectiveness (from strongest to weakest) during the wars, the new realities mean that the relative strengths of the three armed forces are now approximately reversed.

The Shanty by the Minefield

The Shanty sits on the edge of Sarajevo and at the boundary between the Federation and Republika Srpska. It is typical of the sort of thrown-together coffee joints and snack bars one sees along roadsides and at intersections all over this part of the world. The Shanty has two tables inside and two more outside. The Dobrinja I taxi stand is right out front, at the intersection of a seemingly nameless avenue and the road that runs past the airport and out of town. A half dozen taxis are lined up there, and most of their drivers are hanging out inside and about. SFOR vehicles roll back and forth on the airport road.

A double line of yellow warning tapes runs up the avenue, enclosing the narrow median strip with their fluttering message: MINES! MINES! MINES! MINES! MINES! On the Shanty's side of the avenue, laundry on the balconies shows that a few families are living in the damaged low-rise apartment blocks. There certainly are no signs of habitation on the other side of the avenue. The blown-out and abandoned apartment buildings there are surrounded with the MINES! tape. A large sign proclaims that a Norwegian mine-clearing project is under way.

The Norwegians seem to be the mine-clearing specialists in these parts. I saw on television that they have just cleared the Jewish cemetery in town of mines and unexploded ordinance. They removed 68 mines and 358 other undetonated munitions. During the siege, the Jewish burial ground was on the line between territories held by Serb and Muslim/Government forces. Hundreds of thousands of mines are still in the ground in Bosnia and Hercegovina. Thousands of minefields have been identified, and the clearing work is inching forward. A dozen or more mine casualties commonly still occur in any given month. This work will not be completed for several more years.

•   •   •   •

Mido, a Muslim, and his friend Mišo, a Serb, are sitting at a window table inside the Shanty. Actually, both tables are by windows, but they have the one with sunshine. Mido and Mišo are taxi drivers, and they are just starting in to devour a small table of food. Hearty, round paunches overhang each of their belts. This is not the first good meal they have eaten together. I almost think the middle-aged buddies are in a friendly competition to see who can develop the roundest and best-sculpted abdomen. If times were lean for Mido and Mišo during the war and siege, their physical recovery would appear now to be complete.

As is true of taxi drivers everywhere, it does not take much to get these two talking. "The Shanty" is not the formal name for this bistro, they tell us, but that is what everybody calls it. Mido is from the Federation side of town. Mišo is from the Republika Srpska side. Mišo and Mido point out that they were friends before the wars and that they still are friends. They are eating chicken, peppers and other vegetables from a single platter.

"Trust is important," Mišo says, as several other drivers gather in the small room. The day after the Dayton agreement was signed, he recalls, all the city's taxi drivers seemed to be working and there were no disputes between them. Mišo tells Zijo it is good that he, Zijo, had stayed in Sarajevo through the siege. Even though Zijo was not in the army (he had worked for IFOR and the Red Cross), at least he did not abandon his country and run off to Germany or someplace else.

Mido visited Germany a couple years ago to buy a car. Bosnians there, he says, were getting the message from Izetbegović already then that they should return home. Of course, that was nonsense, points out the Muslim driver, because most of these people did not have houses to which they could return. They still do not.

"There is a future," Mido comments, "but only if all these national parties become history." Mišo nods in agreement with his colleague. If he and Mido did not see eye to eye with one another, he stresses, they could not be sitting together and eating from the same platter. "We know how it was before there were the nationalist parties," Mido says.

The Muslim gestures toward the burned-out and battered apartment buildings. Those, he suggests, are evidence enough of what nationalism and corruption continue to do to their country. The men seem to regard nationalist politics and administrative theft to be two sides of the same coin. It is impossible to prove what has happened to it, Mišo comments, but a lot of aid has come in to help repair those apartments, and much of it simply has disappeared. It has been more than two years (actually, close to three) since Dayton was signed, Mido adds, noting that should be enough time to rebuild all of Dobrinja.

And why, Mido asks, rhetorically, does not some of this aid money go toward building a factory? If one factory were opened to employ 500 people, that would take care of 500 families. Everything will be better when the people have jobs, the friends agree, and there is a lot of work that needs to be done.

Business beneath the Shooting Gallery

Leaving Mido and Mišo to finish their meal, we set out to find the tunnel. A lifeline for besieged Sarajevo and the dark and narrow road to riches for select black marketeers, this tunnel was the city's biggest public secret during the war. Locals say they might not have survived the siege had it not been for the burrow connecting the Dobrinja quarter (inside the city limits) and Butmir (in Muslim-held territory outside the city). Serb forces (known in polite diplomatic circles as "the aggressor") had to have known about it, too. I believe that commercial interests from all sides assured that this lifeline would remain intact. Even as food, military materiel and official personnel flowed into Sarajevo through the tunnel, the dwindling wealth of the inhabitants dribbled out. The trapped people had sold jewelry, family heirlooms, clothing and anything else of value in order to buy necessities.

During the siege, most of the hills surrounding Sarajevo bristled with Serb artillery. One exception, during most of the war, was Mount Igman. UNPROFOR controlled Igman, the foot of which is about three miles or so outside of Sarajevo. Muslim soldiers commanded a small piece of territory between Igman and Sarajevo. To the north, south and west beyond the encircled capital was territory firmly in the grip of the Croat-Muslim Federation. That Federation-controlled territory was the supply zone for Sarajevo, and the goods from there were funneled through the city's sole entry point at the base of Mount Igman.

But there was no such thing as free passage through this entry, and, for the first year and a half of the siege, there was no tunnel. Sarajevo's airport, like Igman, was officially (and loosely) controlled by UNPROFOR during the war, and its runway was a dividing line between Sarajevo and its food supply. The landing strip is nearly a mile long, and Serb forces controlled both ends. Before the tunnel was dug under it, the only way for residents to get in and out of Sarajevo was by dashing across the runway. Crossing the runway was risky business, as it was a shooting gallery for Serb snipers. Meanwhile, UNPROFOR was using barriers and patrols to deter people from crossing. Runway casualties were reported daily on Sarajevo radio.

Although Zijo had himself been through the tunnel several times during the siege, it nevertheless takes us awhile to find the entrance. It is daylight now, it has been a long time since Zijo was there, we are coming in from a different direction (and by car), and the wartime debris which had previously marked his way is now cleared away. The tunnel entrance we know must be in one of the low-rise apartment buildings looking out upon the airport from the south edge of Dobrinja.

Nonexistent Tourist Tunnel to a Real Disaster Area

Dobrinja covers approximately three-quarters of a square mile. That is a lot of apartments, and a phenomenal amount of explosive ordnance was pitched into this residential expanse during the war. Virtually every building was damaged, and hundreds of apartments were rendered unfit for habitation. This is not the kind of structure-leveling devastation that saturation aerial bombing would have left. But literally thousands of hits over several years from tanks, mortars and rockets had slashed through many of Dobrinja's buildings. Everything else had been blasted and riddled with shrapnel and flying debris.

Many of the buildings remain structurally sound; their stripped, windowless and pocked apartments can be repaired. Indeed, some are inhabited again, but many more remain to be reconstructed. Around the edges, Dobrinja looks like a 20th-century ghost town. Within, there is more activity. Unevenly and in fits and starts, the residential area is being rebuilt. There is glass in some of the windows and people are on the streets. We ask directions from several people and zero in on our target.

"There it is, Kirk. Park here. It's over there. For sure," Zijo says suddenly.

He jumps out and heads toward a bombed-out apartment block. Zijo is pleased. This is one of the most important sites for Sarajevo's history. I peer through a partially boarded-up ground-floor window and look down into the terminal end of the shaft that fed Sarajevo. It is, of course, no more than a hole in the ground. There remains a bit of track for small carts that sometimes were used in the tunnel.

By summer 1999, I expect the tunnel to open as a tourist attraction. Plans call for tourists to ride in small carts through a newly concrete-reinforced tunnel. They will hear that the burrow was some 1.2 meters wide, 1.6 meters high and 760 meters long. In official communication between Sarajevo officials and UNPROFOR, it was referred to as the "nonexistent tunnel." Dignitaries, including members of Parliament and the US Ambassador, moved in and out of Sarajevo via the shaft.

As we go around front of the building to see how work is progressing on the tunnel's concrete reinforcement, we encounter a well-dressed man whose apartment is two doors down from the burrow's portal. His first-floor apartment faces out to the airport. It was gutted and badly damaged during the war. The man is repairing his apartment out of his own resources. Two more apartments are on two floors above him, but the upstairs neighbors are not working on their flats.

The structure was built in 1981. It was erected to Yugoslav standards, which were based upon German specifications. It may not look like much just now, but he assures us that structurally the building is very strong. Interest from foreign organizations to assist in reconstructing this neighborhood seems to have dried up, the man says. A homeowner might get some help if he or she identifies a potential aid donor and then goes there and asks time and again. Better, though, he comments, is to contact the "right" person, which is to say one who knows who, where, and how to ask. I imagine it is a pretty good business being a "right" person.

I walk out onto the balcony of the bare and partially reconstructed apartment. The neighbors off to one side are further ahead in their rebuilding. All three floors there appear to be occupied. On the ground below the balconies is a large pile of refuse that once was the furnishings for these several residences. The first-floor neighbor next door is taking no chances: the balcony railing there is adorned with twisted spirals of razor-sharp barbed wire. A huge ball of the nasty looking stuff has been anchored below the satellite television antenna.

Thanking the homeowner for the tour and wishing him luck, we cross the road to the tunnel reconstruction site. There is not a workman around at 2:00 in the afternoon. Actually, I take that back, as here comes one, in blue coveralls, walking down the top of the rectangular concrete shaft that is being created in a trench that is the former tunnel. The project is going very well, he says, and only about the last 100 yards are still to be built.

It looks as though the nonexistent tunnel could be open for tourists well before several hundred blasted apartments will be ready for refugees. I guess that will add to the realism. Tourists like a little of that.

Climbing Mount Igman

"The most dangerous road in Europe" is how Richard Holbrooke describes the old road up Mount Igman in his *To End a War*. Holbrooke, the leader of negotiations leading up to and at Dayton, traveled down the Igman road with colleagues in August 1995 in order to reach Sarajevo. There was an accident along the way and part of the delegation went over the edge in an armored personnel carrier. Three of Holbrooke's colleagues were killed. It is a very bad road, but what had made it particularly dangerous at that time was the ongoing war.

Mount Igman was strategically important and had been taken by Serb forces in August 1993. They had held it only briefly, though, and then had abandoned it under threat of airstrikes. Thereafter, Igman was occupied by UNPROFOR. As was their habit, Serb forces tormented the "Blue Helmets," as the UNPROFOR soldiers were known, by firing intermittently upon the peacekeepers as they crawled up and down the mountainside along the old road with their armored vehicles. Had the Serbs kept Igman, they could have made life even a lot tougher in Sarajevo. Then they could have stopped the flow of food into the tunnel. Of course, that would have been bad for business.

Like several other hills and mountains in the area, Igman has ski slopes that were used in the 1984 Winter Olympics. These once were popular for Yugoslavs and foreigners alike. It is understandable that getting tourism back on track has not been a top postwar priority. After all, there still are tens of thousands of people without permanent residences. But there also are hundreds of thousands who are unemployed. For the sake of the jobs, money and world attention that it can generate, I hope that tourism's redevelopment will be accelerated.

Fortunately for skiers, they never will need to take the old road up Mount Igman. There is a newer, paved road to the top. The new road was there also when Holbrooke and his colleagues were coming to Sarajevo in August 1995, but driving to the capital by that route would have required crossing territory held by the Bosnian Serbs.

Curiosity, plain and simple, is the motivating force pushing me to find that dirt road and to drive up it. I figure it ought to be safe enough now, as there will be no "aggressor" taking pot shots at us. It takes awhile to find the road, which starts up Igman just outside Sarajevo's outlying suburb known as Hrasnica. The most direct route to Hrasnica goes through a cluster of hotels set in a green park at Sarajevo's southwest edge. It turns out, though, that this entire area has been commandeered by SFOR. A young sentry at the roadblock politely advises me to drive around the compound on what looks like a path for strolling pedestrians. He snaps me a very fine salute in response to my thank you.

We continue on our way, asking directions occasionally. One man tells us there will be a checkpoint and that we might not get through.

The last person from whom we inquire is a woman walking alone beside the road. My feeling is that she has been talking to herself for several years and that encountering us just continues the long and unbroken conversation going on in her head. The woman has lost several family members in the war and wants to be sure that we realize it. There is nothing that we can do about this, of course, except to pity her. I do, and I hope that her telling us about her pain somehow helps her to feel less alone.

There is no checkpoint, after all, and we start up the mountain. Under perfect conditions, for an appropriate vehicle and experienced driver, and assuming one would not meet too much traffic along the way, the road is not extraordinarily dangerous. Neither, though, would one characterize it as either fast or safe. It takes somewhat over an hour to make the climb. I rarely take the car out of first gear. The roadbed is generally firm, as it is cut into what is mostly solid rock. But it is narrow, potholed in many places, and surfaced with rocks, many of which are about softball-size. It would be more dangerous to come down this road than to crawl up. The chances of going into a slide, especially if one were in a hurry or if the weather or visibility conditions were less than perfect, could be substantial.

Along the way, I glance over the edge from time to time to see if I catch sight of an armored personnel carrier. I do not. A number of smashed vehicles poke out among the trees, rocks and underbrush. Some of these almost certainly have been abandoned by their owners who pushed them over a cliff. Abandonment is a popular method of car disposal here.

Zijo has told me that some people still use this road regularly to avoid nearby Serb-controlled territory. I am skeptical. I start to wonder, though, when, after just a couple minutes we meet a medium-size truck of a type used to carry goods. We come upon a couple cars that are coming down the mountain, too, but no more trucks. Partway up, we see a pair of twin plaques anchored to the stone wall. They memorialize two French soldiers who perished here during the war. I do not notice any plaques honoring the Americans who died on this road.

Counting out a Dinosaur

The OSCE now says it will be at least another week before the election results are announced. No amount of polishing by the international community can put a shine back on these elections. A European Parliamentary delegation is criticizing the OSCE for technical errors in conducting the voter registration and election. The OSCE did not learn from its 1996 and 1997 election mistakes, says a leading EU election observer, who calls the errors inexcusable. Because of errors, it seems that many absentee ballots will not be counted. At the same time, *Oslobodjenje* reports, other members of the EU delegation voiced their respect for the people of Bosnia and Hercegovina for their patience, discipline and democratic spirit on election day.

Just because election officials are having a hard time counting is not keeping the leading political parties from declaring their victories. So far, though, there seem to be more declared victors than there were races. One apparent reason given for the OSCE's reluctance to announce even preliminary results is that the race for Republika Srpska President is particularly close. Also, the international community regards this race as particularly important. Reports that the parties are leaking out, taken together, point to the SDS-SRS coalition's Poplašen defeating the international community's preferred Sloga coalition in that race. That would mean Plavšić is finished as president in Banja Luka (the Republika Srpska capital) and, most likely, that Dodik will bid adieu as the Serb entity's Prime Minister.

Final count or no, Westendorp seems convinced that the reigning Serb member of the Bosnia and Hercegovina Presidency, Momčilo Krajišnik, is on his way out. In an interview with *Oslobodjenje*, the High Representative states that he expects Sloga's Živko Radišić to beat Krajišnik. In that Radišić is regarded as somewhat more moderate than Krajišnik, a Radišić win will be regarded as a victory (albeit perhaps a small one) for the forces favoring pluralism and tolerance.

"Krajišnik is hopeless. We cannot work with a person having his mentality," Westendorp is quoted as saying. "He represents the past. He is a dinosaur. As a person I like him, but he is not a person who favors Bosnia...Radišić is a very reasonable person. He is honest and not corrupted. He is not an ultranationalist."

Still Alive, But You Do Not Know It

We are on the road this morning to Kiseljak, and Zijo is relating to me what an old man once told him about there being something evil in the Balkan air. Every 50 years or so that evil gets into people's blood. Eventually, it gets them started killing one another. After enough blood has been shed, the urge to kill abates. Then peace may again prevail.

Kiseljak: Central Bosnia's Casablanca

About 20 miles northwest of Sarajevo, Kiseljak is a small city. When Holbrooke had wanted to bring his delegation into Sarajevo in summer of 1995, Ratko Mladić, commander of the Bosnian Serb Army, had offered the US diplomat passage to Sarajevo along this road. He had suggested the US delegation fly into Federation-held Kiseljak. The last part of the drive would have been through Mladić's Serb-controlled area. Holbrooke, who had had a frightening experience traveling this road earlier in the war, decided to come over Mount Igman instead.

During the siege, this had been a supply road along which much of Sarajevo's food found its way to the tunnel entrance. Kiseljak was then a center of multiethnic war commerce. Silber and Little describe the situation in 1992 as Sarajevo braced for its first winter under siege:

> (Hardline-nationalist Croats) had been trading with the Serbs besieging Sarajevo, as well as with Muslim black-marketeers in Sarajevo. For months, Kiseljak became a haven of peace, a land-locked, Bosnian Casablanca, as the Croats there took commercial advantage of their position "in between" Muslims and Serbs. The Croats would buy from the Serbs and sell to Muslim war-profiteers who were, by now, operating a cartel system that kept the price of black-market goods in Sarajevo artificially high...By the winter of 1992–93, the Croat forces there had sound financial, as well cynical political, reasons for ensuring the continuation of the siege."[46]

The construction I see as we approach Kiseljak is not to repair war damage. It reflects a miniature economic boom. Serb forces never made a full-scale attack here. That would have been bad for business. We begin to see small businesses—operating or going up—that are four or five miles out of Kiseljak on the Sarajevo side. A Muslim cemetery is on

---

[46]Silber and Little, pp. 295–296.

the edge of town, but I do not expect to find many Muslims in Kiseljak. Before the wars, the greatest proportion of the population had been Croat. There also had been a large percentage of Muslims, but very few Serbs. Today, locals estimate, 95% of Kiseljak's residents are Croat.

A large and impressive Catholic church on Kiseljak's main hill is the first thing that strikes my eye as I drive into town. The city's name is a reference to "mineral-water spring," but Kiseljak is probably best known these days (as in war times) as a source for consumer goods. I park and we walk to the main open-air market that stretches along one embankment of the river that passes through town.

People from Kiseljak do not generally shop in this market so much as do people from out of town, we are told by a man selling sport shoes. That is because the locals tend to have a good bit more money than average, he says. They do most of their shopping in Kiseljak's stores, where quality is higher. For his customers, though, price is the main decision factor. They think little about quality.

The shoe salesman says he is selling mostly factory seconds (imported from Hungary, Italy and Germany) at cut-rate prices. I have seen a lot of low-priced, brand-name sport shoes on sale over the years throughout the formerly communist world. It is hard to imagine there are so many factory seconds to go around. Maybe. The shoes look genuine, but I doubt that most people passing through this market could distinguish a real *Puma* or *Adidas* from a fake.

A shopper comes up with her young son. Looking at a pair of name-brand sport shoes priced at 35 deutschemarks (about $22), she asks: "Do you have anything cheaper?" Ultimately, the woman decides to buy. She pays in Croatian kunas, though, not with deutschemarks or convertible marks.

Serbs Mix Here with Croats

People here are waiting for privatization to move forward in the Federation, the shoe seller reports. They think then there will be more jobs. Getting the elections out of the way on the weekend, he figures, should help to accelerate privatization. The man expects privatization to move faster in the Federation's Croat areas than in its Muslim areas. It is interesting that he distinguishes between Croat and Muslim zones.

Serbs, too, continue to shop and to conduct business in Kiseljak. The shoe seller says that Serbs come even from Montenegro (the nearest border with which is nearly 120 miles distant) and from Banja Luka (the Bosnian Serb capital, some 100 miles away). We encounter a woman from Pale, who has a stall in the open-air market in that Serb town just east of Sarajevo. She is buying in Kiseljak not for herself but, rather, for goods she can take back to resell in Republika Srpska. The Serb woman is not too fearful to say that she is from Pale. She would be more circumspect about her ethnic identity were she in another city, but Kiseljak is all business.

I ask the shoe man about the prospects for war to break out once again. So long as the foreigners stay, he confidently asserts, there will be no more war.

Midway down the stretch of stalls, I step out onto a simple concrete footbridge spanning the river. It has a railing on just one side. I lean against it and look up at the church on the hill. A man late in his middle-age years slowly shuffles up and speaks very softly. This fellow, it seems, is not sharing in Kiseljak's prosperity. He asks for a deutschemark. He is Croat, he says, but the local people do not like him. I fish in my pocket for a two-deutschemark coin, and we try to coax out his story. He does not want to talk. Another man, larger and more self-confident, who is striding across the narrow bridge jokingly grasps the panhandler by both shoulders and gives him a teasing shake. I cannot tell whether this is an affectionate gesture or an intimidating warning.

Also by the railing, a few feet away, is a young man who looks like a future thug in training. In his early teens but already heavyset, he sports a crew cut and a nylon warm-up suit. He is still too young and soft to be a real hoodlum. At the entry to the bridge, he and his older buddy are selling cigarettes at low prices. A carton of *Dunhill's* is just 17 marks (roughly $1 per pack). Zijo takes a carton. I buy him an extra pack to compensate for those of his that I bummed yesterday and will today. I never carry cigarettes, but smoking is part of the ritual and technique when meeting people on the street and interviewing them on the spot.

Just down the line, another young man is selling cassette tapes and compact discs. We ask what is the best-selling tape. To our surprise, he names the Serbian singer Nedeljko Bajić. A lot of people, he says, like to listen to mixed music from an assortment of Bošnjak, Croat, Serb and other artists. Zijo is very sensitive to music as a gauge of how hospitable is a given environment in which we find ourselves. If an establishment is playing mixed music and the lyrics are standard pop fare, this usually indicates friendly surroundings. But if a bar or restaurant, for example, plays an unremitting succession of all Serb or all Croat artists, and particularly if the lyrics are on strongly nationalistic themes, that is a signal to proceed with caution.

As we are looking at tapes, another man comes by and takes aside our music-merchandizing friend. He is collecting money. When that transaction is completed, I ask who owns this space and how much it costs to keep a stall here. Officially, the stallkeeper relates, the market is owned and operated by the local football club. He shows me the receipt he just received, and, sure enough, it bears an official-looking stamp indicating that the sum was just paid to the football club. And who owns the football club? That is not clear, the music seller says. He pays 60 deutschemarks monthly to rent his space and another 40 deutschemarks for electricity. The space is small, but the rent seems not exorbitant.

Some Serbs, but no Muslims, operate stalls in this market, notes the man, who is a Croat. In general, he says, relations between the national groups are less tense in this area than they were a couple years ago. A Muslim family has moved back into his village, for example. It took a while for the family to settle in but now everything is okay for them.

Possession versus Ownership

Resettlement is an enormous and chaotic problem in postwar Bosnia and Hercegovina. In addition to the difficulties of human relations, there is a complex snarl of administrative and legal issues. Sometimes, as the saying goes, possession is nine-tenths of the law. If the possessor is both vicious and powerful, that fraction might run even higher.

We meet a man who is caught up in such a tangle over property. A dapperly dressed older Croat, he has just made a purchase at a stall offering kitchenware. When he left his house in Zenica in December 1993 and moved to Kiseljak, the man explains, he had arranged for the couple next door, who are Muslims, to watch over it for him. Now, that couple is divorced, the ex-wife lives in his house, she has an intimidating new love interest, and she does not want to move out.

Zenica, which is about 25 miles away, is today almost as strongly Muslim as Kiseljak is Croat. The *opština* office for Zenica has given this Croat permission to return to his house, but that does not solve the problem of the obstinate woman and her daunting boyfriend. The man says he has worked with an ombudsman, taken the case to court, and hired a lawyer. So far, though, it all has come to nothing. There are more and more lawyers in the country these days, it seems. Mostly, however, the Croat remarks, they are just playing games with the law.

A nearby merchant steps over to tell his story in a similar vein. Also a Croat, he left 13 trucks behind in Donji Vakuf when he came to

Kiseljak. With the help of a policeman friend in Sarajevo, the man says, he was able to get one of his trucks back. He is thankful for that.

The Croat with the Muslim squatters in his house goes on to point out that, in any case, life is much better for him in Kiseljak than in Zenica. This is partially a matter of economics and partially one of ethnic relations, although the two really are interrelated. "In Zenica," he asserts, "there is no future for Croats."

By the time this man from Zenica had arrived in Kiseljak, in December 1993, this town's Serbs already had been pushed out. War in central Bosnia between Muslims and Croats had raged since spring. If everything is relative, then Kiseljak was paradise compared to most of the rest of central Bosnia. There were shops open here; there was electricity.

The man recalls one of his first evenings in Kiseljak. He was sitting in his temporary apartment and speaking with another man. They talked long. The sun went down and the room darkened. Eventually it was pitch dark. After awhile, the other man asked why he did not turn on the light so they could see one another while they spoke. Having lived in Zenica during the war, this Croat had grown accustomed to darkness. He had forgotten that one could have light simply by flipping a switch.

There is electricity today in Muslim-controlled Zenica just as there is in Croat-run Kiseljak. But there remains a darkness over central Bosnia. Croats and Muslims huddle, fearful but at the same time obstinate, in their separate refuges within that gloom, even though they are of the same blood, speak the same language, and have a long history in common here in central Bosnia. The old gentleman worries about what will happen if and when SFOR and the IPTF leave. Kiseljak is not an absolute refuge from darkness.

To Be Completely Safe

We pass through Visoko on the way from Kiseljak to Vareš. While the countryside around Visoko shows plenty of damaged and destroyed farmsteads, the small city itself is almost unmarked. Have they repaired the town so thoroughly? "No," Zijo explains, "to reach Visoko during the war was to be safe completely." This is a Muslim town. In medieval times, before there were Muslims here at all, Visoko had sometimes been Bosnia's leading city.

Visoko is best known today for *suho meso*, a local meat specialty enjoyed by Bosnians of all ethnonational groups. Thinly sliced, this dry and cured beef goes well with *šljivovica* and tastes like ham when topping a pizza. The Croat and Serb armies might well have been reluctant to attack and destroy this town wherein lies the secret to producing this favorite delicacy. Visoko's Muslims always have had good relations with the Croats and Serbs in the area. It is Zijo's understanding that the town is more strongly Muslim now than before, as many more Muslims have come here as refugees from other parts of the country.

Near Ilijaš, we offer a ride to a middle-aged, red-haired woman. She is on her way to Breza, a small town whose name means "Birch." A Muslim, she has been in Ilijaš to buy 10 cubic meters of firewood for the winter. She is unhappy about her trip. First of all, the price of wood is high. This much wood, she says, costs at least 250 deutschemarks. That is a lot compared to her old mother's monthly pension of 120 deutschemarks (about $75), which is their primary source of income. That price does not include the cost of hiring somebody who has a chain saw to cut it into shorter lengths that actually can be burned. Secondly, our passenger is frustrated because, in the end, she found no wood in Ilijaš to buy at any price. There had been wood for sale earlier in Ilijaš, and she is convinced that a speculator had gotten there ahead of her. The woman believes this unseen trader is hoarding the wood and will sell it for a higher price when people are more desperate.

Because this woman has taken a ride with us, Zijo says, we can know for sure that she has no husband. Were she married, she would have been afraid to take a ride with complete strangers. That is not because she would fear us. Rather, out here in the small towns, a married woman would fear her husband's suspicions if she were seen riding about with other men.

We ask how she and her mother manage to make ends meet. The woman says she has a cow and makes cheese from its milk. Once each week she goes into Sarajevo and sells the cheese. By the time she pays for the bus ticket, though, there is very little of the money remaining.

After visiting Vareš, we will be going to a village called Stupni Do. We ask this woman about what happened there and how to find the village. She begins immediately to cry. The poor woman says that she had friends there and that her brother's son died there. "It was hell there," she says, not speaking the name Stupni Do.

Only Existing in Vareš

The seat of an *opština* by the same name, Vareš is a medium-sized town. The road leading to Vareš is narrow and twisting. It jumps from one bank to the other of the Stavnja River along which it runs. In this respect, the way is very much like hundreds of miles of Bosnia and

Hercegovina's paved roads. They follow the rivers to avoid climbing the steep hills and mountains and because most of the cities are located in valleys. The more poorly surfaced roads are those that run up into the hills. These connect the villages often hidden there to the larger towns, cities and main roads.

Villages often suffered the worst damage in the wars. Traditionally, villages tended to be less ethnically mixed than cities. They are small and often isolated. Once ethnic conflict breaks out and one group gets the upper hand, its most fanatical local elements, often reinforced by roving nationalist paramilitaries, could wipe out a small village in a matter of hours—or even minutes. Should the balance of power subsequently shift in favor of another ethnic group, retribution can be expected and the first group's villages might well be destroyed in turn.

Vareš as Microcosm

A mining town for hundreds of years, Vareš is a long and wide strip along that road through the Stavnja valley. Its steelworks is now very old and very quiet.

Silber and Little call Vareš and the development of conflict here a "microcosm" of the broader interethnic struggle in central Bosnia. Vareš was an almost evenly mixed town of Muslims and Croats. Those few Serbs in the town left early in the wars. Croats and Muslims, meanwhile, tried hard not to begin fighting amongst themselves. But the waves from disturbances in distant areas eventually hit here.

The difficulties actually began when Muslims from eastern Bosnia and other parts of the country, who had been forced out of their homes by Serbs, began flooding into such central Bosnian towns as nearby Visoko, Breza and Zenica. Eventually and in turn, Croats in these communities fled their homes and began pressing into Vareš. Croats in Vareš felt threatened here. When an HVO unit arrived from Kiseljak in October 1993, the growing tension reached a critical mass and the Muslims were driven out. Most did not go far, however. Determined not to lose Vareš, the fearsome Seventh Muslim Brigade, headquartered in Zenica, retook the town. In the last instance, the Croat population fled before the approaching Muslim army even reached Vareš. Soon the town was repopulated with Muslims.[47]

Arriving in Vareš, I first drive the length of the town. Compared to many other places, there is less indication of massive property damage.

---

[47] Silber and Little, pp. 300–301.

Vareš is filled with firewood. There are piles near the homes, and wood is stacked in other areas as if to be transported away for sale. I hope that some of it will make it from this heavily forested area to the poor woman and her mother in Breza just about 12 miles down the road.

We are looking for the center of town and a restaurant. Typically in such long and narrow valley towns there is almost no place wide and flat enough to develop much of a downtown. I turn the car around at the far end of Vareš, drive back for a minute or so, and park in front of a building marked as the *opština* administration. Several youngish men are hanging about out front. We ask one who looks most like he has some official reason to be standing there where to get a pizza.

Salko and Ramo from Unsafe Žepa

As we walk down the street, we meet brothers Salko and Ramo Budić. Both look approximately 40 years old. They are Muslim refugees from Žepa and have been living here in Vareš for more than three years, since late-1995.

Žepa is one of the Muslim enclaves in eastern Bosnia (the others being Srebrenica and Goražde) which the UN in spring 1993 had declared "safe areas."[48] These enclaves became collection points for eastern Bosnia's Muslim refugees. Although armed UN troops were present in these zones, the foreign observers were harassed and bullied by Serb forces surrounding the areas as well as by the Muslims within. These UN troops were virtually prohibited from using their weapons. The Muslims squeezing into these so-called safe areas were far from safe. Finally, two years after the UN declaration, in July 1995, Srebrenica was overrun and Žepa was forced to surrender.

Salko is the more talkative of the two brothers. He has the bearing, though, of one who is naturally modest and introspective, the type who speaks only when he has something worth saying and knows that somebody really wants to hear his view. Ramo is a man who still has the gaunt look of a prisoner of war, which he was in 1995. We invite the brothers to join us for coffee in Klub Napredak, a Croat pizzeria. One can tell this is a Croat establishment by its nationalistic markings.

Along with 16 other Muslim families, the extended Budić family lives in a formerly Serbian village, named Brgule, which is about 10

---

[48]Srebrenica was the first city, with its surrounding area, to be declared "safe." As Srebrenica was overrun and thousands massacred, it symbolizes perhaps the most notorious failure of UN policy in Bosnia and Hercegovina. Other declared safe areas were: Sarajevo, Tuzla in northeastern Bosnia, and Bihać in northwestern Bosnia.

miles out of Vareš. Both brothers are married, and they have five children between them. Another brother, Ismet, disappeared in the war. The brothers do not know what happened to Ismet, but they are sure that he is dead. Ismet's wife and two children also live with them in Brgule, as do their parents, a sister and a brother-in-law.

The Budić family was dispersed when Žepa fell. Women, children and the elderly left together. But men of fighting age had fled earlier. Ramo was captured and held in a camp for six months. Some international organization discovered the camp, and he was moved to France. Ramo was there six months before coming to Brgule. After Salko left Žepa, he spent 22 days hiding in a small village in the forest with a group of other men. Eventually, he heard that his family was near Vareš, and so he came here.

No one in Brgule has work and almost all would like to return to Žepa, the brothers relate. Although he says he knows neither when nor how, Salko is of the opinion that these families one day will go back to Žepa. There is no doctor and there are no shops in Brgule. Even if there were, the brothers point out, there would be no one there with money to buy anything. Once daily, a small bus comes into Vareš.

Most of the Serbs who formerly lived in Brgule now are temporarily settled in a village near Bijeljina, a city in northeast Bosnia almost on the border with Serbia.[49] From time to time, some of those Serb families return to visit their houses and cemeteries. The brothers relate that the Serbs expected trouble when they came back, but there have been no difficulties. Brgule's former, Serb residents say that living conditions are very bad, too, where they now live. The Budić brothers report that those Serbs say that they also expect one day to resettle in their former village. Salko says he does not know much about politics, but it seems to him that, under terms of the Dayton agreement, those Serbs have a right to return to their homes (which they do under Annex 7). So far, though, the Serbs are not coming back to stay.

---

[49]Bijeljina also is just south of Croatia's eastern-most end, known as Eastern Slavonia. This is traditionally a territory of mixed ethnic groups, including Croats and Serbs. Eastern Slavonia was the site of Croat-Serb warfare in 1991. Prior to spring 1992, Bijeljina *opština* had been nearly two-thirds Serb and about one-third Muslim. That spring, which was early in the Serb offensive in Bosnia and Hercegovina, Bijeljina was the site of a sort of pilot project for the Serb paramilitary Arkan and his Tigers. They were testing in Bosnia the model of ethnic cleansing by intimidation that they had developed and applied in Eastern Slavonia. For a discussion of Arkan's terror campaign in Bijeljina, see Silber and Little, p. 224.

Some Muslims from Žepa but now living in and around Vareš went to visit their homes earlier this year. They brought back photographs showing that much of the town is burned. They found nobody living there. Grass is growing up around the houses. The brothers report that their friends and neighbors who visited Žepa sat in front of their houses and cried for two hours and then returned to Vareš.

Nevertheless, the Žepa Muslims were able to vote in this last election for people to represent them as if they still resided in Žepa. Most of these refugees did in fact vote. Formally, Ramo notes, they had the opportunity to go to Žepa for the voting. In fact, they remained here and voted by absentee ballot.

Locally, the situation is different for the Vareš-native Muslims and Croats than it is for the Muslim refugees and for the Serbs who come occasionally. More of the original Croat population is returning every day. The situation must also be hard for many of them, though, and certainly there are housing tangles to work out. Croats and Muslims seem to be living together without many serious problems in Vareš. But Ramo says that almost none of them are working and they have a hard time envisioning any kind of positive future here.

"We only exist," Salko adds. "We live on assistance—and we need help because we have no money and the *opština* does not support us." There is in fact very little foreign aid, although the Red Cross and Catholic Relief Services do have offices here in Vareš. An Italian organization is said to be planning to begin operating here but has not yet done so. There are about 30 families here from Žepa, and some of those get 40 or 50 deutschemarks (i.e., $25 to $30) in monthly assistance. It is mostly the elderly and wounded who receive aid.

Salko reports that a lot of the young Bošnjaks are going to the US and elsewhere abroad. They emigrate because they cannot see a future here. "And those of us who remain," he remarks, "we live on what we can get. What the world sends, we have." Other than that, he says, they have only hope. Salko's hope now is to go abroad, preferably to America. But he does not know how to arrange it. His teenage son will soon need to start a career and build a life, and Salko sees no prospect at all for that to happen in Bosnia and Hercegovina.

I ask about SFOR. It strikes me that the international troops do not have a very strong presence here. Just then, though, an SFOR armored personnel carrier (or "APC") rolls by on the road out front. Salko and Ramo say they see SFOR units from time to time, typically in convoys of three or four vehicles. It is not real clear to them just what is SFOR's function in the Vareš area. They indicate that they have no apparent need for SFOR protection on a day-to-day basis.

Ramo and Salko must run off to catch the only bus of the day back to Brgule. As Zijo and I eat lunch, I muse to myself about their name, "Budić." The -ić is a standard South Slav ending for a family name. In Slavic tongues, the word stem "Bud-" has a sense of "future" or perhaps even of "awakening." Some friends say I think too much about such things. Maybe they are right. It is just a name, after all. There is no point in trying to find any symbolism in it. What would it be, that I have met the future and that the future is bleak and confused? I try and turn my attention back to my pizza.

At *Klub Napredak*

As we finish our meal, another APC rolls past on the road through town that is outside the window and across the Stavnja, which is more a creek than a river. Zijo and I are the only real customers in the restaurant. A husky man nearing middle age sits at a corner table, smoking and drinking coffee. The waitress and a second woman, who I presume is the cook, join him at the table when they are not attending to us.

I assume the man at the table is the owner of Klub Napredak, which would mean, of course, that he is a Croat. I assume wrong. He is in fact a Muslim from Vareš. The two women are Croats. They explain that the restaurant is owned by a cultural association for Croats in Bosnia and Hercegovina. That organization is named Napredak. The local Catholic priest, a Franciscan, is in charge of the restaurant.

The Muslim explains that SDP had come out on top in Vareš in the 1990 election. That indicates considerable local opposition to extreme nationalism. When the HVO showed up in 1993, though, the democratically chosen leaders became irrelevant. By that time, Croat and Muslim military forces in central Bosnia were at all-out war with one another.

Now, the man remarks, Muslims and Croats rule Vareš together. The situation is much improved. Rebuilding Vareš will be a long and terribly difficult process, he says, but the first priority must be to prevent war from breaking out again. Before the wars, there were about 24,000 people in Vareš and the *opština's* surrounding villages. Now, he estimates, there are perhaps 15,000 people living here. Most are Muslims, and there are probably no more than 100 Serbs. Several thousand Croats live in and around Vareš. These are mostly the same Croats that lived here before the fighting broke out. In some cases, the Croats' villages have been destroyed and so they now live in Vareš.

The steel mill here previously employed about 3,000 people, the guest at the corner table goes on. Today, there are just a few people out at the plant. They make stoves, and the number of jobs that provides is almost insignificant. The steel mill's technology is very old. It would be impossible to modernize what exists there now. There is a machine-parts factory on the edge of town, and that employs maybe 100 people. A fairly new wood-products factory provides some 300 jobs.

I do some rough arithmetic in my head: It sounds like the population here could end up stabilizing in the medium term at 15,000 to 18,000 people. If one figures a factory job can support five people directly plus one additional job in the retail and service sector (which itself supports five people), then something like 1,500 factory jobs are needed here. Fewer than one-third of those needed jobs are here now. In these forests and hills, agriculture can help to keep people alive but cannot add much to the local economy.

Not Easily Impressed

Down the street, we encounter a middle-aged man of mixed ethnic background. His father is a Serb and his mother a Croat. The man has lived amidst Muslims all his life. He says he never cared about nationality before. So long as the nationalist parties are in power, the man contends, there future is bleak for Bosnia and Hercegovina. Not surprisingly, this man is an SDP supporter. In fact, he is a party member.

I remark upon reading recently an article that remarked favorably upon the power sharing between this town's Muslim mayor and Croat deputy mayor. It says they were enemies during the war, but now they are learning to cooperate. (The article also notes that Western governments are using promises of aid as a carrot to encourage this kind of cooperation. An international official is quoted as saying, too: "It troubles me that the less democratically we act, the more success we have. But the results are good.")[50]

The SDP man is not much impressed. Yes, he explains, the two officials cooperate. In fact, every six months they swap job titles with one another. They do so in order to assure they are able to concentrate into their own hands control over such things as who is allowed to conduct business in the town. The two officials' friends and supporters are able to open shops, but it is not easy for others to do so.

---

[50]Bosnia Action Coalition, *This Week in Bosnia-Hercegovina* (Boston: Bosnia Action Coalition, 7 May 1998). The Coalition is citing the *New York Times*.

Paradise Ravished: Stupni Do

At the edge of Vareš, we turn left at a signless intersection. We go through the dark viaduct beneath the railroad tracks, then turn right onto a dirt road that goes around back of the machine-parts factory. The road gets even smaller and cuts through a couple farmyards.

"Is this the way to Stupni Do?" I ask, through my window to a group of people by a house that sits right up next to the road.

"Yes," says the man, "but there are no people there. It was destroyed in 1993."

We know, Zijo explains, but we want to go there anyway. Three women who are with the man ask for a ride. They, too, are going up the hill to Stupni Do. The women pile into the back seat.

I drive on a bit, the road makes a bend, and all at once we are peering through the entry to a thick evergreen forest. Several gray, cone-shaped haystacks stand guard over the forest entrance. We start up the hill and through the woods. The women explain that they are going to Stupni Do to collect food from their gardens. They live in Vareš, and each is from a different family. Virtually all the survivors of Stupni Do live in Vareš, they say. The women, who seem dully to cast an emotional numbness, come up here just about every day and try to make the best of what they have left in this world.

The road climbs another mile and a half, occasionally switching back across the hillside. It is a rough road, much like the one leading up Mount Igman. I drive slowly. No one is in a hurry to get to Stupni Do. As the road levels off, we encounter an old military truck that is parked on the narrow road. Several men are loading firewood from a pile. They guide us, and we squeeze around the truck. We pass the first house on the edge of Stupni Do. Nine people were killed and burned in that house, one of the women says quietly.

Growing up to Grass and Weeds

Many people, it seems, would like just to forget about Stupni Do. One would be hard-pressed to find a road map with a dot for Stupni Do. There are no signs pointing the way to Stupni Do. When one manages to find what remains of this village buried in the hills, there is no welcoming sign. Stupni Do is either too remote and its story too horrible even for international relief workers to take on, or local officials, at some level, either want to forget about it or have other reasons of their own for preventing aid from getting through.

It now has been five years since hell was visited upon the little corner of paradise known as Stupni Do. Not much has changed since. The grass and weeds grow up a little higher and thicker each year. A memorial has been constructed to the 38 people who were murdered here on the night of 23 October 1993 by a band of Croats, some of whom almost certainly were the longtime neighbors of the dead and dispossessed. A handful of people are trying to move back, but they have poor prospects for doing so without aid. There is little to suggest that assistance is forthcoming.

Laura Silber and Allan Little describe how Stupni Do was ravished:

> (A)fter a day of unrelenting bombardment...Croat militiamen wearing balaclava masks, or with their faces painted, entered the village and dynamited, or torched, every house. Those villagers unable to flee were shot, or had their throats cut. Some were burned alive in their homes...Some bodies were thrown on to bonfires in the gardens of the homes in which they fell. By the end of the killing spree, the village lay littered with bodies and every house was in flames...Some of the bodies were never recovered.[51]

I stop the car, and our passengers disappear down a path. Save for the babble of a nearby but hidden brook trickling down the hillside, this place is quiet like death. Stupni Do is a collection of ruined houses set into a horseshoe-shaped bowl of a valley that is hewn into the upper reaches of these hills. A few more ruined houses stand at the top of the ridge, facing out over the others.

The bowl-shaped clearing is surrounded by green forest. In addition to the wrecked houses, only a few of which show signs of attempted repair, the clearing is marked by orchards, a few gardens, meadows for grazing and for haymaking. Small haystacks poke up here and there, but there is not another human being in sight. Were it not for the violence implied in the scattered ruins, this would be just about as peaceful and unspoiled a place as one might ever wish to find.

Stupni Do is a lovely name for an idyllic setting. "*Do*" is a diminutive form for the noun *dolina*, which means "valley" or, more poetically, "dale." "*Stupni*" is an adjective, and almost certainly in this usage has an archaic meaning. It conveys to me a sense of "stairway" or "stair step." Loosely translated, then, I would call this village "Stairway Valley."

---

[51]Silber and Little, pp. 301.

One year ago, on the fourth anniversary of the slaughter, Vareš municipality, to which Stupni Do administratively belongs, dedicated a monument to those who died here. The memorial is in the form of a *sebilje*, which is a kind of large fountain at which Muslim men wash their hands and feet and heads before their prayers. It is hexagonal and with an inscribed black-granite tablet on each side at eye level.

Five of the stone plaques are engraved with the names and birth dates of the 38 people slaughtered in Stupni Do. Thirty-three of the victims are named Likić. Below each of the tablets is a waterspout. When, and if, the *sebilje* ever is made functional, and if there ever is a population in Stupni Do to make use of it, those who perform their ablutions at this fountain will do so while bowing towards the names of the villagers who died in the Stupni Do massacre.

The sixth granite plaque's inscription says: "In memory of the victims of the genocide that was carried out 23 October 1993 by the criminals of the HVO." There is an inscription, too, from the *Koran*: "And never say for the people who died on Allah's road that they are dead. No, they are still alive, but you do not know it."

As I am reading names on the memorial, I am startled by the voice of a child. A little boy has come out of a tiny, patched-up house that is just down the hill from me. I later will see two people who I assume are his parents, working around the house. Just then, a car comes up the hill and stops beside the *sebilje*.

"Peace" Is across the Valley

The driver's name is Vejsil Mahmutović. Vejsil is from Stupni Do, but his wife and children now live in Vareš. He formerly had a good job in town. Now he is a shepherd. Vejsil's 50 sheep are pastured above Stupni Do. His hope is to get a loan so that he can rebuild his house and move his family back here before they are finally expelled from their temporary place in town. Vejsil's hope against hope is that he can somehow borrow a little more, perhaps 20,000 deutschemarks (about $12,000), so that he can build up his sheep operation.

Seeing our interest in the memorial, Vejsil walks with us around the *sebilje*. Pressing his finger against each inscribed name, he tells us who they were: four members of this family, four members of another family, an entire family of seven (ranging from grandparents to grandson), two from this family, three from that family, a mentally ill old woman, a visitor from Dubrovnik, and on and on. Many of these people were like family to him, he says. In fact, Vejsil will tell us only

later, his mother's maiden name was Likić, and he lost a brother and
nephew in the carnage of Stupni Do.

Vejsil has been luckier than the others to get some international
assistance, albeit small. A Spanish agency arranged for him and one
other man each to receive 10 sheep. That, he says, is the only aid that
has come to Stupni Do. Several people have visited the decimated
village and hinted of possible future aid, but nothing has materialized. I
self-consciously feel that he sees in us another weak glimmer of hope.

It almost is hard to say what makes Vejsil more angry, the atrocities
that were committed against his family and neighbors or the fact that
the municipality, his country, and the world at large have done almost
nothing to help Stupni Do's struggling and homeless survivors to
rebuild their lives and village. It seems impossible, he notes, even to
get the road to the village properly maintained so that people readily
and safely can get here.

As is true all over the war-torn communities of what once was
Yugoslavia, there exists here great jealousy and suspicion. There are
rumors that funding has been arranged to rebuild another village, a
Croatian one, just over the hill in the next valley. Vejsil bristles at the
thought. Croats from that village, named "Mir" (which means "Peace"),
were recognized by people here among the participants in the Stupni
Do massacre. It is possible that the men of Mir were provoked or even
compelled by HVO extremists either to destroy their neighbors or to risk
losing their own homes. But that excuse will carry no weight with Vejsil,
nor, one can be sure, with most of his longtime former neighbors.

In my travels around Bosnia and Hercegovina, I will encounter a
number of angry and strongly nationalistic individuals. The worst of
these, in fact, have such vicious auras about them that one is hesitant
even to provoke them by conversation. Vejsil does not strike me as
such a man. Nevertheless, he is angry, and one guesses there are others
from the village who are even more enraged. Vejsil wants us to see the
village of Mir, and, if we wish, he will take us to the top of the ridge
from where it is visible. We join him.

Vejsil points his car up the steep, brown-clay lane leading to the
top of the valley. This is a go-for-it road. Once the clutch comes up,
there is no backing off. If one were to try and make the climb too
slowly, his car would not make it. Maneuvering through and among
axle-breaking ruts, rocks and gravel washes, Vejsil scrambles to the top
of the valley's rim. As we bounce about in the car and skirt the
dangerous edge of what is more a cow path cut into the hill than a

roadway, I am glad that Vejsil (and not I) is driving and that it is in his (and not my) car.

As the incline levels off, the road ends and spreads out into a narrow, grassy meadow that is the top of the rim. Vejsil's uncle has a house at the rim's inside edge. In what remains of that building, they have fixed up a room or two sufficiently that Vejsil can sleep there in order to be close to the flock at night.

Standing at the hill's edge, looking down into Stupni Do and beyond, I realize that there was a genuine military objective in capturing Stupni Do. From the top of this ridge, one peers down into Vareš from about a 40-degree angle. The district center is distant, but the view is clear and the distance is easily within artillery range. From the main part of the village, below, Vareš had not even been visible. I am reminded of Žuć, that hill with the birds-eye of Sarajevo, which was held at the cost of so many Muslim lives.

Looking the other direction, and from the very yard of the uncle's house, we gaze across another valley to another village, itself partially destroyed. This is Mir. Immediately below us, meanwhile, are the vacant remains of three stuccoed-block, white houses that formerly were occupied by Croats. These homes, like most houses and barns in Bosnia and Hercegovina, were built too solidly to be demolished by mere fire. Unless thoroughly blasted with explosives, structures here do not burn to the ground and disappear. Either they stand as lasting, ghastly memorials or they are reconstructed and reoccupied. In some cases, the new residents could even be those who had killed the former owners

These three houses stand stark and symmetrically. They are equally spaced from one another, in a perfect row. It is like three friends or brothers had agreed to work together and to build each of their houses in the same way. In the softening light of approaching dusk, these look like stage props constructed of matte-finish white cardboard and spray-painted with black splotches of smoke and flame damage. The roofs are gone, as are the door and window frames. I peer down and into them. They are empty boxes, roofless dollhouses. All the toy furnishings have been put away before bedtime.

Before the wars, Vejsil recalls, there were 218 Muslims and 40 Serbs in Stupni Do. "We had good relations with the Serbs and with these Croats," he says, gesturing broadly toward the surreal row of empty boxes and the more distant village of Mir. The Serbs already were long gone by the time Stupni Do was destroyed. Vejsil recalls how the Serbs had cried when they were ordered to leave.

In retribution for what was done to Stupni Do, of course, Muslims burned the houses of Mir. If Mir is rebuilt and Stupni Do is not, it is easy to imagine that Mir one day will burn again. Or vice versa. Meanwhile, those living in rebuilt homes will lie in their beds at night and wonder when and how it might all start up once more. Perhaps the only thing that would keep some of the most bitter from killing their neighbors or burning their houses is the fear of mutual assured destruction. Once it starts, there may be no stopping the circle of violence. If some trust is not built up, along with some houses and lives on both sides, even an accidental fire could set off a murderous cyclone.

Only at the end of our conversation does Vejsil's voice begin to break and tears come to his eyes. I do not sense that this is from grief. My feeling is that the former residents of Stupni Do cannot grieve any longer. They are numb from anguish, but their frustration continues to grow day by day. All he needs is a loan that will allow him to buy a few more sheep, to build some proper facilities for their care, and to set up a small cheese-making operation. If he could get that, Vejsil says, he could rebuild his house, feed his family, and work to build a future. He would not need to ask anything for free.

We say goodbye to Vejsil and walk down the rutted road and back toward my car. I look up and see several sheep come over the hilltop. They line up abreast of one another atop the ridge—above us and above what remains of Stupni Do. They are watching us leave. The sheep stare at me intensely, angrily, and eye to eye. I look away, shiver, and pull my collar up around my neck.

Up in these hills, it gets chilly quickly as the sun goes down.

Neither Forward nor Back

The interview with Westendorp continues in today's *Oslobodjenje*. He looks toward the year 2000 and beyond. At present, he notes, SFOR in Bosnia and Hercegovina consists of between 32,000 and 35,000 troops, and the country still needs military protection. Although he does not specify how many troops will be necessary a couple years from now, Westendorp says a military force is and will be needed that "will provide the same effectiveness as that which we have now."

Westendorp is asked what disappoints him most in the way Republika Srpska has been run under Prime Minister Milorad Dodik. He mentions first the lack of progress on returning refugees to their homes. In fact, there has been almost no progress on that in Republika Srpska. The situation in the Federation is not much better.

When the Gypsies Return

We are on the road today to Hercegovina. Now, if the outside world understands little about Bosnia, it knows next to nothing about the southern region that is Hercegovina. Indeed, foreigners typically use "Bosnia" to denote the entire country and ignore the rest of the name. Muslims in Bosnia proper are not much better in that regard. They tend to refer to themselves and to their coreligionists in Hercegovina as "Bošnjaks," a term deriving from the local word for Bosnia. A man from Hercegovina, though, is a "*Hercegovac*" (and a woman is a "*Hercegovka*"). His being Muslim does not make him from Bosnia.

Hercegovac conveys only a regional, or geographic, identity. In today's Bosnia and Hercegovina, where people feel obliged to have an ethnonational identity, a regional identity may be regarded as politically insufficient. Of course, if a man wants to emphasize that he is a Bosnian but that the nationalists can go to hell with their ethnicity, he can say that he is a "*Bosanac*." As *Bosanac* carries no sense of ethnicity whatsoever, such a person could be Croat, Serb, Muslim or of some other or mixed ethnic background. *Bosanac* might seem like a nice, neutral word that no one should have a problem with. But even this seemingly impartial term now carries a political overtone. No patriotic Croat or Serb in Bosnia and Hercegovina wants to be known as a *Bosanac*. He is a Croat, or he is a Serb. Thus, his patriotic Muslim former neighbor insists that he is a Bošnjak.

That all may sound like a lot of nonsense and nothing to get worked up about. Around here, though, people care about that sort of thing. Some care about it now even though a decade ago they did not. Many care about it even though they would rather not even think about it. Where I am going today, people think about these things a lot.

Mostar's Wall Symbolically Replaces Bridge

Mostar once was best known for its 16th-century bridge. Some say that single-peaked stone arch across the Neretva River symbolized multiethnic Mostar—and even multiethnic Bosnia and Hercegovina as a whole. Croat bombardment purposefully destroyed the bridge on 9 November 1993. Mostar's Croats, some of whom are among the most virulently nationalistic in all of Bosnia and Hercegovina, began to build a new symbol: a wall between the Muslim and Croat sides of the city. They called this their "Berlin Wall." The barrier was not completed, but neither was it torn down. Today, much of Mostar is a blown-out mess, and it remains an ethnically and politically divided city.

Fighting broke out in Mostar at an early stage in the struggles for Bosnia and Hercegovina. At that time, the fight was primarily between Croats and Serbs. The Croats came out on top. Extreme Croat nationalists intended to create a new state, to be called Herceg-Bosna, and for Mostar to be their capital. That made another round of fighting inevitable. This time, Croats aimed to destroy Muslims. They fought to a standstill, which reigns still today. Now, Croats occupy the western side of Mostar and Muslims the eastern part.

Westendorp recently declared in his *Oslobodjenje* interview that Mostar must be reunited. This will not be easy. In today's paper, the vice-president of HDZ in Mostar Canton is quoted as predicting a new war in Bosnia and Hercegovina. The article is headlined: "Brajković's New War Cry." It was such loose talk that earlier caused Mijo Brajković to lose his job as cantonal president. I am not at all convinced that he is going to care much about being fired, particularly in that Brajković is also the director of an important industrial enterprise in Mostar.

This Is Hercegovina

Although there is a threat of rain, the drive to Mostar is scenic and pleasant. The first part of the trip winds through the villages and green hills south and west of Sarajevo. After roughly 45 minutes, we reach the valley through which flows the exquisitely jade-green Neretva River. The hills become more thinly forested. To our right now is the manmade Lake Jablanica. I am reminded that Ramiz had told me this morning (and CIA figures confirm) that Bosnia and Hercegovina has plentiful hydroelectric capacity. This is one of the few economic advantages that nature has bestowed upon this rugged country.

This is Hercegovina. Lake Jablanica rises up at a bend in the Neretva. Although there is no official boundary between Hercegovina and Bosnia, the lands of Hercegovina lie south of this lake and river bend. We follow the long lake and then the Neretva all the way to Mostar. Every few minutes I see a man or boy alongside the road holding out a fish for sale or who has two or three fish hanging on a stick. The trees on the valley sides become smaller and scrubbier as we continue south. Near Mostar, the hillsides scarcely have topsoil at all. The vegetation is low scrub, and precious little of that. The scars from war increase. I stop to buy fresh figs from an old man selling against a backdrop of burned and shot up farmsteads and houses. I guess that

Ramiz and Vahida will enjoy these. They were born in Hercegovina, and one does not see figs for sale farther north.

Mostar is built along both banks of the creamy-green Neretva. I have seen very nice pictures of the city from before the wars. It was quite a shock when I first visited Mostar a few weeks ago. I will see today if my first impressions of Mostar were exaggerated. My 1980s-era guidebook describes Mostar as "surely one of the more beautiful Turkish cities of Yugoslavia." In some sense, Mostar was not so lucky as Sarajevo. Physically, the guidebook version of Sarajevo largely still exists. The buildings and cultural monuments are battered but, for the most part, not totally demolished. That is not true in Mostar.

Linden Trees for Šantić Street

We park on the Muslim side and walk through a sprinkling rain to the Carinsky Bridge. This new bridge, whose name means "Customs," had been completed just before fighting broke out. Damaged in the intense fighting, it was repaired during 1995 and 1996 with assistance from the EU. On the bridge, we meet a Serb about 55 years old. He formerly lived in Mostar, but today he resides in Nevesinje, a town some 25 miles to the east and just across the IEBL in Republika Srpska.

Some Serbs, he says, are beginning to return first to Mostar's outlying areas. As people become accustomed to seeing—and perhaps even interacting with—those from the other ethnic groups, this refugee figures, then Serbs will begin also to return to Mostar proper. But this will take time.

At present, this man observes, life on either side of divided Mostar—or on either side of the inter-entity line, for that matter—is only barely sufferable. Still, there is progress. There is also contradiction. This old Serb can come to see his old friend here in Mostar, and nobody gives him any problems. Many people in Mostar (and by this he is referring to Croats and Muslims), he says, want the former residents to come back. Overall, though, relations between Mostar's Muslims and Croats are still poor, and that impedes a return to some kind of normalcy.

For example, the Serb refugee explains, the French want to invest in reopening Mostar's aluminum factory. At the same time, though, they are telling Croat leaders that there is a precondition: the Croats must allow—and encourage—Serbs and Muslims also to work in the factory. Some of the Croats here, he implies, are very militant in their nationalism. (Indeed, the director of that plant is one Mijo Brajković, the war-mongering HDZ man written about in today's *Oslobodjenje.*) At that moment, another old Serb passes by on the bridge. The two men greet one another. The refugee says he formerly worked in a plant that produced airplanes and airplane parts. The factory barely operates now. A textiles plant also was important here in Mostar before the wars. It does not operate at all. Until the factories open and there are jobs, the Serb emphasizes, there cannot be any prospects for the future. But investment and jobs will only come when the peace is permanent and everybody regards it as enduring.

The sprinkle is turning to drizzle as we walk the last few steps across the bridge to the Croat side of the river. Along the opposite embankment, though, where we see the crumbling ruins of shot-up and abandoned buildings, we are still in the Muslim zone. The Berlin Wall is set back some from the river. We turn left by the Ero Hotel, whose name is a folklorish word used to indicate a native of Hercegovina, and walk down Aleksa Šantić Street. This street is the dividing line between the Muslim and Croat sides of the city. It is named for a Serb poet who was Mostar's literary favorite son.

If ever there was a true *Hercegovac,* it was Šantić (1868–1924). Rarely leaving his beloved Mostar for more than a few days at a time, Šantić once was described by a contemporary as a patriotic, but not a political, poet. Šantić "was more the northern Slav, kindly and good-natured than the complicated and critical southern Slav…Šantić did not believe that there was any evil in men." This Serb poet also enjoyed a mutually close and fond relationship with Mostar's Muslims.[52]

The buildings on Šantić Street are in a bad state. They look as though they have been abundantly blasted with artillery and then, as if for good measure, have been shot up by hundreds more rounds of machine-gun fire. One small building stands out, as it is the only one that has been completely reconstructed. It is freshly painted. Care International is setting up its Information Center here. In front of the Care building, we encounter three Muslim men who are planting linden trees.

The trees are a gift from the Italians, the men explain. Approximately 100 of them will go on this street and about 3,000 will be planted in the city altogether. The men all previously worked at a company building high-rise apartments. Their former employer has no work for them. One shows us his pay receipt, indicating that he, like

---

[52]Jovan Dučić, "Aleksa Šantić," *Collected Works,* trans. Michael B. Petrovich (Chicago: Palandech's Publishing House, 1952).

the others, makes 166 deutschemarks (about $105) per month. They work six or seven days a week to earn that salary. Planting trees is not their customary line of work, but the men are happy to have jobs.

Hercegovac Votes for a Bošnjak

Lunch is at Pizzeria ET, on the Muslim side of town. It is very chic by local standards and would be regarded so even in Sarajevo. Half coffeehouse and half restaurant, really, it is sparklingly clean, light and airy. Its colorful environment contrasts sharply with that of Mostar as a whole on this gray day. We take a table in the second-floor, half-open dining area. The drizzle has turned into a hard and steady rain. Fortunately, the dining area has a solid roof. The establishment is full. The clientele are well dressed and mostly young. Although it is lunchtime, few of the customers are eating. Rather, they linger over drinks. Pizzeria ET is a place to see and be seen.

I ask our waiter, who is perhaps 20 years old, how Hercegovinians feel about the cultural current emanating from Sarajevo and which encourages the country's Muslims to identify themselves as Bošnjaks. The young man points out that he is *Hercegovac* and neither a *Bosanac* nor Bošnjak. He says, too, that Muslims here speak a different dialect than do those in central Bosnia. Others have told me, in fact, that the most beautiful Serbo-Croatian is spoken in this land of Šantić.

The waiter says that nationalism—including Muslim nationalism— among the political parties is a real problem. So, for whom did he and his friends vote? "Alija," he says, referring to Izetbegović, the SDA and the Coalition. Is that not a contradiction, to say that nationalism is a major political problem and then to vote for a nationalist ticket? Yes, the young man agrees, it is contradictory. To cast one's vote for any other party, he suggests, though, would effectively be to help the Croat and Serb nationalist parties. So there really seemed little choice.

Downstairs, we have coffee and speak with the 30s-something headwaiter. Although there are growing numbers of pubs and small shops, he says, there are almost no industrial jobs here. Numerous among Mostar's and Hercegovina's Muslims now live or work abroad. Many of the young people in this establishment, the waiter says, probably are spending the money that their fathers are earning abroad. Some of the luckier ones among the young people can get jobs working in shops. There are a few jobs (mostly for young women, he notes) in the international aid organizations. Of course, some of the customers earn their livings from various shady activities.

A small portion of Pizzeria ET's clientele is Croat. This Muslim side of town is poor, the waiter explains. They will take anybody's money. It is not the same on the other side, he says, and the Muslims do not go to cafés over there. Sometimes, SFOR troops visit the pizzeria. They spend their money, the girl behind the bar says of the foreign soldiers, and the locals like that. Other than that, though, she has nothing either positive or negative to say about the foreign military presence.

So long as SFOR is here, the waiter adds, there will be no more war. There is another signal of that, too. According to an old folk proverb, war is over when the Gypsies begin to return. The old people really believe that old adage, he relates, and the Gypsies are in fact coming back to Mostar.

A Suspended Work in Progress

We are crossing a bridge, heading over to the Croat side, when we encounter a middle-aged Muslim man who is just returning from there. He formerly lived in what is now the Croat zone. It is bad enough for him that his house is just across town and he cannot live in it. Adding insult to injury, the man tells us that his car is over there, too. He has seen somebody else driving it about, and it seems there is little that he can do about it. The Muslim says he has filled out paperwork to recover both house and car. He keeps checking up to see how his case is progressing, but always hears from the officials that, well, they are very busy, there are many claims to settle... The man has spoken, too, with international officials, but they have no means by which to force the Croat officials to resolve the matter.

This man was in the Bosnian army during the wars. He was captured by Croat forces and imprisoned for 45 days at Dretelj, a nearby village where the area's most notorious prison camp was established. A Red Cross unit from the Netherlands eventually got him and his fellow prisoners liberated. Married and with three children, he has been gathering copper and brass to earn some money. Now, though, all the copper that could be stripped from ruined houses, factories and motor vehicles has been collected. The spent shell casings all have been picked up.

He would like to go abroad—preferably to America—but that is not so easy. His wife does not want to leave. If he could find a job in some other country, the former soldier and prisoner says he would go abroad alone for a few years.

It is raining hard now. Our umbrellas are in the car. We dodge in and out of doorways, reaching the car just as we are thoroughly drenched and the rain lets up. This puts me in an appropriate disposition to go looking for the Berlin Wall.

We find our way through town to the main road that comes into Mostar from the south. This was once the entry to Mostar for tens of thousands of tourists annually. From the Adriatic coast, they came to see Mostar's famous bridge, to stroll through the old town, then to travel on to Sarajevo up the same scenic Neretva valley that we came down through this morning. This entry had given me my initial impressions of Mostar when I passed this way a few weeks ago.

The damage along this road is among the worst that I will see in any urban setting, although it pales in comparison with the total destruction of some smaller villages or the enormity of that in Sarajevo. Making it particularly striking, I suppose, is the fact that very little has been done along this stretch to repair the damage. This strip had been the front line; it still has the look of a no-man's-land between opposing forces who may not yet have given up options for continued violence. Among the skeleton remains of buildings riddled with mortar blasts and gunfire, there is one new structure that looks like a suspended work in progress. This is the several hundred feet of Berlin Wall. The new symbol of divided Mostar is solidly constructed of stone and is as tall as a man. The wall is far from complete. So far, it divides nothing. I hope it is never torn down. The unfinished wall between South Slavic nations could have an appropriate symbolism.

"We can change nothing."

Damage is less severe here on the Croat side. We decide to stop into some shops. The first is a food store. I order a couple items from the courteous but guarded woman in her 50s who is behind the counter. I pay in convertible marks; my change comes back in Croatian kunas. Both currencies circulate here, but the kuna is the more common. Prices here, she tells us, tend to be a bit lower than across the Croatian border, just 30 miles away. Some Croats from Croatia therefore come here to shop. A few prices (on bread, for example) are lower still on the Muslim side of the city. Muslims and Croats go back and forth across the river to shop, the shopkeeper says. The woman is not much inclined to talk about politics, but the war, she summarizes succinctly, was "something stupid."

A couple doors down, in a tiny clothing shop with a "Season Reduction" sign in the window, another saleswoman of about the same age echoes precisely that sentiment about the war. She generalizes her assessment, though, to include all war. Be that as it may, "only God knows," she says, whether the fighting will start up again.

The shopkeeper has an apartment across the river in the Muslim zone. It is so close, yet she can neither live there nor feel safe even visiting it. She has not seen her apartment in six years. Former residents are applying to get their residences returned, of course. Serbs coming to Mostar to see about getting back their apartments and houses sometimes come into the store to shop. Prices are lower here than in Republika Srpska, she says.

At one time, this saleslady made clothes rather than to sell them. She had worked in the local textiles factory. It is closed up now. Rumors are going around that perhaps an Italian firm will buy the factory and reopen it. Maybe. But she is not setting her hopes too high on ever seeing her apartment again, on getting her old job back, or on lasting peace.

The rain has almost stopped. We turn down a side street and stroll, talking. We approach a small, open-air market, consisting of a double line of fixed tables in simple, roofless stalls. There are neither sellers nor customers at this hour and in this weather. At the near end of the now-empty market, though, there is a small shop. Offering soaps and detergents, household cleaning supplies and toiletries, it is a solidly constructed but transportable structure. This is, though, not one of those kiosks, so common here, in which the shopkeeper sits surrounded by iron bars and making all exchanges through a small opening framed in the same metal bars. There are irons over the windows, of course, but this is larger than a kiosk. It is better lit, and with a bigger selection of colorfully labeled consumer goods. A simple but pleasant ambience invites customers to come inside.

As we near the open door, the shop girl steps into the doorway and lights a cigarette. She is a pretty young woman, perhaps in her mid-20s. There are no customers just now, so we stop to talk. Zijo strikes up a conversation about laundry detergent. He once did some work as an interpreter and guide for an executive from a western consumer products company who was in Bosnia and Hercegovina to do some grassroots market research. Now Zijo can talk soap with the best of them.

As they discuss the prices, merits and popularity of the leading local-brand laundry detergent and its imported competitor, I look at the shop girl. She is beautiful, albeit in a common and not-stunning way.

Her eyes and lips are fully but tastefully made up. I observe one imperfection. A long but small scar is etched into her lovely face. Issuing forth almost indiscernibly beneath the young woman's right eye, the blemish flows in a delicate streak down to mid-cheek, where it splinters and widens into a pale smear.

Moving off the general theme of brighter colors and whiter whites at a better price, we ask her about the postwar present and future. Relations between nations never can be the same as they were before the war. How can they be, she asks, when members of people's families have been killed by the other side, when some of their old friends, too, have been lost in the war? The shop girl has turned her back on the past, lives in the present, but is not yet ready to contemplate the future. She has left to fate the question of whether war will or will not come again, as that does not concern her existence today.

"If you think about war and wait for war all the time," the pretty woman comments, "you will not do anything. We can change nothing. We should just work, and without thinking about the future. If war comes again, it will come."

A customer arrives. The shop girl has finished her cigarette. We continue down the street.

At the Croatian Rose

We stop in at the *Hrvatska ruža* for a cup of coffee before getting back on the road. One can be quite certain that very few Muslims ever have set foot in this coffee shop. Zijo is nervous, although he tries not to show it. I understand. *Hrvatska ruža* translates literally as "Croatian Rose." One does not christen one's establishment *Hrvatska ruža* in order to evoke a sense of peace, love and understanding.

It is easy to imagine that on a sunny day the tables on the sidewalk out front would be crowded with people spiritedly discussing business, politics and culture. Warm sunshine and the open air nurture congeniality, even when the talk turns to controversial subjects. Today is cold and wet. *Hrvatska ruža's* few patrons are seated at the several stool-height tables inside, at the back of the small space, as far as possible from the open doors. We take one of two half-booths near the door.

Hrvatska ruža is comfortable in the sense of its being a clean and well-lit place. One aspect of its décor, though, assures that nationalistic Croats will be most comfortable here and Muslims and Serbs enormously less so: The interior walls are painted in a large red and yellow checkerboard pattern. Every South Slav recognizes that pattern as derived from the *šahovnica,* the checkerboard crest which is a Croat national symbol and which generally is associated with the *Ustaše,* the pro-fascist Croat collaborators of World War II. It is not quite so belligerent, perhaps, as would be decorating a German coffee shop in a swastika theme, but it is in that ballpark.

A half dozen casually well-dressed men are there when we arrive. Attractive women accompany two of them. Some carry cell phones. These appear to be young men of some substance, who, in some ambiguous way, have business to which they must attend. Some most likely had been soldiers in the war. None look particularly unfriendly. The waiter is polite to us.

Be that as it may, this is not a good time and place to insist that my interpreter, a slightly built Muslim man from out of town, strike up a conversation about ethnic relations in divided Mostar. Were we to do so, I believe, most probably everything would be just fine. The low probability outcome is that the discussion would become heated, and we might draw the local police. Caution in this case seems the better part of valor. We drink our coffee, continue our conversation in English, and then go on our way.

I would have liked to have had that conversation. These people's viewpoints—individually or collectively—would have interested me. In a very real way, though, the owner and patrons had communicated something by their choice of name and symbols. Their message: "This is our place, in our territory. The door is open. Come in if you would like, but do not expect necessarily to feel welcome."

Driving out of Mostar, I compare in my mind my first and latest visits to this city. My first impressions had not been entirely accurate. I had seen only the most badly damaged parts of Mostar on my first time here. The Croat part of town is less severely ruined. On my first walk about Mostar, I had sensed that the predominant emotions were those of sadness and discouragement. That is just the first layer. Now I realize that loathing and anger also are important elements in the mood and that some people feel these even more deeply.

Heroic Jablanica

The heroic city of Jablanica lies some 30 miles up the river Neretva on the road back to Sarajevo. The city probably is best known for the remains here of a bridge blown up during World War II by Tito and his Partisans. The Partisans needed to get to the other side of the Neretva, and they blew up the bridge before crossing it. The casual observer might well ask: "What's wrong with this picture? They wanted to get to the other side, so they blew the bridge?" War creates its own realities. I imagine that it did make sense at the time. Nevertheless, I suspect that the stories of this event have been embellished more than a little. In Yugoslav days, this destroyed bridge was made a symbol for Tito's reputed military brilliance and deep human compassion.

"Jablanica," according to a patriotic, Communist-Yugoslav telling of the story, "was one of the glorious battlefields of the great epic liberation war and revolution of the peoples and nationalities of Yugoslavia. At this place, in 1943, the most humane battle of the II World War (*sic*) was fought—a battle to save 4,000 wounded."

Tito's army had liberated and was holding territory in an area near Bihać, that is to say, in the regions known as Krajina, Kordun and Lika. Under intense pressure from German and *Ustaše* forces, though, the Partisans moved to the south and east toward Montenegro. They stopped at the Neretva, as did "an enormous number" of civilians who were abandoning their homes and following the Partisans. The entourage was conveying also 4,000 wounded Partisan soldiers. *Četnik* forces lay in wait on the other side.

At that point, Tito, "assuming personal responsibility," ordered that the bridge be knocked down, even though it seemed the only way for his army and the train of refugees to cross the river. "It was a daring and ingenious move—a deception which gave the enemy the impression that the Partisan Supreme Command had altered its plan." Then, "in a dramatic race against time," the Partisans fashioned a narrow footbridge on pontoons and braced by the wreckage of the railroad bridge. They crossed during the night and battled the *Četniks* on the other side, "thus defeating the German and Italian fascist formations and their allies, the *Ustaše* and the *Četniks*."[53]

Under an Old Man's Umbrella

I stop the car in steady rain near the auto bridge that today spans the Neretva. A hundred yards downriver is the jackknifed trestle of the old rail bridge. It had been blown in the center such that its two lengths had dropped straight down into the river while their embankment ends had remained on shore. The condition of the wrecked bridge is not so good as it is in my picture book. One of the

---

[53]Ivan Lovrenović, *Bosnia and Herzegovina*, 2nd ed. (Sarajevo: Svjetlost, 1986), pp. 101, 207.

halves has shifted, so that it has been carried downstream some and is more submerged than would be picturesquely ideal. Like any historical object, the broken bridge needs its maintenance. With wars and reconstruction to think about, and as Tito's image is undergoing revision, to maintain a wrecked old bridge that is a memorial to socialist heroism has not been a priority. The museum on the embankment above the broken bridge is closed.

A man elderly enough to have been here when the bridge was blown is strolling in our direction. We greet him, crowd under his umbrella, smoke and chat. He is a Muslim, but two families of Serbs live right next door to him and they never left during the recent fighting. The old man says, too, that he knows of two Croat families that stayed here. In Jablanica, neighbors neither killed nor even fought one another. The situation in the surrounding villages was quite different, though, and several of them were burned.

The *opština* of Jablanica previously had a population near 15,000 and that was roughly 70% Muslim. Croats accounted for 15–20%, and there were few Serbs. Some 500 to 600 people were killed here in the wars associated with Yugoslavia's collapse, according to the old man. The population is still ethnically mixed, although predominantly Muslim, but it has fallen to perhaps only about 3,000 people in total.

He Saw War Coming

I ask the old man if, having experienced World War II, he had ever thought there would be another one. Yes, he answers, quite a few years ago already he was starting to get a sense that another war of Yugoslavs against Yugoslavs was possible. By 1990, the old Muslim says, he was almost certain that war would come. He could see and feel the problems and tensions, especially between Serbs and Croats.

At the time war began, the man recalls, the Croat HVO and the *Armija* of Bosnia and Hercegovina both were here. While they had separate command structures, the Croat and primarily-Muslim armies had good relations and cooperated with one another. Some of the Muslim soldiers fought in the HVO in the early days of the war because the pay was better. Later, though, they switched over to the army of the Bošnjaks. About that time, the HVO was bringing in heavy weapons from Croatia. The Croat units were moving up into the hills, where they destroyed several Muslim villages. The HVO imprisoned some Muslims. Some of these they eventually killed and others they released.

The Croat HVO had enough heavy weapons, the old man notes, that they also could have completely destroyed Jablanica. He is not sure why they did not. One possibility, he says, is that the Croat nationalists had hoped this city and area would become a part of their Herceg-Bosna. The most-concentrated area of Croat settlement within Bosnia and Hercegovina lies in 10 *opštinas* that are just west of Jablanica and along the border with Croatia.

Serb nationalists, too, had hoped early on that this might be part of their Republika Srpska. Once the Serbs had been pushed out of Mostar (which lies straight to the south), the old man continues, they knew they would not get this area, and they focused on consolidating their hold on eastern Hercegovina.

There is little here to keep the dwindling population from diminishing even further. Other than a few jobs in shops, cafés and the like, Jablanica has few employment opportunities. There is, the old man says, a stone-cutting quarry which produces black granite for headstones, monuments and construction. Then, too, there are three hydroelectric plants. These are important economically to Bosnia and Hercegovina as a whole, but they do not generate a lot of jobs where they are located. The old man, who has been on a pension since 1990, formerly worked for a company that builds hydroelectric plants. His work had taken him to Iraq and Libya. It is common that people from here have worked in foreign countries. If opportunities for work abroad ever disappear completely, it would be very difficult for Bosnia and Hercegovina to absorb the locals into its own economy.

Watchful Eyes in Open Konjic

It is a 15-mile drive from Jablanica to Konjic. The road follows Lake Jablanica, which is a widening of the dammed Neretva. The dam at Jablanica has been built where the smaller Rama River flows into the Neretva, serving to push the waters even higher up the Neretva's steep, rock-walled valley.

We stop for gas as we come into Konjic. The station attendant, a Muslim, says he only has this job today because he was a soldier during the war. "All of them attacked us," he says, "but the Croats made the most violence here."

From a picture in a coffee-table book and from my guidebook, I know that Konjic is supposed to be a beautiful city in a magnificent setting and with scenic mountains, hills, lakes and rivers all about.

Today is gray and rainy, though. Darkness soon will be upon us, and I am tired. The beauty escapes me.

Staying on the main road through town, I park across from a *ćevabdžinica* that the gas station attendant had recommended. The restaurant is roomy, and just two of the tables are occupied. At each sits a man in late middle age. We take a table across the room. Although their tables are close together, the two other customers do not seem much interested in one another. One, who is a little older and slightly built, stares into space. The other gazes at his coffee cup. I sense that the latter is interested in our quiet conversation. Soon he and Zijo are speaking across the room. We ask him to join us at our table. The other man continues to stare into space for a few minutes and then drifts out.

Ismet is a bus driver by trade. Over the years, he has driven tour buses all over Europe. Ismet has been as far south and east as Saudi Arabia and so far west as France. He wants to talk about democracy, about economic development, about ethnonational relations, and about the future. The first three of these are closely interrelated in his mind, and the fourth hinges on the other three. Ismet has great faith in democracy. After 50 years of communism, though, he says it will not be easy to build democracy here. Ismet points out, too, that Bosnia and Hercegovina's poverty, in various ways, inhibits democracy from growing here. Under present conditions, he adds, the politicians' interests are quite different from those of the common people.

Konjic is essentially a Muslim town today. According to 1991 census data, the *opština's* population was 55% Muslim, 26% Croat, 15% Serb and 4% people identifying themselves as Yugoslavs or other nationalities. Now, Ismet estimates, the population is no more than 10% Croat and perhaps 7–10% Serbs.

There was hard fighting here between Croats and Muslims. It seems the ugly memories are still quite fresh. Ismet relates that some of the Croats who have been given permission to come back to their villages are reluctant to do so. In some cases, that might be because they have found better houses to live in as refugees than they would have in their former villages. Many of Konjic's Serbs are now returning, he says. During the wartime, of course, there had been fighting with the Serbs also. Serb forces had carried off to Republika Srpska (the boundary with which lies just to the east from Konjic) quite a lot of manufacturing equipment and other productive property.

Ismet is proud to report that Konjic has declared itself an open city. That makes it exceptional among most other cities in the area. It means, he says, that Serbs, Croats and ethnically mixed families all can return and that their human rights and safety are guaranteed. The city's police are mixed Croats and Muslims under a unified command. The police officers, he says, did not themselves object to working together. Perhaps the politicians, though, made some fuss about it. If the politicians can be convinced to agree on things and to behave themselves properly, Ismet suggests, then the common people will do likewise.

The bus driver insists that Muslims in Konjic had never wished to push out the people of other ethnonational groups in the first place. They left on their own or because the political and military situation forced them to go. Now, the economic situation here is difficult for all. People who would be willing to help one another cannot even do so, Ismet says, because they do not have anything themselves.

With its Lake Jablanica and the mountains, tourism should be the Konjic-Jablanica area's natural industry. But the infrastructure here is insufficient, Ismet says, and there is no possibility to finance that sort of development. There had been porcelain manufacturing here before the wars, he adds. Investment is needed to get that restarted, though, and there seems to be nobody willing to provide that capital. The area also has forests and plenty of electricity, Ismet points out.

In his mind, an economic development program is needed that will be targeted to private businesspeople. The investments should not be channeled through the government of Bosnia and Hercegovina, Ismet cautions, and it certainly should not go into Yugoslav-style worker-managed enterprises. The emphasis he believes, must be on small businesses. It would be wonderful to have a new firm that employs 1,500 people, Ismet allows, but who would own it? Who would be responsible for it? Worker self-management is not the solution. Indeed, he believes that the failure of self-management even was a factor contributing to the outbreak of war here. "You can imagine," Ismet says, "something belonged to everybody, and that meant that it belonged to nobody. It did not work."

To fund and to operate a well-run loan program to support small business, he declares, could be one of the best ways for Western countries to help Bosnia and Hercegovina. I comment that I have seen such programs up close, and they tend to be fraught with difficulties: Entrepreneurs may not have the skills to run businesses. Many businesses fail and the money does not get repaid. Risks are high that there will be fraud and outright theft. Monitoring program investments in many small businesses is time-consuming and requires a lot of skilled, honest and dedicated staff.

All of these difficulties would exist in Bosnia and Hercegovina, he allows, while insisting that they could be overcome. Ismet's view, I think, is that such problems and challenges simply must be overcome. There are not, after all, so many options for an area like Konjic, which is starved for local sources of capital and in various ways is not well-suited to large-scale industry.

In the scheme of things that Ismet imagines, he, for example, could get a loan to buy a bus. Then he could support himself and provide jobs for a couple more people. Of course, Ismet says, to qualify for the loan, he should be required to show that he has some expertise in the bus business. He should be obliged to produce a reasonable business plan. The program officers would need to monitor him closely to make sure that he is using the money properly and is running his business well. All that is only smart and reasonable.

The discussion turns to politics and last weekend's election. Because voting in Bosnia and Hercegovina occurs along nationalist lines and the elections pit nationalist parties against one another, Ismet remarks, people's votes often do not reflect their real thinking. Voters support the party of their ethnonational group just because they are afraid of seeing power go to the other group. There are too many parties, he says, the result of which is that those votes going to the non-national parties are scattered too diffusely. The country cannot, then, elect a credible alternative political force that is moderate and blind to ethnicity. Still, Ismet remarks, in the Federation, at least, progress toward democracy is being made.

Now Ismet surprises me a little. He begins to talk about Alija Izetbegović in the most glowing terms. For the first time in his life, Ismet says, he sees in Izetbegović a president that he loves and for whom he truly wishes to vote. The SDA leader will be able to establish democracy in Bosnia and Hercegovina. World leaders, especially those in the US, recognize Izetbegović as a strong and moral force who is deserving of their support.

Zijo will inform me later that a policemen has just come into the restaurant and has taken a seat nearby. The policeman is not visible from where I am sitting. I have noticed, though, that a couple more customers have come in and seem to be taking a strong interest in our conversation. I begin to think it might be best to wrap up this discussion and to move on.

Ismet wants to tell me also about Milošević. European leaders, he remarks, are absolutely afraid of the President of the Federal Republic of Yugoslavia. They will not stand up to him. Just as Serb nationalists killed and burned and pillaged in Bosnia and Hercegovina, so will Milošević behave in Kosovo, and perhaps later in Macedonia. If the US does not stop Milošević, Ismet assures me, nobody will. Many people in Bosnia and Hercegovina, he adds, were surprised that the US stood by so long as it did during the wars here before using its strength to stop the killing.

I do not know if Ismet would have started to talk next about Tudjman and the Croats. Perhaps not, as that might be particularly sensitive. There is a future for Konjic and for Bosnia and Hercegovina, Ismet concludes, but it is very important "to stop the dictators."

Pressed Between Croat and Serb Nationalisms

Outside, it is dark and raining hard. A police car with one person inside sits across the street from the *ćevabdžinica,* behind and to the side from my car. We seem to have attracted a bit of attention. Probably, Ismet will be having a little discussion with the local cops tonight. Particularly as he was not too careless, I do not expect him to face any seriously negative consequences for having spoken with us.

The rainy drive back to Sarajevo is difficult. The road is hilly, twisting and poorly marked. As I pick my way along, though, I think of the day. I realize now, that Konjic and Jablanica lie wedged between a proverbial rock and hard place. To their west is Bosnia and Hercegovina's most densely populated, and most strongly nationalistic, Croat area. To their east is Republika Srpska. It will be difficult for Muslims, tolerant people of whatever nation and ethnically mixed families to live here. To the south, Mostar, represents the tip of that wedge—and the point where the pressure is strongest. The forces of Croat nationalism pressing from the west and of Serb nationalism pushing from the east will try to squeeze this wedge of Muslims up and out of Hercegovina.

Feeling Good about Democracy

I was right about the figs. Ramiz and Vahida are pleased to receive this taste of Hercegovina. They have family in Mostar and so are interested also to hear about the situation that I found there.

This evening, we watch leaders from three of the major parties participate in a postelection talk show on local television. They are joined by Robert Barry, the OSCE's Head of Mission in Bosnia and Hercegovina and the chief supervisor of the elections. The program begins with a stirring tribute to the voters, to the elections process and to Bosnia and Hercegovina. To the accompaniment of Queen's "We Are the Champions," a video montage recollects the campaigns and the voting. It is supposed to make people feel good about democracy.

The program seems to me a bit ridiculous, though, considering that the voting was nearly a week ago and election outcomes still have not been announced. Barry explains why there are no preliminary results. The races in Republika Srpska are very close, the counting is complicated by the high proportion of off-site and absentee ballots, and various parties already are claiming victories. The OSCE does not want to confuse matters further, he says, by putting out preliminary results. Barry assures voters that there is absolutely no way for any cheating to occur during the counting process, which he describes as "very transparent."

Jealousy, Lies and Deception

"In Madame Tussaud's museum, just one of the figures is kept behind glass. That is the sculpture of Adolph Hitler. If there were such a museum here, I would stand up behind that glass Momčilo Krajišnik." That quote, cited in *Oslobodjenje*, is attributed to Biljana Plavšić, the current President of Republika Srpska and Sloga's candidate in last weekend's elections. Earlier in the week, of course, Westendorp had called Krajišnik a dinosaur. It has been a bad week in the name-calling department for Krajišnik, who is waiting to learn whether or not he will be reelected as the Serb member of the Bosnia and Hercegovina Presidency.

Everybody waits. While they wait, the politicians call one another names and the newspapers speculate and print rumors. Half of *Oslobodjenje's* front-page headlines yesterday were questions instead of declarative statements: "Will Sloga Demand Annulment of Elections in Republika Srpska?" "Is Gradimir Gojer in as President?" "Is Krajišnik's (war crimes tribunal investigation) Dossier Being Opened?"

That was yesterday. Today, we read that Sloga did not request that the Republika Srpska election be voided, but it does look like Sloga has a legitimate complaint against the other Serb nationalists who are its rivals. It seems that, in spite of the round-the-clock campaign blackout that OSCE imposed upon all parties during the voting period, SRS and SDS managed to get some airtime for their messages anyway. OSCE's Media Experts Commission (MEC) is to investigate.

Creating the MEC and its strengthened successor, the Independent Media Commission (IMC), was a good idea. With a few notable exceptions, the media here are a hate-mongering and pretty unprofessional lot (unprofessional, that is, if one thinks the media should contribute to a well-informed public and functioning democracy). It remains to be seen, though, if the IMC has any teeth. The MEC could not actually prevent SRS-SDS campaign violations. *Oslobodjenje* reports today, too, that the MEC has just ordered a magazine that published unsubstantiated accusations against the leader of the SDP to print a correction. Muslim nationalists control the magazine. It is a case of slamming the barn door after the horse has escaped. Any electoral damage that might have been done by the apparent disparagement has of course already been done.

That SDP leader who was accused without substantiation, Zlatko Lagumdžija, is predicting that SDP's candidate for the Croat seat in the

Bosnia and Hercegovina Presidency, Gradimir Gojer, will end in a photo finish with HDZ's Ante Jelavić. In that the race may be close, Lagumdžija is unhappy that the Republican Party, one of two parties in *Koalicija Centra*, had reneged on an agreement it supposedly had made with SDP that it would not put up a candidate for the Croat presidential spot. That Croat seat in the three-member Presidency represents the non-nationalist opposition parties' only real chance to break into the presidential body. To achieve that, though, would have required more unity than the scattered opposition parties could muster.

Until non-nationalist opposition groups join forces against the various nationalists, they will exert little influence over day-to-day politics. Non-nationalists, too, must prove to the electorate that they are viable as political forces and that pluralism, democracy and toleration offer voters something better than do the nationalists and their programs of fighting against one another in the collective names of their ethnonational groups.

As to the third headline question: There is growing public speculation as to whether Krajišnik will be indicted for war crimes. He undoubtedly has been investigated and is the longtime number-two man for Radovan Karadžić, who was himself indicted long ago. Having served since 1996 in the Presidency, Krajišnik has enjoyed some *de facto* immunity. That will melt away if he loses this election. On the other hand, international forces here have shown little interest actually in arresting Karadžić or most of the other indicted war criminals at large in and around this country. They do arrest relative small fry from time to time.[54] An *Oslobodjenje* editorial cartoon today suggests that

---

[54] SFOR's reluctance to assist the International War Crimes Tribunal to do its work by arresting indicted suspects is perhaps disturbing but should not be surprising. Holbrooke explains, for example (*To End A War*, pp. 220–223), how, during planning for the Dayton negotiations, the US military vehemently opposed suggestions that IFOR, and even the IPTF, should have responsibility for policing or civilian aspects of the peace accord's implementation. The concerns relate to so-called "mission creep" and to security issues. The military fears to be assigned tasks for which it has not been allotted sufficient resources or which fall outside its specific expertise. At the same time, military brass recognized that arresting war criminals could cause civil unrest. That would add to an already volatile situation and make peacekeeping more difficult. My own view is that stronger efforts should be made to arrest war criminals but that the current level of international troops deployment may be insufficient to deter those nationalists who would stir up civil unrest in response to such arrests.

Krajišnik's time is running out and that he will soon be in The Hague. I am skeptical.

Another subject that feeds my skepticism is that of refugees returning to their homes. I always am pleased to see the occasional article reporting that a resettlement is in progress. An article in *Oslobodjenje* today states that 300 Bošnjaks have returned to Hodbina, a settlement near Mostar. The refugees of course found their homes destroyed or damaged and so are hoping to receive help from international organizations. According to the article, two additional settlements in the Mostar *opština* have occurred since the war ended. I regard this as good news. I am rather cynical about it, though, because I know that such instances amount to a drop in the bucket relative to the number of displaced people who as yet have no prospects to go home. I know, too, that political leaders like to make a big show of such exceptional cases in order to divert attention away from their much larger failures.

Sarajevo and Bosnia and Hercegovina face a growing new problem: refugees from Kosovo and from Sandžak who are fleeing Serb aggression. One might think that, as these ethnic Albanians and Slavs are Muslims, Sarajevo's Bošnjaks would welcome these unfortunate coreligionists with open arms. One might expect wrong. Two of the headlines in today's paper: "Refugees (from Kosovo) Cannot Stay in Sarajevo" and "Cantonal Government Decides: Refugees from Kosovo Are Not Our Concern."

The UNHCR has demanded that Sarajevo's cantonal government help. It is of course true that Sarajevo has plentiful problems of its own without more refugees. It has made little progress toward returning displaced non-Muslim Sarajevans to their homes, as was pledged under the Sarajevo Declaration.

An official says it is difficult to know how many Sandžak and Kosovar refugees are in the city now but that the figure could be as high as 10,000.[55] The Federation is helping as much as it can, the official states, especially in light of the fact that it has more than 800,000 refugees of its own still in foreign countries. Altogether some 1.5 million Bosnians and Hercegovinians are either refugees abroad or remain displaced within Bosnia and Hercegovina. It scarcely needs to

---

[55]This observation was in September 1998, about six months before Serbia began its massive offensive to depopulate Kosovo of its ethnic Albanians.

be said that the Republika Srpska half of the country is of no help whatsoever in regard to this problem of Sandžak and Kosovar refugees.

The officials may not say it publicly, but another part of the problem is that many Bošnjaks are prejudiced against Muslims from Sandžak and Kosovo. These refugees are seen as foreigners who did nothing to assist people in Bosnia and Hercegovina when there was war here. Some also regard these people to be backward. Sarajevans tend to have similar views even toward rural Bošnjaks who have come to the city from their pilfered farms and destroyed villages.

Best Seen from the Outside

Zijo is giving a tour about town today to Nancy from Alaska. She is one of these election-monitoring junkies that the fellow from the US Embassy told me about. A nice and interesting lady, I meet her for coffee at the Hotel Saraj. So long as I am in the neighborhood, I decide to walk up to the fortress that is on top of the hill and above the hotel. No one in Sarajevo ever has spoken to me of this centuries-old structure that looks out over their city.

Stopping nearly at the crest, I turn to gaze down and across the valley. I count 29 minarets. As I get closer to the hilltop citadel, I discover where Sarajevo's stray dogs hang out. Apparently, a bunch of mutts live in the castle and that motley crew is allowed to run about that small neighborhood. One bored-looking soldier guards the entrance. The closest thing he gets to excitement, I suppose, is when the rare tourist comes through, thinking that he or she will look at some paintings, cultural relics and imperial treasures from the Ottoman or Habsburg days. The castle is a military installation. It has a sort of attractiveness from a distance but up close its aspect is filthy and foreboding.

In retrospect, I realize that this fortress has a long history as a prison—run first by the Turks and then by the Austrians. Most likely, this is the very fortress that plays a central role in Selimović's novel *Death and the Dervish*. The author's citadel reeks of evil, intolerance and injustice. Rare is the man who, having been taken in, comes back out. Rarer still is he who comes out alive.

Good Life

Ramiz will live to be 100 years old, his brother-in-law once remarked to me. I will not be surprised if that turns out to be true. Ramiz lives a personal philosophy that seems a formula for longevity. It involves fresh air, exercise, a diet that is hearty but healthy, a sanguine attitude toward life, an appreciation for friends and family, and a glass of *šljivovica* now and again. Ramiz is always introducing me to the *fino* things in life.

My dictionary translates *fino* (FEE-noh) as "fine," "first-class" and "refined." Nice weather is *fino*; good food is *fino*; tasty beer is *fino*. An attractive and sympathetic woman is *fina* and fresh air is *fin*, but the difference is just a matter of grammar. The sense is that something *fino* is just exactly as it ought to be, the way God or Nature intended.

We are going today to the *vikendica*, and I am expecting a weekend filled with much that is *fino*. Even though it is cold, gray and raining, thoughts of the *vikendica* and his plans for the weekend put Ramiz in a jolly mood. He is singing snippets of Bosnian folk songs about green mountains and how rain makes the grass grow. Ramiz throws in a bit from a drinking song here and there, too, betraying additional thoughts on the weekend. I do not understand completely what he has up his sleeve for the next couple days, but I know it will involve roasting meat in two or three different ways, walking in the forest and various occasions for the moderate but frequent intake of alcohol.

A stick-to-your-ribs breakfast is crucial ahead of a weekend in the out-of-doors. This morning we have *pura*, also known as *palenta* or *kačamak*. This food with three names is like an oily cornbread cooked on the stovetop in a frying pan. It is a simple food, consisting of corn meal, water, butter, and oil. It is not a pasty mush. Rather, it is spooned out of the pan in soft chunks. The grainy but chunky consistency reminds me more than a little bit of mortar. But the color is a dark yellow going on orange. It probably is only my imagination that makes it taste just a little like pumpkin. To appreciate *pura*, and as is true for many staple foods, one must like it for its consistency and the way it complements what is served with it. In this case, we eat it with thick sour cream and cultured milk. Ramiz insists that it is "very good for the organism." For good health, one should eat *pura* one day out of seven, he says, urging me to be generous in applying the cream and milk. This is good stuff, but I think eating it once weekly is indeed often enough for those of us who do not work all day in the fields or forests.

Ramiz has been looking forward to this weekend since our brief visit to his *vikendica* a week ago. He wants everything to be done properly. We buy meat at the butcher shop around the corner, tomatoes, onions and peppers at the neighborhood green grocer, and today's bread at another shop. Most of what we eat this weekend will be cooked, in one manner or another, over a wood fire. There will be no gas grill with artificial coals, and not even charcoal. Nothing will be cooked on *Teflon*, and we will use no fat substitutes, artificial sweeteners, or new-age "light" foods.

Life as a *Balkanac*

Having arrived at the *vikendica*, taken care of a few housekeeping matters, drunk a touch of cognac and a serving of coffee, we feel sufficiently fortified to set out in search of edible fungus. Now, mushroom hunting is a favorite and traditional pastime in just about every Slavic culture. The earliest and only partially differentiated Slavs living in their primeval homeland must already have been mushroom eaters. Particularly if they learned by trial and error to distinguish the edible mushrooms from the poisonous (and it is hard to imagine any other way), then I suspect the Slavic race has a degree of inbred mycological knowledge. This very weekend, in fact, friends of mine in the Czech Republic are on an annual outing in search of mushrooms. In that I am missing that event, it is wholly appropriate that I tromp through a damp, Bosnian forest in pursuit of the same objective.

Ramiz and I stop in at another cottage on our way to the forest. We visit there with two brothers who are some sort of in-laws or relatives of Ramiz. The older one is a widowed pensioner. Over drinks and a bite to eat, the older brother's efforts to find a new wife are discussed. All regard this as a serious matter. It is not easy to find a suitable mate, although all agree that just about any woman would count herself lucky to hitch up with this man. He reports meeting one woman recently who shows promise. She, he assures us, is "*fina, fina,*" but it is still too early to predict how that particular prospect might play out.

Both brothers have worked for Energoinvest, the Sarajevo-based engineering-and-manufacturing enterprise. The younger brother, a manager by training, has worked abroad in Arab and African countries. His former employer does little business these days, and its facilities were much damaged in the war. He works now in a small, private company. Lucky and energetic, he and his family seem to be doing well.

Farther on toward the forest, we encounter a woman in a paddock who is minding about 30 white sheep and one black one. With her, too, are her young son, small daughter, two goats, and a large, friendly dog. She and Ramiz are acquainted, although they have not seen one another for a long time. Ramiz is convinced that the dog remembers him, and that makes him happy. The shepherdess and her children live in the village that sits in the valley below. She is a widow. Ramiz says her husband hung himself in the forest several years ago and that the death apparently had nothing directly to do with the wars here.

We continue on our way and Ramiz, without regard to his age, leads me through the brush, over fences, up and down hills. I am thinking about the State Department's warning in regard to landmines and unexploded ordnance. I ask about mines. There is nothing to worry about, Ramiz says, assuring me that "there were never any *Četniks* here." I notice a couple large bunker-shaped holes dug into the forest floor. And what, I ask, are those? Bunkers dug by soldiers, I am told. Of course I believe Ramiz when he says there are no mines here, but I let him lead the way for a while and I follow at a respectable distance.

Two of the first things a neophyte mycophile learns are that the forest is filled with mushrooms and that most of these are poisonous. The third thing the beginner realizes is that the prettiest mushrooms tend to be the most deadly. We are searching today for a mushroom with a smooth and chocolate-brown top surface and a creamy-yellow spongy flesh below. This species is not easy to spot, but it is worth the effort. These mushrooms are excellent for frying, drying and, if they are large enough, even for roasting. I find the biggest one of the day—a roaster if ever there was one—but Ramiz wins hands-down in the total-units-found category.

In that the *vikendica* has no electricity, our activity is fairly regulated by the sun. As darkness falls, we sit down to a meal of meat kabobs (*šašlik*) roasted directly on the wood coals of the kitchen stove, peppers and fresh bread. Vahida has outdone herself. Not only has she prepared a fine meal, she also has cleaned and sliced the mushrooms. These now are drying in flat pans spread about the kitchen. We turn in early and sleep soundly.

●　　　●　　　●　　　●

A misty rain on Sunday morning makes gathering plums a dampening business. We are determined, though, to complete the harvest. My job is to climb into and shake the trees and to knock down the fruit clinging in the upper reaches. With that job done, there remains one more harvest to complete. The widower relative has a solitary crab apple tree. I am told that its hard, sour fruit can be used to produce a beverage that is supposed to be good for one's cholesterol—which I assume means to lower it. The process is simple: Whole and with skins intact, the crab apples will be left to soak in water through the winter. After a few months, then, the water will be drained off and is to have been transformed into the health-fortifying drink.

Sunday lunch is a production and an event. Ramiz prepares a Balkan specialty known as *meso ispod sača* ("meat under an iron pan"). This involves a special wood-fired apparatus that is set up in the garden shed. Vahida's brother and his family join us. The sister-in-law has prepared a pan of tasty *burek*. This meal reminds me once again of what is for the outsider one of the great Balkan mysteries: how people in this part of the world are able to use their fingers so directly when they eat and yet keep their clothing and bodies reasonably free of grease. Even close observation has not yet revealed to me the answer. An American, trained on fast food and accustomed to having paper tissue in its various forms close to hand, does not know the technique. On this occasion (and as often occurs), the locals, noticing my hesitancy and difficulty, produce paper napkins. (I suspect they do that to distract the foreigner from learning their technique.) Then they urge me to dig in and to eat "like a *Balkanac*." Only later will I realize that the word "*balkanac*" differs in meaning from "*Balkanac*." With a lower-case "b," *balkanac* is an idiomatic reference to a "crude person." In that the word "Balkan" itself comes from a Turkish word meaning "mountain," I suppose one could say we were eating like "mountain men."

On the Drina

Zijo's mother is crying when he leaves the house this morning. She is frightened about the trip he is taking with me today. We are going to Republika Srpska. It does not help matters that it is a miserably cold and rainy morning. Since the wars, Zijo traveled once to Pale and to Mostar to interpret for a visiting western businessman. Other than that, he has not been outside of Sarajevo and, certainly, not in this part of his country since Serb nationalists consolidated their hold, killed or expelled the non-Serbs, and began to create a state within a state.

In anticipation of our travels to Republika Srpska, I had proposed to Zijo that perhaps we should bring along a Serb. My thinking had been that might make it easier for us to establish trust with the other Serbs we would meet and to facilitate conversation. My suggestion had hurt Zijo's feelings a bit, but he asked around some anyway.

As the two of us drive out of town, Zijo explains that he was not able to find any Serb in Sarajevo willing to make this trip. A Serb living in Sarajevo, he had been told, might not be well received in Republika Srpska. Such a Serb, who is living willingly among Muslims, might be regarded as a traitor to his or her nation. They also do not like Americans and journalists out in those parts, he adds. It almost can go without saying that some of the folks out there probably are not going to be too fond either of a Muslim from Sarajevo who is traveling with an American writer.

Oh well, we will be careful. We assure one another that we will get along fine.

Just east of Sarajevo's city limits, we pass a road sign, printed in Cyrillic, welcoming us to "Srpsko Sarajevo." We already have crossed the IEBL. This "Serb Sarajevo" is one of six new political regions created within Republika Srpska. Within Srpsko Sarajevo are 11 *opštinas*, one of which is called New Sarajevo. New Sarajevo is where some Serbs envision they will build their own Sarajevo. They have not started yet.

Bosnian Serb nationalists want to have a Sarajevo of their own. Early in the Bosnian Serb offensive, Karadžić had planned to split Sarajevo into Serb and non-Serb parts. During the siege, of course, Serb forces had held Grbavica and Ilidža. At Dayton, Krajišnik was still pushing for partition of the city.

Unable to obtain their Sarajevo by military or diplomatic means, Serb nationalists may try to build it. In any case, they have good reason to pay the concept lip service. We will visit Pale a few days from now; reports are that many of Sarajevo's Serbs are crowded into that small city, a few miles up the Miljacka River from Sarajevo. After Dayton was signed, Serb-nationalist leaders had commanded Serbs in Grbavica and Ilidža to abandon their homes in Sarajevo and to set them ablaze on the way out the door. Unless life in Pale is a lot more prosperous than I expect to find it, there presumably are many people there who are unhappy about abandoning their Sarajevo.

Just a quarter mile into Serb Sarajevo, I see an OSCE caravan stopped along the road. There are soldiers and a sort of checkpoint there, but our car is not waved over. There had been very little fighting in this area during the war. Serb forces had taken the territory between Pale and Sarajevo early and had held onto it. That is not to say, of course, there had not been ethnic cleansing. We pass through a village named Zumbulovac, which I guess must once have been a Muslim settlement. The name has a Turkish root, and the sign announcing the village's name is still written in the Latin alphabet.

For several miles, we pass through green and rolling countryside. Then the road turns steeply upward and climbs into the rain and clouds of Mount Romanija. Nowhere in Bosnia and Hercegovina can one travel very far without climbing into and over hills or mountains. As we come down off Romanija, we cross a high plain. The soil is thin and rocky, showing the wear from centuries of hard overgrazing. The land in Bosnia and Hercegovina is ungenerous. Life here always has been a hard struggle for the common people and their livestock. Each generation wears down the thin soil a bit more before passing it on to the next.

During 1990 and 1991, Serbs living on and about Romanija had been secretly armed from Yugoslav army stocks. The area had been declared a Serb autonomous region before the Serb offensive began in Bosnia and Hercegovina in spring 1992. The Yugoslav army, which by that time was well on its way toward becoming an essentially Serbian force, was well established here when war broke out in Bosnia and Hercegovina.

A policeman waves us down just outside Stjenice, a village whose name, perhaps appropriately enough, alludes to a stony place but nevertheless sounds to me like the word for bedbug. This is a standard checkpoint and there is nothing special about our being pulled over. I dig out from the glove box an international driver's license, which, just to be on the safe side, I had obtained right before this trip but had never yet used. We are on our way again in not much more than a minute. The anxiety with which we had begun the day's journey dissipates in our first brief encounter with the policeman. We roll on down the road to and through Rogatica.

Rogatica is situated in the green valley of the Rakitnica River. Zijo notes that eastern Bosnia begins at Rogatica. Ethnically, eastern Bosnia means predominantly (and until recently) mixed Serb and Muslim. There also had been thriving Jewish and Gypsy communities at Rogatica before World War II. These were destroyed in that war.[56] This is not traditionally a strong Croat area, and Zijo points out that, since World War II, there have been virtually no local-origin Croats in this part of Bosnia. Rogatica *opština* was roughly two-fifths Muslim and three-fifths Serb in 1991. There must be very few Muslims here now.

We are on the western fringe, too, of a region known as Podrinje, which name refers to the land along the Drina River. As we pass through Rogatica, I begin to watch out for people selling *šljivovica*. Podrinje, Ramiz had told me this morning before I left, is where the best plum brandy is produced. The small farmers here distill it themselves, and I should see them selling it along the road. Ramiz asked me to pick up two or three liters. Probably, it has been a long time since my landlord has had the real stuff from Podrinje.

Outside Rogatica are the ruins of scattered houses and a destroyed Muslim village. The road leaves the Rakitnica valley and leads us back up into the hills. In a few minutes, we enter the Prača River valley. The road ducks frequently in and out of dark tunnels as we follow the Prača valley downstream toward the Drina. We reach the Drina at Ustiprača, a wide spot in the road whose name, very prosaically, means "mouth of the Prača." Ustiprača once was a Muslim town. Almost all its houses are destroyed.

At Ustiprača, the traveler faces a choice. The main road goes up the river toward Goražde and Foča. It also tracks downriver to Višegrad and then continues on to Serbia. Goražde is best known as one of the UN's three infamously declared "safe areas" in eastern Bosnia. It has the distinction, though, of being the only one of the three that did not fall to the Serb aggressors. Foča, meanwhile, is remembered as the site of one of the worst Serb massacres of Muslims during World War II. In the 1941–1942 period, thousands of Muslims were killed in that area.

---

[56]Noel Malcom, *Bosnia: A Short History, paperback* (London: Macmillan, 1994; Papermac, 1994) pp. 113, 118.

Today, Foča is said to be a safe haven for indicted Serb war criminals and assorted riffraff.

We turn north, toward Višegrad. The road follows the Drina through verdant, mountainous terrain. The scenery is marred here and there by the crumbling remains of "cleansed" Muslim villages and a string of damp and unlit tunnels. Nobody is selling *šljivovica*, although there are a few men along the way offering fish they had just caught in the river below.

Setting for an Ethnic-Cleansing Drama

Višegrad is the setting of *The Bridge on the Drina* by Yugoslav author Ivo Andrić. When Andrić was awarded the Nobel Prize for Literature in 1961, this novel was cited as one of the major reasons for his receiving the honor. The bridge at Višegrad, with its 11 arches and some four centuries old, is the main character in Andrić's novel. The bridge is a witness to centuries of uneasy coexistence between Slavic Muslims and Orthodox Slavs as well as of struggle between the Ottoman Turks and a ruptured Christian world. As a literary device, a bridge naturally lends itself to symbolizing a link between people, ideas or principles otherwise divided. That is not the case for Andrić's Višegrad bridge.

The literature-inspiring bridge at Višegrad is a rugged and massive structure, thus it is quite different from the delicate and graceful arch that was destroyed in Mostar. The Drina bridge was built in the 16th century on the order of Mehmed Pasha Sokullu. Mehmed Pasha had been born a Christian here in eastern Bosnia. As a boy, he was carted off to the Ottoman Empire and brought up to serve the Islamic Turkish world. His bridge would witness horrendous bloodshed over the centuries—up to and including the late-20th.

The Bridge on the Drina tells us a lot about the relations between Serbs and Muslims in eastern Bosnia. They have lived together for centuries, but their relations were not always warm. Andrić must have had a deep understanding of Bosnian history in the context of the competing imperial and nationalist forces. Born a Bosnian Serb, he grew up among Serbs, Muslims and Croats, then earned a doctorate in history in Roman Catholic Graz.

Although Andrić was no Serb nationalist, his novel is not a favorite work of literature among Bosnia and Hercegovina's Muslims. They object to the fact that he refers to the Muslim Slavs as "Turks," regarding that as a derogatory term. The term was not, though, necessarily derogatory as used in the local vernacular at the time when the novel is set. Andrić's book does not paint a particularly positive picture of society under Ottoman rule. Some Bosnian Muslims would regard Meša Selimović and his novel *Death and the Dervish* to be more representative of their literature. Selimović, though, also presents an altogether unflattering portrait of life in Ottoman and Islamic Bosnia.

Tomorrow Is Today a Day Later

Višegrad is on the right bank of the Drina, and the road comes in on the left bank. I park across the river from the town. An Orthodox church sits prominently above Višegrad on the opposite bank. It is a symbol of Serb control, just as the Catholic church that I saw above Kiseljak is a territorial marker. I see no minarets, even though in 1991 Višegrad *opština's* population had been two-thirds Muslim and one-third Serb. If there are any Muslims here today, my guess is that they keep themselves inconspicuous. Serbs viciously cleansed Višegrad of its Muslims in spring 1992. Reportedly, some Muslims were beheaded on the bridge and their bodies dumped into the river. According to at least one source, so many Muslim bodies were thrown from the famous bridge that they clogged a hydroelectric plant on the Drina.[57]

Before I even can get myself organized and the car locked up Zijo has found someone with whom to speak. The man accepts our invitation to join us for lunch in the town. Conversing, we walk across the bridge. Serb refugees from all around Bosnia and Hercegovina now live in Višegrad, he says. There are many from Sarajevo and from central Bosnia, including the Zenica and Konjic areas. Quite a few Serbs came here from near Mostar. More than 50% of the population in and around Višegrad is now made up of refugees, he relates.

Our new acquaintance is a Serb from Vogošća, a town just north of Sarajevo. This man had both a house and a flat when he lived there. Now, he lives in a burned-out house in Višegrad and is doing what he can to fix it up. He has filed by post an application to have his property in Vogošća restituted to him. The man says his wife actually has gone to Vogošća and Sarajevo today to try and move that process along. He is worried about her and is just killing time until she will return.

The Muslim who legally owns the house in which this Serb lives now resides in Sarajevo and also has applied to have his property back.

---

[57]John B. Allcock, Marko Milivojevic and John J. Horton, eds., *Conflict in the Former Yugoslavia: An Encyclopedia* (Santa Barbara: ABC-CLIO, Inc., 1998), p. 319.

If his property is returned, the Serb refugee tells us that he might go back to Vogošća. He also points out, though, that he has no family or friends there anymore. The man says he should be receiving a pension from his former employer, but that enterprise and its management are either unable or unwilling to pay.

Equipment was stripped from the factory in which he formerly worked. Some of that equipment was sent to Višegrad, in fact, and some of the same workers who were operating that machinery in Vogošća now are working with it here. This Serb says his son, who has a wife and daughter, also lives here as a refugee. The son lives in a different house than the father and officially is unemployed. In fact, though, the son earns 100 deutschemarks monthly working in a bread shop.

Although the Muslims are gone, Višegrad still is made up of two distinct groups: those Serbs who are native to the *opština* and those who came here as refugees. There is perhaps a small middle group that includes relatively well-to-do newcomers. The refugees, our lunch guest tells us, are not satisfied with the city and *opština* officials. The local authorities strongly favor those born and long living here.

Among the better off, he says, are those who have shops in the town. At the other extreme are those refugees living in temporary shelters. The shelters range from barracks to a former school building. Several of these house 50 to 100 people. The largest is temporary home to some 500 people. Three or four families may be sharing the same space. Some families have been living in such conditions for two to three years, perhaps more.

Meanwhile, the man reports, some of the natives each have two or three apartments or houses. When the Muslims all left in 1992, the local Serbs seized their former neighbors' living spaces. Now, the refugee explains matter-of-factly, these Serbs do not want to let go of what they have stolen.

Just on the other side of the bridge, we walk into what turns out to be a pretty dodgy excuse for a restaurant. The place is empty except for the staff—and the poverty of the people in Višegrad may not be the only reason. The ambience is, well, squalid. Once we are in the door and have greeted the waitress, though, I am reluctant to turn on my heel and walk out. I do not want to be rude or unnecessarily to draw attention. What's more, we are hungry and there might not be a better place. We sit down and order *ćevapčići* and drinks.

There turns out to be a lot of pork in the *ćevapčići*, and they are not particularly good in any case. The servings are substantial, though.

The man from Vogošća tells us that it has been five years since he last ate *ćevapčići*. He cannot afford it now. The Serb remembers well his last plate of *ćevapčići*, because he was sitting under a table in Vogošća at the time and wondering what would become of him and his family. Zijo takes just a few bites of his meal and passes the rest across to our guest. The man is thankful and eats it all.

Refugees in Višegrad need food most of all, he says. They obtain plenty of clothing from the aid centers. Two months ago humanitarian assistance was cut back here by about 50 percent. Nobody seems to know why that occurred. The food supply for refugees was dramatically affected.

The aid varies somewhat according to where a given package comes from. German aid packages, which are supposed to last for one month, typically contain three tins of food, sugar, cooking oil, spaghetti, salt, some clothing and washing detergents. If one gets a French box, it is likely to include some jam and sweets. American aid comes in the form of bread flour. The pensionless pensioner says he has never heard of any other US aid coming into Višegrad. Assistance from Italy has included live chickens and pigs. The livestock have gone especially to those aid centers outside of town. The government of Republika Srpska and some international aid organizations provide some aid in the form of building materials.

In summer, people were able to grow some food in gardens. But summer is now over. My sense is that, three years after the Dayton agreement was signed, Višegrad is going into another tough winter. There are not enough jobs even to support all of Višegrad's allegedly favored natives. There is very little cash here. Indeed, our lunch guest is quite curious to see the convertible marks with which I pay for our meal. Although this is the official currency of Bosnia and Hercegovina, he has never seen it before. Yugoslav dinars and German marks are the most common currency here.

"I am afraid to think about the future," remarks this man. "People always say that maybe tomorrow will be better, but tomorrow they will say the same thing."

Have You a Honey-Sweet Heart?

A few steps down the street from this restaurant that is best forgotten we step into a store selling food and mixed consumer goods. The lady behind the counter is a middle-aged refugee from Mostar. Her husband spent three years in the US during the warfare in Bosnia and

Hercegovina. As I have been unable to find *šljivovica* along the road, I hope that maybe this store will have it. She has one bottle that is made in eastern Bosnia, but it is made in a factory, not by a farmer. I take it. I do not want to go home empty-handed. It seems odd to me, though, that I am not seeing *šljivovica* for sale along the road. It is too early, one person tells me today. My feeling, though, is that population dislocations and social disorder have somehow upset this cottage industry. Considering the potential profit to be earned from selling home-brewed alcohol, that strikes me as strange.

Zijo asks the sales lady if she has *Medeno srce*, a brand of soft cookies made in Vojvodina and which are not easy to find in Sarajevo. The name means "Honey-Sweet Heart." My interpreter just loves these things. He is not lucky at this store, though.

The woman says she is quite satisfied with her job and with her life in Višegrad. She makes about 200 deutschemarks (around $125) per month. We will find out over the next few days that, by Republika Srpska standards, that is quite a good salary. She recognizes that, relative to most other refugees here and even though her husband does not have a job, they are doing okay. Still, she wishes to return to Mostar and has applied for the opportunity to do so.

Some of the Serbs from Mostar have returned, she relates. The woman, who owns a house and an apartment there, visited Mostar a month ago. Although she describes the situation in Mostar as sad and difficult, this refugee does not seem surprised by what she found in her old hometown. Their house in Mostar is now occupied and needs to be repaired. She and her husband are waiting for the legal and administrative details to be worked out.

"We are the same nation, and we must live together," this woman states, referring to Serbs, Muslims and Croats.

Just down the street, we step into another, much smaller shop. Two men are sitting in the corner drinking beer from bottles. They look like they have been there awhile. It is cheaper to sit and drink in a store than it is to go to a pub. Zijo asks the pretty shop girl for *Medeno srce*. I am starting to think there is an implicit subtext when he asks, "By the way, Miss, do you have a honey-sweet heart." She is as polite as she is pretty, but the answer is still no. The girl directs us to the shop across the street.

A middle-aged woman from Čengić Vila, a section of Sarajevo, is keeping shop at the next store. She has *Medeno srce*. We are talking about *šljivovica* and struggling to kindle a conversation when another customer comes in. She is an elderly woman, dressed all in black. The old woman is from Ilidža, the suburb on Sarajevo's outskirts which was under Serb control throughout the siege.

This old woman tells us that her husband had died in the war. Her daughter, still in Ilidža and three months pregnant, had been shot in the head four months after the Dayton agreement was finalized. That timing corresponds to the period of violence and general bedlam coincident to Sarajevo's so-called unification. The daughter's husband was still living in Ilidža. This son-in-law, who had a business there, was killed just two days ago. The woman says she does not know how or why he was killed, and she is too afraid to go to the funeral. Through her sobbing and tears, the old woman tells us that she now is completely alone in this world.

"And now they want us to live together," she exclaims. "No way! Never!"

The woman behind the counter speaks up at this point to tell us that she, too, has lost almost everything and that she, too, has no interest in living with people of other nations. This woman, who lost her husband in the war and is raising two children, says she has no thoughts to return to Sarajevo and to her apartment there. "Especially for the people who have lost somebody," the sales lady explains, it is impossible for Serbs to live with Muslims and Croats.

Muslim Island in a Serb Sea

In a sense, I am taking my interpreter home today. Zijo was born in Goražde, although he has lived in Sarajevo almost all his life and has not been to his birthplace for 11 years. Goražde's recent history is rather heroic and it is an important symbol for Bosnia and Hercegovina's Muslims. Goražde is today the last Muslim island in the Serb sea that is eastern Bosnia. Realizing this, and thinking about that island in the context of my ethnic map based upon the 1991 census, I see in stark relief the extent and efficiency of the ethnic cleansing that occurred in eastern Bosnia.

The census data show that eastern Bosnia's population in 1991 was about evenly divided between Muslims and Serbs. One group dominated here, the other group there. The *opštinas* of Goražde and Srebrenica contained the highest proportions of Muslims (70 percent and 73 percent, respectively). By autumn 1992, thousands upon thousands of eastern Bosnia's Muslims already had been cleared out. Bosnian Serb forces at that time held even more territory in Bosnia and

Hercegovina than they ultimately would control after Dayton. The Serb nationalists' war here had been going pretty much their way up to that point.

But Goražde, Srebrenica and Žepa were problem areas for the Serb forces. Here, there were just too many Muslims for them to be cleared out quickly and by intimidation. These cities and their vicinities also became uncertain sanctuaries for Muslim refugees fleeing eastern Bosnia's other communities. Nevertheless—and even though all three cities were declared UN safe areas in 1993—these islands were subject to battering and erosion from the sea of Serb forces surrounding them. Srebrenica and Žepa fell to Serb nationalists in 1995. That humiliated NATO, the UN and the international community of the world's supposedly most powerful nations.

Goražde never fell. Serb forces did, though, surround and squeeze this enclave in 1994. That was in spite of NATO air strikes—which were too little coming too late—against the Serb forces as they took the heights and closed a ring around Goražde. By the time of Dayton, Goražde was the only Muslim part of eastern Bosnia that Serbs had not overrun entirely. At the peace talks, the Serb side ultimately agreed to allow the Goražde pocket to be a Federation island within Republika Srpska. Also agreed was to allow the Federation a narrow corridor through the hills of Republika Srpska to connect this Muslim enclave with the main body of the Federation.

Sunshine for All or for None

Two or three miles outside of Goražde proper, we come upon a sign announcing our entry into a village that once was known as Kopači. Zijo recalled Kopači as having been mixed Muslim and Serb, but with more of the former than of the latter. Now, the sign says Srpsko Goražde. This "Serb" Goražde is long, stretching a couple miles toward the city. The village is heavily damaged and little repaired. We know when we are leaving Srpsko Goražde. Another sign tells us so. At its very edge is a small Orthodox church and Serb cemetery.

There is a half-mile sort of transition zone before we reach Goražde. Houses are repaired in this space. As Goražde comes fully into view, I am struck by the multitude of new roofs. I am not surprised, then, to see a sign at the entry to Goražde announcing an EU reconstruction operation consisting of various projects. Some 225 houses are to be repaired when the operation is completed; sewer, water and electricity services are to be improved; and various public buildings are to be reconstructed.

I park in front of the *Goraždanka* department store. A half dozen wounds from artillery shells still scar the store's front facade. Two of these are huge and gaping holes out from which impact-splash marks radiate. The holes have been covered over from the inside but not repaired. There is a surreal aspect about these monstrous wounds, accentuated by the fact that most other visible damage in that immediate area has been repaired.

Just around the corner is a street suitable for promenading. On one side is a reconstructed municipal building, freshly painted in lime-green. Across the street are several attractive coffee shops. The street, which is a pedestrian zone, leads down and across the City Bridge over the Drina. We stop in to one of the coffee shops. From that narrow perspective, looking out through a plateglass window at the municipal building and the strolling passersby, one might momentarily forget that there had been a war here and that there is still much rebuilding work to do in Goražde.

Zijo tries to strike up a conversation with four young men sitting around the next table. Only in their late teens, they are too young, though, to have many real and serious thoughts of their own. They seem most concerned with getting the modern James Dean look down, which is to say they probably are pretty normal young guys. Some of the young people are leaving Goražde, they tell us. For the best prospect of getting a job here, they add, one should try to make sure he has friends in the organizations that rebuild houses.

The waiter behind the bar and a customer in front of it (also a young man, but several years older than the four at the table) are only slightly more communicative. They are cautious. We are told of two Serb families that have returned to Goražde. Their houses had been repaired by humanitarian organizations. One of the major factories in town is operating. It is a munitions plant and now manufactures street lamps as well. A clothing factory also is working. Zijo asks about an old friend, who was, last he knew, a policeman in a neighboring village. He is told that the friend survived the war.

We leave the café and walk down the street to the City Bridge. As I step onto the bridge, an approaching man, approximately 20 years old, stops rather abruptly before me. He says something in slurred and what seems to me incoherent speech. His bearing is peculiar and insistent. I am startled and embarrassed because I cannot understand him. I do not know if he is drunk, mentally retarded, a little bit crazy, or if he just has a serious speech impediment and a rather indelicate panhandling style. Coming to my senses, I dig in my pocket for a two-deutschemark coin and give it to him. Zijo tells me afterward that the man had said, "Brother, do you have a mark for me."

Zijo is frustrated because he is having a hard time getting any conversations going. He figures it should not be so difficult in Goražde, the town of his birth. Our luck turns for the better when we walk into a small food shop near the bridge. The shop owner, a clean-cut man, 35 or 40 years of age, is informed, articulate and open. He seems the type who might naturally emerge as a community leader were the field not so crowded with egotists actively courting the public. A bit of a local patriot, this man, who is Muslim, wants us to know that Goražde can and should return to normal and that the nations can live together here.

The shop owner, who formerly had worked in a factory job, points out that he travels with his truck all over the former Yugoslavia to buy goods for his store. He never has any difficulties with people. Economic questions are now most important, the man emphasizes, pointing out that people in Republika Srpska need help, too. He has traveled about, I realize, and is keenly aware that much more aid flows into the Federation than into the Serb part of the country.

Privatizing industry is important for the long term, in this man's view, just as aid to the people is for the immediate term. In both cases, he is concerned as to where the factories and humanitarian assistance go. Charity should be channeled as directly as possible to the people who need it. Too much seems to get lost along the way when it passes through government officials' sticky fingers.

People are optimistic that privatization can help to jump-start local factories and to provide jobs that are badly needed. This man's fear, though, is that industrial ownership will pass to those who are powerful and politically connected rather than to those who have the capability and resources to make the best of them. It would be better, this small-scale capitalist observes, to sell the factories to foreign firms who are able to pay the real value of the businesses and to make the investments necessary to realize that value.

I tell him about privatization in the Czech Republic, where I lived and worked in the capital markets through much of the privatization process. There, hundreds of enterprises were sold to their former managers or to others who were equally unqualified to run the businesses but who were somehow able to hustle up enough cash, credit or influence to get control of the companies. Most of the time, these individuals had neither the access to additional capital nor the managerial skills to make the firms succeed. More than a few were just plain criminals. Privatization here, the man fears, could follow a similar pattern.

Leaving his assistant to tend the store, the merchant leads us off to meet a Serb who he knows and who has recently returned to Goražde. We do not have to go far, as the Serb is one of a group of three friends walking down the main street toward us and the City Bridge.

A senior citizen, the Serb had left Goražde in 1992. He returned a few months ago, in May 1998. The man says he has no difficulties with the other people here. "I was born here," he tells us, "and everybody knows me. Nobody has said a bad word to me." Until his old apartment can be repaired, the man is living in a home for pensioners. The other people here are good to him, the old man says, adding that he knows of other Serbs, too, who are settling peacefully back into the towns, villages and homes from which they had fled.

The man, who spent part of the war in Serbia digging ditches for 3 deutschemarks per day, says he is very concerned, though, about the general economic situation. Money, and to earn money, he contends, is fundamental to the respect people have for themselves and for one another.

As we speak, a couple more old friends, who are Muslims, join our little knot of people. My feeling is that, in old times, these men spent many hours drinking coffee together. If the peace holds, they will settle back into their old ways. They will have even more stories to tell now.

One of the older men has no left arm. He lost it in World War II. A Muslim, he heads an organization to assist civilian victims of the latest war. He says he had had the same job and position after World War II. The one-armed man observes, rather poetically, that "there will be no sunshine" for any of the people unless there is sunshine for all. His view is that, ultimately, all of Bosnia and Hercegovina's ethnonational groups must live together. In the long term, it is inevitable. Realistically, then, he figures, people should just get on with it.

We were in Višegrad today, I relate, and some Serbs there told us that they never again could live together with Muslims. Those people in Višegrad, the old Serb says, probably have taken over other people's houses. They cannot expect to be happy when they are trying to live in homes that do not belong to them. Then, too, he adds, there are—and always will be—some fanatic nationalists within each group. There is no life together for fanatics, remarks the Serb.

It is foolish, contends another of the friends, to blame an entire group of people for the evil deeds of anonymous or extreme individuals and for much of what happens in time of war. This man is a Muslim. He is married to a Serb, and their son was killed in the war. The man says he knows that somebody killed his son. Quite probably a Serb did that. But the killer was not this man, who is his friend, he says. So how foolish would it be to blame his son's death upon another man just because he is a Serb?

Rogatica's Rednecks

I am not sure how many fanatic Serb nationalists there are in Rogatica, where we stop on the return trip, but there are a few. Even more drop by or pass through from time to time. Probably it was a fanatic nationalist who spray-painted the Serb paramilitary leader Arkan's name on several walls along the main road through town. Most probably, too, they were not open-minded pacifists who pasted up along this same thoroughfare Serb Radical Party campaign posters featuring the name and image of Vojislav Šešelj.

Just down and across the main street from Rogatica's heavily sandbagged SFOR post is the Pensioners' Restaurant. Zijo gets a bad feeling as soon as we enter. The pub's music is all Serbian and the lyrics very nationalist, he tells me. (I personally do not know the music and cannot make out the lyrics.) The establishment is nearly full, and there are no women here at all. Several customers are quite inebriated and talking loudly. The loudest and nastiest-sounding patron seems upset mainly about a piece of machinery he bought for his business and which was inadequate for the job. The waiter who brings us *Cokes* seems pleasant enough.

My feeling is that this is not so much different from some backwoods, redneck bar in Wisconsin or Georgia or Arizona. Of course, I do not generally feel too at ease in those places, either. I have a feeling the SFOR guys up the street do not come here when they go off duty. To his credit, Zijo does his best to start up a discussion about a calendar on the wall advertising hunting rifles. It does not come off, though. It is pretty hard to find some common ground here upon which to build up to a conversation. We decide to try somewhere else.

A fruit and vegetable shop down the street seems more hospitable. Maybe they will have locally distilled *šljivovica*. The lone shopkeeper, a girl about 20 years old, has no plum brandy but she does have time and is willing to talk a bit. She tells us she earns about 100 deutschemarks (about $60 or so) monthly. That is more than her mother and father make. Her mother has a job but has not been paid for seven months. Her father earns a little less than does his daughter.

This young woman did not vote last week—or at least not directly. She let her cousin vote for her and does not know to whom her vote went. The shop girl admits she neither knows nor cares too much about politics.

A year ago, the woman had wanted to leave Rogatica. Now, though, she says, it looks as though it will be impossible to do so. She does not make clear just why it is impossible, but we suspect it has to do with the boyfriend that she also mentions. Her career goal is to land a job in a state-owned company so that she can earn a pension and receive additional benefits.

The next people we meet do work in a state-owned company. They are two middle-aged women minding the miserably stocked grocery store down the street. These women say they are satisfied with their work, but they wish they had a wider assortment of better-quality goods to offer their customers. I have no success here, either, in my quest for *šljivovica*. One of the ladies suggests we go down the street to the Pensioners' Restaurant and ask if anybody there knows where to buy the local hooch. That is an excellent suggestion and I wish we would have thought of it earlier, but I do not think we are going to visit there again. Zijo does land a couple bags of *Medeno srce* at the state-owned store. When he gets his cookies back to the car, though, he finds they are stale and hard.

Overlooking Something?

Getting back in the car, I mentally review my impressions. From the main road passing through town, Rogatica looks not very inviting. The shopkeepers were a bit suspicious but pretty friendly. That they are cautious seems not too surprising. After all, we are two strangers who are asking a lot of questions about things that surely must seem to be none of our business. The Pensioners' Restaurant, which must be a popular local watering hole, does not give me any warm feeling, but it is not the other patrons' fault that we tried only halfheartedly to speak with them. Maybe I need to see more.

Instead of heading out the main road toward Sarajevo, therefore, I backtrack to Rogatica's only main intersection. The leg of this

T-intersection leads northeast out of town. According to the map, there are no substantial towns out that way. As it turns out, there is not much more of Rogatica out there either. We see off to our left the neighborhood where I figure Rogatica's Muslims formerly lived. Numerous houses have been burned or otherwise damaged. Most of them look as though they now are being repaired. To our right is the Orthodox church and a couple small shops. I see no mosque, but then I suspect the only Muslim in town is the one sitting in the passenger seat of my car. Zijo surmises that Rogatica's Muslims probably did not put up much of a struggle. By the time they had been forced out the handwriting was on the wall. Most probably, they had just gotten onto the bus and quietly left.

Recognizing that second impressions of Rogatica are no more positive than first impressions, I turn the car around at the edge of town and come back toward the main, Sarajevo-Višegrad road. I pull over across from a shop behind the church. Maybe I still can get lucky and find some *šljivovica*.

The man who runs the shop comes from his house across the road to wait on us. I guess business is a little slow at this time of day. Come to think of it, there was not much activity in the other shops we visited either. He does have *šljivovica*, but it is *Manastirka*, a brand from Serbia that comes in a rather fancy bottle. He has but one bottle. Zijo says it is a good product. I buy it.

About 70 percent of the goods he sells here come from Serbia, the shopkeeper tells us. In fact, he must buy goods from Serbia. That was one of the conditions under which he was allowed to open up in the first place. When goods come in from Serbia, the merchant must pay customs duties at the border. It is not any different in that regard, he explains, than it would be if he were importing them from Sweden. It would be easier, of course, to buy goods in the Federation, which is, after all, supposed to be part of the same country. The man says his brother has visited Kiseljak and seen goods there priced lower than what he pays for imports from Serbia. Apparently, though, there are considerable, if invisible, barriers to trade between the Federation and Republika Srpska.

Clearly, the residents of Republika Srpska are being pressed, in spite of their poverty, to help support the economy of rump-Yugoslavia. The people here are caught in a scissors of low incomes and high prices. The shopkeeper tells us that monthly salaries in this area typically are just 50 to 100 deutschemarks (Roughly $30 to $60).

He has a woman working for him who is displaced from Sarajevo, and her life is very difficult. A few weeks ago, she finally received the house of a Muslim former resident in which to live.

Kicking out Muslims makes room for Serbs, but it does not leave them jobs. Arkan and Šešelj, with their knives and slogans, will not be solving this problem.

Avoiding Starina Novak

As night approaches and we work our way back over Mount Romanija, the rain and fog are not so bad as conditions had been on the trip coming out. Still, it is no picnic. Driving in these hills and mountains (and it is really difficult to say which is which), one gets an appreciation for how difficult it must have been over the centuries for any outside power truly to control this land. Today's main roads must generally correspond roughly to ancient trails and roads, and for every village one sees along the main routes many more settlements are hidden in the hills.

Ivo Andrić tells the tale of Starina Novak, an old highwayman who had made his name and livelihood robbing travelers passing through these very mountains. Nearing the end of his career, this bandit of Romanija was training a young successor to take over his franchise. He advised his young apprentice:

> When you are sitting in ambush, look well at the traveler who comes. If you see that he rides proudly and that he wears a red corselet and silver bosses and white gaiters, then he is from Foča. Strike at once, for he has wealth both on him and in his saddlebags. If you see a poorly dressed traveller, with bowed head, hunched on his horse as if he were going out to beg, then strike freely, for he is a man of Rogatica. They are all alike, misers and tight-fisted but as full of money as a pomegranate. But if you see some mad fellow, with legs crossed over the saddlebow, beating on a drum and singing at the top of his voice, don't strike and (do) not soil your hands for nothing. Let the rascal go his way. He is from Višegrad and he has nothing, for money does not stick to such men (*sic*).[58]

---

[58]The Bridge on the Drina, p. 21.

A Banshee with a Handicap

It is just dark when we reach Sarajevo. We decide to stop into the old town to eat. One can be sure there will be no pork in the *ćevapčiči* there.

As is true in old towns everywhere, the streets in Sarajevo's old town are narrow. Many of them, too, are being rebuilt or repaired. I park on one such street, which, due to there being a large pile of mixed sand and gravel placed in its middle, has been turned into a dead end from each side. The situation has created a nice, if informal, parking lot with room for a half dozen cars. Only one car is parked there, and that at the very entry to the street. Courteous man that I am, I park with care, being sure to leave sufficient space for other drivers to share my fortune in having found this wonderful parking place.

Upon returning, however, I discover that at least one of Sarajevo's drivers is not so forward-thinking and courteous as me. This individual has, in fact, parked also in the very entry to the narrow street, thereby blocking off all possibility either for others to get in or, perhaps most importantly, for me to get out. Naturally, I am struck by the apparent inconsiderate nature and general low intelligence of the driver who had plugged off the street. My observation as to this individual's intelligence is reinforced by the fact that he or she also has left on the car's headlights. That is an easy enough thing to do during the daytime, of course, but it seems rather extraordinary that one should do so on an unlit street in total darkness. Being compassionate by nature, though, I moderate my contempt when I notice that the automobile also has a sticker with an international handicapped symbol in the windshield. Perhaps the driver is blind.

Well, what to do? I go wandering down the street, stopping into cafés and shops, and looking for an unfortunate, handicapped, and perhaps not very intelligent individual. Such a person, though, is nowhere to be found. Nor do I have immediate success in finding the owner of the other car, which, quite innocently (as it was there first), also was blocking my exit. After a half hour, I blow my car's horn and hope that will roust one of the two cars' owners from one of several nearby apartment buildings. After an hour, I began to try, using a plank found nearby as a shovel, to move enough of the pile of sand and gravel to get past it. Having given that up, and after what is now 1-1/2 hours, I resort once again to the horn. This time it works, and the owner of the innocent car is alerted.

A very nice young lady comes down from the top floor of a nearby apartment building. Just as the polite woman is about to move her car to let me pass, who should show up but the owner of the offending vehicle with the fading battery. Actually, four people show up—two men and two women. It is difficult to ascertain which is the actual owner of the car, as none of them appear to be physically handicapped, with the exception, perhaps, that their motor skills have been somewhat impaired by the consumption of substantial quantities of alcohol.

Two of these individuals set about immediately to the task of confirming my earlier judgments in regard to the intelligence of the car's owner. One of them, a stout and well-dressed woman, seems to be the leader. Quite unprovoked, she begins at once to scream out a horrendous stream of obscenities, the basic thrust of which is to denounce me for being a foreigner who has come to her country for the sole purpose of exploiting it for my own enrichment. This volatile woman goes on—for reasons not apparent to me, and I suspect not clear to her either—to chastise also the nice young lady who is moving her car for me. Soon there is a great cacophony of screaming. One of the men in the banshee's retinue roars out that he "had fought to be able to park here." I gather from his remark that he had been a soldier. This is the first I ever have heard of parking places and the right to block others from leaving their parking places as objectives of war. But, well, one learns new things all the time.

Particularly interesting is that the screaming leader of this unmerry band wants to be sure that everybody present realizes that she is none other than the beloved sister of former Prime Minister (and now leader of the centrist Muslim Party for Bosnia and Hercegovina) Haris Silajdžić. As it turns out, though, the pleasant woman upon whom the reputed Ms. Silajdžić has been venting her rather bilious spleen is the sister of one of Sarajevo's top governmental officials. Oops! Upon recognizing this, the banshee calms quickly and even apologizes. The whole unpleasant lot rather sheepishly crawls into the car (the battery of which, fortunately, still has just enough juice to start the engine) and slips away.

Apparently this tempest in a teapot was not worth starting a battle between two powerful Muslim political families. It strikes me as terribly ironic that I could spend the whole day in Republika Srpska without conflict and then come back to such a demonstration of intolerance, contempt and open hostility among Muslims in Sarajevo.

The Bloodiest Corner of Bosnia

As we roll, once again, down the eastern slope of Mount Romanija, I decide I had best stop at the first gas station I see before pushing on to Srebrenica. The farther we get from the main road, I figure, the less likely it will be that filling stations will sell lead-free and the more likely they are to accept payment only in Yugoslav dinars (of which I have none). There is an impressive-looking station at the foot of the mountain and at a fork in the road known, appropriately enough, as Podromanija (meaning "below Romanija"). That is where the main road continues on east, toward Belgrade in Serbia, while the smaller road to the left takes one toward Zvornik and the bloodiest corner of Bosnia.

Sixty miles to the northeast, in that border city of Zvornik, Serb forces had first launched their war against Muslims on 8 April 1992.[59] The battle for Zvornik had begun with shelling from Serbia proper, which is just across the Drina River that flows past the city. Arkan had demanded that the Muslim-majority city surrender. It did not. Zvornik was taken on 10 April.[60]

The UNHCR's most senior official for Yugoslavia chanced to be passing through Zvornik on that day and was detained. He recalled afterward what he saw in Zvornik:

> I could see trucks full of dead bodies. I could see militiamen taking more corpses of children, women and old people from their houses, and putting them on trucks. I saw at least four or five trucks full of corpses. When I arrived, the cleansing had been done...It was all finished. They were looting, cleaning up the city after the massacre.

Zvornik was the Serb nationalists' dress rehearsal for the 44-month run of their highly successful tragedy *Ethnic Cleansing*. That production's climax performance in Bosnia, of course, would be staged in the UN-declared "safe areas" of Srebrenica and Žepa three years later.

The gas station at Podromanija is out of no-lead. Not to worry, though. The attendant assures us we can buy gas in the next town on

---

[59]The offensive against non-Serbs began in Bosnia and Hercegovina one week earlier with a less bloody but nonetheless violent terror offensive in Bijeljina, a major city in the northeastern corner of the country.

[60]Silber and Little, pp. 222–223.

the road toward Zvornik and Srebrenica. The man's information is accurate, and his counterpart at the station in Sokolac even accepts the official currency of his own country. We are on a roll.

A Polite Passenger

About 100 yards from the filling station, we pass a police officer who is trying to hitch a ride. I go right past. Zijo and I look at one another, though, and we figure what the heck? Police officers are okay, Zijo says. They are monitored by the IPTF. Policemen make relatively good money, and they are unlikely to do anything to risk messing up the deal they have going. I turn the car around and come back.

Just do not pick up soldiers, my interpreter advises. "And why not," I ask, "are they dangerous?" No, he answers, they are just boring to speak with, as they generally have little to say. What's more, they tend to travel in groups. You pick up one and you are liable to get a car full of uninteresting people.

The policeman is on his way to Vlasenica, which is about 35 miles up the road and more than half of the way to Srebrenica. Vlasenica, according to my *Blue Guide*, should be "a village set amidst high mountains and dark forests, (which) was a centre of partisan resistance in the Second World War." First, though, we must climb up and over the Javor ("Maple") Massif, which is supposed to be known for its bear and chamois. Vlasenica also was headquarters of the so-called Drina Corps, a Serb military unit that is believed to have been primarily responsible for overseeing the grisly mass murders of thousands of men at the time that Srebrenica was overrun.

A polite man, the police officer also seems happy. And why not? He is on his way home to see his family after working the night shift for 10 days straight. It is a damp and chilly day, and he is getting a ride all the way home.

When the war broke out, our traveling companion had been about 20 years old. He says he had wanted to get married, have a home, a job and a normal life. Fighting delayed all that. The policeman finally married last year. He earns 120 deutschemarks monthly, and that salary is about to be raised to 200 deutschemarks or maybe a bit higher. The current salary only supports his family for about 10 days out of the month. He is hopeful that pay for policemen in Republika Srpska eventually will catch up to that of officers in the Federation, who receive about twice as much. His first child, a daughter, was born six weeks ago.

The new father loves his baby very much. He says he misses her terribly when he needs to be away for 10 days at a time. His parents love her, too, and the cop admits he gets a little jealous sometimes. This is their first grandchild, and, since she was born, it seems like his parents hardly know that he exists anymore. It is, he jokes, as though his sole purpose in this world was to bring her to them.

"After all that I went through in the war," the policeman says, "I deserve a job." He does not tell us what all it was that he did go through, and we do not ask. According to 1991 census data, his Vlasenica *opština* formerly was populated 55% by Muslims and 42% by Serbs. Today, the policeman confirms, there are virtually no Muslims in his hometown. It is not hard to imagine that the work in the army was pretty grim.

Police Are There to Help

Nevertheless, he assures us, regardless of one's nationality, everybody is safe here today. Our passenger, in fact, delivers a rather strong public-relations message for the men in civilian uniform. If we are looking for directions or help of any kind, he advises, we should go first to the police. The man on the street might be suspicious of outsiders, but the police are there to help.

I ask about the IPTF training. He says he has completed one course and must go through two more. The first course was about human rights. "Most of these things I knew before," the policeman remarks. "But it is not bad to review and to learn a little more." The trainers in the first course, he adds, were from the US, Germany and Ghana.

As we approach Vlasenica (which is larger than the "village" promised by my guidebook), I remark about how pretty it is here. I found on the Internet some promotional materials for tourism in Republika Srpska. If the people here spend as much energy on drawing in tourists as they did in war, I gently lecture, life here might be much better. Yes, the Serb says, the Republika Srpska government needs to support tourism. He says nothing about the unified, central government of Bosnia and Hercegovina. Serbs in Republika Srpska do not recognize as legitimate very much of what happens in Sarajevo at the supposed top level of politics and policymaking in this two-entity country.

Before he gets out of the car, the policeman makes sure we know where we are going. We will find many people in Srebrenica, he tells us, but Žepa will be completely empty.

"He was a pretty nice fellow, eh?" I ask, as we drive off.

"Yes," Zijo answers. "Very polite. He even saved all his cigarette butts in an empty box and took them out of the car with him."

"Did you like him?"

"No," says Zijo.

It is not an easy job to be a policeman in this country, Zijo comments later. There are a lot of rules and procedures to know. If a police officer screws up, he can lose his job instantly. Meanwhile, if, for example, some Muslims want to visit, or even return to, their former homes in a Serb-controlled town, SFOR and IPTF require that the local police protect these people. The local people might object to this vociferously, but it is the job of the policeman, newly trained in the importance of human rights, to explain the situation to the neighbors and to try to control their reactions.

In this environment, I now understand, it must be terribly difficult both to be a good cop and, at the same time, to earn the respect and trust of the people that one is responsible to protect. It is almost too bad that not all citizens—and especially politicians—are not required to sit through human rights training.

Among Mass Graves

We continue on our way to Srebrenica and, a few minutes later, pick up another rider in the village of Milići. Actually, I just stopped to ask directions of a young man about 20 years old. He is going the same way, though, so he joins us. The man is a Serb refugee from Ilijaš, the city just 10–15 miles north of Sarajevo on the road to Visoko. He now lives with his sister in a tiny village here in Republika Srpska called Konjević Polje, and he has just begun to study law at a university that is being created in Pale for Serb students. Were it not for the wars, he probably would be studying in Sarajevo.

The aspiring lawyer knows some English but says he gets very little opportunity to practice. Especially in comparison to Sarajevo, I guess, there probably are not many English speakers in Pale and in Konjević Polje. The young man's parents died a couple of years ago—the father in an industrial accident. His sister is absolutely opposed to returning to their house in Ilijaš. The student comments that he, too, is afraid to attend a Muslim school and to live in an area controlled by Muslims.

He and his sister live with the help of family members who reside in Serbia and abroad. Other members of his extended family, along with many more Serbs from Sarajevo, live in Konjević Polje and another village nearby called Dušanovo. That second village formerly was called by the half-Arabic (by way of Turkish) and half-Slavic name Nova Kasaba, meaning the "new market town."

Nova Kasaba's new name honors Serbia's greatest king, Dušan, who came to the throne of Serbia's medieval state in 1331. Dušan is credited with nearly doubling the territory under his control. Over the course of the century after his death, though, much of Dušan's empire was chipped away and it slipped increasingly under Ottoman control.

Hard Times in the House Market

Our passenger and his sister live temporarily in a Muslim house. Meanwhile, Muslims from Srebrenica occupy their family home in Ilijaš. Many Muslims from Srebrenica now are in Ilijaš. Effectively, then, this has been a sort of population swap, as Muslims from eastern Bosnia moved to central Bosnia and Serbs from the central part were relocated to the eastern edge. The young man notes that he has visited the house in Ilijaš. He would like to sell it and to buy something here. He is waiting to sell, believing he will get a better price in the future. His reasoning seems well grounded. Although there is great need for housing, the Bosnian economy is short on cash and, in light of the continuing turmoil, potential house buyers are hoping to buy at fire-sale prices.

Letting our rider off in his village, I turn the car east toward Bratunac. We are now just a few miles from the Serbian border. It is a devastated and ethnically purified area that is now packed with unhappy Serb refugees from other parts of the country. Muslims previously constituted two-thirds of the Bratunac *opština's* population and three-quarters of that in neighboring Srebrenica *opština*. It is estimated that no fewer than 7,000 Muslims lie in mass graves in this area. Most of these are the men massacred at and around Srebrenica. A mass grave site has been positively identified and exhumed at Nova Kasaba (Dušanovo). The site was exhumed in 1996. In a few minutes we will pass through Glogova, where there is reported to be another mass grave.

For the first six or seven miles out of Konjević Polje (which means about halfway to Bratunac), the route is framed by burned-out, badly damaged and ruined houses. In nearly all of these, there once must have lived Muslim families. Some have been stripped for building materials. Near the road and up into the hills of the valley we are winding through, I guess I see 200 to 300 such houses and farmsteads by the time we reach Bratunac. As we get closer to Bratunac, I see first one camp of temporary refugee housing, then I see several more camps. One of these has perhaps 25 wooden barracks.

Bratunac itself has about it a look of shock, although, on the whole, its physical structures (other than mosques and other Muslim cultural monuments, one can be sure) perhaps were not badly damaged. A certain shabbiness and an indescribable pall hangs over the city. It is difficult to say, though how much of the gloom that I feel is reflected from the community and how much is in my own mind. All through Bratunac, but especially on its edge along the road to Srebrenica, people are selling gasoline, diesel fuel and heating oil from small plastic and metal containers. That seems to be a major business here. It is six more miles to Srebrenica as we pass out of Bratunac through an industrial zone. The factories look mostly intact, but inactive.

A Drink in Srebrenica's Market

Srebrenica is nestled into a terrain of emerald gumdrop hills. The city is long and narrow, stretching a couple of miles up an angular, V-shaped gorge. The houses, streets and shops hug close to the floor of the steep-walled valley.

The single main street runs the extent of the town. I first drive its full length. Several people push new wheelbarrows down the street. Most are moving building materials. One old woman transports a large bag of flour. Neat piles of firewood stand in front of patched-up houses.

Near the far end of the town, the road doubles back as it climbs up into the hills. Very quickly I find myself in the countryside; the city below me disappears. At the top of the hill, I stop the car by a partially reconstructed house. Alone, it is set almost into the road embankment and looks out over a dramatic valley view.

From this higher perspective, the terrain's gumdrop appearance gives way to a look of random hilliness. There are hills of various shapes and sizes, hills on top of hills, hills and more hills. Scattered about the forested vista are patches of meadow. In some of these clearings are the remains of houses and tiny farmsteads. All is green and lush.

I am looking west and southwest, with Srebrenica behind and below me. During the war with the Serb forces, everything that I see before me had been under Muslim control until July 1995. All this had been well within the confines of the so-called safe area. During summer of 1995, though, Serb forces had advanced from the south side of the safe zone. That south boundary had been about five miles farther down this road. The Serb soldiers had overrun the several UN outposts along that boundary. They simply had strong-armed the UN-commanded Dutch soldiers, who had not been authorized to resist the advance. The foremost point of the advancing Serb line had been on this road.

I turn the car around and drive back down the road and into town. An old woman holding a large water canister shouts across the road to her neighbor as we pass by: "Has the water come yet?"

Scattered about are campaign posters and graffiti promoting Šešelj and his SRS. The pictures of Serbia's Deputy Prime Minister posted in Srebrenica demonstrate that the Radical Party is in fact run from Belgrade, not Banja Luka and not Pale. From the founding of the SRS in Bosnia and Hercegovina in 1993, Šešelj's party called for unification of Republika Srpska with Serbia. Although the SRS in Bosnia and Hercegovina remains a hard-line, right-wing party, its official public stance is now that Republika Srpska should seek to maximize its independence within the existing realities of Bosnia and Hercegovina.

I stop the car by a small marketplace and in front of the Red Cross center. The market is not busy. Indeed, the town as a whole seems not very active. That is not to say Srebrenica is not full. It is, and virtually everybody is a Serb. We stop at a stall in the market. The stallkeeper and three customers are drinking *šljivovica*, which the proprietor sells by the shot or the bottle. Two of the customers drift away as we arrive.

Most of the people here are from Sarajevo, the vendor tells us. So is he. His wife was wounded by an artillery blast during the siege of Sarajevo, but she died of her wounds only after the peace accord was signed. The middle-aged man is now left with two children. He is doing his best to raise and to support them. Dealing in the smattering of goods that he has on his table cannot provide much of a living.

Very little international aid is being distributed here. Old people and families who lost their fathers during the war get some assistance. It even is difficult to bring in goods for resale, the stallkeeper says. The state-owned stores supply most of those consumer goods that come in, and the largest percentage of that merchandise must come from Serbia—and through the organized channels.

Some sort of mafia controls those distribution channels, as it does most other economic activity in the town. Meanwhile, remarks the man, the bulk of the people suffer. Expressing his agreement is a weathered, gray-bearded customer who is still sipping his *šljivovica*. If you are enough of a troublemaker, quips the customer, eventually you can come to power. The man with the overgrown gray stubble expresses himself in a string of vacuous figures of speech, never seriously disagreeing with anyone else. He seems terribly chameleonlike, as though he would be equally at home whether among extreme nationalists or tolerant pacifists.

The gray-whiskered man is a Srebrenica native, but he fled the town early and spent the wartime in Serbia. His house in Srebrenica was burned (by Muslims, almost certainly), and he lives now in someone else's house. The man seems sincere, though, when he comments that national extremists, from all sides, are responsible for destroying Bosnian society. He notes, too, that extremists use intimidation, including even threat of death, to prevent people of one ethnonational group from helping, or even associating with, members of another group.

Zijo buys a round, remarking that he likes to have a drink every now and again although he is a Muslim. A good man is a good man, no matter what his nationality, remarks the customer, assuring that he is perfectly willing to drink *šljivovica* with a Muslim. He says he is afraid, though, of those Muslims who are fundamentalists.

The vendor recalls a bit of his life in Sarajevo. He had good neighbors there of varying ethnic identities. The nationalist parties, he says, though, cultivated hatred between the groups. "I could not believe that a man could hate his neighbor or would be able to kill his neighbor's child," the proprietor says. He recalls how, during the wars and while he was still in Sarajevo, somebody attempted to rape his daughter. Fortunately, she was able to get away. The stallkeeper seems to want to dismiss blame for his wife's death. The guilt lies with the artillery shell, he says.

"We lost the trust that we had."

Before the wars, this Sarajevo refugee recalls, his best friend was a Muslim. They helped each other, confided in each other, and even called one another "brother." He would like to see this old friend again, but he fears that to do so is impossible. "We lost the trust that we had," the man says. "I don't trust him, and he doesn't trust me. There are many cases like this." Most of the other Serbs he knows, says the vendor, are even more reluctant than he is to seek out old friends who are Croats or Muslims.

"This hatred of the nations," he says, "is a kind of disease of the nerves, and then it gets into the blood." The man insists, though, that he himself still does not hate. Nevertheless, relationships cannot be as they once were. Because people now have learned to hate, he says, only a powerful central authority working within a strong legal framework could enable Bosnia and Hercegovina's groups to live together again.

So far, virtually no Muslims have come back to try and live in this area, the men confirm. Some have come to look, but not to stay. The stallkeeper says, though, that if the Muslim owner of the house where he now lives were to come back, he would welcome that visitor and make coffee for him. He may be saying that to be diplomatic, for foreign consumption, as it were. I do not think so, though. My feeling is that the disasters which war have brought down upon this man have left him defeated, humbled as never before, introspective because nothing that he sees outside of himself makes any sense, and hungry to know and to give human love and caring. Here is the same character type that I saw in Salko, the Muslim father and refugee from Žepa with whom I had had coffee in Vareš.

Sometimes, the vendor concedes, he asks himself why he was even born. He does not know which way to turn, what to do to try and build a future. His home is burned and far away, his wife is dead, his old friends are scattered, dead or beyond a seemingly insurmountable wall of mistrust. The father of two momentarily snaps out of his despondency, though, when he remembers his children. The most important thing in his life, he says, is to send his children to school. Maybe he will take them abroad, but he just does not know.

"We all are waiting for something," concludes the man with the gray whiskers. "It may be bad, it may be good. We don't know. We're just waiting."

I buy a bottle of the *šljivovica*. Ramiz will be pleased, as it is good, homemade plum brandy. We drive slowly back through the town and back to Bratunac, then backtrack farther to Han Pijesak.

Where No One Goes

The locals in Han Pijesak know where is the road that leads only to Žepa, but they have no reason ever to travel it these days. I drive down the hill from the main part of Han Pijesak, go through a viaduct, and pass a few houses set in small yards. A couple farms are a bit beyond that point, and there is the occasional lumbering truck rumbling down the potholed road. Otherwise, it is quiet and empty. The road is poor to begin with and gets worse as it goes. The bushes alongside the disused road crowd in more and more, making the way seem to narrow. According to the map, it is some nine or 10 miles from Han Pijesak to Žepa.

What must be a couple miles from Žepa, we come upon a pole across the road and stop the car. Off to the left side is a small shack, outside of which is a roughly constructed table. Two young soldiers sit at the table and a third approaches the car. We tell him that I am an independent journalist and that we would like to go to Žepa.

The commander is called to the car. About 30 years old, slender and of average height, he is young but has the look and demeanor of a true soldier. The others are younger still and, with blue coveralls over their uniforms, look less like soldiers than they do farmers or mechanics. The officer politely explains that only former residents of Žepa and those with specific permission from the Republika Srpska government are allowed entry. There are no people in Žepa, he says. The commander tells us to back the car away from the gate and then to get out and speak with him.

As this is a very empty place and far from town, I am a little nervous. I am sure that Zijo is, too, but he disguises it well. The commander asks for our identification. He examines my US passport and studies Zijo's papers. There is no denying, of course, that my interpreter is a Muslim from Sarajevo. Zijo confirms this to the commander. In light of his ethnic identity and residency, he then adds, honestly, he is not quite at ease in the present situation.

We are asked then to join these Serbs in a drink. Out comes a bottle of inexpensive cognac, which is passed around. This seems a genuinely friendly gesture, and the tension eases.

A group of Muslims visited Žepa a couple weeks ago, the commander says. The Republika Srpska government organized that visit, and the former residents retrieved some personal things. No more than five or 10 percent of Žepa's former residents want to come back now, he insists. Rather, they prefer to live in whatever new places they have found. Some of the Muslims burned their own houses before leaving Žepa, he adds.

"It's too bad about this war," the young commander says near the end of our conversation, explaining that he had a Muslim girlfriend before the war. Her name is Fatima, and the young man had wanted to marry this girl. Does he still love Fatima? That was a long time ago, six or seven years, he says, waving his hand to indicate that all of that is over now. Still, he knows what city she lives in now. This Serb officer never is going to forget his Fatima.

You Can Never Go Home

Just outside of Han Pijesak, on our way back to Sarajevo, we stop to pick up a soldier. He is on his way home to his village, which is about 20 miles down the road. Although a father of two sons, the man's naive and almost cherubic face makes him look younger than his years. It is true, of course, that we had spoken just this morning about the various reasons why one should not pick up a soldier, but, well, what can I say? He was clearly alone, it was late in the day, and he looked like a nice fellow.

"It's the only job I can get now," he volunteers, settling into the seat, "so I have to go into the army." He seems almost apologetic about it. The army in this case is that of the Republika Srpska. The man is a contract soldier, which means he did not enlist but was hired on. He says he earns 200 deutschemarks per month. That is not so much, our passenger notes, but at least it covers some of his family's basic needs. (At the equivalent of $120–$130, it is more than twice the average salary we were told yesterday is paid in the Rogatica area.) The term "contract soldier" sounds a lot like "mercenary," but this man is no hired killer. Indeed, he points out that he is not even a nationalist. The man would prefer, in fact, that the extreme nationalists in his country would somehow just disappear.

This soldier's parents both died before the war broke out, and he lives in a house that they had had in this village. He had himself lived in a house in one of the poorer sections of Sarajevo, but left there before the situation got too bad in the capital city. It turns out that this is the very section of town where my interpreter still lives. Zijo says nothing of this, though, and I keep quiet about it, too.

Our passenger has never again seen that house in Sarajevo since he left it more than six years ago. The man remembers his many friends in Sarajevo and in his mixed but largely Muslim neighborhood. He now has lost track of nearly all those people. He wishes he could see them and could speak again with the old friends, but he does not seem optimistic that such an opportunity will soon present itself.

As we approach the soldier's village, Zijo decides to speak more openly. The two men, who were not quite neighbors but almost certainly had some common acquaintances, speak briefly about the neighborhood in Sarajevo, what has happened there, and what is going on now. The Muslims, Zijo reports, plundered, burned and destroyed the contract soldier's former house. The roof tiles were stripped off and put on other houses. There is nothing left there to come home to.

We reach the man's village and stop the car. He gets out and thanks us for the ride. We wish peace and best of luck to him and to his family. If we hurry, we can get over Romanija before total darkness sets in.

Bad Boys Finish First

Šešelj, Poplašen and their Radical Party will pay a price for violating campaign and election rules. *Oslobodjenje* reports today that nine leading SRS candidates have been stricken from the party's candidate list for parliamentary slots because their party leaders broke the election-period silence rule. During the blackout period, Poplašen spoke on TV Belgrade and that message was beamed into Republika Srpska homes. Šešelj gave an interview with a Republika Srpska radio station.

Meanwhile, Sloga leaders had their first postelection press conference yesterday. Although Plavšić, Dodik and Radišić must be gloating some over the punishment meted out to their Serb nationalist competitors, all is not well for Sloga. Plavšić has all but conceded defeat in her bid for reelection to the Republika Srpska Presidency. If she did in fact lose, Plavšić suggested, it is because living conditions in the Serb half of Bosnia and Hercegovina are particularly hard. That, she implied, might have caused Serbs to vote in an irrational manner that is against their own best interests.

After two days of traveling in the eastern portion of Republika Srpska, I am convinced already that the economic situation there is worse than is generally the case in the Federation. That is not saying much, of course. Without international assistance to Republika Srpska that difference will widen. Unless Poplašen changes his tune once he gets into office, an SDS-SRS victory does not bode well for aid to Republika Srpska.

Through a Twilight Zone to a Focal Point of Conflict

It is three minutes past six, and the *mutaveliji* are calling Sarajevo's Muslims to prayer. It is not yet light out, but it must be soon. Muslims are supposed to pray at sunrise, and the call to prayer would not be heard if the time were not right. I woke up thinking about the fact that my visit is approaching its end and about a conversation from last night.

When I returned to Sarajevo yesterday evening, I ran into an acquaintance, a middle-aged professional from a middle-class Muslim family. She asked me what I had found in Srebrenica. I see a lot every day, and I really still needed time to ruminate upon my impressions and to form a view. I told her, though, that the town was filled with Serbs, that the houses were mostly occupied and were being repaired in a fashion, and that the people had looks of great loss and bewilderment. It is very sad to see.

"So," she asked, "it was like a living ghost town?" Yes, in fact, that is quite a good description. "Good," she said.

Why does this women hate the Serbs in Srebrenica? She does not even know them. My acquaintance was quick to point out that she does not hate all Serbs. She in fact still has a close friend who is a Serb. This friend is married to a Croat and no longer lives in Sarajevo, but the two women remain in contact with one another. Almost everybody seems to have a story of a cherished friend from another group who is the exception to the rule. Bosnians and Hercegovinians of all identities have been conditioned to hate their abstract enemies, people who are distant, faceless and nameless. Individually, most also are blameless. But so long as they are anonymous, they are guilty by ethnonational association.

Where Siamese Twins Join

"I am going to America today," I joke to my hosts, "to the USA in Bosnia." My main destination is Brčko, the diplomatically and militarily much fought over city on the northern border. Brčko is situated at the narrowest point of Republika Srpska's so-called Posavina Corridor. The city couples the eastern and western bodies of the Siamese twinset that is Republika Srpska. Brčko lies in the US Operational Zone.[61] The US SFOR zone's headquarters is at Tuzla, which is on the road to Brčko.

Today and tomorrow, I will be in lands lying south of the Sava River that delineates Bosnia and Hercegovina's northern border with Croatia. Posavina means "along the Sava," and the name applies to both the Croatian and Bosnian sides of the river. The Bosnian Posavina was hard fought over during 1992–1995. The flatness and fertility of these low-lying lands contrast with the country's generally rugged terrain.

Brčko represents a terribly emotional issue. Serb forces had a tenuous hold on Brčko when peace talks began in Dayton in November 1995. Leaders in both the Muslim-Croat Federation and Republika Srpska badly wanted the town. The talks nearly foundered over Brčko. In the eleventh hour, all parties agreed to a US proposal that Serbs be allowed temporarily to retain control of the city but that the issue's final resolution would be settled through binding arbitration. An independent arbitrator was to make a decision in early-1997. In fact, the arbitrator postponed the decision in 1997 and deferred it again in early-1998.

Why is this one city such a big issue? There are several reasons, the most important of which are strategic. Brčko's prewar population was thoroughly mixed, although Muslims constituted the largest group. Present and former residents want to live there. The city also is important as a Sava River port. The Sava is itself navigable and flows into the Danube in Belgrade, Serbia. The Danube, then, flows to the Black Sea. Upstream from Belgrade, the Danube connects with Budapest (Hungary), Bratislava (Slovakia), Vienna (Austria) and southern Germany. So Brčko is important for Croats, Muslims and Serbs alike as a transshipping point. For Croatia, it is important also as a spot to cross the Sava, thereby connecting Bosnia and Hercegovina to eastern Croatia.

Serbs counter, though, that they must keep control. Without Brčko, they argue, Republika Srpska is not a single, unbroken entity. Although Muslims and Croats do not say so publicly, to weaken Republika Srpska by severing it at its center is a worthwhile objective in and of itself.

Today's drive will be entirely through Federation territory until I reach the very outskirts of Brčko. Then I will hit Republika Srpska. As I am on my way out the door, Ramiz mentions to me that some of the locals produce *šljivovica* up around Tuzla and Brčko. It is some of the

---

[61]SFOR's operations have been organized into three zones. These are under UK, US and French commands.

best there is. If I see anybody selling it, I might just pick him up a couple liters.

A Twilight Zone and Beyond

Today is the first day of autumn. Sarajevo's morning haze burned off quickly, rendering us a lovely day that will become increasingly resplendent as it progresses.

Just north of Sarajevo, I pass the road to Vogošća. I read last week that Volkswagen has a new production line in Vogošća. The first *Škoda Felicias* to be assembled in Bosnia and Hercegovina rolled out of the German company's Vogošća plant on the day I was in Mostar. Production is only 10 cars daily just now, but I guess it is a start. Output is supposed to reach 60 cars daily by the end of the year. There is said to be a plan in the works also to assemble the *Škoda Octavia*.

The *Felicia* and *Octavia* are Czech-branded, lower-priced copies of the *VW Golf* and *Passat*. The *Felicia* should do well here, as its first cousin, the *Golf*, is one of the most popular cars in the country. Volkswagen had produced *Golfs* in Vogošća before the war. Ramiz owns a *Golf*. His son, who now lives abroad, bought it for him. My host once had a nicer *Golf*, but he says *"Četniks"* stole it during the siege.

Between Vogošća and Ilijaš, I turn north and drive up the Ljubina River valley. We are headed toward Olovo, a medieval lead-mining center and site of one of four Franciscan monasteries established in Bosnia in the 14th century. At that time, Catholicism had not been catching on and sticking among the Bosnians so well as the powers that be in Rome felt that it should. The Pope, therefore, had sent in a substantial mission of Franciscans to put things in order.

Although traffic has not been a problem up until this time, that situation changes beyond Olovo. We must cross some seemingly anonymous mountain. Surely, the locals have a name for it, I figure, but it is not on the map and I do not stop to ask. The road over the mountain is well paved but narrow. It is heavily congested with creeping trucks and military vehicles.

A Picture of Peace

On the other side of the mountain is Kladanj. As we come down off the mountain, we see a piece of Bosnia that is not wholesale ravaged by war. For some 50 miles, there are no destroyed houses along the way. The towns and farms present a picture of peace and a simple but relative prosperity against an autumnal and almost alpine background. Hiding on the far side of that nameless mountain is a rare face of Bosnia and Hercegovina that I have not yet seen. Zijo is snapping pictures. He had forgotten how beautiful his country could be.

About 15 miles out of Brčko, we see the first tell-tale signs that we are leaving this twilight zone. There is a house with mortar scars and a seriously damaged church. The mountains are well behind us now, and even the foothills have melted into the broad and flat bottom of the Sava River valley. Near the city, the markings of violence are more numerous. We pass through a haggard-looking village that is too small to be Brčko but which seems as though it ought to be Brčko. The village is Muslim and must be administratively attached to Brčko. Between the village and the city, a large military compound sprawls before us on the flat plain.

We stop on the periphery of the compound to speak with a large and muscular man in camouflage fatigue pants and a colored T-shirt. A local Muslim, he is a civilian SFOR employee working in grounds maintenance. This encampment, he explains, is shared by troops from the Federation, Republika Srpska and SFOR. The maintenance worker says he is waiting for his house on the Serb side of Brčko to be repaired and is living in a Croat's house in the meantime.

An amiable and particularly diplomatic character who says he is quite satisfied with his salary of 23 deutschemarks (about $15) per day, the SFOR employee tells us that Serbs, Muslims and Croats live together in Brčko. Often, their houses are side by side. Many Muslims have returned to Brčko, he remarks, and some Croats also are coming back.

Brčko: A City in Limbo

A deeply potholed road skirts around the base and leads into the city. Residential areas outside the central core have been devastated, but many houses are now under reconstruction. We stop for lunch at the Pizzeria Stella. A rather large establishment but nearly empty now, it offers one style of pizza. The waitress is as near to indifferent toward us as she can be while still taking our order and bringing us our food. The place is not unfriendly, just spiritless.

After lunch, we speak outside with a woman about 50 years of age. A Serb, she leads us to the nearby marketplace. Asked what are her expectations for how the Brčko issue will be resolved, the woman tells us she anticipates the city will be divided between the Federation and Republika Srpska. However the territorial question is resolved, she would prefer to see people of the different identities live together in a mixed community. That is not to say that she expects relations to work out that way in the future. Were this to be a mixed community, the Serb remarks, there would certainly be "incidents." Memories of the wars are still too fresh, and it will take a long time for people to get over what has happened. That especially will be the case, she stresses, for those who lost family members or close friends.

Why Otherwise All the Bloodshed?

In the market, we meet another Serb woman of about the same age. Like the others here, she is shutting down her stall as the market is supposed to close at 2:00. All of Brčko will remain under Republika Srpska control, she predicts, but adds that Serbs, Muslims and Croats will then live together here. In this market, the stallkeeper points out, people of all nations are welcome to operate stalls and to shop. There are practically no industrial jobs in Brčko, she adds.

This woman is a refugee from Sarajevo, where she formerly worked for the state telephone company. She never expects to return to Sarajevo. Nor does she want to. Her husband was there a couple days ago. After that visit, it became clear that they could not move back. The bureaucrats in Sarajevo's municipal offices refused to accept his Republika Srpska identification card. Nobody would even speak with her husband, she relates, once they knew he was a Serb. There are legions of displaced Serbs in Brčko and many of them, like this woman, do not know where they will go from here.

"All of our men visited our former houses in the Federation," relates another Serb woman, also near 50 years of age, who is closing down the next stall. "And all of them came back disappointed...We have no rights anywhere in the Federation." When a driver carrying Republika Srpska identification is stopped by Federation police, she insists, the driver knows he will be fined for something.

Some are even more unlucky. Several weeks ago, says the woman, a Serb refugee from Zenica, a man living in Brčko, traveled to Ilijaš, near Sarajevo, to visit his son's grave. He was stabbed to death there.

My impression is that this woman is earnest in her segregationist view but is at the same time uncertain about her justification for holding that opinion. She prefers not to meet Muslims here in Brčko. "If we could have lived together before," she asks, "then why did we split up?" It is a rhetorical question meant to justify the conflict, but she is herself puzzled over what is its answer. Before war came to Zenica, the woman recalls, after all, there was no fighting between ethnonational groups there. Problems began to arise for the Serbs only when ethnic relations became politicized.

The Serb says she had never had particularly close relationships with any Muslims when she lived in Zenica, and she does not intend to go back there now. "Muslims," the woman remarks, "speak very sweetly, as if honey were flowing from their mouths," when they talk of living together with Serbs and Croats, "but they are thinking something different from what they are saying." She is hopeful that once the territorial issue of Brčko is decided the Croats and Muslims among them here will sell their homes and move away.

It will be a great tragedy, in this woman's view, if things turn out such that the Serbs do not get Brčko. If the two parts of Republika Srpska ultimately are not connected, she asks, what would have been the purpose then of all this bloodshed? Only now do I find out that this woman's husband was a soldier and died in the fighting. Several other members of her family also were killed. I understand much better now why this widow feels as she does—and why her views never will change.

Look Not to the Future

A few stalls down the line, a reserved and petite woman just on the lower side of 40 years old does not want to speak with us at first. She opens up slowly, though. Zijo asks her view of the future. Giving the answer she thinks we want to hear, the woman says she expects a better future. Once she opens up a bit, she gives her truthful answer: She has stopped thinking about the future.

Only after a few minutes does she quietly tell us that she is a Muslim. She has a husband and child and remained in Brčko all throughout the fighting. The woman notes that she never had any life-threatening difficulties with Serbs or Croats during that time. She did, though, have a child die of leukemia in the course of the war. Before the war, this woman had had a job in a local government office. She has applied to get her job back but has heard nothing. Today, Muslims and Croats have about 30% of the jobs in the local municipal offices.

I ask what is her view on SFOR. "They came," she observes simply, "and things are better." This woman says she does not know what would happen if the foreign soldiers left. But then, to think about that would be to look to the future. This she does not do.

"It is not important what happens in January. We will remain here," declares the merchant across the way. A Croat married to a Serb, and not at all reserved, she proclaims that she loves Serbs and would never trade her husband for any other man. "A man is a man, a human being. It is not the point whether he is a Muslim or a Croat or a Serb."

My understanding is that many ethnically mixed marriages did not survive the war years. She insists that those marriages that could not endure were never strong to begin with. The woman and her husband moved here from Tuzla, which is now in the Federation. It had been her husband's wish to relocate, and Republika Srpska has given them a temporary place to live.

"There is some competition here in our market," pipes up a man 35 to 40 years old a couple stalls down the line, "but the relations are good. Nation is not important. We are all the same here." Whatever decision comes down on the territorial issue, he says, the people here will live and work together and will make the best of it. More important, the man emphasizes is to create jobs for people. They cannot all live by selling goods to one another, after all.

A gregarious Serb, this merchant is a natural for his line of work. He clearly likes to talk, but says he does not like politics. He gets a dig in at the local politicians, though. Every month, the man remarks, he must pay 400 deutschemarks in rental and taxes to operate his stall. "All that money goes into their pockets," he says of the local public servants.

Another, slightly younger man now approaches. He does not like to hear this criticism of the officials. Nobody, and especially not a Serb, should be speaking against the SDS, the young man emphasizes. No one here actually has criticized the Serb Democratic Party by name, which goes to show how sensitive is this man about such matters. Whether or not they really trust or like SDS, Zijo explains to me later, most Serbs here are going to identify with Karadžić's party.

"Americans don't like Serbs and they always write against SDS," the suspicious young patriot charges. "And they always write in favor of the Croats' HDZ and the Muslims' SDA." But these parties, he says, are far from being democratic. From all indications I have seen and heard so far, I see no reason to take issue with the young man on that criticism.

Sometimes, It Hurts to Hate

We set out from the market to find some Muslims. This part of town seems pretty clearly to be Serb-dominated, but I have an idea that there should be a Muslim part of town.

Two late-teenage girls are minding a store where we stop to buy *Cokes*. They are Serbs from Orašje and Novi Travnik. Orašje is a medium-sized but very significant town. It lies just north and west of Brčko, also on the Sava. Orašje and its surrounding area were predominantly Croat before the wars and still are today. That area, known as the "Orašje pocket," is the only piece of Federation (and Croat-held) territory between Republika Srpska's northern corridor and the Sava. If war were to break out, the military strength packed into the Orašje pocket would pose a considerable threat to the Serb forces' narrow corridor. Novi Travnik, meanwhile, is in central Bosnia. It is a sort of industrial suburb of Travnik. Muslims and Croats have long been the largest groups there, although Serbs, too, had their traditional villages in that area and lived in its cities. HDZ and Croats control Novi Travnik now.

The two girls are embarrassed when Zijo insists upon buying them *Cokes*. They tell us they get along okay with the locals here in Brčko. Both insist that they know nothing about politics and have no interest in politics. One voted in the recent election, the other did not. They agree with one another that there is no future here for young people. The youth here talk a lot about going abroad.

Her shift over, the girl from Novi Travnik leaves the shop. The one from Orašje, who is less shy, goes on to say that she only thinks about leaving Bosnia. She looks like a college freshman and comes across as bright and determined. Her education must have been disrupted by the wars, though, and, when she finds her way abroad one day soon, she is likely to take a job not much different from the one she is in now.

Brčko is not her home and never could be, the shop girl makes clear. After all, she lives here in a house that does not belong to her family. Orašje is now a purely Croat town, and Croats (who do not wish to leave) live in the house where she grew up. She does not hate those Croats. She does not hate anybody. In fact, her greatest wish is for all the people in her country to stop hating one another. But how to stop the hate? That, she says, is the question that seems to have no answer.

Many have told me in recent days that they wish to leave for straightforward economic reasons. Hundreds of thousands left during the wars, and the outflow continues. Some, though, are fleeing not poverty but hatred and intolerance. For some, it hurts as much or more to hate another as it does to feel that person's hatred towards oneself. Who wants to live in a country where hatred for others is a defining element in one's identity? Faced with a mandate to hate, some will decide just to live elsewhere. Nationalists of all stripes are driving many of the most civilized and compassionate citizens from Bosnia and Hercegovina.

I think back to a comment made by the widow from Zenica who I had spoken with in the market a few minutes earlier. The common people, without regard to ethnonational identity, pay the price of war and, she had emphasized, the children pay the greatest price of all. The thinking youth of Brčko, Sarajevo, Pale, Kiseljak and hundreds of villages across the country feel they have paid enough—more than enough. I am not optimistic that they can be encouraged to stay and to rebuild what they did not themselves destroy. When I hear them say "no future," I recognize now, they are not referring only to economic prospects.

One Cannot Just Kill Oneself

We drive out past the same residential area, devastated but in early stages of reconstruction, that we had passed when we came into town. It seems the Muslim part of town should be out this way. We stop near a large house, not yet habitable, where several men are working up on the second and third floors. An old man comes by pushing a bicycle. The bicycle's basket is full of scrap wood and the man has under his arm and supported across the handlebars a six-foot piece of galvanized eaves trough. He is a Muslim. Zijo asks him what he will do if Brčko finally and officially becomes a part of Republika Srpska. "I will have to leave," he responds. "I can't just kill myself."

The man with the bicycle has directed us back toward the village we had passed through on our way into Brčko. Just down the road past the multinational military base I see something that makes me pull over to the side and to get out and gape. "Shit, it must be a joke," remarks Zijo, who now is also standing and staring.

"Worldwide Market and Business Center" is bannered across the top of a large billboard-sized sign that stands in a cleared area and faces out to the potholed road. The clearing looks like a construction site, or, more accurately, the site of a future construction site. The ground has been cleared and there is off to one side a trailer that looks like an office, which is locked. On another side has been placed a temporary building of the sort one sees at construction sites.

A schematic drawing shows what are either somebody's big plans or somebody's big scam. Phase I, the sign reads, is to include: a 30,000-square-meter shopping area, 10,000 square meters of warehouse space, a 5,000-meter business center, a 27,000-meter gas station and auto center, parking for 3,000 cars and 500 trucks, and (as Dave Barry would say, Really, I'm not making this up!) a slaughter house. Later additions are to include a hotel, theme park, exhibition center and a new highway.

We drive on and stop in at a restaurant just down the road. A distinguished-looking man in his 50s and two women sit at the table nearest the kitchen. Several guests at the only other occupied table, over by the window, are just finishing their meals. The younger of the two women comes over to take our order and collect payment from the other guests. The older one goes back to the kitchen. The man now sits alone.

Zijo asks him about the Worldwide Market and Business Center. That sign went up just before the election, relates the man, but nobody around here takes it very seriously. He has heard that some Germans are to invest $65 million over six years.

The man's neatly trimmed and coal-black hair is salted with just the slightest metallic flecks of silver. His temples are pure silver. Bright eyes that look directly but softly into those of the person with whom he is speaking are set into a warm and sincere but sad face. Dressed well but casually, his blue dress shirt and cardigan sweater are properly proportioned to his tall and solid frame. This man's tone of voice and words convey the same calm confidence as do his eyes and gaze. A Muslim, he has the look of a respected member of the community, quite possibly a community leader. Of course, little remains of his community.

This gentleman runs the restaurant. Probably, he owns it, the waitress is his daughter and the cook his wife. He leaves the room to retrieve something from the office in back. I notice a sign prominently displayed at the bar, declaring: "Drunken guests not served."

He returns with a colored, glossy brochure. "Brčko: Forming a Link Between East and West," proclaims the cover. Noting that Brčko is situated virtually at the common borders of Croatia, Bosnia and Hercegovina and Serbia, it says the city's Sava River port offers access to the Danube River and to the Black Sea. Brčko, the brochure concludes, should be an important trading center for the entire Balkan region.

Brčko perhaps can be an important shipping and merchandizing center one day. Such an idea seems quite ridiculous, however, when I consider Brčko's ravaged housing and commercial buildings, speak with disheartened and distrusting residents, and recognize how far from truly settled is the territorial question. Even when the arbitrator announces terms of a settlement, the question may not be truly resolved.

The restaurateur tells us he believes the decision as to who gets Brčko will be delayed another year. But he asserts that a decision is needed now so that people can get on with their lives. The best solution, in this man's view, would be to allow all former residents to return to their own homes. He recognizes though, too, that this can only be possible if economic conditions allow people to return. And if Brčko is turned over to Republika Srpska? "In that case," he predicts, "there will be another war. It cannot be otherwise. Can I come to your house and steal your home? Can I steal your car?"

Fairness May Be Irrelevant

Of course, during the wars, many houses and cars were stolen—and even much more than houses and cars. But I see no point in debating details. This man is speaking of course about fairness. Alija Izetbegović, too, has never stopped talking about fairness. He did so all through the wars in his country, at the talks in Dayton from beginning to end, and ever since. That is fine, but, in the end and as a practical matter, what is fair may not be very relevant.

The Muslim businessman pulls out an ethnographic map. In 1991, the figures show, Brčko *opština's* 82,768 residents were 53% Muslims, 17% Serbs, 7% Croats and 22% people declaring themselves to be Yugoslavs and of other ethnic groups.[62] These figures include not just Brčko proper but also all the villages and countryside within the *opština* for which Brčko is the administrative seat. Today, he estimates, less than 5% of the population within Brčko proper is Muslim.

Most of Brčko's Muslims were pushed out in 1992, during the early weeks of the struggle for Bosnian territory. Croat and Serb nationalist bosses had agreed that the Serbs could have the city.[63] The Serbs quickly got down to the business of creating an outwardly Serb city. Roughly 20,000 Muslims were pushed out, our host says, and were replaced by thousands of Serb refugees. Brčko's five mosques were destroyed. Parking lots are in their places now. Although the lone Catholic church was not leveled, he says, naturally Brčko today looks more like a Serb city than a Muslim one. In the 1996 elections, Serb refugees voted but non-Serbs from 18 villages in the *opština* were not allowed to do so.

"And after that," the man relates, "they say to the foreigners—because you don't know the situation—that this is a purely Serbian town...But there are photographs, and we can prove what we had here before."

The OSCE, he says, is responsible for the fact that potential voters from Brčko's surrounding villages were not allowed to vote in 1996. When it came time to vote, these people's names simply were not on the lists of registered voters. That situation was improved for the elections that occurred this month. Nevertheless, the man notes, many

---

[62]My own ethnographic map, also based upon official 1991 census numbers, indicates the population was 44% Muslims, 25% Croats, 21% Serbs and 9% Yugoslavs and others. In both cases, percentages do not add to 100 due to rounding.

[63]Silber and Little, pp. 232, 256, 308.

of the *opština's* Muslims now live in Australia, Canada, the US, Germany and elsewhere. Most of these did not vote, and this created a big disadvantage for the non-Serb political parties here.

During the wars, he explains, conditions were such that it was easier for Muslims to get passports and, therefore, to go abroad than it was for Serbs to do so. Now, those Muslims are settled outside the country. Some have jobs abroad and their children are with them. Here, meanwhile, there are no jobs, much uncertainty and plenty to fear. "Under these conditions," he remarks, "they have no reason to come back. There is no way to get food for your children here." If Brčko becomes part of Republika Srpska, the man adds, Muslims will not be allowed to file official documents in the public administrative offices.

SFOR and the other two armies based in the sprawling camp nearby must now constitute the largest industry here. As occurred elsewhere, Serb forces stripped equipment from some of Brčko's factories. One of these had employed some 1,000 people. Even the local agriculture has been undermined—literally. There still are hundreds, perhaps thousands, of mines spread about the area. It is not safe to go into the fields and forests. Last year, there was mine clearing around the military base and the Worldwide Market and Business Center site. "But when the other places will be cleared," the man wonders aloud, "who knows?"

My guess is that maybe the SFOR and other military presence helps his restaurant business. After all, he runs a clean and pleasant establishment that is just down the road from the base. But the SFOR people do not come to his restaurant, the man says. They have a special restaurant of their own in a different village and another one right on the base. The local people have almost no money, meanwhile, so his business is poor. I guess he is not holding his breath until the Worldwide Market and Business Center opens.

"I don't believe in the international community."

"I've lost all hopes," the Muslim businessman says quietly. "I don't believe in the international community. I don't trust anybody." Like so many other Muslims, he once had hung his hopes on the US—upon its military might and what he had regarded as America's support for justice. He still cannot understand why the US and its allies do not stop Milošević, who, he maintains, is doing the same thing in Kosovo that he and the other Serb nationalists did in Bosnia and Hercegovina. But the international community, the restaurateur observes, mostly makes empty threats and the entire world watches as Serbs kill more people.

The hour is getting late, and I am hopeful that maybe we can still get to Tuzla. As I pay the bill, I am sorry to leave. I feel that I have been speaking with a voice of reason, albeit one colored with naiveté arising from the Muslim fixation upon justice. The Muslims here do not hate Serbs, this man with the sad but clear eyes tells me, but they are afraid of Serb nationalism and to live under Serb political domination.

Two Talkative Croat Women

About halfway between Brčko and Srebrenik, we pass through an informal marketplace that has been set up. In about a dozen or so stalls on both sides of the road people are offering locally produced food items. This is the (most recent) territory where Ramiz has told me there ought to be good homemade *šljivovica* on sale. I pull over to the side. Sure enough, two talkative Croat women in one of the stalls have plum brandy for sale. The women are neighbors. One of them, who is dressed in black and has two gleaming gold teeth, explains that her husband produces the *šljivovica*. The woman says she used to send her husband out here to sell it himself, but he was more interested in drinking than in selling. It is better, she had decided, to let him stay at home and for her to take care of the business at this end.

The women recall that there had been fighting in this locality only briefly. The women and children had fled and stayed away for just 21 days while the men had stayed behind to fight. Once the Croatian and Bosnian armies had pushed the Serb line back a couple miles from the village, the women and children had returned.

Earlier, when war had begun in Hercegovina but there was still no fighting in this part of Bosnia, these Croats recall, they had sensed a change in relations with their Muslim neighbors. It had been subtle but real. Muslims and Croats no longer greeted one another when they met, for example. Today, however, the women assure us that Croats and Muslims in this area get along well. Apparently, the good relations do not reach so far as Tuzla and Sarajevo. The villagers here used to sell their wares in those cities. The roadside market was created when these urban markets were closed off to them. Even if SFOR were to leave, one of the women says she believes there would be no fighting here. Nevertheless, both prefer that the foreign troops stay on for now.

I buy two liters of *šljivovica* and resist the women's spirited efforts to sell me just about everything they have left in their stand. Ramiz will be pleased. It is now too late, and I am too tired, to stop in Tuzla. Tomorrow is another long drive.

An Enemy for Some, a Brother for Others

This time they really mean it, maybe. OSCE is to have a press conference today at noon to announce results of the elections conducted almost two weeks ago. The suspense is minimal. Having pulled together data in bits and pieces from polling places, the political parties and press pretty much know what to expect. People mainly will be watching out to see if there are any surprises indicating that international officials had cooked the numbers.

The fact that some of the least democratic of the electoral candidates are already declaring and celebrating victory goes to show that the international community did not "engineer" these elections, as some have charged. That is according to Robert Gelbard, special US envoy to the Balkans. Gelbard was up in Banja Luka yesterday meeting with Milorad Dodik and Biljana Plavšić. Although it is now generally taken for granted that Plavšić is on her way out as President of Republika Srpska, I doubt that Gelbard was there just to tell her thanks, good luck and goodbye. The Sloga coalition and her Serb People's Union should remain powerful in the legislative bodies. The US and others surely will attempt to continue playing the Serb parties of Dodik, Plavšić and Radišić against the Serb parties of Poplašen and Krajišnik. After meeting with the US envoy, Dodik told reporters that he and Gelbard agree the foremost goal of the new government must be to protect the peace and the rule of law.

Meanwhile, Nikola Poplašen the Serb extremist candidate (and expected winner) for the Republika Srpska Presidency, has told a Croatian newspaper that he is pleased that nationalist Ante Jelavić will be the Croat member of the Bosnia and Hercegovina Presidency. "With HDZ we will easily agree on policy and everything important," Poplašen reportedly said.

One of the things that makes Bosnia and Hercegovina's Muslims most nervous is to hear about good relations between Serb and Croat nationalist leaders. When they catch wind of meetings between top Serb and Croat politicians and they know that the subject is Bosnia and Hercegovina, Bošnjaks tend to think of plans to divide their country: with one piece for Serbia, another piece for Croatia, and nothing for Bošnjaks. This concept is summed up in a single word: "Karadjordjevo." That is the name of a formerly royal hunting lodge where, in March 1991, Tudjman and Milošević are widely believed to have agreed in principle to divide Bosnia and Hercegovina. It is sometimes likened to the secret protocol of the 1939 Molotov-Ribbentrop Nonaggression Treaty in which Stalin and Hitler agreed to split Poland between their countries.

While we were in Brčko yesterday, SFOR and visitors from The Hague's war crimes tribunal were having a busy day in Mostar and in Vitez. *Oslobodjenje* reports that investigators made surprise visits to collect evidence in the city hall and HVO headquarters in Vitez, as well as at HVO buildings in Mostar and in a smaller town nearby. SFOR and local police provided stiff security for the investigators.

The investigators were looking for evidence in the cases of Dario Kordić and nine other Croats who had turned themselves over to tribunal authorities in autumn 1997. The men are charged with war crimes relating to the 1993 anti-Muslim rampage in the Lašva valley that included the Ahmići massacre. Kordić had been the HDZ leader for the Lašva valley area and is alleged to have ordered the massacres, destruction and expulsions. A spokesman for the tribunal prosecutor's office has said more cases will be opened in relation to incidents in that area.

Bringing war criminals to justice is one important part of a healing process in the Lašva valley and central Bosnia. Returning the displaced to their homes is another. Neither occurs easily.

I read of one central Bosnian village, near Vitez, where attempts are being made to resettle Muslims. Croats there have been physically blocking Muslims from returning. They also put out a list of seven Bošnjaks who they say committed war crimes and may not return under any circumstances. An international representative has noted, however, that only the tribunal in The Hague may list war criminals. *Oslobodjenje* reporters covering the story got a good taste of the bitter conflict. While trying to conduct interviews, they were forced to flee when attacked with stones and verbal abuse by people on both sides of the conflict.

In this particular case, a compromise solution was reached that allowed some Muslims to return. For the time being, however, those Muslims named on the Croats' list will not come back.

Summer Becomes Autumn

It is a gray and hazy morning as we leave Sarajevo and follow the Bosna River valley west and north from its very beginning in the outskirts of town. The water in the Bosna is running high, swiftly and muddily after the recent rains. It is completely different from the beautifully lazy and green Bosna along which I had driven northward to Croatia on a much briefer visit two months ago. That was summer. This is autumn.

My perspective also will be different on this drive from what it was when I first followed the Bosna on its course to the Sava. I know that the worst of the visible wreckage will be between the cities of Doboj and Derventa, but this time the devastation will not astonish me.

We pass Ilijaš, with its gray cement plant. I think of the Muslim woman we met near here a few days ago and her unsuccessful effort to buy firewood. Near here, too, is where, according to the story we heard yesterday, the Serb refugee from Brčko had been killed while visiting his son's grave. We follow the Bosna past Visoko, that strongly Muslim town known for its cured meat and as an island of relative safety during the years of war. Well east of Vitez, we turn north where the Lašva River flows out of its bloodstained valley, past Ahmići, and into the Bosna.

Road and river now lead to Zenica, a steel town, formerly an ethnically very mixed city, but a Muslim stronghold during the wars and today. Zenica was home base for savage *mujahedeen* paramilitaries that had been active in the Croat-Muslim struggle in central Bosnia. Partially recruited, financed and directed from Iran, these units not only struck terror in the hearts of the enemy but also terrified the local, secularized Bošnjaks. Mirsada's family lives here until they can return to Ahmići. In Zenica are the recalcitrant Muslim divorcee and her formidable lover who occupy the home of the dapper, old Croat I met in Kiseljak. This is the former home of the Serb widow now living in Brčko and who wants never to return. Zenica's Serbs are spread about Republika Srpska. Many have gone far to the east, to Višegrad, where they displace Muslims.

When we emerge from the second dark tunnel beyond Zenica, the sun is shining onto a mountainside that looks out at us from the distance. A bit of sky-blue is spattered directly above us. That azure propagates itself hastily as it devours the clouds. In a few minutes, it has overrun the entire sky and we have a gorgeous day. At Žepče the Bosna River turns east, but we continue straight north. The river will loop around and meet us back in Maglaj, just 10 or 12 miles up the road. Within this loop, and between Žepče and Maglaj, we are in a small patch of Croat-controlled territory. This is an isolated fragment of Herceg-Bosna, the Croat nationalists' would-be ministate.

We see only light war damage between Žepče and Maglaj, but that changes abruptly as we approach Maglaj from the south. Croats, Muslims and Serbs all had fought one another around Maglaj. All sides had much to lose or to gain here. We are near the easternmost flank of Republika Srpska's western lobe. The IEBL is a ragged line north of Maglaj, and there are distinct Croat and Bošnjak territories on this side of that line.

New Asphalt through a Wasteland

Traffic stops south of Doboj, where the Usora River joins the Bosna. Only a one-lane, temporary military bridge crosses into Republika Srpska until the smashed main bridge will be reconstructed. It seems odd to me that almost three years after the Dayton agreement was reached this bridge, on a major north-south road and on the edge of a substantial city, has not yet been rebuilt. The broken highway bridge reinforces the *de facto* boundary separating the Federation and Republika Srpska. While we wait to cross, droves of vendors walk up and down the line of cars offering bootleg music tapes, sodas, candy bars and cigarettes. I find this annoying. Others view it as a shopping opportunity.

Across the bridge, the signs are lettered in Cyrillic. We stay on the main road that skirts around the main part of Doboj. On the far side of town, a policeman on foot waves me down. It is a quick stop. I think he just wants to get a quick look at who is driving this car with foreign plates. "Drive carefully and watch out for the children," he cautions and sends us on our way. His warning is appropriate enough. The sides of the road are crowded with children, some of whom are hitchhiking. In this country, children go to school in two shifts. The morning students now are going home and the afternoon students are arriving.

Immediately beyond Doboj's city limits we begin to see ravaged farmsteads, houses and villages. Very few of these are being reconstructed so far. According to my most-detailed ethnographic map, Muslims had previously owned most of this land between Maglaj and Doboj. Republika Srpska obviously is not encouraging the owners to return. We are driving on a good two-lane road, but there is very little traffic. If my memory from the summer serves me correctly, this landscape will be with us all the way to Derventa. As we drive, we are waiting to hear the election results on the radio. These are supposed to be announced at noon.

What we hear at noon is that the election results have been delayed again "for technical reasons." Those words smack of socialism and backwardness. Having lived and traveled for years in the lands of crumbling communism, I can recognize the words "Closed for Technical Reasons" in several languages. A well-worn sign bearing those words seems to be within easy reach in every shop, ticket counter and government office wherever communism has been. There is little hesitancy to hang that sign in the window and to lock the door.

I am disappointed that the OSCE resorts to excusing itself with this lame and well-worn cliche. Everybody in this country knows those words mean either that somebody screwed up or is too lazy or incompetent to get the job done on time. An important part of the OSCE's task in running these elections, as near as I can tell, is to build confidence in democratic processes. Repeated delay in announcing the election results does not help achieve that goal. Many in Bosnia and Hercegovina regard the OSCE as a weak organization. I do not know what is going on behind the scenes, and I am certain that the political parties here are causing plenty of problems, but I nevertheless am concerned that the OSCE cannot complete the process in a more open and timely manner.

My memory of this road is right on the mark, except for one surprising thing. Suddenly I recognize that I am driving on brand-new asphalt. This definitely was not the case only a few weeks ago. We catch up to the paving crew just south of Derventa. A worker tells us that foreign aid money is paying for part of the work. I am surprised at the apparent efficiency with which the crew must be working. They have put down quite a few miles of new blacktop in a relatively short time. Cynical after hearing the latest news from OSCE, I wonder if there is a rush to get the work done before the donor realizes what the money actually was spent on (or before aid gets cut off because of the election outcome in Republika Srpska).

All Sides Devastated Derventa

After I had driven through Derventa that summer evening a few weeks ago, I had described it in a letter to a friend as "almost a ghost town." Arriving here now, I am jolted into reminding myself not to be too quick in making judgments and to be modest about my conclusions (particularly those that are based on little evidence). Derventa is not at all the abandoned town I had thought it to be. At midday today, the city is absolutely full of people.

We are looking for the hospital. We expect to find working there a blind man from Ilidža, that suburb of Sarajevo that had been under Serb occupation throughout the siege. I am very interested to hear this man's perspective. I am a bit uncomfortable about the circumstances of our visit, though, because it involves a small deception. It is a sort of mission of love, too, and that makes it seem nobler. This man is a Serb and he has left a wife, also blind, in Ilidža. She is a Croat and lives on a pension. Zijo has become acquainted with this woman. She has asked him to speak with her husband and to gauge whether or not he is likely ever to return home. The wife in Ilidža has regular telephone contact with her husband. She has assured Zijo that her husband knows many people in Derventa and understands very well the situation here.

Neither the hospital nor our interview subject are difficult to find. A man near retirement age, he is indeed knowledgeable. He is soft-spoken but responsive. His mind works quickly, and his answers are diplomatically formulated.

There are greater than 13,000 refugees in Derventa, he explains. That these are Serbs is clear and does not need to be said. The largest groups of refugees are from the areas of Bosanski Petrovac, Glamoč and Sarajevo. Those who came here as refugees traveled far. Bosanski Petrovac and Glamoč are in the far west of Bosnia. More than 75% of the populations in these two *opštinas* had been counted as Serbs in 1991. When the shooting stopped, though, Bosanski Petrovac and Glamoč were not within Republika Srpska.

Derventa *opština* must be almost purely Serb today. Serbs constituted a 41% plurality even before the wars. At 39% of the population, Croats were nearly as numerous then. We are, of course, very close to Croatia. Just up the road and across the Sava River is Croatian Slavonia, from which many Serbs fled or were forced out. Muslims, at 13% of the 1991 population, were the smallest group in Derventa *opština*.

Among Bosnia and Hercegovina's major towns, this refugee from Ilidža tells us, Derventa is physically one of the most devastated. All sides had a hand in destroying parts of this city. The main fight was between Serbs and Croats, and the city changed hands a couple times. Muslims were caught in between. Many of them here sided with the Croats and fought against the Serbs, which put them on the losing side. A few of Derventa's Muslims, though, stayed here throughout the fighting and are still here now. Some even had joined the Serb army. "If the Muslims stayed on the Serb side," the blind man maintains, "nobody touched them." It is true, though, he allows, that some Serb refugees have wanted to push the remaining Muslims out of Derventa.

Not surprisingly, one feels here that Derventa is a very unsettled place. Of course, that feeling exists throughout Bosnia and Hercegovina and varies only by degree from one place to the next. While Serb nationalists undoubtedly were the principal aggressors, the dislocation and havoc that they created hits ethnic Serbs very hard.

This hospital worker tells us that the woman who owns the flat in which he now resides is living in Sweden but wants to return to her apartment. As of today, he believes he could return to Ilidža and be safe there. But how long would that be the case? There are many "fundamentalists" in Sarajevo, the man insists, and the situation there is not yet completely settled, either.

Others in Derventa also contemplate returning to their former homes. But there are many who are too afraid and say they never will go back. It is usually the old people who most wish to return, the blind man relates. The young people, though, talk more about leaving. There are many mixed marriages here, he says, and those people especially are inclined to quit the country altogether.

"Tito's children" is the term he uses to refer to the mixed marriages and their offspring. I know, of course, that he, his wife, and their two daughters who are living in Serbia all are Tito's children. Still, it becomes clear to me by now that this man also has very strong feelings of Serb nationalism. "If the Republika Srpska continues to exist," he declares, for example, "then there is a future."

This man was part of the mass exodus of Serbs from Sarajevo that followed the Dayton agreement but preceded the official unification of that city. Up until Dayton, he had hoped that the peace settlement would leave Ilidža within Republika Srpska. Now, he says he has permission from the municipal office in Ilidža to return, that he intends to return and that, ultimately, he and his wife must be back together. Maybe. But the way he describes his intentions is not very convincing.

Life in Derventa is difficult. The man earns 60 deutschemarks per month (less than $40), and he says he is very lucky to have a job. Before he began to work, he had received some aid as a refugee. Now, he no longer gets assistance. There is very little aid available, and what assistance there is goes only to those in the most dire need.

How, I wonder, does one survive on 60 deutschemarks per month? "You must eat only what you have," he states, simply. You cannot eat more. And if you have 60 deutschemarks, you can spend only 60 deutschemarks." People find ways, he allows, though, to get a little extra money and to survive.

There are a couple factories here that are running at fractions of their capacities. Some agricultural enterprises provide a few additional jobs. Overall, though, there is very little work in and around Derventa. It is especially difficult for those with handicaps, and this man is actively involved in organizing the blind. In Derventa and nearby Bosanski/

Srpski Brod there are some 70 blind people, he notes. Before the wars, most of these had earned their own livings and were self-sufficient. In many cases, though, blind people need special equipment to do their jobs. Most of what they need was lost to the fighting and destruction.

War, which is itself not only blind but also deaf and unfeeling, took most of what everybody here needs. Some will argue that it was worth it. Some even will make that argument and believe it to be true. Most, I suppose, principally want stability, predictability. They want to know where they need to be in order to get on with what is left of their lives.

The Lot of South Slavs

From the hospital we go into Derventa's downtown to have coffee. We are hungry, but we suspect we are more likely to find a good restaurant back down the road in Doboj. We take the last patio table at a perfectly serviceable coffee shop. It is not fancy, but neither is it a place where people earning 60 deutschemarks a month and feeling lucky for it are going to be passing their time. Outside of Sarajevo, I rarely find that I can truly relax in such a place. I am always alert, feeling as though a simple coffee break could turn into an altercation at any time. I have that feeling strongly here. We drink our coffee with little conversation, pay and move on.

Across the street is a privately owned building supplies store. The shopkeeper is a friendly man in his 20s. A Derventa native, he says there are about 3,000 longtime Derventa residents here and, generally confirming the blind man's figure, some 14,000 new residents. Most of the goods in his well-stocked shop, he says, are from Serbia. The prices are marked in Bosnia and Hercegovina's official currency, the convertible mark. This is our first visit to the western portion of Republika Srpska. It may be coincidental, but, in the eastern part, I never saw prices stated in any currency except Yugoslav dinars. I am much more relaxed here among the hardware than in the coffee shop.

A deliveryman, also in his 20s, comes into the store. He tells us he is from Petrovac. His whole family relocated here. In fact, he says, the entire Serb population of Petrovac came to Derventa. He is speaking of Bosanski Petrovac. He does not use the first word in the name, however, which means "Bosnian." Many of those who came here from Petrovac were farmers. These Serbs could not bring their soil, but they did bring their tractors and thousands of horses.

When a family of refugee arrives here, the deliveryman explains, they look around the area until they find a house that they want to live in but which is not yet inhabited. They move in right away and then go to the municipal center officially to declare where they will live. The deliveryman says he earns 200 deutschemarks monthly and that he is quite satisfied about that. His grandmother receives a bit of food aid. Other than that, the family must make do as best it can.

A few days ago, the young man says, his aunt took her family back to Petrovac to live. Another family returned at the same time. His mother went there to visit. She found that their house had been burned. He assures us that he has no intention ever to return to Bosanski Petrovac.

Croatian Serb Regrets Flight

A man about 60 years old and his wife come into the store. They are from Slavonski Brod, which is the twin city on the Croatian side of the Sava River across from Bosanski (now "Srpski") Brod. A Serb, he is not a bit happy to be stuck over here in Bosnia and Derventa. He was pushed out of Croatia, but now he wishes he would have been more assertive about staying. For 36 years he had worked on the railroad in Croatia. Had he stayed in Croatia—and survived—he would have a good pension now. Here, the man says, he has nothing. His hope is that Croatia and Republika Srpska will work out an agreement reciprocally to swap one another's pension obligations. But he is not optimistic.

Nobody over here cares, he says, about people who are poor and who have no power. The retired railroad man emphasizes the words "no power." His wife, too, stresses the difficulties of the powerless. They point out that little aid is available here. Even where there is aid, the husband asserts, the local officials take a big cut of whatever is distributed. He echoes a sentiment that I hear time and again: Foreign aid organizations should distribute assistance directly to the people who need it. Do not pass it through the sticky fingers of local officials.

When I think of this old Slavonian Serb in Derventa's hardware store, I am reminded of a passage in Ivo Andrić's *Bosnian Chronicle.* That story, though, is of an old Muslim whose family, the Karahodjić clan, had been pushed out of Slavonia and into Bosnia late in the 17th century. The story is of a "sullen and pigheaded" old Muslim, encountered outside of Travnik in the first decade of the 1800s.[64]

---

[64]Ivo Andrić, *Bosnian Chronicle, paperback*, trans. Joseph Hitrec (New York: Alfred A. Knopf, 1963; first Arcade paperback edition, 1993), pp. 115–116.

In the 16th century, this fictional character's ancestors, benefiting from Ottoman Turkish advances into Slavonia at that time, had acquired vast lands in the vicinity just 25 miles north and west of Slavonski Brod. Some 120 years later, the Austrians retook those lands and sent this and other Muslim families fleeing into Bosnia.

> Their family still kept a cauldron or copper kettle, which they had taken with them as a reminder of the lost estate and lost lordship when, bitter and humiliated, and led by their ancestor Karahodja, they came back to Bosnia. On this cauldron, Karahodja had sworn them to a pledge: that they would never fail to answer a single war call against the Austrians and that each of them would do everything in his power to get back the lordship they had lost in Slavonia.

The Karahodjić clan is fictional, but the story is based upon historical realities. It had been at the time of the Muslims' flight from Slavonia that thousands of Serbs and Croats had moved in. Some of these were returning families that had been pushed out a century or more earlier by the Turkish advance. Immigrating to Slavonia, too, at about that time were Serbs who were even then being pushed by the Turks out of the old Serbian Kingdom and from Kosovo. The elderly Serb from Croatia who we encountered in the hardware store in northern Bosnia may well have had ancestors in that earlier migration.

Migration and heartbreak seems to be the historical lot of the South Slavs.

Doboj: Full Coffee Shops, Empty Promises

War, goes a saying here, is an enemy for some and like a (rich) brother for others. The sense of the expression is that it destroys many while enriching others. Quite a few of those made wealthy by the wars must live in Doboj. Others among the *nouveau riche* created by war just pop in to drink coffee and to talk.

Doboj contrasts sharply with Derventa, just a few miles up the road. Also Serb-controlled, this town has several advantages. Physical damage to Doboj from the war was only slight. Federation territory is just across the Usora River that is on the south edge of town. SFOR troops stand between the two sides, helping to maintain peace and order. Near the confluence of the Spreča and Bosna rivers, Doboj is situated in a potentially rich agricultural area.

Relatively prosperous, Doboj is a refuge for well-dressed riffraff on the path toward eventual respectability, ranging from small-time smugglers and black marketeers to big-time mafia bosses. They slip back and forth across the inter-entity boundary, coming here to drink coffee and do their deals. Most are Serbs, but, so long as they behave themselves, Muslims and Croats of a similar bent, too, are welcome to make and spend their money here.

Doboj was taken by Serb forces early during the recent wars and cleansed of its Muslims and Croats. A railway hub, the city was, in fact, a collection point for deporting non-Serbs from Serb-held areas.[65] Historical memory no doubt helped to justify the ethnic cleansing. Doboj (like Brčko, Bihać and Mostar) had been the site of atrocities against Serbs during World War II when this area was part of the Independent State of Croatia.

We stop in at the Pizzeria Cezar. The food is good, the music ethnically mixed and the Serb waiters friendly. The prices are denominated in Yugoslav dinars, although it is no problem to pay in convertible marks. Lunch here costs roughly twice what it did yesterday in Brčko, but the prices are about the same as in Sarajevo. From our veranda table, we look out across the street and down a pedestrian mall lined on both sides with coffee shops. Young men come and go from the coffee shops. Some have fast and flashy cars, but most have not-fast and not-very-flashy cars. Whatever they are driving, they like to rev their engines and screech their tires.

The pizzeria's two waiters are youngish men, each maybe 30 years old. Many people come here from the Federation every day, they relate. A few Muslims remain who resided here already before the war. Some Muslims who left during the fighting are returning. Generally, though, these are people who live only on the very fringes of town or in outlying areas. The local economy seems slowly to be getting better. A person cannot expect too much, though, one waiter says, so soon after the hostilities have ended. The other points out that here, close to the IEBL, a good bit of black-market activity adds to the economy.

It is clear that some people here have money. The coffee shops and restaurants are nearly filled with well-dressed people. Those who have money, continues one of the waiters as the other goes off to clear a table, will quickly improve themselves and the town. But those who have no money—and there are many of these—have little or no

---

opportunity even to get a start. Doboj's population today consists perhaps 30% to 40% of refugees. There is very little aid of any kind.

SFOR has three bases here, the waiter says. We will notice a few of the international soldiers on the streets. Generally, those we see will be unarmed. That is unusual. At first, the waiter notes, perhaps some of the locals verbally abused the SFOR troops from time to time. But there are no incidents now. The international soldiers regularly visit Doboj's bars and restaurants. The waiter says he prefers that SFOR is here and patrolling the streets. It means that he no longer needs to carry a gun. At the time he makes that last remark, I assume the waiter means that he no longer needs to be a soldier himself. As I think about it later, I am not so sure that is all he meant in that ambiguous statement.

After having coffee on the pedestrian mall, we leave the café quarter and walk to see if the rest of this town looks just as prosperous. We pass an obelisk erected in memory of those who rose up and gave their lives in the struggle against fascism. That, of course, is a World War II monument. We stroll through a clean and green park. Across the street from an exhibition hall where there is a small-business trade show, two young men are hanging out in the sunshine. About 16 or 17 years old, both are dressed in baggy athletic pants, sport shoes and sweatshirts. One, the more talkative of the two, has a white painter's cap jauntily slung onto his head with the visor down the back. Both are displaced from villages near Doboj.

We decide to walk together up to the ruins of the 13th-century castle that looks out over Doboj. Along the way, we pass near a mosque. Although looted and badly damaged, it has not been razed. I wonder to myself why it has been spared complete obliteration. The talker reads my mind. The mosque will be fixed up, he relates, noting that it is important to those Muslims who still live in the area.

I ask the two youths what they think about their futures. The quiet one tells me his father was killed in the war. Now, he just wants to go away. He does not know to where, nor does he seem to care so long as he can get away from here. (He will later ask me if it is possible to get to America by bus.) The more gregarious one, who is a year older and has finished his basic schooling, says he wants to stay. He was born here, the young man notes. His father is a dentist and so was his grandfather. He hopes that he can follow in their footsteps. In my mind, the two young men become "the Dentist" and "the Sad One."

We enter a gate of the hilltop ruin and come upon three SFOR soldiers, two in their civilian clothes. The third, a black man and sharply dressed in full uniform, is having his picture taken as he sits on the fortification wall and with the city below as a backdrop. "This is Doboj (pronounced 'Dough Boy,' like the little Pillsbury guy)," I can imagine him writing on the back of the photo to the folks back home. "It's where I'm stationed. Doboj isn't Shangri-La, but at least nobody's fighting here anymore."

From the highest point of the castle ruin, we can see all of Doboj and much of the surrounding countryside. The castle needs some restoration work, but it is not in bad shape for a ruin. There is definitely enough here to make it a minor tourist attraction, although tourists these days are pretty few and far between. The city below looks to be in surprisingly good shape, although it, too, needs some work.

I ask the young men how they feel about relations with the other ethnonational groups. The Sad One comments that he never will be able to get along with Croats and with Muslims. How could he? Other families, he says, had even greater losses. Some lost three or four sons and brothers. That cannot be forgiven. The Dentist asserts, though, that the nations must get along. He points out that some Serbs are now returning to his village, which is four miles away on the Federation side.

On the way back down the hill, we walk past several nice new houses. We also pass one that has been stripped of all removable building materials. That house, they say, formerly belonged to the richest Muslim in the town. He does not live in Doboj anymore. The nicest of the new houses, the young men relate, belongs to the richest man in the town today, a Serb.

The Dentist is of an age such that he should be beginning his higher education. It is not clear where he will study, but he is certain that he will go on to school somewhere. The Sad One says he does not think about studying. He assures me that there are no resources for that. His mother plants trees for a living. She earns 150 deutschemarks per month. That is relatively good money for Republika Srpska, but it is not enough to send a son to college. The government, he relates, is always promising that there will be money for education and there will be special assistance to those who have lost one or both parents. The young men agree, though, that promises are all they have seen so far and that empty promises are all they are likely to see in the future.

Hate, Souvenirs and, Oh Yes, Election Results

Today is my last full day with Ramiz and Vahida. Breakfast is something special: *kajgana*. This is delicious and is the perfect meal for days when one suspects one's body might be running in serious deficiency of saturated fat and cholesterol. *Kajgana* is scrambled eggs with young cheese, butter and creamy *kajmak*. Ramiz looks on approvingly as I consume my *kajgana* with thick slices of fresh bread and hot cocoa.

I will go to Pale today. This will be a short visit, though, so that Ramiz and I can go into town this afternoon to shop for souvenirs.

Pale: Betrayed, Abandoned, Angry

Pale is only 10 minutes' drive east of Sarajevo, toward the mountain called Romanija. It is known in the West as the headquarters (sometimes described as "stronghold") of Radovan Karadžić, the Bosnian Serbs' leader and their former president. Pale is not exactly the mountain-village hideout that western media often portray it to be. It is a run-of-the-mill, not very attractive Balkan town. As we are coming into town and crossing the city limits, a half dozen sheep skitter across the road in front of the car. That creates a nice theatrical effect.

Pale's strongly negative image has not been lost on us. We are a little tense about this visit. To read about it, Pale is supposed to be a pretty nasty place. The Muslims in Sarajevo, too, speak of Pale in fearsome terms. They do not come here.

I know there will be only Serbs in Pale. Many of them will have fled here from Sarajevo. I do not suppose they will care much for Americans, writer-types and Muslims. For good measure, we have brought along, too, a Kosovo Albanian. Ajla is a part-time journalist from southern Kosovo, near the Macedonian border. She recently moved to Sarajevo. Her mother tongue is Macedonian. Zijo and I rather think that the less she talks to the people in Pale the better it might be for all of us. In any case, I plan to keep this visit brief. We will go to the market, talk to a few people there, then go back to Sarajevo.

Zijo has a plan. He expects the atmosphere in Pale will not be much conducive to chitchat. His proposal is that we present ourselves as journalists and doing a somewhat formal survey. That seems fair enough. After all, Ajla is a real journalist, I am a former journalist, and Zijo works part-time for a Sarajevo radio station. We have three questions: How do the people here feel about SFOR? What are the prospects for relations between Serbs and Muslims? What should be the relationship between Republika Srpska and Serbia (or rump Yugoslavia)? Of course, we will try to use these questions as a base upon which to build broader discussions.

Now, an outdoor market generally is a pretty good place to stir up conversation. Merchants usually like to talk, and lots of people come out as much to gather news and to spread gossip as they do to shop. Some folks do not like to attract a lot of attention, though, so one must be careful not to try and force people to say too much too publicly too soon. It is always a little slow getting the talk started in such situations, but Pale turns out to be a particularly tough conversational nut to crack.

The first couple people we approach are not willing to speak with us at all. Maybe that is my fault; I do not settle in very readily to this journalist-as-pollster role, and it probably shows. What's more, we are too large an entourage. Ajla does not think too much of our strategy, anyway, so she soon ditches us and goes off on her own. That helps a little. The bottom line, though, is that people here generally do not trust us, do not like us, and see no upside in speaking with us. And why should they, after all?

Our luck improves with persistence. We find that people will talk—if we prod them a little. To summarize, people here are angry. Our unscientifically selected sample of Pale's Serbs feels the world unfairly blames them for all the bloodshed and problems in Bosnia and Hercegovina. Meanwhile, they believe the world is raining charity upon the Federation's Muslims and Croats. That gets under their skin. It does nothing to assuage their anguish that Pale's Serbs live so close to Sarajevo and, in many cases, to their former homes. Sarajevo unquestionably benefits greatly from the foreign presence here.

These Bosnian Serbs are not very happy, either with Milošević's Serbia/Yugoslavia. They feel betrayed and abandoned by their fellow Serbs. Surprisingly to me, there is very little enthusiasm for merging Republika Srpska into Serbia proper and the rump Yugoslavia. Although nobody mentions it specifically, it would stand to reason that people here would be jealous, too, of those Serbs in the other, western part of Republika Srpska that essentially has Banja Luka—and not Pale—as its capital. After all, there must be more foreign aid going there than is coming here to the eastern lobe.

We speak with more than a dozen people. Among them, only a teenage boy, one middle-aged woman, and one female pensioner indicate even moderately positive feelings about the potential for ever having something like normal relations with Muslims. (The object of people's anger and apprehension here is the Muslim community. These Serbs do not seem to think much about Croats. But, then, most are from Sarajevo, and Muslims now control Sarajevo.) Most of the people with whom we speak say they are opposed to having SFOR troops in their country. The general view is that SFOR is an occupying force, and some believe the foreign troops and officials are imposing an unjust peace

There is considerable tension between the local people in Pale and the SFOR troops, reports a teenager, about 16 or 17 years old, whom we encounter on the fringe of the market. While they will not completely forget about the war, he says, young people generally will put it behind them. The young man fears, though, that many older people, and even some younger ones if they lost relatives in the wars, will never reach that stage.

A middle-aged woman, who is selling mixed goods from a stall in the market, says she intends next week to return to Sarajevo. "Both sides lost people," she emphasizes, "and both sides must forgive." There is, the woman implies, no other way. Another merchant in the stall across the way tries, not so subtly, to distract her, to keep her from speaking to us. But the woman, who is about 45 years old, continues. There are now four other families living in her house in Sarajevo, but she expects them to go elsewhere and for her residence to be returned to her. She will try to live among her neighbors. She hopes they will not call her a "*Četnik*" and make her life unhappy.

In any case, this woman says, it will not be possible for people to return to their homes and for the nations to live with one another unless SFOR stays. Down the line of stalls a bit, an older woman also observes that the SFOR presence enables people from here to visit Sarajevo. But she has mixed feelings. "Sometimes we need SFOR and sometimes we don't," she remarks.

This woman is a pensioner and she has a Muslim friend in Sarajevo who also draws a pension. The Serb pensioner admits she is angry because the friend in Sarajevo receives a bigger monthly payment. She believes this disparity exists because rich countries of the world are doing much more to help people in the Federation than they are to assist those in Republika Srpska.

As is the situation at other markets, most of the merchants here operate from simple, makeshift stalls. Around the periphery, though, are more-fixed establishments. Those operating these simple shops are a step up on the merchandising hierarchy. They lock up at the close of every trading day rather than completely to tear down and box up their places of business. We speak briefly to one of these merchants. A middle-aged man from Sarajevo's suburb of Dobrinja, he declares that he will never go back. He had lived there in an apartment owned by the enterprise for which he had worked. Were he to go back now and to ask for his apartment and job, the man assures us, the boss will just tell him: "I fuck your Serbian mother!"

We are standing half in the doorway of this small shop and encouraging (not very successfully) an older woman to speak with us. A man in his 40s comes in. SFOR, he interjects, is not welcome here, and OSCE is appreciated still less. "But there will be war again if the SFOR people go!" finally pipes up the older woman, scolding the outspoken man.

All the better, he shoots back. Then the Serbs can finish the job that they began. The situation for the Serbian nation is "terrible." There are mass graves filled with Serbs everywhere, but the international community never seems to find those! During the war, he points out, Serbs had controlled 70 percent of Bosnia and Hercegovina territory, and then the international community helped the Croats and Muslims to take much of it back. Serbs never should have agreed to a cease-fire. Serbs fought the hardest and suffered the most in both world wars, yet their reward always has been to get the short end of the stick— including this latest unjust peace. Serbs worked hard, too, to build up Sarajevo, and now they have been kicked out. "And now they want me to live with Muslims?!" This angry man has a special hatred for the OSCE. He says he is convinced that OSCE is trying to steal the election. It is no wonder that it is taking them so long to announce the results. Yes, he concludes, the OSCE, "they are the enemy."

Pale is filled with hate and drenched in disillusion. People here have many reasons—and some justification—for their gloom. The way things look to me, prospects for the future do not look good, either.

Shopping in Baščaršija

We have lunch in my neighborhood pizzeria back in Sarajevo, then I go off to meet Ramiz. I leave a somewhat frustrated Zijo to continue conversing with Ajla. She is a pretty lady, I guess, and probably quite clever. Ajla is not very traditional, though, and that seems to bother my poet friend. He just met her today for the first time. They previously had spoken by telephone. Zijo tries to get her to talk about things like love and marriage and family. A hopeless romantic, these are his favorite topics. Such subject matter does not seem to interest Ajla much, or, at least, she does not wish to discuss it with him. She cares more about her career and experiencing what the world has to offer.

•   •   •   •

Ramiz is ready to go souvenir shopping and he is taking the project very seriously. I think he has been looking forward to it all week. I plan to buy just two souvenirs: a copy of Mustafa Imamović's *Historija Bošnjaka (History of the Bošnjaks)* and a traditional copper coffee-serving set. Ramiz showed me his personal copy of the Imamović book a couple weeks ago, and I already have referred to it several times. The coffee set will remind me of my daily ritual with Ramiz and Vahida when I sipped my *jutarnji lijek*, got lessons in local culture and built my Bosno-Serbo-Croatian communication skills.

A retired professional, Ramiz always puts on a suit to go into the center of town. He is dignified but at the same time so open, polite and good-hearted that his tilt to gentility is not offensive. Ramiz is proud of Sarajevo, so, as we ride the streetcar down to Baščaršija today, he is pointing out and explaining things. What great strides in communication we have made in less than three weeks! Ramiz and I delight in speaking with each other. We have worked out how to communicate using a limited vocabulary, by watching and listening to one another very carefully, and, I guess, by reading one another's minds. This is a phenomenon that I have experienced before, but it is rare and it creates a very special closeness. Only people who are very patient, sensitive and curious can create such a linguistic bond with a foreigner.

We stop into several bookstores and get the same answer at each: The Imamović book is very popular. It sold out long ago. Imamović must have written much of his *History of the Bošnjaks* during the wars and it was released only after the siege of Sarajevo had been lifted. There was a second printing of 10,000 copies in 1998. That is not a small press run for a book in the local language of a country this size. There is a strong interest these days in *Bošnjaštvo*, which is the cultural and national identity of the Bošnjaks. *Bošnjaštvo* is a work in progress, and this history must be an important contribution. Imamović, a professor of history at the Law Faculty in Sarajevo, seems well-qualified to have authored this history. Even his name is very Bošnjak, an Arabic word with a Slavic suffix. The name suggests that his family descended from a line of Imams, which are Muslim religious leaders.

We walk slowly together, conversing in our singularly rudimentary fashion as we go. Ramiz shows his interest in all that is new even as he speaks to me of everything that is familiar. As we approach the Markale

Market, he recollects the massacre that occurred when an artillery shell landed here in May 1992. The pavement had been utterly soaked and slick in blood. We go into the Austrian-era market building and survey the meat and dairy products on offer. In contrast to the outdoor market, all is clean, well-lit and orderly. Numerous Muslim merchants from Visoko are selling their highly regarded *suho meso*. They urge us to taste their several varieties of cured meats.

In a tiny store just down the street from Gazi-Husrevbeg Mosque, we find *Historija Bošnjaka*. The shop's pleasant proprietor specializes in works on local history, culture and the like. All of us—Ramiz, the proprietor and I—are pleased with ourselves and with one another for successfully matching supply to demand and completing this important transaction. We are now on the edge of Baščaršija, or what I always am tempted to call the Muslim old town. I try especially not to use that term, though, when Ramiz is in earshot. He wants me to understand that this is everybody's old town. It does not belong just to Muslims.

One souvenir down and one to go. As we search for a coffee set, short supply will be the least of our worries. We know beforehand that our search will both begin and end in the *Kazandžiluk*, that narrow street just off the Baščaršija square where Sarajevo's coppersmiths keep shops cheek by jowl.[66] They, like their fathers and their grandfathers before them, compete to entice the limited tourist traffic.

In front of the first shop, at the very entrance to the coppersmiths' alley, there stands an old man whose sales technique emphasizes superior workmanship and discriminating taste. Dressed in a suit and tie, this master craftsman's hands are clean and mustache neatly trimmed. He speaks English—and not just a little, but excellently. No finer quality is to be found in the *Kazandžiluk*, he assures us. Prices are lower elsewhere, yes. But a fine coffee set from Sarajevo is a once-in-a-lifetime purchase. The decision should not be taken on the basis of price alone. Notice the heavy gauge of the copper and the delicate handwork in hammering out the finish on the copper tray and the pot. This brass coffee mill pulverizes the coffee beans to the consistency of fine talc, he says, as he pours the dark powder out into my hand. The cups are real, high-quality porcelain. Their brims are unblemished,

---

[66]The other basic trades also have their special streets in the Baščaršija, although not all such streets remain so strictly devoted to their traditional activities as once was the case. For example, goldsmiths are in the *Kujundžiluk* and locksmiths have their *Bravadžiluk*. Tailors and furriers traditionally have worked in the *Abadžiluk* and the *Ćurčiluk*.

smooth. Other shops will try and scrimp on the cups, as they will, too, on the tiny brass spoons.

This man is very smooth and very convincing. When I decide to move on, though, and to comparison shop, he knows that he has lost the sale. His prices are high, perhaps the highest on the street. But he generally has told the truth, and I learned from him to pay attention to the details. No other merchant we visit will have the high-quality spoons that he offers. And the other craftsmen have two styles of porcelain cups. Only when pressed will they offer the better-quality ones.

A young man runs the second shop we enter. His selection is limited, and he has no coffee grinders. The proprietor disappears down the street to get a coffee mill from another shop. As we wait, a troika of French SFOR soldiers are strolling in the street. One is a tall, attractive woman. She is, in fact, exceptionally tall and strong for someone from France (either man or woman). All three are dressed in camouflage fatigues and are lightly armed. The young coppersmiths stand in their doorways. They gawk, and, each in turn, make smiling but puzzled faces at one another after the soldiers pass them. The temptation to whistle or catcall is so strong I can feel it in the air. No one has the nerve to do so, though.

The third establishment has a functional sort of feel about it. Although it is probably an illusion, this shop feels even smaller than the others. It is crowded with inventory, both of raw materials and of finished goods. The room looks more like a workshop than a showroom. The smith's tools and partially finished work are in the back, and pictures of his family are on the wall. The quality of his work is good and the prices fair. When the proprietor steps to the door and asks some previously invisible person on the street to bring us coffee, the deal is as good as done. "We do not need to look further. You will not find better," Ramiz tells me quietly.

The coppersmith bids us find a spot to sit in the back of the shop, which we do by moving a few things about. The coffee arrives quickly, in three tiny, long-handled pots. One is never far from a coffee maker in Baščaršija. The conversation is unhurried and steady. As it turns out, Ramiz had been acquainted with the craftsman's father. In due time, the proprietor begins carefully to wrap the etched copper tray, boiler and cup holders. The porcelain cups are of the good kind. He wraps up two spare cups and tucks them into the package. After all, this is a coffee set to use, not just to look at. If a cup is broken, well, it may be some time before I can come back to Sarajevo to replace it.

• • • •

Our business successfully completed, Ramiz and I walk back to the square called Baščaršija. I suggest cold beer is in order. We take a table on the upper end of the square and I order two bottles of *Sarajevsko pivo*. Looking out across and through the pigeons around and about the fountain, I admire for the final time of this visit the Baščaršija Mosque and the Brusa Bezistan, a covered market for textiles and other luxury goods. Both had been built in the 16th century. Raising my gaze to the minarets rising above Baščaršija's low buildings, I marvel that so little damage was done to the mosques during Sarajevo's bombardment. Oh, but there was damage, Ramiz notes. But compared to the leveling of mosques in other cities, I remind him, Sarajevo's houses of prayer came through the turmoil splendidly. Our conversation falls silent. For the second time since we sat down, a boy about 10 years of age comes by and asks for a mark. Earlier in the month, I had given him one on the first occasion that I sat at a table on this square. There is something strange about the begging on Baščaršija. I rarely (if ever) see Gypsy children here, although I would expect to see them. But this preteen panhandler is always here. He seems to own the franchise for Baščaršija.

Ramiz and I walk the few paces to the Baščaršija streetcar stop. While we wait, Ramiz is gazing at a large hole which an artillery shell left in the side of a nearby building. A slight old Muslim man standing near, wearing a suit and over that a tweed sport jacket, wants to make conversation. He tells us of being forced out of Pale and leaving behind two houses, gardens, several cows and horses, and the like.

On the streetcar, Ramiz and I quietly discuss the old Muslim's story. When I make reference to the "man from Pale," several passengers turn to look at me. Those words their ears had caught. Ramiz, also sensing that we have become the center of silent but focused attention, goes on to repeat (a little louder) something to the effect that: "and then the *Četniks* took all his cows and horses and they burned his house." Somehow, I could sense that everybody around us relaxed after hearing that.

Drinking to Democracy

A small social event is planned for the evening. This is partially a sendoff for me but is justified, too, by the fact that the election results are to be announced on television. Ramiz explains to me that he (with Vahida's help, of course) is preparing a *meze*. This, as I will learn, involves several types of thinly sliced cured meats, cheese, vegetables, some cooked meat, all of which is to be consumed with moderate quantities of *šljivovica*, *rakija* and beer. In that I misunderstand just what is meant by a *meze*, I commit a *faux pas* by initially eating too heartily. This event is intended to unwind slowly over several hours' time, Ramiz patiently explains. One is supposed to drink a little, then eat a little, then chat a little, then drink a little more and so forth. This is not a meal meant to be wolfed down. Neighbors come over in time for the election-returns show. The *meze* continues at a more moderate pace.

There are no major surprises in the official election results. The outcome carries mixed good news and bad news for the international community and the friends of pluralism. The good news is that some of the non-nationalist parties, such as the Social Democrats have done reasonably well in the legislative races. Then, too, the leading Serb and Croat nationalist parties now face viable and more moderate opposition parties (or coalitions) within their own ethnonational domains.

Nikola Poplašen is the worst piece of bad news, from the international community's point of view. A veritable *Četnik* Pride poster boy, this black-bearded leader of Šešelj's SRS has defeated Biljana Plavšić to become President of Republika Srpska. The race between the SRS-SDS and Sloga coalitions was fairly close, especially if one considers that fully 13% of the total ballots cast in that race were declared invalid. Poplašen took 44% of the valid votes to Plavšić's 39%. Interestingly, a multiethnic and far-left socialist party made a reasonable showing in this race. With its ethnically neutral name, the Bosnian Party (*Bosanska stranka*) and its presidential candidate drew 15% of the valid votes.

One might have expected for Republika Srpska's absentee Muslim voters to support Plavšić, regarding her as the better of two bad choices. That does not appear to have happened, and Muslims pretty much cast their ballots straight down national lines or perhaps voted for the leftist Bosnian Party. Unlike Americans, Bosnians and Hercegovinians have not yet learned the electoral practice of holding their noses and voting for the least-poor choice. Then, too, they might truly have a hard time seeing any substantive difference between Plavšić and Poplašen.

The good news for the international community (and which just goes to show that everything is indeed relative) is that the Sloga coalition's Živko Radišić is the new Serb member of the Bosnia and

Hercegovina Presidency. That means he effectively will be president of the country for the next eight months. Radišić took 51% of the valid votes to Krajišnik's 45%.

Izetbegović will, of course, remain as the Bošnjak member of the Bosnia and Hercegovina Presidency. The SDA/Coalition candidate took 87% of the valid votes. Izetbegović's enemy, Fikret Abdić drew 6%.

Ante Jelavić, the Croat presidential candidate for Tudjman's HDZ, surprised no one by winning that slot with 53% of the vote. The party-changing incumbent, Krešimir Zubak and his moderate-nationalist New Croat Initiative drew just 11%. (In 1996, when Zubak had run on the HDZ ticket, he and the party had attracted 89% of the Croat votes.) The Social Democrat, Gradimir Gojer, made a respectable showing with 32% of the vote. That was not, though, the Jelavić-Gojer "photo finish" that some SDP people had optimistically predicted.

A high proportion of invalid ballots hint as to the difficulties that election officials faced in the Republika Srpska polling. In the voting for the Serb member of the Bosnia and Hercegovina Presidency, for example, that proportion was fully 17% of the total. In the races for the Bošnjak and Croat presidential slots (voting for which was in the Federation only), the proportions of ballots declared invalid were just 11% and less than 1%, respectively.

My *meze* companions (and the women, too, who do not participate directly in alcohol-related events) are satisfied with the election outcome. They are Muslims and naturally do not take well to the likes of a Poplašen. But then, he is in Republika Srpska; if Serbs there want to elect a *Četnik* as their president, that is their business.

Ramiz is not very positively impressed with the way the OSCE has run the elections, though. Echoing a common sentiment, he calls the organization "weak." Also not very pleased is a foreign journalist who criticizes OSCE during the televised press conference. The journalist begins his question to Robert Barry, the OSCE's Head of Mission and chief supervisor of the elections, with a critique. He virtually calls management of the electoral process scandalous. Is it not necessary, he asks, for there to be a complete change of OSCE staff in the country? Barry points out that, despite some difficulties, these elections went much better than the previous ones. High Representative Westendorp adds a general defense of OSCE.

I understand the journalist's frustration, as I once was a journalist myself. A reporter wants to provide solid information to his or her editor and readers—not the rumors and half-baked, hit-and-miss data that journalists have had little choice but to dig up and spread about over the past two weeks. The men and women in the press also are sensitive to the skepticism that excuses and delays create in the public mind. In the end, I guess my opinion on this subject tends toward the golden mean. I have read of the challenges and errors that occurred in the 1996 elections.[67] It does appear that these came off much better than did those. Still, the process has not gone well and does not reflect positively upon the OSCE and the international community.

I suppose the results of the election would have been the same in any case, and the outcome points to more of the same that exists now: political deadlock. It is difficult to imagine that those elected will do much real governing in Bosnia and Hercegovina. Mostly, the three camps of nationalist politicians will continue fighting amongst themselves. That is why Westendorp and the Office of the High Representative must remain. With no king standing over and, when necessary between, the princes and their petty quarrels, there would be no government at all in this country.

Oslobodjenje recently ran an editorial cartoon that depicts a toga-clad female figure attempting to cross a shark-filled expanse of water. She represents democracy. On the shore behind her is the shattered Bosnia and Hercegovina. A line of symbolic stepping stones lead to the distant opposite shore, where lies a free and prosperous Bosnia and Hercegovina of the future. Each stepping stone symbolizes an election and an increment of progress. Democracy has gotten over the Elections-1996 and Elections-1997 stones and now stands on Elections 1998. Looking to the faraway shore, she sees that many more stones lie between 1998 and Bosnia and Hercegovina's promising future. The sharks show no signs that they will swim away.

---

[67]See, e.g., Noel Malcom, "Observations on the Bosnian Elections (14 September 1996) and on the Post-Electoral Situation," *Bosnia Report*, Issue 17 (November 1996–January 1997).

Tito's Home

As this is the last morning that I will drink coffee with Ramiz and Vahida, I must examine how my *jutarnji lijek* is brewed. Into a pot for six small cups go four heaping scoops of the finely pulverized coffee. Vahida pours boiling water onto the powder, then sets the coffee boiler over the stove's flame for a few seconds. A rich foam rises above the rim. Pretty simple. I think I can do this at home. Now I have all the necessary equipment but not a supply of the active ingredient.

After coffee and while I eat breakfast, Ramiz goes out to run a couple shopping errands for me. He returns with two kilos of coffee and today's *Oslobodjenje*. On the front page is a photograph of the toppled minaret and smashed mosque in Ahmići that is just up the hill from Mirsada's house. Ahmići's broken and tumbled minaret is one of the few things I photographed during this visit. The scene seemed to me symbolic.

Every Place Belongs to Somebody

I say goodbye to Ramiz and Vahida and am on the road just after 10:00. It is another beautiful day. I drive through three police control points even before I get beyond Sarajevo's outskirts. Probably that is a coincidence and is not at all related to last night's announcement of election results. The reported outcome brought no important surprises, so there was no reason to expect special problems. I pass a couple organized soccer games and the occasional person looking after one cow, a few goats or a small flock of sheep grazing the hillsides. The cone-shaped haystacks are as big as they are going to get for this season. Hopefully, they are sufficient to feed the livestock through the winter. The green is fading from the small corn plots and giving way to a slowly brightening glow of golden brown.

The Bosna is clearing this week's rain out of its system, and the water is slowly recovering its customary gray-green hue. Along the road to Zenica, a chalky plume billows from the cement plant's enormous smokestack, drifts down the valley, and disperses into a spreading haze. In the dirty cloud I see not pollution but jobs. How much more polluted the Bosna valley must have been before the wars, though, when more factories were operating.

Outside of Kakanj, a crew of nine men, some clad half in army fatigues, is tidying the sparse gravel of the shoulders on either side of the road. Around the next bend there is new pavement. A line of three men dressed in bright white coveralls is strung down the middle of the fresh asphalt. They are tracing out where the center line will be painted. Farther on, a woman sits in a sunny and green hillside clearing. She stares out not toward her five colorful cows grazing calmly but away from them and into the distance. If she is lucky, perhaps the woman is merely bored. On a good day, one's thoughts do not get stuck on the past. But for many people here, I have learned, what is worse than to recollect the past is to be forced to think about the future.

South of Zenica, I turn off the northbound road along the Bosna and take that which runs west and northwest along the Lašva River through Vitez and Travnik to Donji Vakuf. I pass the Christian cemetery that is across the way from the entrance to Ahmići. The first time I was here, I drove past that entry road three times before I realized that the remains of the village lay there. No doubt, I will today drive unknowingly past many more tragic stories. As isolated incidents, these are unimportant in the full picture of world history. Only collectively do they matter to the rest of the world. Locally, though, every tragedy will be a lingering poison in these communities.

A couple of ragged, old Croat national flags hang limp in windless Vitez. I notice today something that I had not observed when I was in Vitez before. There is a great deal of building here—including new construction. A new shopping center and other shops are going up. Ordinary villages that are nameless to me line the road along much of the 15 miles between Vitez and Travnik. Here, too, I see much rebuilding in progress, although there is almost no new construction. Zijo once explained to me that every city, town or village "belongs to somebody." Here in central Bosnia, they are divided between Croats and Muslims. Those I see rebuilding here most likely are Croats, could be Bošnjaks, but are unlikely to be Serbs.

At the edge of Travnik there hangs a Federation banner. Travnik, then, must be still a predominantly Muslim town. Croats do not display Federation symbols, and I am not yet in Republika Srpska. I count six minarets poking up around and among Travnik's imposing castle. Women on the street wear the *dimije* (baggy trousers) and scarves of Muslims, and the men wear their distinctive hats. Travnik once was a minor tourist attraction. A banner over the main street announces an upcoming "cultural festival," and SFOR trucks are abundant today.

Important as a trade-route town already in medieval times, Travnik had been the seat of Bosnia's viziers after these Islamic rulers, their powers weakening, were pushed out of Sarajevo at the close of the 18th century. Since those days, Travnik has been among the most Muslim of Bosnian towns. But Travnik's history and traditions are woven from long multiethnic threads. This is the birthplace of Ivo Andrić and the setting of his *Bosnian Chronicle.*

Winding up into and through the hills west of Travnik, I am surprised that I do not remember this scenery, even though I traveled this road when I drove to Sarajevo at the beginning of this month. It was hazy then, and perhaps even foggy. The setting is splendid today; the country feels more familiar, less perilous. In spite of all the fear and hate and destruction that I have seen here, I can say that now I see a potential—albeit fragile and ever imperiled—for nonviolent resolution of conflicts and difficult issues. From a distance, from outside Bosnia and Hercegovina, I had not seen this potential. I had not come here expecting to find such hope, but I did look for it.

These are my thoughts as I enter Donji Vakuf, a place with a thoroughly Bošnjak name. A *vakuf* is a traditional, Muslim charitable endowment. Theoretically established in perpetuity, these foundations once supported educational, cultural and social-welfare institutions. *Donji* is simply a Slavic adjective meaning "lower" or "in the valley."

I am near to the loop in the IEBL known as "the egg." I can tell by their clothing that at least some of the people in Donji Vakuf clearly are Muslims. As for others—those, for example, taking advantage of the sunny day to dig potatoes in fields on the outskirts of town—I cannot judge their identities. I see no minarets. This had been a hotly contested area, both militarily and, at Dayton, diplomatically. Their position strengthened by NATO air strikes in late-summer 1995, Croat and Muslim forces had retaken Donji Vakuf from the Serbs even as the final cease-fire was negotiated that would open the way to the peace talks at Dayton. When and if war breaks out again, this is the sort of place that again will be fought over fiercely.

The main road turns north from Donji Vakuf. From now on, I will be driving up the Vrbas River valley. One of Bosnia and Hercegovina's major rivers, the Vrbas will lead me to Banja Luka and well beyond. In my travels here, it has been the exceptional case when I have not been driving along some river or another. If not, it usually is because I am going over a mountain.

I am reminded that when King Aleksandar, in 1929, got fed up with the bickering between ethnonational groups, he renamed his country, reorganized local political divisions, and gave the names of rivers to most of the new regional units. This part of the country was included in the Vrbas region; Sarajevo fell into the region named for the Drina River.

The new political unit boundaries cut across traditional political boundaries. One aim was to create conditions for unifying this place called, for the first time, Yugoslavia by denying Croats, Serbs and Muslims their own provinces. Like Aleksandar himself, his plan to cultivate Yugoslavism died violently. Tito was more successful against nationalists, but only during his lifetime.

Ruined Castles, Obliterated Culture

Jajce lies still in Federation territory, but Republika Srpska lies beyond the IEBL that loops around this city on its north, west and south. Jajce had been under Serb control during much of the armed struggle over Bosnia and Hercegovina. The town had fallen to Federation forces just a couple weeks before the final cease-fire was declared in October 1995. Today, a Croatian flag flies above Jajce's imposing castle. Refugee return and resettlement have gotten off to a rough start here. Mobs of angry Croats have sometimes been reported to block Muslims from returning to their homes in and around Jajce. Muslims have done the same thing in their cities, including in Sarajevo. Serbs do it, too, in their twin quarters of Bosnia and Hercegovina.

Jajce is historically important. It was the last capital of the medieval Bosnian Kingdom and was conquered by the Ottoman Empire in 1527. Under the Turks, Jajce's Catholic monastery was converted into a mosque and this became a loyal Muslim town. Jajce fought off the Austrian army that was occupying Bosnia and Hercegovina in 1878. The city hosted Tito's beleaguered Partisans for several months in 1943. It was the site, late in that year, at which the communist-dominated Anti-Fascist Council for the National Liberation of Yugoslavia declared itself the government of the country. There is much in that history to stick in the craw of Croat nationalists. I have read, too, that Croats and Muslims each blame one another for Jajce's fall to the Serbs in autumn 1992.

Jajce was one of Rebecca West's favorite towns when she traveled through Yugoslavia on the eve of World War II. My guidebook describes it as "a picturesque Oriental town situated amidst the wooded mountains of central Bosnia, at the confluence of the Vrbas and Pliva." Uh-huh. The scenery is beautiful everywhere around here, no doubt, but my first impression is formed in seeing a burned-out factory on the edge of town. Another factory is just up the road. It appears to be in only marginally better condition, but there is smoke rising from its smokestacks.

The turn toward Banja Luka is not well-marked in Jajce. Banja Luka is in Republika Srpska, and I suppose there is very little love lost between the folks around here and those Serbs. Be that as it may, when I pull into a gas station to ask for the road to Banja Luka the two men there are friendly enough to me. As I am backtracking through town, I pull over, too, to double-check my bearings with a couple police officers on foot patrol. They also are very polite and helpful.

Leaving Jajce, I meet four enormous SFOR tanks headed into town. This is the first time since I got to Bosnia and Hercegovina that I ever have encountered tanks on the road. The lighter and more mobile APCs are typically more abundant, and there are all sorts of military-style trucks. North of Jajce, the terrain is exceptionally rugged and there are few signs of human activity. Alongside me is the Vrbas, which is flowing so sluggishly as to seem almost stagnant. I cross a military bridge. On the other side, there are signs written in Cyrillic—a sure indication that I am now in Republika Srpska. A police checkpoint (through which I pass unhindered) provides further confirmation.

I cross another military bridge. People are fishing from it. The Vrbas now is turning into a lake that is narrow, deep, green and set into a valley that is in some spots strikingly lovely. It is carved into limestone cliffs, solid and sheer. I pull over to the side to look at the map and guidebook. This is the Vrbas Gorge. A star beside its name in the guidebook indicates that this gorge is a must-see for tourists. The book notes that this "wild, narrow canyon" is "guarded by ruined castles." One of the castles in fact is just down and across the river from me. It must have been destroyed and abandoned centuries ago. Had I not known there were to be castles hereabouts, I might not even have recognized it as a manmade structure. A sign at this lookout forbids photography.

A hydroelectric dam at the north end of the gorge explains why the water was so deep and moved so slowly. Beyond the dam, the Vrbas is much smaller. The valley broadens out and I find myself surrounded by good agricultural land. I am in a region that Serb nationalists around these parts have come to call Krajina. For historical reasons, the term Krajina implies certain Serb claims. In applying the historical term Krajina to this area, though, Serb nationalists are taking considerable liberty in redefining the word. The *Vojna krajina*, or Military Frontier, to which it refers did not extend to the territory I am driving through now. In fact, the Krajina primarily was in lands that now are in Croatia and in Serbia's formerly autonomous Vojvodina.

In spring 1991 more than a dozen of the Serb-dominated *opštinas* here in Northwest Bosnia had declared this territory the Serbian Autonomous Region of the Bosnian Krajina, with Banja Luka as its capital. The previous autumn, just across the border, Serbs in Croatia had voted to assert their autonomy from Croats and from Croatia. There, too, they had declared the Serbian Autonomous Region of Krajina (in what was truly the historical Krajina). Croats fought hard to keep these Serbian autonomous regions in Croatia and in Bosnia from becoming one.

The Serbs' referendum on autonomy was a response to the fact that Tudjman and his HDZ had won Croatia's first multi-party election and then demonstrated the danger inherent in democracy that a majority might tyrannize minorities. Tudjman quickly had made clear that Croatia would be run by its Croats and for its Croats. It seems not too surprising that Krajina Serbs declared autonomy in response to Tudjman's menacing nationalism.

As I approach Banja Luka from the south, the valley widens out. The Vrbas will continue on to the Sava, north of the Republika Srpska capital, and the topography will blend into the flat Posavina lowland. This is (or at least had been until last night) Biljana Plavšić's Republika Srpska. In return for cooperating with the US and the international community generally, her western lobe of Republika Srpska has gotten more financial and technical support. Although itself poor, parts of this western lobe are pink and healthy alongside the inflamed eastern lobe with the festering lesions that are Srebrenica, Pale and Višegrad. Unless Poplašen changes his ultranationalist tune, I fear the economic prognosis for the entire organ will not be good.

There is today in Banja Luka relatively little physical evidence of war damage. One needs to dig well below the surface to learn about what has been destroyed. In any case, the worst damage from war is not to buildings and infrastructure. It is to human beings and their society. Buildings can be repaired or, as in the case of Banja Luka, wiped without a trace from the face of the earth.

Banja Luka's apparent normalcy is veneer over a depraved reality. More than 60,000 non-Serbs were driven from their homes here between 1992 and 1995. Few have had the courage, patience or temerity to return. In May 1993, all of Banja Luka's important cultural monuments of Islam were obliterated. UNESCO had designated some of these as historical sites important enough that they be protected for all the world to appreciate. During just two nights, 17 mosques were blown up. Most Catholic churches and monasteries also were destroyed. About one-half of today's approximately 300,000 Serb residents are displaced persons or refugees.

Driving Banja Luka's main street through town, one gets the impression of a peaceful and normal but not wealthy European city. ("And after that," the words of the Muslim businessman in Brčko remind me, "they say to the foreigners—because you don't know the situation—that this is a purely Serbian town.") I do not stop, as I want still to reach Tito's birthplace, Kumrovec, in daylight. I see a bit of new road construction on the edge of the Republika Srpska capital. Some luxurious houses are going up on the outskirts. A continuous string of villages stretches all the way to the border. A temporary military bridge has been stretched across the Sava. The original bridge, like most other bridges across the Sava, was destroyed.

Neither Brotherhood nor Unity

Across the river is the portion of Croatia known as Western Slavonia or Croatian Posavina. Prior to May 1995, the ethnic-Serb population and occupiers here knew it as a part of the so-called Republic of Serb Krajina. It also lay within a United Nations Protected Area named Sector West. This Serb-held and ostensibly UN-protected area was strategically important. At that time there was still a bridge across the Sava into northern Bosnia.

I stop for gas in Novi Varoš, the second town on the Croatian side. It is badly damaged and appears still to be mostly depopulated. The people in the gas station are not very friendly, but somehow that does not surprise me. A couple miles north of Novi Varoš is the major highway that runs from Zagreb, the length of Slavonia, into Vojvodina and on to Belgrade. It formerly was named the Brotherhood and Unity Highway. Early in the war in Croatia, Serb forces had held territory on both sides of the highway. They had closed down the Brotherhood and Unity in 1991, but agreed early in 1995 to reopen it.

On 1 May 1995, and in spite of a cease-fire agreement, Croatian forces launched Operation Flash (*Bljesak*), a surprise attack that cleared out most of the Serbs in the area. *Bljesak* was a dress rehearsal for Operation Storm (*Oluja*), which was to follow in August and to drive most remaining Serbs from Krajina. *Bljesak* sent Serbs fleeing by the thousands into northern Bosnia and Hercegovina. Novi Varoš was in the spout of a funnel that opened onto the Sava bridge. Accounts differ as to what happened, but the operation was certainly vicious. During the first days of May 1995 tiny Novi Varoš had been crowded with cars, tractors people and their belongings. This human train was under fire from Croat forces.

In a few minutes I am headed toward Zagreb on the former Brotherhood and Unity. This highway passes through some of the flattest and best farmland in all of Croatia. Few settlements are visible from the road. To look about, one would never know this had been a war zone.

Disappointed but Not Surprised

Tito must have enjoyed driving to Kumrovec, the village in which he was born. Kumrovec is 10 or 12 miles off the Zagreb-Maribor highway, just on the Croatian side of the border with Slovenia. It lies among some of the most gorgeous countryside one ever could wish to see. I am arriving in the early evening. The road to Kumrovec traverses hills and forests, passing quaint villages, tiny fields, neat orchards and steep vineyards. It is a scene of corn drying in shocks, hay piled high in bushy pillars, chickens and geese in meandering flocks. A few cattle graze the patches of still verdant meadow, but vacation homes tucked in here and there suggest that recreation vies with farming as an economic activity. From within and around Kumrovec, one catches sight of several isolated hilltop churches. It is distinctive that there are so many of these churches—mounted like trophies or idols on their natural pedestals—concentrated in such a small area. This is not very practical in the sense of making places of worship readily accessible, but these are very effective everyday reminders of the local religious identity.

Kumrovec remains small. The open-air museum-village that centers on Tito's boyhood home still is the main attraction. The buildings and grounds are well-maintained, there is no admission charge, and, even at this late hour and season, several families and groups are strolling through.

I go first, naturally, to the preserved home of Franjo and Marija Broz, whose seventh of 15 children would make such a name for himself as the father of communist Yugoslavia. Tito was a Croatian (on his father's side). He generally made reference to that only when it was expedient to do so. He also could point to his mother's Slovenian heritage when that better suited his purposes. Tito preferred, though, to be seen as a Yugoslav. His wish, in fact, was that all of his countrymen would regard themselves first and foremost as Yugoslavs. Sometimes, people joke that Tito was the only Yugoslav and that Yugoslavism died when he did (in 1980). These days, Yugoslavism is not well regarded—at least not openly so—in Croatia. But neither is Tudjman's extreme brand of Croatian nationalism held in high esteem by all. At least privately, some disagree.

The Croatian flag hangs limp in the still evening air in front of the house in which Tito was born on 7 May 1892. He would not be pleased to see the *šahovnica* on a flag outside his front window. The house is small for such a large family. There appear to be just five rooms and a loft. In the entry room, there is a photograph of Tito showing the house to Richard Nixon in 1970. "*Živio Franjo Tudjman* (Long live Franjo Tudjman!)," reads one note in the guest book. "*Ali ne dugo* (But not too long)," another visitor has written below.

Well-preserved and with buildings exhibiting traditional trades and village community activities, this is one of the finer open-air museums I have seen in Europe. Kumrovec's museum does much more than just to honor Tito's memory. It celebrates the Zagorje region in which it is located and emphasizes the importance of preserving cultural heritage. An exhibit in one building is devoted to promoting 13 other ethnographic museums and makes an appeal for creating additional museums in order to preserve the heritage of abandoned villages.

An exhibit text laments the loss of villages: "The problem of the decline and disappearance of villages in Lika, accompanied by a loss of material culture, can be traced through the unfolding of historical events, particularly over the past 70 years." That is putting it pretty diplomatically. In this decade, Serbs and Croats have been driving one another out of their villages, then pillaging and burning one another's villages. In spite of the irony left unsaid, I certainly take the point: the loss of cultural heritage is tragic.

Tito was a brutal dictator, and so one should not romanticize him blindly. Nevertheless, I ponder what he would be thinking were he to look down upon his former Yugoslavia from some Marxist-Leninist Paradise. He certainly feared the sort of violence and disintegration that followed his death. The system of ethnonational checks and balances that was part of his legacy was intended to prevent from happening exactly what has occurred. He had hoped there would be no Tudjmans, no Miloševićes, no Izetbegovićes, no Jelavićes, no Poplašens, no Šešeljs. Tito is disappointed, but I think he is not surprised.

Turning out Extremists

Maribor to Graz to Vienna and Brno... I speed through the darkness and the old Austro-Hungarian Empire. Five countries in one day. Were I to take the route through Bratislava, it would be six. When this decade had begun, the six countries were three. At the beginning of this century, all had been within a single empire.

I am waiting in line for my final border crossing when I pick up a radio station reporting the preliminary outcome of parliamentary elections this weekend in Slovakia. Vladimir Mečiar, the nationalist prime minister and a man of despotic and antidemocratic tendencies, is seeing his ruling party lose by a narrow margin to an opposition coalition. That is in spite of the fact that Mečiar and his party used the government-controlled media to dominate the election campaigns.

Mečiar falls somewhere between Slovenia's Kučan and Croatia's Tudjman on the scale of nationalist radicalism. Under Mečiar and his Movement for a Democratic Slovakia (HDZS) Slovakia has fallen into international disrepute and become estranged from the circle of democratic countries. Mečiar has pledged to stand by the election outcome.

Slovak voters, it seems, may finally have had enough of Mečiar. Having succeeded in taking Slovakia out of Czechoslovakia, perhaps the time for Mečiar and his HZDS has passed. That thought gives me hope for Bosnia and Hercegovina and helps my trip to end on a positive note. Perhaps there, too, a time will come to de-emphasize nationalism.

Still, Czechoslovakia was less complicated than was Yugoslavia. It will take the South Slavs longer to turn out the extremists. That Czechoslovakia came apart without violence while Yugoslavia did not has to do with differences in emotional disposition between the West and South Slavic cultures. Czechs and Slovaks are much less bellicose by temperament than are Croats and Serbs. Common Slovaks and Czechs let their politicians do the fighting over questions of nation and state, but they do not allow themselves to be drawn too deeply, energetically or actively into such issues.

Serbs especially, Croats as well, and Muslims by their fate of being mixed among and caught in between the other two, have not been able to stand aside from the troubles that their contemptible leaders create for them.

Part Two:

Bosnia and Hercegovina Revisited

Good Timing, Perhaps

It is March 1999. Five months have passed since the day I drove home to Brno from Sarajevo. Winter has come and soon will be gone. Little information has been available about goings-on in Bosnia and Hercegovina since the elections. The daily newspapers have turned their attention to a budding crisis over Kosovo. Even the Internet seems to have had little to offer. The best way to find out what is really going on will be to jump in my car and run down there.

Poplašen Fired, Brčko Decided

On Friday 5 March, I am driving from Brno to Vienna and thinking about next week's trip to Bosnia and Hercegovina. To my surprise, I hear on the radio two news stories out of that country. Rare has been the day recently that there is even one news item from there. Today began with Carlos Westendorp announcing that he had removed Nikola Poplašen as President of Republika Srpska. Poplašen, the High Representative charged, has been obstructing Dayton implementation. Poplašen has been unable to form an acceptable government. Since the election, Milorad Dodik has stayed on as acting prime minister. Westendorp has wanted Dodik to be reappointed, but the Radical Poplašen only has put forward candidates that cannot win approval in the relatively more moderate Republika Srpska National Assembly.[68]

A problem for Krajišnik and Poplašen is that their SDS-SRS coalition came through the September election with just 30 seats in the 83-seat Republika Srpska National Assembly that must approve Poplašen's nominee for prime minister. Plavšić, Radišić and Dodik's Sloga coalition, meanwhile, took 28 seats and picked up support against SDS-SRS from Assembly members in the SDA-led Coalition and SDP. Altogether, that gives Sloga and the antiradicals a 45-vote majority.

A few hours after Poplašen was asked to clear out his desk, the international arbitrator on the Brčko question at long last announced his decision. The arbitrator declared that the disputed and pivotal city—until now under Serb control—shall be jointly administered by Serbs,

---

[68]Poplašen even brought his political godfather, Šešelj, from Belgrade to Banja Luka in an effort to whip up support for one prime ministerial candidate, Dragan Kalinić, president of SDS. In short order, though, Westendorp expelled the inflammatory Šešelj from the country.

Muslims and Croats. Brčko, the arbitrator ruled, is to become a neutral and self-governing district in which former residents of all groups will be able to live. International supervision will continue, and neither the Croat-Muslim Federation nor Republika Srpska will control that Sava River port city.

British, German, UN, NATO and US diplomats quickly praise and support the decision on Brčko. Not surprisingly, the arbitrator's ruling does not go over well with Bosnian Serb leaders and Serb nationalists. A dramatic day in Bosnia and Hercegovina is just beginning. The country is back in the news, although not much of that news will show up in the US press. One needs to be in Europe or, most especially, on the Internet in order to follow developments.

In Banja Luka, Dodik says he will resign as acting prime minister over the Brčko ruling. Reportedly, other members of Dodik's caretaker government will follow him out the door. Poplašen immediately states that he will not step down from his position, calling Westendorp's attempt to sack him "illegitimate and undemocratic." Republika Srpska Vice-President, Mirko Sarović, also a hard-liner, refuses to take over as president. Before the day is over, outside a restaurant in northeastern Bosnia, an American SFOR soldier has shot in self-defense and killed a local deputy chairman of the Serb Radical Party. That killing occurs after the SRS official and some of his buddies attack several SFOR soldiers. In Brčko, stepped up SFOR patrols are noted but no incidents are reported there.

Later, Živko Radišić, who currently chairs the rotating, collective Bosnia and Hercegovina Presidency, says he will suspend his participation in the Presidency because of the Brčko decision. Radišić's Socialists also run the Republika Srpska Assembly in the person of Speaker Petar Djokić. On Sunday, in an emergency session called by Djokić, the Bosnian Serb parliament votes to withdraw all Bosnian Serb representatives from the central governing bodies. Early in the new week, Bosnian Serb leaders stage several public rallies to protest the Friday announcements.

These developments come at a time when peace talks appear to be breaking down between Yugoslav/Serbian officials, Kosovo's ethnic-Albanian leaders, and representatives of the international community. An agreement has been drafted in the negotiations taking place at Rambouillet castle in France, but irreconcilable differences remain between the Serbs and ethnic Albanians. The US and NATO are threatening to bomb Serbia if the Kosovars sign the agreement but

Milošević refuses to do so. For his part, meanwhile, Milošević has stepped up military operations in Kosovo. This is characterized as police action against terrorists, but it is beginning to look more like ethnic cleansing.

Kosovo-related matters should have little or nothing directly to do with Bosnia and Hercegovina, of course, but all politics are regional in the former Yugoslavia. Then, too, there always seem to be outsiders adding fuel to the fire. Lord David Owen, the United Kingdom's former Balkans mediator, is suggesting publicly that perhaps Belgrade could receive some Republika Srpska territory in return for giving up some land in Kosovo. It is rather irresponsible to be promoting such a scheme, in my view. I guess nobody told his lordship about an agreement that was made in Dayton, Ohio in November 1995 and which assures Bosnia and Hercegovina's integrity within its recognized borders.

Slight Change of Plan

My intent has been to go into northern Bosnia this time via Banja Luka and Republika Srpska. After speaking with Zijo by telephone on Saturday night, I decide that might not be the best idea. Since the previous day's announcements on Brčko and Poplašen, and the SFOR killing of a Serb politician, he says there have been a lot of stories swirling about the country with reference to retribution against Americans and the international organizations. Although it will take an extra day to do so, I decide to drive south through Croatia, as I did in September, and to come in from the west. That route will take me through just a little bit of Republika Srpska around "the egg." I will drive into Sarajevo, avoiding Banja Luka until I get a better feel for the situation there.

Tuesday morning, I call in to the US Consulate in Sarajevo to check on the political travel conditions. I will leave tomorrow. The State Department's latest warning is for Americans to stay away from Republika Srpska altogether. The woman at the Consulate says, though, that there have been no reports of aggressive Serb political activity in the sparsely populated area of Republika Srpska that I will pass through. It is the other, eastern lobe of Republika Srpska that is most dangerous, although there was a large, but not physically violent, demonstration the other day in the western-lobe city of Doboj.

As when I was there during the September elections, I seem to have selected (albeit this time wholly unintentionally) a rather interesting time to be in Bosnia and Hercegovina.

Spring Drive

When traveling, I see and experience the world from the viewpoint of the Wisconsin farmboy that I am at heart. In springtime, that perspective is particularly oriented on the sense of smell. Now, in mid-March, the olfactory essence of little Slovenia's countryside is everywhere that of freshly spread manure. The farmers are cleaning their barns after the winter, and they are moving to the fields the piles that have been heaping up behind the barns through the cold and dark months. In Croatia's Lika region and in Bosnia, by contrast, the dominant odor is that of burning brush and grass. People there are clearing scrub growth on some plots that have not been cultivated for several years. Elsewhere, residents are burning areas of pastureland and the vegetative refuse from last year's gardens and corn crops. To burn the previous season's crop residue seems to me an antiquated practice. This may be necessary, though, if a small farmer does not have modern equipment properly to till that material into the soil.

Both the odors of freshly spread manure and of spring bonfires are pleasant to me, but my nose recognizes the first of these scents as a signal of relatively greater prosperity. In Slovenia's valleys and least-steep hillsides, there is a livestock agriculture that is centered in the farmstead. Many of the steeper hillsides are covered with vineyards. The farmers are already working the fields with their tractors. Some of these tractors are tiny—just one small step up from walk-behind models—but they are tractors and not horses.

In Lika and in those parts of northwestern Bosnia through which I am driving, the agriculture is not so prosperous. Many of these peasant farmers have neither tractors nor horses. The land is either very hilly or is more gently rolling but at rather high altitude. In some of the highland areas, there was very little settlement even before the recent wars, and what farmsteads and villages are there now mostly stand empty and neglected. Abandoned farms emanate no scents of springtime, only a gloomy olfactory silence.

Emil and Almir Face Mecca

I overnighted again in Croatia's Plitvice Lakes area. In contrast to last September's trip into Sarajevo, there is no fog today. My mood is excellent, and it matches the weather. In the area of the park and along the way to the border crossing at Petrovo Selo, a great deal of construction and reconstruction is underway. Before war smashed

Plitvica's tourism, many of these houses must have been bed-and-breakfasts. Their owners will be taking in summer guests again some day. Plitvica's waterfalls and Dalmatia's beaches are not going to disappear, after all, and other opportunities to earn a livelihood here always will be few. Nearer term, diplomatic and military rumblings do not bode well for the 1999 tourist season anywhere in the Balkans.

I stop to buy two large Lika cheeses from one of the many women selling it along the main road that comes from Karlovac and passes the state park on its way to Split. Once I turn from that road to the one leading to Bosnia, there are no women selling cheese. Tourists continue southward from Plitvica to the coast; they do not go east to Bosnia.

At a Bosnian village named Velagići, I stop to photograph a new cemetery. Just off the road, several dozen fresh graves have been laid out in orderly rows. Each of the Muslim burial plots has an identical, simple, wooden marker. Painted green, the markers state names and dates of birth and death. All died in 1992, but they were not buried here in that year. Only recently have they been laid to rest in this place, facing east, toward Mecca. The graveyard's soil is still fresh, dark and uncompacted, like a freshly planted potato field. The earth is formed into ingot-shaped mounds for each grave, as is customary here.

Across the road, in what I guess to be a collective farm, men are working on a construction project. Most of the houses here are being rebuilt. A few stand empty and seemingly ignored. Several children scamper by. They must be the afternoon shift in the local school. They do not dawdle as would children on their way home after spending the morning in class. As I drive away, I am thinking about Emil and Almir Delić. Their remains lay side by side in one corner of Velagići's new cemetery. Both were born in 1974 and died at 18 years of age. If they were brothers, they must have been twins.[69]

---

[69] There is a story behind every destroyed village. Some of these are recorded in investigative documents that have been submitted to the International War Crimes Tribunal. Velagići, as I will learn after further research, is one such case. According to documents prepared by the US State Department and based upon eyewitness reports, Velagići was among a dozen or more villages near Ključ that had come under Serb nationalists' mortar fire in May 1992. Velagići's population had been about 75% Muslim, 24% Serb, and 1% Croat. It was perhaps the wealthiest in Ključ *opština* because many of the men worked in Germany during the summer. In fact, many men were out of the country when shelling and the village's systematic destruction began on 27 May.

When two Federation policemen wave me over on the eastern outskirts of Ključ, I am not nervous in the least. In fact, I rather enjoy the opportunity to practice my Bosno-Serbo-Croatian. A couple kilometers down the road, a sign welcomes me to Republika Srpska. A little farther, and there are two Republika Srpska policemen. They are easily recognizable as such because they have older model cars, painted a dark blue that approximately matches the color of the Republika Srpska flag. Federation police, by contrast, always have new cars that are painted white and green. These two officers already are occupied with a couple of other motorists, so they do not beckon me to stop and chat.

Better with Pear Brandy

It is just 4 p.m. when I reach Sarajevo and cross the highway overpass at the lower end of the valley and which separates Sarajevo proper from its Ilidža suburb. It is that time of day when the sun is low in the sky and the light is perfect, when colors glow at their brightest and everything with the slightest essence of beauty appears most

---

As the shelling started, local Serb radio broadcast a demand that the Muslim citizens of Velagići surrender all arms and property unconditionally to Serb forces. Most of the women and children managed to escape on foot that evening and they hid in a nearby village. A total of 13 people were killed during this attack. Although the bombardment lasted only a couple days, local Serbs continued to torment the remaining Muslim inhabitants with a campaign of random killing, looting, rape, and destroying houses.

In August, the Ključ *opština* government took a census of the area and announced over the radio that those who wanted to leave could do so, but only if they agreed to relinquish all claims to their property. Ključ *opština* officials prepared property abandonment forms and the Muslims were required to sign them. In addition, Muslims were required to purchase certificates, costing 50 deutschemarks each, permitting them to leave the area and to pay for their transportation. On September 11, a convoy of about eight buses and 12 large trucks formed in front of the school in Ključ. All Muslims who had paid and had the proper documentation were transported to Mount Vlašić and Travnik. Velagići was renamed Ravna Gora by local Serbian authorities.

This particular evidence was collected to prove "Mass Forcible Expulsion" and "Deportation of Civilians," which are breaches of the Fourth Geneva Convention. See United States Department of State, *Supplemental United States Submission of Information to The United Nations Security Council in Accordance with Paragraph 5 of Resolution 771 (1992) and Paragraph 1 of Resolution 780 (1992), 8th submission,* 16 June 1993.

beautifully. "Disneyland," the brightly colored but bombed-out and never-occupied home for pensioners stands out brightly against its gray-white backdrop that is the wreckage of the Oslobodjenje building. The diffuse light reflects kindly from red tile roofs and gaily painted high-rise buildings, emphasizing their colors while toning down their wounds and scars.

Ramiz and Vahida and I all are happy to see one another. Only the kiss is cumbersome: I am going for the cheeks, but Ramiz is aiming for the lips. We compromise in the end with a bit of each. Five months away—three of which were spent in German language study—have wreaked havoc on my proficiency in the language that I call Bosnian out of politeness. Ramiz tells me that Zijo was here earlier in the afternoon to see if I had arrived yet.

A *meze* is soon spread. Pear brandy, Ramiz asks, or plum brandy? I go for the pear, to be different. That is "*die Birne*" in German, Ramiz remarks. He is happy that I now know some German. It is not that we can communicate any better in that language than we can in Bosno-Serbo-Croatian, but it adds a new element to our linguistic mosaic. The brandy glides down smoothly, albeit in small swallows. By the time we are into our second or third glass, my language abilities are beginning to revive.

Zijo arrives. He is troubled. The situation in this country is worse than when I was here last, he insists, and it is deteriorating all the time. As to the privatization program in the Federation (which has not really gone forward yet), Zijo declares, people do not even want to hear about it. When all is said and done, he contends, 20 families will end up owning everything. In reality, Zijo says, the economic situation is not so much improved as is indicated by government statistics and by those who would interpret those figures for the general public. As for the political situation, well, that is obvious from developments in recent days. I will be surprised by what I find here on this visit, my interpreter assures me.

Zijo has just come from an SDP meeting. That, I guess, is why he is stirred up. Ramiz suggests he have a little drink. I agree that is a good idea.

Catching up and a Visit to Oslobodjenje

Croats Want Their Own Space

A "third entity" is all the talk these days among Croats in Bosnia and Hercegovina. Croat ultranationalists are not about to let go of Herceg-Bosna, their concept for a Croat ministate that presumably would have Mostar as its capital. Since the autumn elections, they have been agitating more openly and loudly than before about creating their third entity. The Brčko and Poplašen decisions, by stirring up the Serbs, have unsettled the political situation more generally. Croat ultranationalists will try to turn that to their advantage. They thrive on disorder.

The US and international community already have told the Croat nationalists to drop the third-entity idea and have called upon Croat political leaders to speak out against it. Dayton, they say, allows for just two entities in Bosnia and Hercegovina: the Croat-Muslim Federation and Republika Srpska. Even both of those are supposed to be multiethnic.

Using Brčko to Justify Herceg-Bosna

Croat politicians are seizing upon the Brčko ruling to bolster their case. Ivo Andrić Lužanski, the Croat president of the Muslim-Croat Federation and a HDZ leader, had laid the groundwork several weeks ago.[70] Lužanski had testified before the Brčko arbitrator in Vienna that he personally, along with the Croat people of Bosnia and Hercegovina, objected to the idea of creating a special district for Brčko. To do so, he had told the arbitrator, would be to establish a third entity in Bosnia and Hercegovina, which would be in violation of Dayton. The official Federation position in Vienna, however, had been that it (and not Republika Srpska) should get Brčko, but that the next best alternative would be to create a special district.

Croat nationalists now argue that if there can be a Brčko District of Bosnia and Hercegovina, then why not a Herceg-Bosna? After all, is not the Brčko District a new entity? The reasoning is pretty lame, but, then,

---

[70]The Federation President was not elected by direct vote in the September general election. The Federation House of Representatives fills that position by appointment.

stretching logic to the breaking point and beyond is as much a part of local politics as are intimidation tactics, duplicity and brinkmanship.

Croats' Interests Divided

Bosnia and Hercegovina's Croat population can be roughly categorized in two groups according to geography and politics. First are those concentrated in western Hercegovina and from there north into southwestern Bosnia. Croat ultranationalism is strongest in that region. Second are Croats in central and northern Bosnia. The latter are concentrated in their own communities (like Kiseljak and Jajce), perhaps, but otherwise are mixed with Muslim communities. The ultranationalists will have a tough time convincing their politically moderate brethren in the ethnically mixed areas to abandon their homes and move into a consolidated Croat ministate.

Any strong push to formalize Herceg-Bosna in central Bosnia, where many Bošnjaks live, likely would lead to war. It is not pleasant to contemplate thoughts of renewed Muslim-Croat warfare in the Lašva valley.

A third entity is impossible, as without Croats there would be no Bosnia and Hercegovina. So concluded yesterday a group of international agency representatives conferring in Mostar. The international community does not intend to threaten the national and cultural identity of Croats, a spokesperson stated. The Croat nation has the same rights as do Bošnjaks and Serbs, he assured, and their rights must also be protected. Meanwhile, Ante Jelavić, the Croat member of the Bosnia and Hercegovina Presidency has had a meeting with Robert Gelbard, the American special envoy to the Balkans. It is reported that Jelavić told Gelbard that Croats within Bosnia and Hercegovina see their future within a "united, democratic, independent and decentralized Bosnia and Hercegovina."[71]

So, is everybody in agreement? Hardly. I am reminded of the words from the Serb refugee that I met in Brčko's market last fall. Jelavić and other Croat nationalists, to use her words, "speak very sweetly, as if honey were flowing from their mouths...but they are thinking something different from what they are saying." She had been speaking of Muslims, of course, but the same is true of Croat and Serb leaders. The statement coming out of Jelavić's office apparently says nothing concrete one way or the other about a third entity.

---

[71] I am quoting here from the newspaper article and not directly from Jelavić.

While HDZ aims to exploit ambiguity and turmoil arising from the Brčko decision, and as Serb nationalists make threatening noises and stir up the *populus*, the SDP aims to gain by supporting the arbitrator's ruling. The Social Democrats have stated their full support for the decision and pledge their cooperation and assistance to Robert Farrand, a retired US diplomat who is international supervisor for the Brčko District. In Brčko, an SDP official stated yesterday, the groups can create a model of cooperation for building a future, unified Bosnia and Hercegovina. I am reminded that, in 1995, there had been a vision that Sarajevo would be such a model.

It has become difficult for me as an outsider to see in any actions by Bosnian and Hercegovinian Croat leaders anything other than variations on a theme of undermining and obstructing progress in the Federation and in Bosnia and Hercegovina. That puts them in the same category as the Bosnian Serb leaders. Bosnian Croat nationalists are as hell-bent upon building their Herceg-Bosna as are their Serb counterparts upon maintaining an ethnically pure Republika Srpska. Both objectives depend upon killing off Dayton-born Bosnia and Hercegovina in its prolonged infancy. Even if the Bošnjak leaders were capable and incorruptible—which they continually demonstrate themselves not to be—they would have difficulty finding Croat and Serb counterparts with whom to cooperate in building Bosnia and Hercegovina.

An example of Croat duplicity in action is going on today in the coastal city of Neum. This is an economic conference organized by the Croatian Community of Herceg-Bosna. Founded in May 1997, this organization has represented itself since its founding to be a nonpolitical organization. In fact, of course, the Croatian Community of Herceg-Bosna is run by the HDZ and is wholly political. While HDZ does all that it can to keep the Federation and Bosnia and Hercegovina from functioning properly, through such organizations as the Croatian Community and HVO, it aims to construct its own ministate within a state.

The Croatian Community of Herceg-Bosna is headed by Vladimir Šoljić, a Tudjman underling and former Federation President and defense minister. Currently Vice-President of the Federation, he is a signatory to the "Agreement on Special Relations between the Federation of Bosnia and Hercegovina and the Republic of Croatia," about which I will have more to say momentarily. Other prominent

HDZ leaders also attending and addressing the conference include Lužanski, the Federation President.

The Neum conference's stated purpose is to address the problem of slow economic improvement in central Bosnia. The conference is sure to conclude that closer cooperation with Croatia will be the key to economic growth in Herceg-Bosna.

Neum is an appropriate setting for such a conference. It is itself the center of a controversy that has Bošnjaks and the Federation on one side and Croats and Croatia on the other. Croatia has had the Bošnjaks between a rock and a hard place on the issue of Neum.

Powerful Bargaining Chip: Sea Access

Here is the situation: Bosnia and Hercegovina possesses a mere 12 miles of Adriatic coastline, in the middle of which lies Neum. The land both up and down the coast from this strip of shoreline belongs to Croatia. Neum has minor value as a tourist resort, but it is not suitable as a port. The nearest harbor is some 20 miles up the coast at the Croatian city of Ploče. Ploče lies in the estuary of Hercegovina's Neretva River, along which runs the rail line from the country's interior to the Adriatic port. Bosnia and Hercegovina badly needs that access to the sea.

In November 1998, an agreement was reached that allows Croatian highway traffic to pass uninterruptedly through the Neum strip. That is important for Croatia's tourism. The deal also permits Bosnia and Hercegovina access via Croatian territory to the port at Ploče. That seems simple enough, but Tudjman and HDZ wanted more. And they were in strong position to get it. What the Croats wanted they got—provisionally, at least, and also in November 1998—in the form of the "Agreement on Special Relations between the Federation of Bosnia and Hercegovina and the Republic of Croatia."

Bošnjak leaders would have preferred a Neum-Ploče deal without an Agreement on Special Relations. Their fear—not entirely unwarranted—is that such a deal will open channels for Croatia to meddle in Bosnia and Hercegovina's internal affairs and to undermine her sovereignty. Tudjman reminded the Bošnjaks, though, that, in establishing the Muslim-Croat Federation in 1994 under terms of the Washington Agreement, Muslims and Croats had pledged to establish a special relationship between Croatia and the Federation. It was generally assumed that this would be some sort of confederation and would include economic and cultural cooperation as well as military coordination. Tudjman was adamant: until there was an Agreement on Special Relations there would be no Neum-Ploče deal.

Izetbegović, in his role as a member of the Bosnia and Hercegovina Presidency was not a signatory to the November 1998 Agreement on Special Relations. But Izetbegović does head the SDA, and SDA is the power that matters in regard to all political matters of interest to Bošnjaks. His public statements at the time of the November signing suggested no more than lukewarm support. Up to now, the Agreement has yet to be ratified by the Federation parliament. When and if it clears parliament, the Agreement calls for a Council of Cooperation still to work out actual details of the cooperation. This has the look of a deal that is continuing to go nowhere fast.

Big Talk, Weak Will, Little Action

There is another conference also going on this weekend in Neum. This one concerns returning refugees to their homes. It is a joint production of the Federation's Ministry of Social Policy and of UNHCR. There is a plan to return approximately 150,000 people to their homes within the Federation during 1999. With nearly 850,000 people displaced within the country and another 350,000 still refugees abroad, the target of 150,000 returns is not ambitious. If past experience is any guide, though, even this target will not be achieved.

Oftentimes in this country, plans are made and agreements are signed in full knowledge and expectation that the stated ends will not be reached. The Bošnjak side might agree to something, for example, realizing that actions on the Croat side or a Serb refusal to agree or to cooperate at all will render the plan or agreement moot. Nevertheless, such schemes' hopeful beginnings show the international representatives what they want to see and give them something positive to report to the folks back home. If it all peters out in the end and does not amount to much, that fact is not publicized. I do not know if this latest resettlement plan is for show or if it will prove to be for real. In any case, judging by the noises coming from the Croat nationalists and Republika Srpska these days, to achieve the stated goal will be difficult.

For example, an SFOR official recently stated that plans to return 2,000 refugees to each of three major cities—Sarajevo, Banja Luka and Mostar—have been slowed this year because of tensions in Republika Srpska. Those three cities, respectively, are controlled by Bošnjak, Serb and Croat powers. The official also pointed out that, while some 120 Serbs have been returned to a Mostar suburb, very few have been returned to Drvar, a Bosnian city that once was populated almost wholly by Serbs and which now is virtually pure Croat.

Visiting Oslobodjenje

The atmosphere in Oslobodjenje's downtown office has the look and feel of a university newspaper. It is crowded, informal, smoky and hectic. When I arrive, a couple of staff members sit smoking below a No Smoking sign in the reception area. People and work from adjoining rooms spill out into this space, which serves also as a sort of break room. Myself a former newspaper reporter and accustomed to working in makeshift conditions, I quite appreciate this environment. Once upon a time, of course, the staff of *Oslobodjenje* had occupied the large and modern office building that stands in ruins at the lower end of Sarajevo's valley. Now, they make do with this much smaller space and continue to put out the country's most respectable daily newspaper.

I meet here Emir Salihović, a journalist on the international news desk. A man still young but approaching middle age, Salihović grew up in Sarajevo and spent the war in Belgrade. He came back to Sarajevo in 1997. Whether we speak of the past, present or future, Salihović demonstrates that he has thought both deeply and broadly about his country and his people. I explain to him my intent to visit several cities across the country and that I would like in each to meet *Oslobodjenje* journalists. Zijo, meanwhile, is off somewhere else in the office getting contact information for those other meetings.

We speak a bit about ethnicity. Salihović, who has a Muslim name, says he would term his ethnicity "white Caucasian of Slavic origin." By country of citizenship, Salihović says he would prefer to be called *Bosanac*, meaning Bosnian. Muslim political leaders have decreed, though, that he must call himself by the term "Bošnjak," in order to distinguish himself from Bosnian Serbs and Bosnian Croats.

In his student days, Salihović had studied cultural anthropology and, more specifically, the ethnogenesis of the South Slavs. Yugoslavia, meaning "land of the South Slavs," was a good name for the country, he says, because the research he was involved in found that the origins of all these South Slavs were basically the same. The differences between the various groups he had found to be "regional instead of essential." In short, then, there is something quite artificial in Bosnia and Hercegovina's South Slavs picking ethnonational sides and then fighting amongst themselves.

When they isolate themselves from one another, Salihović remarks, nations and individuals may delude themselves into believing that their own ways of life are superior to all others. In such states of naivete, they are more easily pulled in one direction or another by extreme views that are persuasively promoted. Within the social circles he moves in, at least, Salihović says he was surprised when he returned from Belgrade to hear how little the people in Sarajevo speak of hate and think in nationalistic terms. If he were to criticize his countrymen, it would be that people are too passive, that they do not look hard enough for ways to improve the existing situation.

Zijo's More Upbeat Side

Zijo has invited me to his house for coffee. Along the way, we drive past the twin-towered UNIS skyscraper. I am surprised to see that the chump boxers Momo and Uzeir have been transformed since autumn. The windows forming their shining blue-glass hides have been replaced. This is a major improvement in the Sarajevo skyline. The tower of the nearby Parliament Building looks as bad as ever, though, and I suppose incrementally worse with the passage of time. It would be too controversial to repair the Parliament Building just now, Zijo explains. The public view is that there are other, higher priorities.

The road leading to Zijo's neighborhood is mostly paved but in a poor state. Just up from the valley floor, it passes a small and crowded Orthodox cemetery, then takes a sharp right turn and climbs steeply upward but across the valley wall. Instead of switching back 180 degrees to climb farther, the road then turns 90 degrees and straight into the hill. The final couple hundred feet or so, the car scrambles up a slope that seems pretty much straight up.

Zijo and his parents live in a typical clay-block house built into a hillside on Sarajevo's outskirts and amongst a jumble of similar dwellings. It is small, but solidly constructed. During Sarajevo's bombardment, an artillery shell had dropped through the tile roof. Fortunately, the shell did not explode and the damage was limited to a single, upper room. That room remains empty and unrepaired.

The neighborhood is socioeconomically mixed. At the lowest end of the spectrum, a dozen or more Kurd refugees are crowded into a single small house. They stay there—and new Kurds constantly rotate through—while they wait for transit out. The Kurds are a bit noisy, but as the house is overflowing with people, it is difficult to imagine how they could appear otherwise. At the other end of the socioeconomic spectrum is an upper middle-class family with helpful but not extraordinary political connections.

Over coffee, Zijo begins to update me on developments since my last visit. His outlook is decidedly more upbeat than it was when I first saw him about 24 hours ago. I am happy about that. He tells me that regulation of the electronic media has been improving in recent months. Television and radio stations may remain on the air now only with the Office of the High Representative's approval. As a result, extreme nationalist messages no longer glut the airwaves.

Then, too, Zijo observes that the population is beginning to move about more. People from outside Sarajevo are coming into town and Sarajevans are ranging farther outside the city. They still do not generally go far, though. It is becoming more common for people to run into old friends and neighbors. Zijo is speaking now mostly of Serbs and Muslims. His sense is that, although relatively more Croats were returning to Sarajevo earlier in the postwar period, now there are more Serbs coming back and some of the Croats are tending to leave. He sees little interaction, at least in Sarajevo, between Muslims and Croats. Muslims do go to Croat-controlled Kiseljak to shop, but they make their purchases and leave without lingering.

Zijo feels that Serbs and Muslims always have had more in common culturally with one another than either group has had with the Croats. Serb folk songs even are becoming popular again in some Muslim homes.

Karadjordjevo versus Dayton

Fired Serb Supports Croats

In the true but unstated spirit of Karadjordjevo, the officially fired but practically still in office President of Republika Srpska, Nikola Poplašen, says he supports Croat nationalists' efforts to create a third entity in Bosnia and Hercegovina. "It would be more logical to me to be talking about a third entity in which the Croat nation would live and not about a third entity in the Brčko region," Poplašen is quoted as saying in today's *Oslobodjenje*. Poplašen insists that the Brčko decision destroyed Dayton and that he will support the rights of Bosnian Croats to self-determination in creating their own entity. It is, he says, "an unusual situation that one nation has its own entity and the other two live together."

The rub, of course, is that the likes of Poplašen and Jelavić, Tudjman and Milošević care not at all about rights for Muslims.

Meanwhile, HDZ leaders, including Jelavić and Lužanski, reportedly were meeting this week behind closed doors in Kiseljak. They were believed to be discussing their third-entity strategy. Publicly, HDZ says the discussions were about what the Croat nationalists claim to be growing terrorist activities against Croats in central Bosnia.

In today's *Oslobodjenje*, though, there is a report that Tudjman is against creating a third entity. As a signatory to the Dayton accord, and in that to carve out a Croat state within Bosnia and Hercegovina would violate that agreement, a Croatian news service relates, Tudjman strongly opposes the idea. An article in this week's *Slobodna Bosna* (an independent newsweekly known for criticizing the leading Croat, Bošnjak and Serb political parties and leaders) supports the notion that Tudjman truly is angry with Jelavić and the Bosnian Croats on this issue. Zagreb's message seems to be that Mostar and the Bosnian Croats should improve their relations with the international community or face a cut in financial support from Croatia.

It is difficult to surmise whether Tudjman opposes the Bosnian Croats' aim or just their timing and tactics. In any case, I doubt Croat ultranationalists here will obediently toe the line chalked down by Zagreb on this. Meanwhile, spoken support for Croat ultranationalists from the embattled Poplašen will only discourage international donors from assisting Croat communities in Bosnia and Hercegovina.

Brčko Is Bosnia and Hercegovina

The newspapers still are filled with rhetoric about Brčko. This looks like a done deal, and so most of what I see in print is just venting of spleens and blowing off steam. The international arbitrator's decision on Brčko did not much surprise me. During my September visit to that pivotal city, it became clear to me that Brčko was too dominated by Serbs ever to be turned over to the Federation. Nevertheless, the area's economic importance for all of Bosnia and Hercegovina, its former Muslim majority, and Brčko's only tenuous physical connection to Republika Srpska, argued against awarding Brčko to the Serb entity. The decision to create a neutral Brčko seems the only solution, albeit one with which no side (and Serb nationalists least of all) would be satisfied.

Now, as I read through the text of the international arbitrator's decision on Brčko, I see that the case for creating a neutral district in Brčko was built primarily upon evidence of Republika Srpska's failure to run Brčko within the terms of the Dayton accord. The connection between the Brčko ruling and Poplašen's firing also becomes obvious in reading that text, although international officials insist there is no direct relationship between last week's two announcements.

According to the arbitrator's written decision, the parties to the arbitration generally recognized that there had been three possible outcomes: 1) Brčko goes to the Federation, 2) the Brčko corridor remains in Republika Srpska, or 3) "the result most consistent with Dayton's objectives might be to remove Brčko from the exclusive control of either entity and place its governance in the hands of an independent District government under the exclusive sovereignty of (the unified state of Bosnia and Hercegovina)."

The document states that Republika Srpska did not get Brčko because the Serb entity, while it had custody of Brčko had engaged in "systematic non-compliance with (indeed, defiance of) the Dayton Accords in the Brčko area." A preliminary ruling from the arbitral tribunal in 1998 had "explicitly forewarned" Republika Srpska that it would need to demonstrate "very clearly that it has truly reversed course and committed itself to an apparently permanent program of full Dayton compliance." That included specifically a burden to demonstrate "significant new achievements" in resettling former Brčko residents and "strong support for the multiethnic governmental institutions" that were being developed under international supervision.

Serb Nationalists Violated Dayton

The main issue to be decided in the end was whether or not Republika Srpska was honoring these obligations under Dayton and the earlier instructions from the arbitral tribunal. The arbitrator determined that Republika Srpska had not honored those obligations and, furthermore, that it never would "so long as anti-Dayton political elements, particularly the SDS and SRS parties led by newly-elected President Nikola Poplašen, are allowed to remain dominant in that portion of the Brčko area that is in (Republika Srpska) custody." In particular, the tribunal criticizes these "anti-Dayton elements" for failing to encourage and enable refugees to return to their pre-war homes, for failing to help develop democratic multiethnic institutions for Brčko, and for failing to cooperate with the international supervisory regime.

"Only days" before the final award was announced, the text notes, Poplašen was quoted in the press as threatening to respond militarily if the arbitrator ruled against Republika Srpska. Furthermore, "he has recently refused to comply with the High Representative's decision regarding civilian command authority over (Republika Srpska) military forces. These actions have strengthened the Tribunal's conclusion that a change from (Republika Srpska) control is essential. Indeed, Mr. Poplašen must take major responsibility for the result being reached in this decision." The decision also blames Slobodan Milošević, who at Dayton had guaranteed Republika Srpska compliance.

Bošnjak and Croat Nationalists Also at Fault

None of this is to say that Muslims and Croats in the Federation are angels by comparison. Indeed, the tribunal found that Federation officials, too, had by their actions (and inactions) shown themselves unfit to administer Brčko. The arbitrator calls the Federation's efforts to return refugees to their former homes "less than satisfactory" during 1998, and notes that even Federation representatives concede that judgment to be accurate.

The arbitrator's final award comments that settling the Brčko issue "in a sense" marks "the final phase of the Dayton process itself." That is an overstatement. The Dayton process, as originally envisioned, will not be completed until the civilian aspects have been fully implemented and until refugees are resettled. It is not yet time to declare success when little progress has been made on resettling hundreds of thousands of refugees, when there is not yet a functioning economy in Bosnia and Hercegovina, when the country does not yet have an effectively functioning government (not to mention one that is democratic), when rampant corruption surely is siphoning off tens (and perhaps hundreds) of millions of dollars of foreign aid, and when not a single major war criminal has yet been brought to justice.

Brčko exemplifies just how far all of Bosnia and Hercegovina is today from achieving the vision of Dayton.

Where Croat Push Comes to Bošnjak Shove

Zenica: A Muslim Collection Point

One can be sure that Zenica never will be a part of Herceg-Bosna. Not without an awful lot of bloodshed anyway. With a prewar population of about 100,000, Zenica is the third-largest city in Bosnia and Hercegovina (after Sarajevo and Banja Luka). During the wars, as Serbs and Croats drove Muslims from northern and central Bosnia, Zenica filled up with Muslims. Based in the city and its surrounding hills were Islamic *mujahedeen*, fierce fighters who were ready and able to repay in kind the worst atrocities that Croat and Serb paramilitaries could deliver.

Today, in the fourth year since Dayton, Zenica is a steel town with no steel production and remains filled with Muslim refugees. To walk through Zenica's downtown streets, the situation does not look so bad. The appearance is of a place that is rundown but not grubby. Surely, the air is much cleaner than it was when the steel mill was operating.

•　　•　　•　　•

We are waiting in Oslobodjenje's Zenica bureau office for Mesud Djulan, the newspaper's chief correspondent for Zenica. We chat with the receptionist there, a pleasant Croat. One of her colleagues, a man who works in circulation and sales, comes by. The salesman, who as a soldier was wounded in the fighting here, is proud of *Oslobodjenje* and of his country and people.

Three major daily newspapers compete in Zenica, he relates: *Dnevni Avaz* ("Daily Voice"), *Večernje novine* ("Evening News") and *Oslobodjenje*. *Dnevni Avaz* is privately owned but actively supports SDA. *Večernje novine*, also privately owned, is editorially more independent. Although *Oslobodjenje* has an editorial policy of independence, an ethnically mixed staff and a Croat editor, the salesman reports, nationalist Croats like to insinuate that the newspaper is supported by SDA.[72] Few Croats in the half-virtual Herceg-Bosna read *Oslobodjenje*, and fewer still would admit to doing so on a regular basis.

---

[72] *Oslobodjenje* strives for editorial independence, but its ownership and control are somewhat ambiguous and unresolved. For a description of *Oslobodjenje's* founding during World War II as a communist organ, its break from the communists in 1990, its incomplete privatization and struggle with the ruling SDA, see Tom

I remark that I have never noticed *Oslobodjenje* on sale in Republika Srpska. Actually, he tells me, a couple hundred copies do go to Banja Luka every day. The level of sales there scarcely justifies the transportation and distribution costs, but he points out that it is important for the independent newspaper to appear in the Republika Srpska capital. *Dnevni Avaz* is the most widely read newspaper in Zenica, while *Oslobodjenje* is the most expensive (costing 1 deutschemark daily, which is about 60 cents) and most sophisticated. It is especially favored by intellectuals and those who can afford it. Of course, the salesman notes, people are so poor that few can buy newspapers often.

We speak about the privatization program for the Federation. Many people here are eager for that program to move forward, although they also are a bit afraid about it. Privatization is a necessary step toward getting the economy on track and growing. At the same time, though, it will result in many people officially losing their jobs. A lot of these people are not working now anyway, of course, but they hold onto some hope that they might one day return to their former positions.

The salesman, who also does some photography work for the paper, says *Oslobodjenje* also will be privatized. Perhaps then even he might lose his job. In any case, he is confident that *Oslobodjenje* will continue to set a good example of independence and professionalism.

•　　•　　•　　•

Djulan, a man nearing retirement age, has been a journalist for some 30 years. He recalls that at one time in the prewar days he was the only Muslim journalist in Zenica. All the rest were Serbs, even though Muslims constituted the largest group.

For many people here, Djulan remarks, the possibility to have a normal life, rather than drawing closer, is moving ever farther into the distant future. Because the local situation is bad and deteriorating, he fears that some sort of social uprising could occur. Nothing like that ever has happened here before.

In better times, the steel mill produced some 2 million tons annually. Now its output is negligible. All of Yugoslavia once received steel from Zenica, so all of Yugoslavia helped to support the city and its heavy industry. A couple thousand people do have jobs at the mill, but their salaries are very low. These must mostly be maintenance jobs. About 20,000 people are waiting for production to begin. The Kuwaiti

Gjelten, *Sarajevo Daily: A City and Its Newspaper under Siege, paperback* (New York: HarperCollins, 1996; HarperPerennial edition, 1996), pp. 46–47, 51–52, 56, 247–249.

government has discussed taking over and investing in the steel factory, Djulan relates, but the Kuwaitis insist upon employing just 4,615 workers.

On local politics Djulan says that, "It is a one-party system, just the same as before." In short, SDA and the Coalition run Zenica. The Zenica-Doboj Cantonal Assembly includes 28 members from the Coalition, 11 from SDP, four from HDZ and seven members divided across five additional parties.[73] Although the Coalition has a majority, there is at least an appearance of pluralism. There is no pluralism behind the appearance, though, Djulan assures.

The success or failure of democracy can be a function of what those who have power do with that power. It is a tragic fact, Djulan explains, that personal politics and personal economy are one and the same here: People not belonging to SDA or to Haris Silajdžić's Party for Bosnia and Hercegovina have poor prospects to find paying jobs. There can be no prosperity so long as the nationalist parties rule, he believes.

Djulan reports that there are today, in early-1999, some 30,000 refugees within Zenica. There are 48,000 refugees in the canton as a whole. Approximately 70% of these refugees are displaced from other parts of the Federation. These refugees, he notes, fall into two categories. The first group is made up of Muslims living in Zenica who had been run out of nearby and Croat-dominated Jajce and Serb-controlled Doboj. Some of these are beginning now to return to their homes, although the younger members of the families tend to stay in Zenica. Those who remain here live in houses and apartments that do not belong to them. So long as they do not leave—and there is little pressure upon them from the local ruling SDA to do so—then the Croats or Serbs that those residences belong to cannot return.

The second group consists of refugees living in the five refugee camps set up near Zenica. These are Muslims from Goražde, Doboj, Banja Luka, Bijeljina, Žepče and Jajce. Thus, again, some are from Serb-controlled areas within Republika Srpska and others are from Croat-controlled areas within the Federation. The conditions in these camps are very bad, Djulan reports, and people there are forced to beg and steal in order to survive. These camps are home to some 3,500 to 4,000 people. The Norwegians built the camps back in 1992 and 1993, and some of the refugees have been there ever since.

---

[73]The seat-allocation numbers cited here differ slightly from those mentioned in the interview. My numbers come from an official OSCE source.

Djulan figures it will take at least 10 years to bring some degree of normality to this area. It may be necessary virtually to build a new city to accommodate some of the refugees, and he expects that only about 20% of these displaced people ever will go back to their earlier homes. People who formerly lived in villages and who now live in the city often do not wish to return to village life. They present a special problem, as quite a few of them are poorly educated and therefore not well-suited to working and living in an urban environment.

Before the wars, Djulan recalls, there were some 23,000 Serbs and perhaps 20,000 Croats in Zenica.[74] The latest count shows that there are about 14,000 to 15,000 Croats here now and between 5,000 and 6,000 Serbs. I actually am surprised to hear that the non-Muslim population here is so large as it is—especially that there are so many Serbs. The future for those Serbs, though, is perhaps particularly bleak. Djulan points to an example of four large villages near Zenica in which Serbs formerly made up some 90% of the population. When those Serbs fled their individual houses, non-Serb families from Jajce moved in. These newcomers now refuse to go home, and so the Serbs cannot return to their rightful places. Of course, he says, even if these Serbs were to come back, they can never get work here. The best they can hope for is to return, assert their property rights, sell their property, and then go to Republika Srpska.

•　　•　　•　　•

We make a couple false starts down wrong roads to get out of Zenica and headed toward Travnik. Maybe it is just Zijo and me, but folks here seem to have a different concept of the term traffic light ("*semafor*" in Bosno-Serbo-Croatian) than we do in America or even than do people in Sarajevo. Two or three times today, we have been directed to make a turn at such and such a *semafor* only to find that there is no traffic light at which to turn. In any case, after driving about a bit, we finally pick up a middle-aged man in a suit who wants to go more or less the same direction as we do. He directs us, taking what is surely the scenic route.

---

[74]One set of official numbers that I have put the prewar number of Croats within the city at 16,000 and of Serbs at 18,000, but there also were 19,000 people classified as Yugoslavs and others. Most of the latter could be considered Croats, Serbs or to number among the 43,000 Muslims. Comparison of Zenica city and *opština* figures suggest that most of those regarding themselves as Yugoslavs lived within the city, rather than in the villages and rural areas.

Our passenger has just made his regular monthly visit to Zenica's steelworks to let his former—and, he hopes, future—employer know that he is still available and interested to come back to his old job. Just outside of Zenica, we pass the village of Čajdraš. Turkish SFOR soldiers are standing guard along the road and patrolling the settlement. Croats are beginning to return to their houses in that village, our passenger tells us, and the Muslims who had occupied those houses are in no hurry to move out. The Bošnjaks are waiting until their houses near Vitez are ready for them to move back into. SFOR is here to prevent clashes.

At the Foot of Mount Vlašić

Driving in from the east, one does not see Travnik in the distance. Rather, we round a bend in the road and the city springs up before us. Travnik is nestled into a valley cut by the Lašva River into the foot of Mount Vlašić, one of the tallest peaks in central Bosnia.

Muslims and Roman Catholic Croats have for many centuries been the dominant groups here, but the Serbs, too, have had their villages in these hills. Travnik's ethnic roots are a typically South Slav snarl. The very name of Mount Vlašić reminds me that some of the Serbs who have lived here, and likely, too, a few of the Bošnjaks and Croats have some non-Slavic ancestry. "Vlašić" is a reference to Vlachs, that ancient nomadic race that is related to the Romanians. Frequently Orthodox by faith, Vlachs migrated into central and northern Bosnia centuries ago and mixed with the Slavic population. In this locality and over time, the terms and identities of "Vlach," "Serb" and "Orthodox Christian" became intertwined.

Travnik as It Was

Reading Ivo Andrić's *Bosnian Chronicle* first aroused my interest in Travnik. Since then, I have become acquainted, too, with a man in America who had grown up in Travnik some 60 years ago. He is a Serb but says he still thinks of himself as a Yugoslav. He has shared with me stories of that time and place. Muslims, Catholics, Orthodox and Jews lived together in Travnik in those days. On market day, Travnik would swell with people coming from the surrounding villages. After the market had closed, the Serb and Croat villagers would crowd into the taverns. As their inhibitions would naturally diminish in that setting and their bravado heighten, pretty soon they would be brawling with one another. The Muslims, who, if they did so at all, did not drink in public places, just tried to stay clear of the commotion.

It probably is not accurate to say that people in and around Travnik had learned to live together so much as that they just knew how to live together. As a practical matter, after all, they always had lived together. A certain amount of bickering, distrust and even fighting was a normal part of life in equilibrium. In such a community, though, an overdose of potent demagoguery, a provocative external stimulus or an extraordinary local incident of some sort could upset the equilibrium.

A passage from *Bosnian Chronicle* sticks in my memory. It is one in which Andrić describes "in general outline...the origins, the evolution, and the end of a typical riot in a Bosnian town." This is something much larger than a bar brawl but smaller than total war. Travnik's bazaar is the epicenter of this particular riot (perhaps only partially fictional) in 1807. There has been a change of regime in Istanbul, the distant Ottoman capital. Mehmed Pasha, the Bosnian vizier and who rules from Travnik rather than Sarajevo, sees the handwriting on the wall. He, too, will lose his job and position. If he uses his wits, perhaps Mehmed Pasha can avoid also losing his head. The vizier slips away before his successor arrives.[75]

Although the vizier's flight catalyzes the ensuing melee, the bazaar has been building up to a riot for some time. At first, there had been only a tension, "a vague general mood." People in the market had gone about their own affairs, but all the time gossiping and murmuring and "making mental notes." After many months, as the mood has approached a sort of climax, "the bazaar whispered, braced itself, waited, as bees wait for the hour of swarming."

The riot in the bazaar begins on a calm day, like any other. Even the vizier's departure is not sufficient to trigger the outburst. For this there must be one or two instigators: "noisy, violent, disgruntled cranks and have-nots whom no one had ever seen or known before and who, when the riot subsided, would vanish once more into the nameless squalor on the hillside outskirts from which they had emerged, or remain pining in some police jail." After a few days of chaos and violence, then, the situation calms down and people, a bit ashamed for their lapse into barbarism, settle back into their customary routines.

---

[75]Andrić, *Bosnian Chronicle*, pp. 143–144.

There was in Travnik, too, a lapse into barbarism during the time of my acquaintance's youth. It was when the *Ustaše* took over the town as World War II was beginning. From the time the autonomous Croatian *Banovina* had been created in 1939, many Croatian flags were flying in Travnik. But one Serb, named Mahmut Robović, who operated a newspaper kiosk in the town, proudly flew a big Serbian flag instead. It was not even a Yugoslav flag, but a Serbian one. When the *Ustaše* came in 1941, Robović was the first person killed in Travnik. His killers then dragged Robović's body down the street.

"But his name was Mahmut," I pointed out when I heard this story. "That is a Muslim name. Surely he was no Serb."

"He was a Serb of Muslim religion," my acquaintance from Travnik explained. "He never changed or hid his historical background. He traced it far back and was also at the same time religiously a good Muslim. For his Serbian roots and political activism and his opposition to the *Ustaše*, he paid with his life."

In this man's Travnik, there were, in addition to the town's 14 mosques, both Catholic and Orthodox churches as well as a synagogue. (I will find out today that the synagogue is no longer here; only a Jewish cemetery remains.) There were so many Catholic churches and monasteries in the surrounding villages and hills that people sometimes called Travnik "Little Rome." My acquaintance's father was a government official in the Kingdom of Yugoslavia. Once, on the official Unification Day holiday (1 December), his father, representing the government, was to attend special worship services in each of the town's major houses of worship. The royal official took along his small son on this mission.

Father and son came first to the Catholic church. Before entering the House of God, the father warned the boy to be respectful and to take off his hat. Next, they went to the synagogue. The little fellow solemnly removed his hat. The father reproached him, pointing out that they were inside the synagogue, after all, and so he must cover his head. Then father and son came to their own, Orthodox church. When the boy (who was by now quite confused) left his head warmly covered, his father snatched the cap—and gave the youngster's ear a good pinch besides. The last stop was the mosque. As the lad got it wrong again, his exasperated father sharply scolded him and told him to put his hat on. The boy learned a lesson that day about religious and cultural differences: It has a lot to do with hats!

An Apparent Island of Peace

Travnik, like Zenica, filled up with fleeing Muslims during the 1992–1995 wars. Beginning in 1992, there was an influx of Muslims from northern Bosnia, as well as from areas cleansed by Serb forces. Croats and, especially Serbs, were by then leaving Travnik. By spring 1993, with Croats and Muslims at war in central Bosnia, Muslims from that area were concentrating in Travnik and Zenica while Croats were amassing in the likes of Kiseljak and Vitez. Driving in, I see the usual Bosnian countryside, with its enduring evidence of earlier violence: rugged hills pocked by mile after mile of burned-out and abandoned houses and farmsteads. When we leave Travnik tomorrow and drive to Banja Luka, capital of Republika Srpska, the landscape on the other side of Travnik will show us that same ravished face.

But Travnik itself is something markedly different. We are surprised to see and learn how calm, albeit impoverished, is life here now and to see how little war damage occurred in this ancient city. That Travnik harbors less hostility today than many other cities outside of Sarajevo is palpable. People here, the majority of whom are Muslims, seem relaxed and friendly. There is very little nationalistic graffiti, and, as we walk around in the city center, I see no political posters. A kiosk sells newspapers of various and independent views and offers even cassette tapes by Serb musicians.[76]

I am surprised, though, in that this is the first place in all of my travels within Bosnia and Hercegovina that I see women in full, conservative Islamic garb. That is to say, these women are dressed entirely in black, including a full face and head covering. I see only a couple of these. The first sighting shocks me, as the woman comes around a corner and is walking toward me. A dark-bearded man who

---

[76]In former Yugoslavia, calm, like truth, is relative. Little should be accepted at face value, although there ordinarily is little point in debating local reality with those living within it. Unbeknownst to me during this visit to Travnik, there reportedly had been an attempt to murder a Croat policeman here just a few weeks earlier. This incident is one which Croat nationalists point to as evidence of Muslim violence against Croats in central Bosnia and to justify their demands for a third, Croat entity. Unfortunately, the Croat nationalists cry "Wolf!" so frequently, frenetically and indiscriminately that they have destroyed their own credibility. Several weeks after my visit, I will read of a HDZ proposal to divide Travnik *opština* into six micro-*opštinas* so that Croats would not need to live with Muslims. The idea is to turn Travnik into another bitterly divided Mostar.

also looks out of place here accompanies her. Seeing the second such couple jolts me as much as the first.

During the war, *mujahedeen* from several eastern Islamic countries had come to central Bosnia to fight alongside Bosnian Muslims. They were known as fierce fighters, and they quite frightened the local Muslims. Nevertheless, a few married local women and stayed in the country. Fundamental Islamic influences are far from prominent here, though. For example, some of the young women here dress less conservatively than they typically do in Sarajevo.

We walk to a line of taxis in the center of town. A small group of drivers is passing the time. One of them, named Mesud, helps us to line up accommodations for the evening in a hillside home. Mesud has a son living in Prague. When he sees that my car is registered in the Czech Republic, then finds out that I live there, he is eager to talk. We agree to meet later for coffee.

•   •   •   •

"We all get along fine here now," Mesud assures us when we later go together to a coffeehouse. "You can ask anyone, and they will tell you the same thing." Some of Travnik's Serbs and many of its Croats never left the city during the wars, he says. Some who did leave have come back. Mesud's understanding is that some Croats left because Croat nationalists ordered them to leave. Early on, when the fighting had been against Serb forces, Croats and Muslims had fought side by side. But then, Mesud recalls, the Croat soldiers betrayed their Muslim comrades.

There were many mixed marriages in Travnik before the wars, and Mesud says these generally have survived. New interethnic marriages have come to be since then, too. As a practical matter, though, young people do not regard marrying and settling here in Travnik to be very advantageous. If they have a chance to go abroad, he notes, they do so.

Mesud admits that it is easier for him to have an open attitude toward his Catholic and Orthodox neighbors than it is for some others. After all, none of his family was killed in the fighting here. I ask Mesud about SFOR. The foreign soldiers, he answers, have a base "up on Vlašić, thanks be to God," and they come around sometimes. The "normal" local people get along fine with them.

•   •   •   •

We leave our taxi driver friend and take a long *korzo*. The main street through Travnik is long and clean and quiet. Not many people are out walking, although the coffee shops are doing a good business. We stroll past several mosques, a white Catholic church, the prominent graves of two of Travnik's viziers.

At an open newsstand, I buy a copy of *Dani* ("Days"), a weekly newsmagazine which bills itself as independent. *Dani's* editorial content seems aimed to offend extreme nationalists of all stripes. On the cover this week is a now-famous photo from Poplašen's campaign for President of Republika Srpska. The photo depicts the recently fired president in his *Četnik* Pride pose: Black-bearded and in military uniform, Poplašen poses in a forest clearing. His right foot is raised on a stump. The uplifted knee props up a machine gun. A long and proper throat-slitting knife hangs on his belt. Dark eyes glare fiercely into the camera.

In this case, though, as if painted with two quick swipes from a paintbrush, a red "X" is splashed across Poplašen's fearsome image. "Brčko a District," reads the cover banner. "Poplašen Fired. Carlos for President." *Dani's* cover is a reference to events of the week earlier. The main story inside is entitled: "Black Friday in Republika Srpska." The author compares Poplašen to Che Guevara, Fidel Castro's right-hand man, who had hoped to serve his revolutionary master by carrying Havana-centered communism into Latin America. The Argentine Guevara, of course, fought a hopeless cause and was captured and executed in Bolivia in 1967. Guevara's legend grew quickly after his death. Poplašen is not likely to take that road to fame. He will linger. While the international community can discredit and threaten Poplašen, SFOR will no more enforce Westendorp's order against Poplašen than it will arrest the most nefarious of war criminals.

Although one should be cautious about taking things at face value in Dayton Bosnia and Hercegovina, Travnik is today an island of relative calm. There is plenty to remind one, though, of just how fragile and rare is that peace.[77]

---

[77]Although Travnik has indeed been a relative success story in terms especially of Croat returns, those returns themselves have not pleased ultranationalist leaders. Returns interfere with their efforts to concentrate Croats in communities under HDZ/HVO control. According to an International Crisis Group Report: "The HDZ relentlessly portrays Travnik as a municipality in which Croats are subject to constant threats and intimidation. This image is used both to discourage Croat return and to distract attention from other areas, such as Drvar, where the HDZ has been criticized for encouraging violence against returning minorities. There was some justification for this negative image. Four Croats were murdered in Travnik in August

Travnik as Federation Capital?

Ante Jelavić is quoted today in *Oslobodjenje* as saying that there is now a "nearly universal consensus among Croats" that "the best course is to define a new strategy for resolving the Croat question in Bosnia and Hercegovina." Jelavić had added that he, Tudjman and this country's Croats oppose the concept of a third entity. The HDZ leader and member of the Bosnia and Hercegovina Presidency proposes to form smaller cantons that are ethnically more compact and homogeneous. The Croat cantons among these should have their own educational programs, their own mass media, their own Croatian language, and local regulations. Jelavić also suggests that Travnik should be made the provisional capital of the Croat-Muslim Federation. Eventually, he thinks that capital should be Mostar.[78]

The great patriots of Herceg-Bosna in western Hercegovina are not buying into what they regard as a watered-down separatism. In an opinion piece headlined "Cheated Hercegovinians," a former general in the Croatian Defense Force (HOS), Ante Prkačin, criticizes Tudjman and his policies toward Croats in Bosnia and Hercegovina. Prkačin warns the Croats of Hercegovina that Tudjman will not help them to merge their territory into Croatia. The HOS general urges Croats in Bosnia and Hercegovina to ditch the HDZ and to elect their own leaders who will not lie to them.

Prkačin is to Tudjman among Croats as Šešelj and Poplašen are to Milošević among Serbs. That is to say, he is even more radical in his nationalism. The HOS should not be confused with the HVO (Croat

---

and October of 1997 and the culprits were never found. However, evidence appears to suggest that the crimes were not ethnically motivated. Moreover, the negative image is no longer accurate. The 2,500 Croats who have returned to Travnik since the end of the war have reported few incidents. See International Crisis Group, *A Tale of Two Cities: Return of Displaced Persons to Jajce and Travnik* (Brussels and Washington: International Crisis Group, 3 June 1998).

[78]Jelavić's comments originated in an interview with *Jutarnji list* ("Morning Herald"), a new and independent daily newspaper. *Jutarnji list* is published in Zagreb for distribution both in Croatia and in Bosnia and Hercegovina. Until this independent paper hit the newsstands in 1998, there had been little practical freedom of choice in Croatia's mass media. Croatia's three television networks are state-owned, as are two major newspapers. All these media, plus another private but not independent newspaper are generally regarded as mouthpieces for Tudjman and his HDZ. Improved press freedom in Croatia would be a positive development for democracy and tolerance also in neighboring Bosnia and Hercegovina. See Reuters, "Croatia's First Private Daily Out to Stir Market," 6 April 1998.

Council of Defense). The HVO is the HDZ's army. The HOS is a former militia, a rival to the HVO, and associated with the extreme Croatian Party of Rights (HSP). At least since 1992, HSP leaders have accused Tudjman of being too soft. That is a pretty scary thought.

Augmenting the bellicose clamor from HOS/HSP and HVO/HDZ extremist Croats is the collective voice of HVIDRA, an association of Bosnian Croat veterans and invalids. It probably is not wholly coincidental that the acronym for this organization sounds so much like the word for Hydra, that many-headed and monstrous serpent from Greek mythology that sprouts two heads wherever Hercules cuts off one. HVIDRA sees in every violent or, merely unfortunate, incident involving a Croat justification for its position that Croats in Bosnia and Hercegovina cannot be secure without having their own entity. HVIDRA recently staged a rally in the Croat-occupied west bank of Mostar where the demonstrators carried signs reading: "No Identity without an Entity."

At first sight, this incessant agitation among Croat ultranationalist looks like paranoia. As the smallest of Bosnia and Hercegovina's major ethnonational groups but effectively holding territory disproportionately large relative to their numbers, these Croats have reasons to be anxious. There is more to it than that, though. I believe these chauvinist eccentrics draw their venomous lifeblood through long and twisted roots thrust deeply into an outdated and essentially fascist tradition. The civilized world sees especially Serb ethnic-cleansers in Bosnia and Hercegovina and in former Yugoslavia. Croatian extremists, though, scarcely are less vicious.

This Land Is Our Land, This Land Is My Land

Travnik's old fortress squats on the hillside across the valley from our makeshift pension. Just beyond is Mount Vlašić. The morning is still cool and damp and quiet. The sun's rays have not yet found their way directly into this hollow. I count five mosques around and about the citadel. Their white minarets sprout up from the hillside, like new shoots reaching for the early spring sun. Had I time, I would enjoy this morning to walk about this scenic town, to visit the museum in the center, and to search out Andrić's house. Unfortunately, we have a long day ahead and no time for tourism.

As there is no coffee here, I drive down the hill, following the owner of the house, to a coffee shop near the central marketplace. Our host formerly was a special forces soldier in the Yugoslav army. Now, his primary occupation is to run a private detective agency. These days, he tells us over coffee, there is plenty of work for him. He specializes in providing protection and in potentially dangerous investigations. This is work for a young man, which he certainly still is. But one needs also to have a plan for the longer term. That is why he is turning the house where he has his detective agency into a bed and breakfast.

The detective's long-range plan makes sense. If peace holds, and Bosnia and Hercegovina is rebuilt within its existing borders (an outcome which today is by no means assured), then Travnik will one day be an important tourist destination. Zijo is surprised to hear me say so, and I am puzzled that he does not see the touristic potential in this scenic former seat of the viziers. Travnik is historically very important, has literary associations, is reasonably safe, and was not physically destroyed in the fighting. After Sarajevo, it is today probably the most interesting city in the country for tourists. That distinction perhaps once belonged to Mostar, but no longer.

Make No Mistake: HDZ Owns Jajce

From Travnik, there are two roads to Banja Luka. The shortest route to the Republika Srpska capital goes over Mount Vlašić. On the map, it is a fine red line. I decide to opt for the longer, bold red line and a route that I already know. This is the road that I had driven in September and which follows the Vrbas River north from Jajce.

We stop for lunch in Jajce, last capital of the medieval Bosnian Kingdom, before continuing on to Banja Luka. Jajce is within Federation territory but near the IEBL. There is no mistaking that Jajce is today a purely Croat city. The fact that the flag of another country, Croatia, flies over Jajce's imposing castle makes a clear statement. We park on the outskirts of the walled old town and walk into the center in search of a pizzeria.

The first restaurant we pass is called *Oluja 95*. The name, meaning "storm" or "tempest," refers to the Croat military operation in summer 1995. That was a ferocious—and very successful—campaign in which Croat forces took huge areas of Bosnia and of Croatia that Serb forces had conquered early in the wars. Tens of thousands of Serbs had been driven both from their ancestral villages and from homes they previously had commandeered from Croats and Muslims. The *Oluja* operation was an important factor forcing Serb nationalists to negotiate in Dayton and ultimately to sign the peace agreement. Be that as it may, only a Croat nationalist could regard *Oluja 95* as a pleasant name for an eating establishment. A hundred years from now, maybe, but not while the memories are still fresh.

The gate leading into Jajce's old town and many of the buildings along this main thoroughfare are prominently tagged with the stenciled initials "HDZ." Also to mark Croat territory, in Jajce's main square there is an impressive, new monument to Croats who died fighting Serbs and Muslims. Constructed as a fountain and in black granite, the memorial is topped by a *šahovnica* carved into the stone.[79] The names of Croat war heroes are cut into the granite, as are the words "He will live forever who has died with honor."

All countries have war memorials. That is normal. The US, too, has even its Civil War monuments. This one in Jajce might well be appropriate were it constructed in Croatia. Its presence, though, is incongruous with Dayton's objectives and the specific local situation. This is a district in which the prewar population was just 14% Croat. The warring parties—including Croat leaders—committed themselves at Dayton to allowing displaced persons to return to their prewar homes and to live without harassment.

Not all is nationalism and bellicosity in Jajce, of course. I am surprised to see that the newsstands here have *Oslobodjenje* on sale. Then, too, the women who serve us pizza in Croatia Grill (actually spelled in English) are friendly enough.

---

[79]I will learn later that this monument is constructed across the street from the site where Jajce's mosque used to be. That site is now an empty lot. As occurred in many other cities, the mosque was destroyed during the time that Jajce was under Serb control.

Zijo and I are alone in the small restaurant at first. When a couple more customers come in, we lower our voices and speak less in English. We do so not out of fear but from politeness. One of the other customers, a young man, leaves without finishing his meal. I hear the waitress comment to the cook about this odd behavior. If our presence destroyed his appetite, I figure that is his problem.

Banja Luka: An Unexpected Rally

The US State Department has advised Americans to avoid Republika Srpska just now. But I have a meeting planned with an *Oslobodjenje* journalist in Banja Luka, and it is important for me to go there. I do not mean to stay long, and I do intend to keep a low profile.

I arrive to find that loudspeakers have been set up on Banja Luka's main square. These are blaring Serb pop songs. Everywhere are plastered large posters announcing a public rally, set for 2 p.m. today, "For the Defense of Republika Srpska." A similar rally was held in Serb-dominated Doboj a few days ego. Unbeknownst to me just now (as was this planned rally), several other such demonstrations are set today for other cities in Republika Srpska.

We are looking for *Oslobodjenje's* Banja Luka correspondent, Gordana Katana. We find her at the International Press Club, where a press conference called by representatives of the international community is just ending. "We can't cooperate with a government which is consistently sabotaging the peace process," a representative of the international community is saying in response to a question. A NATO spokesperson—the last to speak today—then comments briefly. His message is to welcome Poland, Hungary and the Czech Republic (whose admission has just become official) as full members of NATO. He notes, too, that this will be his last press conference in Banja Luka (as he apparently has been reassigned) and wishes this country "a peaceful and prosperous future."

As the press conference breaks up, we locate Katana. She has only a few minutes to speak with us, as she will attend the rally just taking shape down the street. Katana is a Serb. She is married to a Muslim, who also is a journalist. Katana says she and her husband are "floaters," people who, as a practical matter, cannot live in their own houses. A court ruling says they can return to the home from which they earlier had been pushed, but the police can do nothing to enforce that decision.

I ask about ethnically mixed marriages, noting that Mesud, the Travnik taxi driver, had said these had generally survived in his town. In this area, too, Katana says, few mixed marriages dissolved over war pressures, but many of those families have gone abroad to live.

In just a half hour's time, Katana tells me, I will see firsthand what is the political situation in this country. If less than 10,000 people attend today's rally, she says, "then the national option is finished." A low turnout would demonstrate that the nationalist forces are rapidly exhausting their influence. Pressures to pit Serbs against other ethnonational groups would be diminishing.

Today's rally is to protest the Brčko decision, Poplašen's firing, and Republika Srpska's "occupation" by foreign forces. All these are related issues. In the Serb nationalist's mind, to lose Brčko is to see Republika Srpska broken and divided. Poplašen is a uniting force. The foreign occupiers (who, by the way, bring not only military might but also economic aid) are seen as the force that would destroy Republika Srpska.

I have seen that this country's people—be they Serb, Muslim, Croat or ethnically undeclared—generally are sick and tired of war, poverty and international opprobrium. Be that as it may, if the pull of Serb nationalism is stronger than is the exhaustion from struggle, then Katana fears that the international community will cut off aid to Republika Srpska. After Poplašen was elected, assistance for economic development to the Serb half of Bosnia and Hercegovina was reduced. But aid for social programs continued, Katana says. That, too, might now be terminated.

There can be no peace here, Katana remarks, until refugees are allowed to return to their homes. Annex 7 of the Dayton accord promises displaced people the right to return home safely and either to regain lost property or to obtain just compensation. It states, too, that all persons have the right to move freely throughout the country, without harassment or discrimination.

Reality is something else. None of the powerful political parties in Banja Luka support the right for refugees to return to their homes, Katana explains. On the contrary, all are agreed that there will be no returns. When the international community threw its support behind the likes of Plavšić, perhaps there was an expectation that progress would be made on resettlement. If so, that belief was not well founded. Nor has SFOR done much to facilitate resettlement, Katana observes.

Unless and until SFOR flexes its muscles to enforce Annex 7, and until greater pressure is brought to bear on political leaders in Bosnia and Hercegovina, Annex 7 will remain the same farce that it has been over the first three years since Dayton implementation began.

•   •   •   •

The rally is just beginning as we pick our way through the crowd assembled on Krajina Square. Many people appear to be here more as spectators than as active participants. A good bit of the crowd is just milling around on an extended fringe. Most of the enthusiasts—and enthusiasm—seem to be up front and near the television cameras. Probably, passions will intensify as the rally continues. Poplašen is to address the crowd at the very end. I will be in another town by that time. In her reporting tomorrow, Katana will estimate attendance at today's rally at 12,000. One western media report will say 7,000. My guess is that the higher figure is closer to the mark.

No One Is at Home in Drvar

Titov Drvar was a celebrated city in communist times. During World War II, Tito at one point had been holed up here (quite literally so, as he was hiding in a cave) with his Partisan forces. In May 1944, the German command had launched an air attack on the city, and Tito had barely (and, one must assume, heroically) escaped. Today, the Croats who control this town within the Federation have dropped the earlier name's reference to Tito. They call it simply Drvar, which means "woodcutter" or "lumberjack."

Sitting in an isolated valley in western Bosnia and on the Unac River, Drvar is boxed in by tall mountains. It today has the look of a near ghost town, although several thousand Croats—including a couple thousand HVO army troops—live in and around Drvar. Mine is about the only car on the streets of this city, which once had a population of some 17,000 people. No more than half the buildings on the main strip of the town are inhabitable and inhabited by businesses. Most of the apartment buildings in the flat river bottom that is the main part of Drvar still stand empty and spoiled but not totally destroyed. Single-family houses cover much of the lower hillsides on the west side of town. There is more activity there.

By whatever name, (Titov) Drvar stands high on the list of the most uninviting places that I have visited in Bosnia and Hercegovina. Perhaps that should not be too surprising. After all, this probably does not seem much like home, either, to most of the people who live in and around Drvar. When the last prewar census was made in 1991, Drvar and its surrounding district were more than 90% populated by Serbs (97% in the city proper). They are gone now, having been driven out in the Croat offensive for which Jajce's *Oluja 95* restaurant is named. There must have been more of Drvar's Serbs at today's rally in Banja Luka than there are here this evening.

Drvar, like Jajce, is a Croat town. Several Croatian flags fly on the main street. In Bosnia and Hercegovina, the Croatian flag is more than just a symbol of civic pride. It is flown and displayed as a message of hatred and intimidation. That flag declares as it waves: "Muslims and Serbs, you are not welcome here." After visiting Drvar, I now realize that it also declares to foreigners of all other stripes that they are not appreciated either.

Feeling Drvar's Threat

This visit to Drvar represents a case where I will learn a lot more about the town after I return home and do a bit more research. I know already that there is a small political party, based in Banja Luka, which is called the Party of Drvar Residents. I am aware of no other city in Bosnia and Hercegovina whose displaced residents are so politically well organized in order to return to their homes as are Drvar's Serbs. In the September 1997 municipal elections, Drvar's displaced Serbs won theoretical absolute power over Drvar. Today, though, there is no more democracy in Drvar than there are Serbs. Croat nationalists run Drvar. An HVO military threat substitutes for politics. Neither the OSCE, SFOR nor any other part of the international community has been willing or able to implement the 1997 municipal election outcome here.

Drvar has the distinction of making the Brčko arbitrator's list of Federation municipalities where Croat or (in other locations) Bošnjak army forces are most threatening to potentially returning Serbs. Jajce is on that list, too. The arbitrator's decision emphasizes that resettling Brčko hinges upon moving Serbs displaced to Brčko back to their original homes in such places as Drvar. An incident in spring 1997 demonstrates why Drvar made the list. On that occasion, an international mediator had come to Drvar to discuss returning displaced Serbs. His welcome was less than warm and the meetings unproductive. During that and the following evening, some 25 Serb-owned houses in and around Drvar were set ablaze. A similar message by vandalism had been delivered several months earlier. On that occasion, 35 Serb houses were torched when Serbs attempted to begin returning to Drvar.

A few days after the 1997 arson offensive, Drvar's Croat police chief had joined Federation Deputy Minister for Police, Jozo Leutar, in attempting to play down and to put some political spin on the incident. "The violation of the right to return to one's own house is not only happening in Drvar," Leutar, also a Croat, had stated. "There is not much difference between the burning of homes in Drvar and refusing Croats who have proper documents to return to their apartments in Sarajevo. I guarantee that there are more human rights abuses in Sarajevo than in Drvar."[80]

In absolute numbers, Leutar may very well have been right in his Drvar-Sarajevo comparison. The unease is more palpable and all-embracing, though, in Drvar. If one imagines a town out of a *Mad Max* movie that is run by the Ku Klux Klan, that gives a pretty good sense of what Drvar is today.

An Unpleasant Meal

As I say, I do not know quite all of this about Drvar when I arrive. Neither, as it turns out, does Zijo. Indeed, we will find that a lack of proper information is a general problem this evening. I drive over a mountain and into Drvar in search of a village which I later will figure out really is not near Drvar at all. It is about 40 miles away. That mislocated village is home to an *Oslobodjenje* correspondent.

We ride around a good bit looking for a restaurant and an accessible public telephone. We pass the Croat military installation that has been set up within the town. Several times we stop and ask people on the street about the village for which we are searching. The blank stares are not purely out of rudeness. The people here all are refugees from other parts of the country, after all, and they would be unlikely to know. One kind man, who is leading a small child by the hand down the street, wants to be sure we understand that he would help us if he could, but he really is quite sure that no such village lies near Drvar.

There are two public telephones on Drvar's main street. These accept only payment cards for the Croatian national phone company. It strikes me as queer that the state-owned telecom of a neighboring country should provide the only public phones in this corner of Bosnia and Hercegovina. On the other hand, were it not for the Croatian

---

[80]International Crisis Group, *House Burnings: Obstruction of the Right to Return to Drvar* (Brussels and Washington: International Crisis Group, 9 June 1997).

company, there might be no public phone here at all. For our purposes, as we have only Bosnia and Hercegovina telephone cards, the result is the same. We give up on telephoning and walk down the street to the first place we see presenting itself as a pizzeria.

By the looks of the predominantly male clientele, this establishment caters especially to the local military population. The waitress tells us there actually is no pizza served here, only coffee and other drinks. In a manner curt but not overtly rude, she recommends we go down the street a couple blocks to another pizzeria, which, she assures us, does sell pizza. This young woman is Miss Congeniality relative to the boorish brute of a waitress we encounter at Pizzeria Rimini.

I guess they do not often get out-of-town guests here (and probably not a lot of repeat business from those who do stop in). Apparently, that suits everybody just fine. Well, it turns out they do not have any pizza here at Pizzeria Rimini, either. Rather than to discuss our ideas about why the management might wish to change the name of its restaurant, we just order something else from the menu. We do so, that is, once our waitress has served those who came in after us, smoked a cigarette, made a phone call, and spent some time flirting with several thuggish-looking types who perhaps have come around to create atmosphere.

Zijo is quite upset. He cannot completely conceal this fact, because he feels his unhappiness and unease so strongly. Naturally, Zijo is more sensitive to the looks and remarks of the other customers and hangers-out than I am. I try to do as much of the talking with the waitress as I can and to overcompensate with politeness. I am treated just as rudely as he is. I am determined, though, that we will eat in this restaurant. We do, and, in the end, we get a good meal.

Our original plan had been to spend the night in Drvar. We now decide, though, to drive back over the mountain to Bosanski Petrovac, which we expect will be more hospitable.

As I drive, Zijo tells me about some of what was making him so uncomfortable back in Pizzeria Rimini. In contrast to some of our other trips, he explains, this time he has not tried to adjust his Sarajevo speech to local dialects. The waitress and others, Zijo figures, had responded negatively to that fact. Also, he had observed that people in Drvar seemed to speak quite unnaturally, as if they were trying very hard to modify their own language in order to speak as they perceive that Croats should speak.

Zijo remarks, too, that he overheard several people in the restaurant talking about a bomb attack that took place today in Sarajevo. There is some confusion in that regard. The talk seemed to be about an attack on a prominent and politically active Roman Catholic priest. In fact, as we will learn in the morning, it is a Croat member of the central government who was severely injured today by a car bomb. The wounded official is the very Jozo Leutar, who in 1997 had compared the human-rights situation in Drvar to that in Sarajevo.

Warm Hospitality in Rainy Bosanski Petrovac

Bosanski Petrovac lies just off the main road running from Bihać in the northwest to Sarajevo in the central part of the country. Spread out on a high plain that is otherwise only sparsely populated, there is a remote, Route-66 feel about the town and its environs. Darkness has fallen and a light rain is coming down by the time we enter Bosanski Petrovac. Unlit streets cause the town to seem much emptier than it in fact is. We roll gropingly around the streets until I find what we think must be the center of town. I park in the rain and the darkness. We get out and walk, looking for a warm and dry place.

We are drawn to a pale blotch of light that a small shop selling mixed goods is casting into the general murkiness. Across the street, a coffee shop emits its own weak light and muffled but lively music into the glow. Inside the coffee shop, two young, Muslim waiters are tonight conducting a good but not bustling business. The ambience is that of a small-town corner tavern somewhere in the American Midwest, except that everyone is drinking strong, sweet coffee instead of weak beer and the odd shot. The white-shirted waiters are a gregarious pair. We stand at the bar, smoking, sipping coffee, and chatting with the waiter who is spooning sugar from a bucket into tiny porcelain cups and working the coffeemaker. The second fellow, who is waiting tables, joins the conversation when he sporadically comes by for more drinks.

I have driven past Bosanski Petrovac on several occasions previously. My first impression—a gut feeling—had been that this was a Serb city. Subsequently, I noticed a couple minarets poking up from the town, which would not be very normal where Serbs are in control. The reality, in fact, is somewhere in between. Serbs came back to vote in the September elections or voted by absentee ballot, the waiter tells us, as he scoops sugar in a fluid motion. That has created the curious situation wherein Bosanski Petrovac has a Serb mayor and generally

Serb-dominated local administration even though the majority of the population today is Muslim.

There formerly were more mosques than the couple that I have seen from the road. Serb nationalists destroyed the others. The waiter says, though, that Muslims did not destroy the Orthodox churches in retribution.

Before the wars, the district of Bosanski Petrovac had been populated 75% by Serbs and 21% by Muslims. Croats were few and far between in these parts. Until the *Oluja* offensive, this area had been under Serb military control from 1992 into summer of 1995. It was during that time, the waiter tells us, that several mosques were wiped away. Although Bosnia and Hercegovina's Croats and Muslims were formally united into their Federation at the time of *Oluja*, that had been primarily a Croat operation. Driving the Serbs from the Drvar-Bosanski Petrovac area in 1995 had created conditions for Croats and Muslims to grapple over the spoils. In the end, the Croats had gotten Drvar and the Muslims had taken a weak grip on Bosanski Petrovac.

Considering the prewar population distribution, it is not surprising that absentee voting could put Serbs in control of Bosanski Petrovac's administration. In fact, that is approximately the way Dayton is supposed to work. Foreign observers generally hope, though, that voting and local administration will not be driven by ethnonational considerations. There has been precious little in actual fact to support that hope. As Drvar exemplifies, and perhaps Bosanski Petrovac does, too, elections are one thing and day-to-day life another.

The waiters ask about Sarajevo. It seems they do not get a lot of news out this way about goings-on in the capital. They have not yet heard, for example, about the assassination attempt in Sarajevo today. People from a friendly cluster of other locals join in the conversation from time to time. We talk also about America, about politics and about the upcoming privatization. I tell them about the privatizations that I have experienced in the Czech Republic and Ukraine. The general view seems to be that people here are more concerned about jobs than they are about who owns the enterprises that create those jobs. Zijo asks about accommodations, and we are advised to spend the night at the Motel 9 that is out on the highway.

After a day of potentially hostile environments, it is a pleasure to chat over coffee in a friendly café. Were we Serbs or Croats, though, rather than a Muslim from Sarajevo and an American, I suppose we would not have been welcomed here so warmly.

Last Stop: Bihać

A few minutes after 5:00 a.m., I finally give up on the idea of getting any more sleep this night. I have been awake for an hour or so. The booming bass-and-drum beat from the motel disco is still going strong. Covering my head with a pillow does no good, as the beat is resonating through the floor and bed, as well as through the flimsy door. I am surprised there are enough people ready to party all night to justify an all-night disco. Somewhere in this remote and seemingly impoverished town on the high plains there must be more wealth than first meets the eye if the party crowd passes the night at the Motel 9 out on the edge of town. They must do a good business in the disco, if that is more important than the sleep of the motel guests.

Forty minutes earlier, I had heard another guest wake his colleague in the room next door. "Get up. It's 4:30. Time to get going." Probably, I had figured, the nightclub closes at 5:00. Even the party animals in Bosanski Petrovac must sleep sometime. But the booming continues. Rising, I touch the stone-cold radiator next to my bed. I dress, and walk down the hall to use the toilet. If the disco is still open, then there must also be a place to get coffee. So I continue on down to the bar and restaurant on the ground floor.

Bleary-eyed, I ask the nicely dressed young man behind the bar where this music is coming from. Is the disco next door? There is no music, he says, gesturing toward an empty bandstand on one side of the room. It is only on weekends. Then where is that music coming from? He points to a small stereo speaker fastened to the ceiling. Aha! There is the all-night discotheque. The explanation is in thin, wooden floors and the night clerk's need to entertain himself.

I complain a little in an ugly mixture of Slavic tongues. My command of the local language is poorer than usual at this hour and before coffee. He turns the music down a little, then brings coffee and a *Fanta* to my table by the window. As I sip my morning stimulants, he reduces the volume a little more. Outside, a light snow is falling. I see my reflection in the window, realizing then that I do not look friendly at this hour. My visage even shocks me a bit. After seeing the nasty slits though which my eyes blearily squint, my nasty scowl and my hair all akimbo, I am surprised that the clerk did not turn the music off completely. I look down the long room at the sole other patron. He looks a lot worse off than I do, actually.

I am not upset, really. I had slept pretty well for several hours. How much more can one expect when for 35 deutschemarks one gets a double room, sufficient blankets to keep from freezing to death, the promise (albeit unfulfilled, in my case) of a hot shower and breakfast? This is not the *Hilton*, after all.

Testing the Rubicon's Waters

A breakfast of greasy eggs and bread has ameliorated my mood only minimally. Fortunately, Zijo is in rather better form. The phantom disco had disturbed his sleep, too, but he has the benefit of having gotten a hot shower before going to bed. He suggests some music in the car, perhaps thinking that I will sing along with the tape, as I sometimes do. The Allman Brothers playing "One Way Out" does perk me up a bit, but I do not sing.

Intermittent and generally light snow is falling as we cross the high plain, then drop down to Bihać in the Una River valley. I have one meeting planned in Bihać, then I will head home and Zijo will find his way back to Sarajevo by bus. The intended subject of my interview, Dika Bejdić, who is *Oslobodjenje's* correspondent in Bihać, is not in her office when we arrive. We go off to find a coffee shop, cutting through a small market square. Shoppers are few on this cold and raw morning. The merchants tamp their feet and glance about hopefully. We stop on the fringe of the marketplace so that Zijo can humor two talkative women selling cigarettes. For their efforts they get only a couple minutes' conversation.

We end up in the smoky Café Mustang, which is a popular place this chilly day. I pull out today's newspaper to read through the headlines and skim the main stories. Yesterday's assassination attempt in Sarajevo tops the news. Organized demonstrations in Banja Luka, Doboj, Brčko, Bijeljina and several other cities in Republika Srpska get second billing.

Leutar, who is Federation Deputy Minister for Police, was gravely injured when his *Volkswagen Golf* was blown up by a remote-controlled bomb. The car was parked near the US Embassy at the time of the explosion. Leutar's driver and bodyguard escaped with minor injuries. The Croat official has been responsible for efforts to root out corruption and to attack organized crime. Last summer, he had created an antiterrorist unit within his ministry.[81]

Croat nationalists from Jelavić on down were quick to blame Muslim political leaders for the attack, although there is apparently no evidence to support those accusations. Predictably, some Croats cited the incident as further evidence that, for the sake of their security, they must have an entity of their own.

In a sidebar to the bombing story, *Oslobodjenje* cites seven additional cases over the past two years in which Catholic churches and schools, Croats' police cars and other objects were either bombed or when explosive devices were discovered. In a front-page editorial, the newspaper expresses a fear that "Bosnia has crossed a Rubicon and has entered into the hell of systematic terrorism."

Testing the waters at a Rubicon of their own, perhaps 20,000 Serbs were out at various locations yesterday to protest. While all the protestors are angry about Brčko and Poplašen's firing, their leaders differ slightly in their views on the situation. At least three views were presented at the largest rally, in Banja Luka, according to Gordana Katana's report. A vice-president of Dodik's Independent Social Democrats called for peaceful methods of passive resistance as taught by the Indian nationalist Mahatma Gandhi. Then a political adviser to the fired Poplašen asked the public to "immediately break all forms of relations with the occupying powers." The radical then added that "Whoever is not with us is against us." A leader of Živko Radišić's Socialist Party, though, declared that only "by democratic methods will you preserve your democratic rights."

Life in the Big Lie

A middle-aged Muslim, Dika Bejdić is direct and plainspoken. She is displeased with both today's governing officials and with the international community, and Bejdić is not afraid to say so. She is angry that foreign countries and interests almost certainly contributed to Yugoslavia's breakup. I think she is correct in seeing guilt beyond the

---

[81]Leutar will die almost two weeks after the bombing. Westendorp's office will issue a statement at that time praising Leutar for his "courageous efforts to advance the cause of justice under difficult circumstances." By that time, HDZ will have boycotted Federation and joint government institutions for one week to protest the attack. HDZ also will call for the resignations of the Federation's prime minister and interior minister, who are Muslims. Responsibility for the murder remains unexplained.

borders, although I think I would apportion that blame somewhat differently than she does.

Bejdić describes the social situation in and around Bihać as "catastrophic," and says many people here are near to financial and emotional collapse. Thousands of Muslims from this area have moved abroad, both before and during the wars. Perhaps it is money flowing in from these Bošnjaks abroad, she surmises, that has forestalled social uprising here.

In and around Bihać, she relates, more than 90% of the people are Muslims and probably less than 1% are Serbs. Serbs formerly made up one-fifth of the population. About one-tenth of the population formerly was Croat. Many are now gone, and there is still an outflow of Croats to nearby Croatia. All the fine words about returning and resettling refugees Bejdić characterizes as a "big lie." Political leaders do not want the refugees to return to their homes.

She does not say so, but I get a sense that she has practically given up on the idea of restoring multiethnic communities in Bosnia and Hercegovina. The international community's first priority now, Bejdić tells me, should be on creating jobs. She says that if they do not get jobs soon, people will begin to "work against society."

I ask about the privatization. Bejdić is pessimistic about that, too. Privatization will go forward, as she acknowledges it must, but only criminals and nationalist politicians will gain control of businesses. Her expectations are that the outcome will be most unfortunate. Bejdić says she is no expert on economic matters, but she does feel that some enterprises should remain under state control so that normal people will have places to go for jobs.

Bejdić dreads the thought that war criminals and profiteers—who are about the only ones having money in large quantities today—will become the new bosses of industry. The state allows them to continue enriching themselves. As these people pay neither taxes nor social security, the government loses out on potential revenues and even those fortunate enough to have work do not build security.

Bribery and corruption, Bejdić observes, exist even at the highest levels in society and government. She points to the example of a leading official in SDA and the government who is supposedly responsible to help clean up corruption. This man reportedly has purchased a luxurious house in Sarajevo at a price that is a fraction of its market value. He controls businesses and sends his children abroad for their educations. How are people to believe that this man is going to fight corruption and to work for improving other people's situations? Journalists, Bejdić notes, can spend many months investigating, documenting and writing about cases of corruption, only to watch as the accused officials rise to higher and higher positions.

How Professionals See It

During this second and briefer trip I have spoken with four *Oslobodjenje* journalists in four cities and four distinct parts of the country: Sarajevo, Zenica, Banja Luka and today Bihać. My conversations on the whole have been something quite different in contrast to those of my previous journey. Earlier, I aimed to speak with a large cross-section of common people. This time, I spoke with a more select group of what I regard as professional observers. Good, professional journalists are trained to observe but at the same time are accustomed to repressing their opinions. So, to request such a journalist for an interview is to ask that person to step outside his or her customary role. I appreciate these professionals' willingness to share their thoughts and allowing me to use these to prod my own thinking. In opening up to me, they of course were not speaking for *Oslobodjenje*.

I admire those journalists who strive to work to high standards in Bosnia and Hercegovina. It is no easy matter to practice professional journalism in an environment where the principles of professional journalism—things like objectivity, balance and accuracy—are not much seen or appreciated. *Oslobodjenje* comes closer to what we in Western democracies would regard as professional journalistic practice than do most news media in Bosnia and Hercegovina. It is for that reason that I have used *Oslobodjenje* as my primary source for published information in the local language.

There are several subjects about which I have asked in each of these meetings. Brotherhood and Unity is one of these. The proper role for SFOR and the international community is another. I have tried also to draw out my informants on some big-picture issues.

On Brotherhood and Unity

An American friend of mine is absolutely convinced that Yugoslavs of her generation believed in the Titoist ideology of Brotherhood and Unity. This was not just an empty slogan for them, she insists. My friend is a South Slavic specialist. I have a lot of respect for her opinions. Perhaps, she says, some in the World War II generation did not buy into Brotherhood and Unity, and maybe the younger generation that fought the wars of Yugoslav succession did not, but there is a middle generation that did.

When I drive through Bosnia and Hercegovina, however, and see broken Serb village after smashed Croat village after devastated Muslim village, it is difficult to believe, frankly, that this mind-set ever had much force. When I walk through the towns and speak with people, the sentiments of hatred and vindictiveness often make a stronger impression than do any of reconciliation. Genuine forgiveness is rare.

What's more, the nationalities question had remained an important issue of communist ideology and public policy all through the period from World War II to the disintegration of Yugoslavia. If the notion of Brotherhood and Unity had been internalized by a substantial majority of Yugoslavs, one might reasonably ask, why then were ethnic relations always near the top of the political agenda?

The top-level leaders who began and conducted the wars of Yugoslav succession were members of that generation born immediately after World War II. That fact, pointed out Salihović, in Sarajevo, naturally makes one somewhat skeptical about how influential was the slogan, philosophy and guiding principle of Brotherhood and Unity. After all, these people are the age of Tito's children. Many of them were members of the League of Communists of Yugoslavia. Of course, it is also true that these nationalist politicians scarcely represent a cross-section of Yugoslav society.

Emphasizing that he was giving me a very personal view, Salihović likened Brotherhood and Unity to a plant whose roots had grown not so deeply as some people previously had thought. The principle did have its adherents, though, and some internalized it much more profoundly than did others. Brotherhood and Unity, Salihović observed, took root most deeply within what he calls the "Rock 'n' Roll Generation." By that term he refers not so much to an entire generation, though, as to its educated and cultured urban elite. For many of those people, Brotherhood and Unity was something very real. But views in rural villages were often quite different from those in the cities and among the most educated. Many villagers lived in worlds that were isolated from the urban elites by mountains and by their traditions. Salihović admitted that he himself was surprised to see in retrospect how great had been that urban-rural contrast. Because of its shallow roots, Salihović remarked, it was relatively easy "to take that young plant and to pull it out."

To establish something like Brotherhood and Unity now will not be easy. That is particularly true, the Sarajevo-based journalist noted, because the urban intellectuals largely have emigrated to other countries.

Brotherhood and Unity, says Bejdić, here in Bihać, "was at one and the same time a lie and the truth." This was demonstrated during the wars over Bosnia and Hercegovina. While some were trying to drive their neighbors out, there were also many examples of neighbors who helped—or tried to help—one another and without regard to ethnicity. She cites an example close to her heart: While some Serbs were trying to force her parents from their house, other Serbs were trying to help them.

Yugoslavia was built upon friendship between peoples, Bejdić maintains. She feels in her heart that there are many good Serbs, formerly from Bihać, and from elsewhere in Bosnia and Hercegovina, who are now living as refugees in Vojvodina, in Belgrade and elsewhere. These good Serbs never would have intended harm to non-Serbs here. Many people in Bihać, she believes, share her opinion, but most of them are not yet ready to say so.

Brotherhood and Unity, Djulan remarked in Zenica, "was just an excellent slogan, and Yugoslavia was built upon that slogan...Yugoslavia could survive only on slogans and by the repeating of those slogans." People used those words all the time in their day-to-day public speech, he said, but they often did not believe in those words.

Of course, one need not like, or even believe in, rules of conduct in order to live within them. "We must live together now, though," Djulan noted. Unless all the nations coexist in the spirit of something like Brotherhood and Unity, there will be no country here at all. A Greater Croatia, a Greater Serbia, a Muslim nation, he insisted, these are not real options for Bosnia and Hercegovina.

In my own view, it is unrealistic to portray Bosnia-Hercegovina within Yugoslavia as a land of ethnic harmony. There was tolerance, yes, but that tolerance was enforced from above. There were countless individual examples of intergroup friendship, but there also were tensions between and within communities. Neither is it accurate to portray the old Bosnia-Hercegovina as a land on the verge of ethnic explosion at every moment. The reality is somewhere in between, and extremely complicated.

In any case, there is nothing like Brotherhood and Unity in Bosnia and Hercegovina today—certainly not with a capital B and a capital U. Nor will there be anything like Brotherhood and Unity in the foreseeable future. Hatred is now real and fear is great. The war, ethnic cleansing and post-Dayton politics have been conducted in such ways as to maximize interethnic separation and discord. Certain forces of toleration and decency have lost to those of bigotry and ignominy. That is an ugly reality. But it is reality, and no amount of wishful think will change that.

On the International Community's Role

From protecting the peace to paying public-sector salaries, rebuilding bridges and houses to running elections, the international community seems to have its hands (and money) in everything here. Many people regard preventing war in the immediate term as the foreigners' most important function. Education, refugee resettlement and jobs creation are other roles for the international community that are important in the minds of the journalists I interviewed.

It is not a good thing that Bosnia and Hercegovina needs to have SFOR here in order to prevent renewed fighting, Djulan told me, but in fact SFOR is needed.

Perhaps there would be war without SFOR, said Salihović, but it is really difficult to know for sure what would happen if the foreign military forces left. In any case, he commented that it would be ridiculous to think that SFOR should remain here for decades on end. Steps must be taken to assure that will not be necessary.

Salihović told me that, in his view, education is one of the most important tasks for the international community. Salihović meant by this that people here need to be taught the principles of modern democracy; the news media need help to learn what is their proper role in an open society and how professionally to perform that role; aid is needed in order to build a good educational system overall. Young people need civic education, he said, to learn to respect and to appreciate one another. Now, some here argue that civic education is hostile to national culture. It is ridiculous, Salihović insisted, to think it is necessary to teach cultural exclusivism and divisiveness instead of appreciation for ethnic differences and inclusiveness. Such narrow views belong to those who want to keep the common people ignorant so that their leaders can more readily manipulate them in order to gain and hold onto power.

Refugee resettlement is a high priority in Katana's mind. If Annex 7 is to be implemented, she believes, then SFOR must demonstrate its strength more. In Bihać and the Federation, Bejdić's perspective on resettlement is similar to Katana's in Banja Luka and Republika Srpska. The political leaders, she relates, are agreed that they do not want refugees to return to their homes. At the same time, Bejdić suggests, lack of jobs is one of the reasons that resettlement is going nowhere fast. That is why she hopes that the international community will make economic development efforts to create jobs a higher priority. If there are no jobs in Bihać, why would the people living here now encourage others to come? Likewise, why would those whose homes are elsewhere go back to where there are no jobs? Djulan told me that he believes a major public works program is needed of the sort organized in the US during the Great Depression of the 1930s.

So, there still is plenty for the international community to do. Keeping the lid on violence is not enough. There is not yet an economic, political and social foundation upon which to build a prosperous and pluralistic society, and there is a great deal of resistance, corruption, inefficiency and poor cooperation within the country. It is frustrating for donors to see the extent to which bad leadership and the lack of unified effort diminish the effectiveness of their donations, efforts and good intentions.

On the Big Picture

I ask about how Bosnia and Hercegovina fits into the regional big picture that is former Yugoslavia, what are the prospects for the country's own political development, and what are the social or political landmines that could trigger renewed violence?

Bosnia and Hercegovina is a country "unnaturally divided," Salihović told me. This unnatural divide is not sustainable in the long run. Circumstances point to two possibilities for the future. The first of these is that Bosnia and Hercegovina will ultimately be divided between Croatia and Serbia. The second possibility is to end the unnatural division of the country by abolishing the Inter-Entity Boundary Line, eliminating the Federation, eliminating Republika Srpska and making Bosnia and Hercegovina whole and unified again. But to continue over the long term as an internally divided country is not viable. The country must go one way or the other. Right now, Salihović thinks the forces working to divide Bosnia and Hercegovina are stronger than are those that would reunite it.

Some think they see a third way, for example to divide the country into three entities (one for each Croats, Muslims and Serbs). In Salihović's opinion, that approach, for which Croat nationalists now clamor incessantly, would leave the country's Muslims in a kind of ghetto. It would be different if there could be a Bošnjak country. But Salihović just does not see a "critical mass" to create a Slavic Muslim state.

From her vantage point in Bihać, Bejdić would agree with Salihović only insofar as she thinks that to create three separate Croat, Serb and Bošnjak entities would be to eliminate Bosnia and Hercegovina as a country. Although Bejdić says she is not a big fan of Fikret Abdić, she does share Abdić's view that if Bosnia and Hercegovina is to remain unified then it should be subdivided along ethnic lines into cantons and with decentralized governmental authority. Such decentralization within the state boundaries, she believes, is the only solution that will maintain Bosnia and Hercegovina as a single country.

Developments elsewhere within former Yugoslavia are felt in Bosnia and Hercegovina, Salihović remarked, but it is not generally true that developments here have effects elsewhere. The breakdown in civic order and war in Bosnia and Hercegovina, for example, was the result of Serbian and Croatian politics. Once Serbia and Croatia resolve their conflicts, then the situation in Bosnia and Hercegovina will be nearly settled.

In the meantime, Salihović is apprehensive that Milošević and Serbia, as well as Tudjman and Croatia, will continue to meddle in Bosnia and Hercegovina. He pointed out to me, though, that people in Serbia are themselves tired of Milošević. Then, too, Kosovo is a big problem for Serbia/Yugoslavia, and so Milošević's attention and resources likely will be focused upon the situation there.[82] In that Tudjman wishes to build Croatia's standing in international circles, Salihović predicted that Tudjman will not sacrifice the progress he has made thus far in that direction by meddling too aggressively in Bosnia and Hercegovina.

Milošević and Belgrade is the power source that drives Republika Srpska, commented Salihović. If Milošević falls from power and Yugoslavia/Serbia becomes democratic, that will pull the plug on Republika Srpska. He pointed out that the first thing that a Poplašen, or

---

[82]This interview occurred on 12 March 1999, just 12 days before NATO began its air campaign against Yugoslavia.

even a Dodik, does when he rises here in Bosnia and Hercegovina is to go to Belgrade. He would not come to power to begin with had he not some level of support in Serbia's capital.

Even if forces, be they internal or external, were to try and stir up trouble here, Bejdić says only some kind of extreme coercion could cause people in Bosnia and Hercegovina to take up arms again. People are tired and broken. With the exception of those who have political connections or business opportunities, she adds, the situations of former soldiers are especially bad. People are poor and unemployed; some are crippled from war wounds. Although there is some risk of social uprising, these conditions contribute to a certain weary stability. It is difficult, Bejdić observes, to destabilize such a situation. She has been also to Republika Srpska. People there have lost their pride and also are broken. The Bihać journalist believes, too, that Serbs are beginning to accept that their nation is largely responsible for what has happened here.

Salihović also had said that he perceives among people a certain "resignation." Political upheaval is possible, but not a military outburst. SFOR and the international community are doing their jobs well, and that will keep the lid on things here. It may be several years, Salihović remarked before it would be possible for the people of any ethnonational group here to be driven to take any wild actions.

Unfortunately, in such an atmosphere, it also can be difficult to motivate people even for positive ends. In the Balkans, Djulan explained, people always need a leader—and a strong one. When there is no such leader, as was the case in Yugoslavia after Tito died, then such foolishness as interethnic fighting can occur. Unfortunately, he does not see a good and powerful leader among any of the people currently holding the most visible positions of power in Bosnia and Hercegovina. The wars have not formed leaders that are suitable for today and for the future.

One might argue that today Carlos Westendorp is the leader. Yes, Djulan allows there is no other way for the time being but to have a strong foreign ruler. Westendorp is effectively president of Bosnia and Hercegovina, he says, noting that the High Representative is doing a good job overall but should exert his authority even more strongly than he does already. Westendorp is in a difficult position, Djulan adds, because all the local politicians lie to him—saying they will do one thing and then doing quite another.

Bejdić, too, comments upon the leadership void. Bosnia and Hercegovina, she says, is like a little Yugoslavia and it needs a Tito— somebody strong and able to keep the country under control. Does she see such a person anywhere in her country? "Unfortunately not." In the long run, this leader cannot be a foreigner. Bosnia and Hercegovina, Bejdić states, needs a leader who is a *Bosanac*. (I note that she does not say a Bošnjak.)

I agree that Bosnia and Hercegovina remains an open question until the larger imbroglio that is all of former Yugoslavia is worked out. What's more, those political leaders in whose hands power is now most concentrated cannot mend this torn country. People here do not believe in their leaders. They acknowledge their leaders, and they want to believe in them. They even are desperate to be led. But they do not believe. Until larger issues beyond but overhanging Bosnia and Hercegovina's borders finally have been resolved, and until modern and capable leaders somehow emerge, an uneasy equilibrium grounded in political inertia may very well tediously endure.

Tricky Weather in Bosnia and Hercegovina

Zijo did not bring a warm coat from Sarajevo, and he has been concealing his chill. It was spring when we left Sarajevo a couple days ago, as it had been when I had come through Bihać a week earlier. Now, though, winter is enjoying its final amusement at our expense. Snow is falling not heavily, but steadily. The cold is not extreme, although it is bothersome. In the Czech Republic, we call this "*aprilový počasí*," meaning "tricky weather." The term is a poetic reference to the mischievous pranks of April Fools Day, when one and all have a sanctioned right to be something less than forthright.

I am wearing an old ski jacket. I no longer need the jacket, which is worn but still functional. I figure the weather will improve along the drive out of this damp river bottom and beyond the high altitudes of Kordun, Zagorje and Styria. As we stand next to my car and say goodbye, I give my coat to Zijo. The jacket is warm from my body. As he zips it up over his light blazer, the glow in Zijo's face is the first outward sign of just how chilled he really was. The jacket hangs well on this poet from Sarajevo who has discovered much about his country by traveling through it with a foreigner.

I turn the car around, pointing it toward home. Zijo walks the other way. When I look into the rearview mirror, he is just disappearing into Bosnia and Hercegovina's *aprilový počasí*.

Epilogue

So It Goes, and So It Goes

On 24 March 1999, one week to the day after I left Bosnia and Hercegovina, the gathering Kosovo crisis burst wide open. NATO began bombing Yugoslavia, and Serb forces launched a massive ethnic-cleansing operation in Kosovo. The bombing and cleansing continued for 78 days. The Kosovo crisis sharply heightened tensions in Bosnia and Hercegovina, and especially in Republika Srpska. Nonmilitary international personnel—including IPTF staff—were pulled from Republika Srpska. Some international offices within the Serb entity were attacked. Nevertheless, that volatile situation did not explode.

The mass exodus of more than half of Kosovo's 1.8 million ethnic Albanians could have been much worse for Bosnia and Hercegovina than it turned out to be. An estimated 10,000 Kosovo-Albanian refugees, and perhaps a similar number of Sandžak Muslims, already were in the Federation before Kosovo blew up. More flowed in during the bombing and ethnic cleansing. When the bombing stopped, UNHCR counted some 22,000 Kosovo-Albanian and 22,000 Sandžak Muslim refugees in the Federation. In addition, there were in Republika Srpska an unknown number of Serbs who had fled Serbia and Montenegro.

During the bombing and ethnic cleansing, the extended Serb nation exhibited to the world an ugly aspect of the mystical Serb nationalism. While horrendous atrocities were being committed in Kosovo by Serbs and in the name of the Serb nation, Serbs absolutely denied responsibility and even the indisputable facts concerning the massive crimes against humanity that were occurring. One would expect complete denial from the oddly mixed former communists and vicious ultranationalists who are Serbia/Yugoslavia's government and political officials. Joining in the blind denial, though, were leaders of the Serbian Orthodox Church, common people on the streets of Belgrade and across Serbia, and some American citizens of Serbian descent. This cannot be attributed to a lack of information and a controlled press. There was sufficient information for those who wished to know, but it was lost on those who refused to believe.

Even as returning Kosovars and international criminal investigators set about the grisly work of discovering, investigating, burying and reburying Kosovo's mutilated and murdered, many Serbs persisted in denial, characterizing the nauseating new evidence as lies and fabrications. In the wake of the Kosovo defeat, the Serbian Orthodox Church joined various opposition groups in denouncing Milošević and calling for his resignation. It has been ambiguous, though, whether Church leaders, who have blessed Serb ultranationalists in their vicious wars throughout the 1990s, felt Milošević should go because of the evil committed in Kosovo or because he had lost Kosovo.

This revolting display by members of the Serb nation powerfully illustrates the generally dehumanizing potential of nationalism and the intensity of nationalist sentiment in the Balkans. As was true of Bošnjak nationalists in Yugoslav Bosnia-Hercegovina, extreme nationalists among the Kosovo Albanians contributed also to the crisis there.

•   •   •   •

Remarkably, the effective unity of the 19-country NATO alliance did not come apart during the 11-week bombing campaign. Milošević was counting on international disunity to save him, as it had done so many times before. To be honest, I also was skeptical that the NATO countries would remain unified, particularly when it became clear early in the campaign that planning for the operation had been inadequate and based upon poor intelligence.

The NATO-led and UN-assisted occupation and protection of Kosovo has gone forward too slowly. Serb forces began pulling out of Kosovo on 10 June. Shortly after midnight on 12 June, a Russian convoy rolled into Kosovo's capital of Priština. NATO forces had not yet begun moving into Kosovo. The 200 Russian early-bird forces secured Priština's airport, where the NATO commander had intended to set up a command center. These Russians were SFOR troops who had been ordered by Moscow to abandon their posts in Bosnia and Hercegovina and had traveled to Priština through Serbia. The "S" in SFOR had been painted over on their military vehicles with "K" to create KFOR, the acronym for the Kosovo protection force. Several days later, the small Russian contingent was still making trouble for NATO.

A month after the international troops began moving into Kosovo, only about one-half of the planned 55,000-plus occupying troops had yet been deployed. Meanwhile, ethnic Albanians were taking their revenge on their Serb and Gypsy neighbors—burning, looting, and sometimes killing. Much of the non-Albanian population was fleeing. Overstretched NATO soldiers were making the best of a difficult situation not of their own making. Only part of the blame for this slow deployment can be attributed to the fact that the militarily inept UN is involved in this peacemaking operation.

•   •   •   •

The crisis in Kosovo has mixed effects for Bosnia and Hercegovina. Most positively, perhaps, it has drawn some international attention back to that country. At the same time, though, it is now clear that Kosovo and other Balkan states (especially Albania and Macedonia, but also Bulgaria and Romania) also need assistance. Resources are limited, and, frankly, Bosnia and Hercegovina has not shown great ability effectively to use those resources which the world has provided it. A secure and economically improving Balkan region is in the best interests of all countries and people within the region, so the people of Bosnia and Hercegovina should not expect to receive an inordinate share of the available aid.

Croats and Muslims in Bosnia and Hercegovina and elsewhere will view Serbia's defeat in and over Kosovo rather positively, if not with outright joy. While Serbia/Yugoslavia has been weakened, though, there is reason for concern that its very weakness might cause the country to become radicalized politically. While Milošević quite rightfully is portrayed as a tyrant, war criminal and failure as a grand strategist, the prospect that such alternative political leaders as Vojislav Šešelj and Vuk Drašković might assume greater power in Serbia should concern Europeans and NATO.[83] Nor should Serbia's weakness be exaggerated. Serbia is down, but it is not out. There is still plentiful potential for Serb extreme nationalists to make trouble in Montenegro, in Macedonia, in Vojvodina, and even in Kosovo and Republika Srpska.

Parallels naturally are being drawn between post-Dayton Bosnia and Hercegovina and postwar Kosovo. To the extent that these are relevant, political and military authorities, as well as international aid and development agencies, should draw upon the experience gained and lessons learned in Bosnia and Hercegovina. The first three to four

---

[83]Milošević looks like a choirboy in comparison to the ruthlessly ultranationalist Šešelj. Šešelj's SRS is the second-largest party in the Serbian parliament, with 82 of 250 seats. Milošević's coalition of socialists and communists has 110 seats. With the Kosovo defeat, Šešelj threatened to leave the government and to take his party with him. He remains in government as of this writing, as Milošević has insisted that all governing officials remain in their positions for the sake of unity and continuity. Drašković leads the Serbian Renewal Movement, which holds 45 seats in Parliament. He is in Yugoslavia analogous to what Plavšić is in Bosnia and Hercegovina: an extremist, cut out of basically the same cloth as is Šešelj, but clever enough to dress up in lamb's clothing to make a good impression on the West. Drašković formerly was allied with Šešelj and, like Šešelj, promoted for himself a *Četnik* image while sponsoring a violent and ultranationalist paramilitary group. Drašković's forces gained notoriety for their brutal ethnic-cleansing activities in eastern Hercegovina.

years of peace implementation in Bosnia and Hercegovina offer some, albeit limited, insight as to what one should expect to see happen in Kosovo. Let us be clear, though: Kosovo is not Bosnia and Hercegovina.

Kosovo, like Bosnia and Hercegovina, is a mountainous and economically poor land. Kosovo is much smaller, with only about one-fifth the land area of Bosnia and Hercegovina. Considered on a prewars basis, Kosovo's population is roughly two-fifths that of Bosnia and Hercegovina. The damage to infrastructure and housing stock is much less extensive in Kosovo than in Bosnia and Hercegovina. Ethnic cleansing was viciously pursued in Kosovo over three months, but in Bosnia and Hercegovina the combatants spent four years destroying their country and one another.

The international community likely will establish a true protectorate in Kosovo. It can and should do so because, as of this writing, no government to speak of exists there. By contrast, the Dayton accords recognized existing governing structures and personalities in Bosnia and Hercegovina. Dayton did not disband and disarm existing Serb, Croat and Bošnjak military structures. Therefore, a true protectorate could not have been created in Bosnia and Hercegovina.

Potentially, Kosovo's lack of government is an advantage for the international community as it tries to help build something there. In post-Dayton Bosnia and Hercegovina, such government as existed was far worse than had there been nothing at all. The assumption had been that existing local leaders would run things with the assistance of the international community and that a basis for democracy already was in place. The reality was—and is—far different. Ineffective governing institutions, free-for-all politics, and political agendas driven by nationalism and maliciousness continue to this day greatly to hinder progress on many fronts in Bosnia and Hercegovina.

On the other hand, in that Kosovo legally remains a part of Serbia and of Yugoslavia, there will be constitutional issues and other legal complications in establishing an autonomous Kosovo. Nevertheless, as it operates in Kosovo, the international community likely will pay Belgrade little heed so long as a government run by Milošević or politicians of his ilk is in power there.

Ethnonational problems will be far less troublesome in Kosovo than in Bosnia and Hercegovina. Whereas in Bosnia and Hercegovina there is a three-sided struggle, with the Croat and Serb sides trying to tear the country apart even as Bošnjak elements attempt to pull it back together under their own discreditable control, Kosovo will now be more than 90% ethnic Albanian.[84] What Serbs and other minorities remain will be practically irrelevant as political forces in Kosovo. On the other hand, divisions between factions within the Kosovo Albanian community will be troublesome and easily could turn violent.

The international community's success or failure in Kosovo, as in Bosnia and Hercegovina, will nevertheless be measured in accordance with how well minorities are protected and their interests respected. After nearly four years, this has not been achieved very successfully in Bosnia and Hercegovina. The international community should analyze why that has been the case and judge what therefore can be done differently in Kosovo.

Another aspect of Dayton implementation that has been disappointing is the slow progress and extent to which the economy there has been put on track. Nonetheless, various parties use economic statistics to portray that situation more positively than the underlying—and, in fact, visible—reality. Figures are cited to suggest, for example, that annual GDP growth in Bosnia and Hercegovina is now as high as 40%. That sounds impressive, but anyone with eyes and ears connected to a brain and who visits can recognize that economic progress there is not astonishingly rapid. A senior Western aid official in Bosnia and Hercegovina has pointed out that a key lesson from experience there is that, in Kosovo, there should be an immediate effort to privatize industry, to establish a market economy, and to attract business investments.[85]

In addition to transferring wisdom, some personnel and resources presently in Bosnia and Hercegovina likely will be redirected to Kosovo. Shortly after NATO forces had moved into Kosovo, IPTF advisors were on their way from Bosnia and Hercegovina to Kosovo to assist in establishing a trained and responsible local police force. This, surely, is an example of how knowledge advantageously can be transferred from the experience in Bosnia and Hercegovina to the effort

---

[84]There are in Bosnia and Hercegovina really more than three sides, in fact. The international community and non-nationalist political leaders are working (and not generally much in concert with one another) toward building a truly multiethnic democracy in which no ethnonational group will tyrannize other ethnonational or ethnically unconnected groups at either the local or highest levels.

[85]Fredrik Dahl, "West Must Not Wait with Kosovo Reform," *Reuters*, 23 June 1999.

in Kosovo. Hopefully, there will not be such a large net transfer of these resources to Kosovo that it occurs to the detriment of Bosnia and Hercegovina.

International donors have plenty of reasons to be frustrated, and even disgusted, with the slow progress made in Bosnia and Hercegovina. It is to be expected that donors will be dissatisfied with local political bosses who stubbornly refuse to cooperate with one another, ignore the great and real needs of the people they purport to represent, and even act outright to thwart progress. Donors may feel it more productive to take their aid elsewhere. It will be difficult to argue against such judgments. The international community has begun to make a fuss about corruption, which informed observers say sucks off millions of dollars from the aid that is pouring into Bosnia and Hercegovina. Alija Izetbegović has responded to the accusations by saying that the donors are exaggerating the problem.[86]

Nevertheless, as smart bombs were flying into Serbia and Kosovo, representatives of some 45 countries and 30 donor organizations met in Brussels to discuss aid to Bosnia and Hercegovina. They agreed to provide $1.05 billion in 1999, which is the final installment of the $5.1 billion program for 1996–1999. The World Bank and EU project that Bosnia and Hercegovina will need about $2.6 billion in additional external funding during 2000–2004.

Even as KFOR is being assembled only sluggishly, NATO is announcing that it will begin in 1999 to scale back the SFOR operation in Bosnia and Hercegovina. Reductions from the 32,000-troop level to a force of less than 17,000 are planned. That does not bode well for refugee resettlement in Bosnia and Hercegovina, because refugees will not return as minorities to their communities unless they are confident

---

[86]As this book was being readied for publication, an article in the *New York Times* reported that as much as $1 billion in foreign aid and local government funds has been stolen in Bosnia and Hercegovina since the end of the wars there. (See: Chris Hedges, "Up to $1 Billion Reported Stolen by Bosnia Leaders, *New York Times*, 17 August 1999.) The *Times* obtained its information from investigators working for and within the Office of the High Representative. The US State Department, fearful of losing support in Congress for foreign aid, disputed the article. In fact, other sources support the substance of the *Times* story. Named in the article as "one of the wealthiest and most powerful men" in Bosnia and Hercegovina was Bakir Izetbegović, son of the Bošnjak member of the Presidency. I had heard Bakir Izetbegović's name mentioned several times in regard to corruption (and generally in hushed tones) during my time in the country. In my opinion, the State Department is wrong for disclaiming the evidence of corruption and outright theft.

that they will be protected. The cost of maintaining the SFOR force is cited as an important reason for the cutback. Many of the roughly 40 countries that contribute troops and other resources to SFOR also will be providing these to KFOR.

Also going home is Carlos Westendorp, High Representative since 1997. His appointment was for just two years. Coming in Westendorp's place is Austrian diplomat Wolfgang Petritsch. Petritsch, who has served as the EU's special envoy for Kosovo, was born in Klagenfurt, in southern Austria where Slovenian and German cultures meet and blend. He was raised bilingually to speak German and Slovenian. With a Ph.D. in East European history, he also speaks Serbo-Croatian.

Although Petritsch's credentials are good, the appointment of an Austrian should raise some eyebrows. The first two high representatives had been from countries well distant from the Balkan region, thereby creating a certain appearance of impartiality. The first high representative, Carl Bildt, is a former Swedish prime minister. Westendorp is Spanish (with a Dutch surname). Appointing an Austrian to the international community's top civilian post in Bosnia and Hercegovina seems to throw that aspect of neutrality to the wind.

While Petritsch brings a practical advantage in his ability to communicate with Serbs, Croats and Bošnjaks in their local language, he will be regarded as a Slovene and an Austrian. In light of their extreme sensitivity to history and Serbia's historical distrust and animosity toward Austria (and, especially more recently, toward Slovenia), Serb nationalists may look upon Petritsch's appointment as a provocative move. From a historical perspective, Croats and Bošnjaks may regard him more positively. In the final analysis, though, Petritsch should be judged only by his performance. Unfortunately for him, as was true for Bildt and Westendorp, his performance will be influenced by many factors over which he will not have full control.

Petritsch inherits from his predecessor a necessity still to contend with Nikola Poplašen, who, more than four months after his supposed firing, has not stepped down as President of Republika Srpska. Poplašen's powers, though, are minimal. Dodik, who continues as acting prime minister in Republika Srpska, reportedly has cut off funding for Poplašen's office. Elsewhere on the political front, OSCE has announced that municipal elections scheduled for November 1999 will be delayed until April 2000. OSCE attributes this delay to the war in Kosovo, noting that it has destabilized the political situation in Bosnia and Hercegovina.

Passing Judgment

Four years of continuous diplomacy were spent in ending the wars in Bosnia and Hercegovina and in Croatia. So far, nearly four more years have been spent in stitching together a peace from the tattered remains. The next stage, that of building long-term security and well-being, cannot move expeditiously forward until the peacemaking is complete. So long as peace is tenuous in Bosnia and Hercegovina, so long as thousands of families remain displaced, so long as the most heinous and high-level of war criminals remain at large and unsought, so long as governmental processes and institutions remain dysfunctional, then prospects are not good for the large-scale investments to occur that are necessary to create jobs, prospects are poor for integrating the country politically into democratic Europe, prospects are grim for healing the emotional wounds in order that coming generations will not also be infected with confusion, fear and hate.

At Dayton, the advocates of pluralism and unity accepted a two-entity Bosnia and Hercegovina because without doing so a deal to end the fighting could not have been made at that time. Otherwise, only continued warfare until the Serb side would be even more badly beaten could have softened the Serb nationalists sufficiently to stop armed hostilities. It was hoped that the guarantees established in Annex 7 would make the IEBL porous and would compel Croats and Muslims also to live together. The expectation, too, was that constitutional structures and protections outlined in Annex 4 had set a course to unity.

Those hopes have so far not been fulfilled. The IEBL is in fact a substantial barrier to the movement of people, goods, capital and services. Although traffic back and forth has become more common, most people still regard crossing the IEBL to be dangerous. Even within the Federation, Muslims and Croats are hesitant to enter towns and villages that are controlled by the other group. What I have seen and heard and felt in the likes of Jajce, Drvar, Pale, Rogatica and Mostar, shows me that their fears are not wholly without foundation.

Local officials and other nationalists are making a farce of Annex 7. Few displaced Serbs, Croats and Muslims have so far been allowed to return safely to their homes, to regain their lost property or to obtain just compensation for their losses. Quietly but effectively, political leaders of all groups are colluding to keep returns to a minimum.

Collaboration to frustrate the Dayton process is not the sort of cooperation between groups that the international community had expected. Meanwhile, military and police forces are insufficient, or improperly commanded, to provide frightened potential returnees the security that they need. Neither by threats nor by inducements has the international community so far been able to achieve the goals of Annex 7. Frankly, I do not see the will on the side of the international community to enforce Annex 7. I think that Annex 10, which assures that the High Representative cannot count upon SFOR to assist in enforcing its directives, is a big part of the problem.

Perhaps more progress has been made in reforming the media. The work of the MEC and IMC has had salutary effects, but the situation remains far from ideal. In the longer term, an unregulated media, which creates a free market in ideas, must be the desired goal. Today, though, an unregulated media would give too-free rein to destabilizing and hateful rhetoric.

Fractionalization in the economy adds to the disunity. Republika Srpska, Herceg-Bosna (officially unrecognized and nonexistent), the various Croat and Muslim communities interspersed within the Federation, and the Bihać region are in various ways and extents economically isolated from one another. Outside pressures to use the Croatian kuna and the Serbian dinar instead of the convertible mark in the miniature economies contributes to the fragmentation. So, too, do poor mobility and pressures to purchase goods from supportive patrons (i.e., from Serbia in Republika Srpska and from Croatia in Croat-controlled areas of the Federation).

The currency issue is one that may work itself out, and trade has its own way of breaking through barriers. Especially since the war in Kosovo, the Yugoslav dinar does not hold its value from one day to the next. The Croatian kuna is not so infirm as the dinar, but the convertible mark, pegged as it is to the deutschemark, surely is better regarded. The official currency will gain in acceptance and importance. The pursuit of profit will assure that goods will flow between the miniature economies. Much of this will occur through black-market and gray-market channels, though, such that the central government will see no tax revenue from that activity.

In and of themselves, currency differences and black-marketeering are marginal problems. The larger issue is the poor economic recovery that, after the resettlement failures, is one of the most disappointing realities in post-Dayton Bosnia and Hercegovina. The country's basket-case economy impedes progress in virtually all other spheres. It is the most dangerous threat to stability.

The economic situation amounts to a slew of vicious circles overlaying one another. High unemployment discourages people from returning to their prewar homes and feeds the suspicion and bitterness between ethnonational groups. Low incomes mean meager demand for goods, which discourages investment needed to create jobs. Instability retards commerce, which limits contact between people and enterprises in the various parts of the country. Business inactivity keeps capital scarce. Corruption thrives in a poorly developed economy and swallows up potential tax revenues. Underfunded and dysfunctional, government can do little to stimulate and to develop the economy.

There is an urgent need to get the economy on track and growing. So far, though, there are few signs that these vicious circles in the economy will soon be broken.

Nothing hinders progress so much as do the grips that the nationalist political parties have on political power and their resistance to tolerance and to reason. The nationalist parties continually act to maintain and even to strengthen the estrangement between ethnonational groups. The urge to alienate seems to be proportional to the amount of territory that each side controls. The Serb nationalist parties are most resistant to pluralism, followed closely by the Croat parties. Even SDA, which speaks positively of pluralism and unity does little to dispel fears that, given half a chance, a Bošnjak plurality would tyrannize Serb and Croat minorities.

Were Croat and Serb leaders able to put their differences aside and jointly to oppose the Bošnjaks, of course, their unified positions could prevail in a democratic Bosnia and Hercegovina. In that light, whatsoever divides Serb and Croat nationalists, strengthens SDA and the Coalition. Likewise, every rift between Croats and Muslims can be seen to advantage Serb nationalists. Thus, for example, we see Poplašen speaking out for the Croats in their campaign for a third entity. And while SDA speaks of a unified Bosnia and Hercegovina, that leading Bošnjak party is stronger so long as barriers are hard and fast between the country's two entities. SDA may regard it to be more advantageous to be the big fish in the smaller Federation pond (while making such trouble as it can with its few votes in the neighboring Republika Srpska) than to be the common prey of Serb and Croat sharks in the lake that breaching the IEBL dike would create.

Voters widely regard the national parties to be at the heart of the country's problems. Yet people vote for those nationalist parties—again and again. The apparently general support for nationalist parties is one of Bosnia and Hercegovina's illusions. Many people—and perhaps most—do not believe in their leaders. Still, they tend meekly to fall into line behind these political masters. Bewildered people do not know what to believe, so they accept what is easiest to believe and they lean with the wind. In the main, though, their political and chauvinist convictions are not so strong as they might appear.

The international community rests its hopes in the opposition parties, which slowly are gaining strength. The opposition is a diverse and splintered lot. The two Social Democrat parties are unwilling to work in concert. The Republican Party and Liberal Bošnjak Organization which make up the *Koalicija Centra* are not strong at present, but they do have potential and have shown their willingness to work with other parties that oppose ethnonational exclusivism. In the unlikely event that SDA ever were to practice what it preaches, it could cooperate with opposition parties. The Croat HDZ and Serb SRS and SDS never will do that. Whatever their shifting public pronouncements, their long-term goals remain the final partition of Bosnia and Hercegovina.

If the nationalist character of politics in Bosnia and Hercegovina is not sufficient to assure that all government is dysfunctional, then the unwieldy structure of governing institutions completes the disorder. It is designed to work on consensus where consensus is virtually unsought and unattainable. That structure borrows some of the worst elements from the post-Tito Yugoslav system that contributed to Yugoslavia's disintegration in the first place. Just as republican governments were able to stymie action in the former Yugoslav government, so, too, can nationalists prevent Bosnia and Hercegovina's central governing bodies from functioning. As a general matter, Serb politicians have been altogether reluctant to participate in the central government, preferring to treat Republika Srpska as a country of their own. Both Serb and Croat members, Radišić and Jelavić, have meanwhile shown their willingness to boycott the unworkable three-seat, rotating Presidency, as well as other joint governing institutions. The boycott and the veto over consensus are too-common political tools. Government cannot function by continuous brinksmanship.

Sooner or later, then, if Bosnia and Hercegovina is to survive as a country, the governing institutions must be reformed. The international community is understandably reluctant, though, to tinker with the constitutional order agreed at Dayton. The fear is that to do so will create new instability and that any new structure might even be worse than the existing one.

Clearly, international officials and aid workers are working here in a tough environment. A major frustration is that there is no dividing line between modest subterfuge for the sake of political maneuver and blatant lying. Virtually nobody with power will obey rules or honor their agreements if it is more advantageous to violate and to cheat on them. All politicians here expect their opponents to be as dishonest as they are themselves. Bosnia and Hercegovina's politics are byzantine, and civility is not much valued in political circles.

It is no wonder, then, that corruption and graft, too, permeate politics, the economy and society at every level. This fact is especially disconcerting when one recognizes that this results in millions upon millions of dollars in foreign aid being wasted, stolen, and used for private profit. Time and again people have told me that international donors should not allow aid to pass through local administrators' hands on the way to the intended recipients. As a practical matter, it is probably impossible to deliver aid through mechanisms and channels that are wholly free of corruption and waste, but, at the very least, monitoring should be improved.

Tens of thousands of Serbs, Croats and Bošnjaks are today much more strongly conscious of their ethnonational identities than they had been before. Those identities give them something to hold onto. Under such conditions as presently exist, unity with one's own ethnonational group rather than reconciliation with members of other groups is, on all sides, generally regarded as the best course. In an environment of much greater stability, personal security and economic well-being, this sentiment might well diminish. That is not yet the case.

It is a basic human characteristic that most people prefer to live among others who are culturally most similar to themselves, and Yugoslav history points to the reality that there is no point in trying to deny the constituent peoples their identities. It also is true, though, that exclusivism cannot work in a multicultural society. In many countries, people with much greater differences than exist between Croats, Serbs and Bošnjaks do live together in peace and harmony. Groups are most likely to clash in an environment characterized by economic distress, manipulated mass media, ineffective government, weak rule of law, chauvinist agitation, and no popularly recognized identity and purpose that stand higher than ethnic or national identities. Bosnia and Hercegovina today suffers from all these shortcomings, although efforts are being made—against considerable odds—to address them.

Prospects are poor that the people of Bosnia and Hercegovina very soon will subscribe to some sort of *Bosanac* identity that transcends their ethnonational identities. Croats and Serbs, in particular, have told me that they do not want to be regarded as Bosnian Croats and Bosnian Serbs. They are more likely, though, I believe, to aspire to a higher "European" identity, if such is offered to them. Members of all three ethnonational groups want to think of themselves as Europeans but feel that they have heretofore been excluded from the European family.

Yugoslavia's breakup, the wars of succession, and the violent differentiation between these groups have reinforced the separate identities of Croats, Serbs and Muslims. Nevertheless, Serb and Croat ultranationalists have failed to deliver on their promises to unite their respective peoples. Bosnia and Hercegovina's Serbs and Croats increasingly feel abandoned or betrayed by their national leaders who are connected to Milošević's Serbia and Tudjman's Croatia. What's more, many people of all groups want to return to their former homes and would do so if it were a safe and economically viable option. Not uncommonly, they are frightened by their own leaders—who want them to live apart from others—as much as they fear their former neighbors.

In contrast to those of the Croats and Serbs, the Bošnjak nation still scarcely exists. Nonetheless, for better or worse, *Bošnjaštvo* nation-building is progressing. In its still unfinished form, it is being forged, as always, by a Serbian hammer on a Croatian anvil. Nothing will continue to shape and to strengthen Bošnjak nationalism more than the threats of Croat and Serb nationalisms. *Bošnjaštvo* is probably strong enough now that Bosnia and Hercegovina's Muslims will never willingly live as a disadvantaged minority split between Croat and Serb states. Even cantonization within the existing borders of Bosnia and Hercegovina will heighten, and even could radicalize, Bošnjak nationalism.

If the will exists, the international community can prevent partition. It is a matter of patient but persistent and forceful resistance to the nationalists while working to offer a pluralistic, functional and outward-looking alternative. It means a long and hard struggle against the very forces that rule the country. Also necessary, of course, is to resolve the wider regional struggles that are beyond—but which are strongly felt within—Bosnia and Hercegovina's borders. If the international community turns that work over to those European interests that abetted Yugoslavia's breakup in the first place, and with no regard for the Muslims, then the integrity of the country will be seriously at risk.

In light of current realities, I see three general possibilities for Bosnia and Hercegovina's long-term development. The country could 1) become fully unified, integrated and politically centralized, 2) be broken three ways, or 3) be cantonized and decentralized within Bosnia and Hercegovina's existing boundaries.

Under the first scenario, which now appears least likely, Serb, Croat and Bošnjak nationalists would need to find a *modus operandi* wherein they could work effectively together in governing the country or they necessarily must altogether lose their legitimacy to rule. In fact, although they have proven their inability to govern and to work collectively with one another, the nationalists are far from losing their grips on power. Since 1990, the people of Bosnia and Hercegovina have time and again manifest their willingness to give the nationalists their votes. Indications are that opposition parties will remain too divided and their ideological offerings insufficiently compelling to overcome this nationalist sentiment at any time soon.

Under the second scenario, western Hercegovina, portions of western Bosnia and perhaps the Orašje pocket north of Brčko would be joined to Croatia. Likewise, the eastern lobe of Republika Srpska would be merged into Serbia and Montenegro. The remainder of the country, then, would exist as a rump-Bosnia. (There would be no Hercegovina, as that region would have been split off to Croatia and Montenegro.) This scenario, I think, is also improbable. The international community is unlikely to allow such a division. It would not solve the problems of Croat-Muslim relations in central Bosnia, would require further relocations of people, and would leave the western lobe of Republika Srpska within rump-Bosnia essentially to be ruled by a Muslim majority. Division also would represent a complete failure of the Dayton peace process.

I regard the third scenario as most likely. There is much precedent for that solution. The Lisbon Accord (1992), Vance-Owen Plan (1992) and Owen-Stoltenberg Plan (1993) all had envisioned cantonal decentralization in various forms. Even the Dayton agreement's acceptance of the two-entity concept is to some extent a precedent for further decentralization. Cantonization will not solve the host of other problems, least of all that of returning displaced families to their homes.

The two greatest threats to Bosnia and Hercegovina today, as always, emanate from Zagreb and Belgrade. In that Tudjman, Milošević and their ilk never will cease in their efforts to destabilize Bosnia and Hercegovina, stability will be in jeopardy and progress slow so long as the likes of Tudjman and Milošević remain at political center stage in their countries. They do not stand alone, of course. Bosnia and Hercegovina has a bumper crop of homegrown Serb, Croat and Bošnjak ultranationalists. Izetbegović, too, is now part of the problem.

Milošević's Serbia is not the only rogue state on the territory of the former Yugoslavia. So, too, is Tudjman's Croatia. That Tudjman and Croat ultranationalists have stirred up somewhat less trouble and committed less violence in the region than have their Serb counterparts probably is just a matter of demographics. Croats were not so dispersed across republic borders in the former Yugoslavia as were Serbs, and Croatia did not have a Kosovo.

The international community must maintain constant vigilance and pressure upon both Zagreb and Belgrade. Until they truly reform their ways, both should be regarded as pariah states. There is a danger, I believe, that the institutionally weak and fractious EU will too quickly establish closer and warmer relations with Croatia. That would effectively reward Tudjman's renegade state for its undemocratic actions, ill treatment of Croatian Serbs, and continuing interference in Bosnia and Hercegovina.

If the international community truly intends to maintain Bosnia and Hercegovina within its present borders, then the policy toward all nationalists should be one of steady and strong pressure. Stiff resistance and a threat of force should stand in the face of Balkan disingenuousness, corruption, belligerence and prejudice. More pressure must especially be brought upon the Croat strongholds that have been established within the Federation.

The international community should accept that an international military and police presence must remain at least for several more years. Those forces should be commanded to work more actively in support of Annex 7 and the International War Crimes Tribunal. Otherwise, the lip service and hypocrisy in regard to refugee returns will continue. In order to break the traditional circle of murderous vengeance and to give war victims the closure they need in order to heal, war criminals must be arrested, tried and punished. Some will say that the time has come to let bygones be bygones, to shift the focus to forgiveness. Such a view reflects a disregard for, or ignorance of, the depth and intensity of feeling in Bosnia and Hercegovina. This process of bringing criminals to justice must be seen to be thorough, fair and evenhanded across the ethnonational patchwork. I am apprehensive that the plans, recently announced, to reduce troops strength in Bosnia and Hercegovina will be accompanied by still more excuses for failure to resettle the displaced and to arrest war criminals.

Substantial economic assistance from the international community still is necessary if the economy is to be put on track. This is a great challenge in consideration of the country's instability and its leaders' great propensity for graft, corruption, bigotry and disingenuousness. Aid must be tied to fulfilling objectives that are part of building a civil society. For example, donors' funds cannot be invested in factories controlled by nationalists who deny jobs to people not belonging to their own ethnonational group or political party. Linking investment to refugee returns in specific localities is a sensible approach. Unfortunately, many nationalist leaders would prefer to see their people remain poor and hopeless than to be employed and working alongside members of the other groups.

Ultimately, peace and stability throughout the Balkans and Europe must be built on a supranational basis. Nationalism and the homogeneous nation-state are 19th-century concepts that are becoming outdated in Europe. The Europe of the future will be characterized by economic and political integration. Bosnia and Hercegovina's best hope is to find its place in the new European order. That European order is itself still evolving, however, and the EU has problems of its own. The EU is institutionally weak, divided and indecisive. Conflicting national interests and even competing national prides too often prevent rational and concerted action. EU responses to the Yugoslav crises of the 1990s certainly demonstrate that. So, too, does the fact that, in March 1999, as I was returning from Bosnia and Hercegovina, in Brussels the European Commission was resigning *en masse* over accusations of corruption and incompetence. EU economies remain shackled by excessive state ownership of industry, subsidies and protectionism, labor market rigidities, along with regulatory and bureaucratic encumbrances.

Nevertheless, Europe's main thrust is in the right direction. The EU should create a secure and prosperous living space for other countries to join. There can be no room in that Europe for nations in whose name genocide is committed or for countries that violate internationally recognized borders.

In that Yugoslavia and Czechoslovakia were both created at the same time, came apart at about the same time, and perhaps because I live in the Czech Republic, I often compare their two situations. I find the political experience in Slovakia particularly instructive. When Czechoslovakia broke up in 1993, it did so without bloodshed but also without public referenda or other concessions to democracy. For most of the next five years, Vladimir Mečiar, a nationalist and former-communist demagogue, ran Slovakia. As a result, Europe turned its back on Slovakia.

Slovakia's nationalists are still there, but their time in the spotlight has passed. Their function was perhaps important when the new country was establishing itself. But in autumn 1998 a majority of Slovak voters turned out Mečiar. They elected reasonably modern, civilized and outward-looking politicians in place of HDZS chauvinists. In spring 1999, then, Slovaks elected a president of similar disposition. Now, Slovakia is on track toward joining Europe and NATO.

In Slovakia, it took five years to get rid of the old thinking and to vote out the nationalists. It is too early to tell but that the country might slip back into its old ways. In Bosnia and Hercegovina and the countries that surround it, the stage of nationalist consolidation may take longer than in Slovakia—perhaps twice as long, maybe three times or four times longer. Probably most important for Bosnia and Hercegovina is that Croatia and Serbia ultimately go the way of Slovakia.

As I am writing these last few words, a Balkan summit, in which some 40 countries are participating, is going on in Sarajevo. The war over Kosovo has created interest in, and perhaps opportunity for, a regional effort to put the Balkans in order once and for all. Leaders from the US, EU, Japan, Canada, Russia and several Balkan countries (excluding Milošević's Serbia) are gathered to discuss a "Balkan stability pact." Some are giving it advance billing as a "Marshall Plan for the Balkans."

It is too early to know whether the Sarajevo summit and Balkan pact will or will not be substantial and successful. Hopefully, EU members will demonstrate a collective commitment to creating a Europe that is an attractive option for countries and nations willing and able to rise above nationalism. In any case, the road to joining Europe will be long and hard. As of today, Bosnia and Hercegovina has not yet found that road.

Glossary

Četniks – ("Chetniks"). Name adopted, formally or informally, several times in Serbian history for Serb military organizations. Also used by non-Serbs as a disparaging epithet for nationalist and militant Serbs.

(The) Coalition – Coalition for a Single and Democratic Bosnia and Hercegovina. The dominant Muslim political force in Bosnia and Hercegovina, led by SDA but includes three other Bošnjak parties.

Contact Group – successor to the ICFY, made up of representatives of the US, Russia, Germany, France and the United Kingdom. Convened in April 1994 in Geneva. Key elements of its plan were carried into the Dayton peace negotiations in 1995.

EU – European Union (formerly European Community, or EC). Includes 15 economically developed and democratic European countries.

HDZ (*Hrvatska demokratska zajednica*) – Croatian Democratic Union. Led by Croatian President Franjo Tudjman, the leading Croat nationalist party both in Croatia and in Bosnia and Hercegovina.

HDZS – Movement for a Democratic Slovakia. Nationalist party of Vladimir Mečiar, former Slovak prime minister.

(Office of the) High Representative – The highest international official responsible for civilian aspects of the peace implementation. Role is to coordinate humanitarian aid, reconstruction, protecting human rights and conducting elections. Dayton specifically denied the High Representative authority over foreign military forces in the country.

HOS (*Hrvatska obrambena snaga*) – Croatian Defense Force. A former militia, a rival to the HVO, and associated with the extreme Croatian Party of Rights (HSP).

HSP (*Hrvatska stranka prava*) – Croat Party of Rights. Founded in Zagreb in 1990 by Dobroslav Paraga, a long-time dissident and extreme Croat nationalist. The HSP's name is taken from a 19th-century nationalist party whose founder advocated overthrow of the Habsburgs and Croatianizing all South Slavs (thus including Slovenes, Serbs, Muslims and Macedonians) with the exception of Bulgarians.

HVO (*Hrvatsko vijeće odbrane*) – Croat Council of Defense. Effectively, a still-functioning army of the HDZ.

ICFY – International Conference on the Former Yugoslavia. Convened in Geneva, Switzerland in September 1992 as a permanent body to address the Yugoslav conflicts. Initially cochaired by Cyrus Vance, a US diplomat, as the United Nations envoy, and David Owen, a British politician and representing the EC.

IEBL – Inter-Entity Boundary Line. Created at Dayton, separates the Muslim-Croat Federation and Republika Srpska within Bosnia and Hercegovina.

IFOR – a multinational military Implementation Force "invited" into Bosnia and Hercegovina under terms of the Dayton peace accords. Later renamed "SFOR" (for "Stabilization Force"), IFOR operated under NATO command and UN authority.

IMC – Independent Media Commission. Created by the High Representative in 1998 to license and regulate the mass media in Bosnia and Hercegovina. Successor to the MEC.

IPTF – International Police Task Force. Created by Dayton under UN administration to train and advise local law enforcement personnel, as well as to monitor law enforcement activities.

Koalicija Centra – Coalition of the Center. Minor coalition of two parties (the Republicans and the Liberal Bošnjak Organization) that oppose national exclusivism. Readily allies with other moderate parties.

MEC – Media Experts Commission. An OSCE-created body intended to regulate and improve the mass media. Succeeded by the IMC.

NATO – North Atlantic Treaty Organization. Military alliance consisting of 19 democratic countries and led by the US.

NDZ (Narodna demokratska zajednica) – People's Democratic Union. Party created in 1996 by Fikret Abdić, a controversial Muslim leader from northwestern Bosnia. Political enemy of Alija Izetbegović.

NHI (Nova hrvatska inicijativa) – New Croat Initiative. Party founded in summer 1998 by then-member of the Bosnia and Hercegovina Presidency Krešimir Zubak as a more moderate alternative to Tudjman's HDZ.

OSCE – Organization of Security and Cooperation in Europe. Supervises elections and otherwise plays a substantial role in administering the civilian aspects of the Dayton implementation.

Opština – A political-administrative unit, similar to a US county.

SDA (Stranka demokratske akcije) – Party of Democratic Action. The leading Bošnjak nationalist political party in Bosnia and Hercegovina. Led by Alija Izetbegović.

SDP (Socijaldemokratska partija) – The leading opposition political party in Bosnia and Hercegovina. Direct descendant of the former League of Communists of Yugoslavia. Opposes all forms of nationalism.

SDS (*Srpska demokratska stranka*) – Serb Democratic Party. Leading Serb nationalist party in Bosnia and Hercegovina, formerly led by Radovan Karadžić.

SFOR – Stabilization Force. Successor to IFOR.

(*Koalicija*) *Sloga* – Coalition Unity. Coalition of Serb nationalist parties in Bosnia and Hercegovina that is supported by the international community as a relatively moderate alternative to the SDS-SRS coalition. Sloga is made up of Biljana Plavšić's Serb People's Alliance, Milorad Dodik's Party of Independent Social Democrats, and the Socialist Party of Republika Srpska that is led by Živko Radišić.

Social-Demokrati – Like SDP, a party of social democrats. This one is associated with Ante Marković, the would-be reformer and last prime minister of Yugoslavia before it began coming to pieces.

SRS (*Srpska radikalna stranka*) – Serb Radical Party. Ultranationalist Serb party founded by the Serb extremist Vojislav Šešelj. Operating in both Bosnia and Hercegovina and Serbia/Yugoslavia, SRS is in a coalition with SDS in Bosnia and Hercegovina.

UMCOR – United Methodist Committee on Relief.

UNHCR – United Nations High Commission for Refugees.

UNPROFOR – United Nations Protection Force. A military force created early in the wars to protect aid convoys and those working for the UN Office of the High Commission for Refugees (UNHCR). Known as the "Blue Helmets," UNPROFOR's mandate did not go beyond protecting humanitarian efforts.

USAID – United States Agency for International Development.

Ustaše – ("Ustashe"). Meaning "insurrection," name of the extreme nationalist Croat political and military organization that collaborated with German Nazis and Italian Fascists prior to and during World War II. Also used by non-Croats as a disparaging epithet for ultranationalist and militant Croats.

Selected Bibliography

Even well before Yugoslavia began to come apart, that country had attracted an interest in scholarly circles probably disproportionate to its size (although perhaps not out of proportion to its importance). The general public took a greater interest in the 1990s, and more has been written in English for the mass audience in recent years. There are now many books from which to choose, as well as a great deal of information that can be gathered by searching the Internet.

I do not mention here every book that I have consulted, but neither have I excluded any which were truly major information sources. This listing tilts toward recent books, which are readily available and up-to-date, even though some older works (especially in the way of history) may in some ways be more authoritative. One should be aware that a great deal of what has been written about former Yugoslavia, its ethnonational constituents and the wars of Yugoslav succession is ideologically and emotionally charged. Sometimes the bias is easy to detect; sometimes it is very subtle.

Akhavan, Payam and Robert Howse, eds. *Yugoslavia the Former and Future: Reflections by Scholars from the Region.* Washington and Geneva: The Brookings Institution and The United Nations Research Institute for Social Development, 1995.

Allcock, John B., Marko Milivojevic and John J. Horton, eds. *Conflict in the Former Yugoslavia: An Encyclopedia.* Santa Barbara: ABC-CLIO, Inc., 1998.

Andrić, Ivo. *Bosnian Chronicle.* Translated by Joseph Hitrec. New York: Alfred A. Knopf, 1963. First Arcade paperback edition, 1993.

———. *The Bridge on the Drina.* Translated by Lovett F. Edwards. Chicago: University of Chicago Press, 1977. Paperback edition, 1977.

Banac, Ivo. *The National Question in Yugoslavia: Origins, History, Politics.* Ithaca and London: Cornell University Press, 1984; Cornell Paperbacks, 1988, 1994.

Blanchard, Paul. *Blue Guide Yugoslavia.* London: A & C Black, 1989.

Bringa, Tone. *Being Muslim the Bosnian Way: Identity and Community in a Central Bosnian Village.* Princeton: Princeton University Press, 1995.

Cohen, Lenard J. *Broken Bonds: Yugoslavia's Disintegration and Balkan Politics in Transition.* Boulder: Westview Press, 1993; second edition (updated and expanded) in paperback, 1995.

Crnobrnja, Mihailo. *The Yugoslav Drama, 2nd edition.* Montreal and Kingston: McGill-Queen's University Press, 1994, 1996.

Dizdarević, Zlatko. *Sarajevo: A War Journal.* Translated from French by Anselm Hollo. Edited from Serbo-Croatian by Ammiel Alcalay. New York: Fromm International, 1993.

Doder, Dusko. *The Yugoslavs.* New York and Toronto: Random House, 1978; Vintage Books paperback, 1979.

Donia, Robert J. and John V. A. Fine. *Bosnia and Hercegovina: A Tradition Betrayed.* New York: Columbia University Press, 1994.

Dvornik, Francis. *The Slavs in Early European History and Civilization.* New Brunswick: Rutgers University Press, 1962.

FAMA. *Sarajevo 1992–1995* (also known as the *Sarajevo Survival Map*). Sarajevo: FAMA, 1996.

Fine, John V. A. *The Early Medieval Balkans: A Critical Survey from the Sixth to the Late Twelfth Century.* Ann Arbor: The University of Michigan Press, 1983; first paperback edition, 1991.

————. *The Late Medieval Balkans: A Critical Survey from the Late Twelfth Century to the Ottoman Conquest.* Ann Arbor: The University of Michigan Press, 1987; first paperback edition, 1994.

Gjelten, Tom. *Sarajevo Daily: A City and Its Newspaper under Siege.* New York: HarperCollins, 1995; HarperPerennial (paperback), 1996.

Halpern, Joel M. *A Serbian Village.* New York: Columbia University Press, 1956.

Holbrooke, Richard. *To End a War.* New York and Toronto: Random House, 1998.

Jelavich, Barbara. *History of the Balkans, vol. 1 (18th and 19th centuries) and vol. 2 (20th century).* Cambridge and New York: Cambridge University Press, 1983.

Judah, Tim. *The Serbs: History, Myth and the Destruction of Yugoslavia.* New Haven and London, 1997.

Kann, Robert A. *A History of the Habsburg Empire, 1526–1918.* Berkeley, Los Angeles and London: University of California Press, 1974.

Lampe, John R. *Yugoslavia as History: Twice There Was a Country.* Cambridge: Cambridge University Press, 1996.

Lockwood, William G. *European Moslems: Economy and Ethnicity in Western Bosnia.* New York: Academic Press, 1975.

Lodge, Olive. *Peasant Life in Jugoslavia.* London: Seeley, Service & Co., 1941.

Lovrenović, Ivan et al. *Bosnia and Herzegovina, 2nd edition.* Sarajevo: Svjetlost, 1986.

Magocsi, Paul Robert. *Historical Atlas of East Central Europe.* Seattle and London: University of Washington Press, 1993; first paperback edition, 1995.

Malcom, Noel. *Bosnia: A Short History*. London: Macmillan, 1994; Papermac, 1994.

Media Plan. *Guide for Journalists in Bosnia & Hercegovina: Elections '98*. Sarajevo: Media Plan, 1998.

Mihailovich, Vasa, ed. *Landmarks in Serbian Culture and History*. Pittsburgh: Serb National Foundation, 1983.

Rhode, David. *A Safe Area (Srebrenica: Europe's Worst Massacre since the Second World War)*. London: Simon & Schuster, 1997; Pocket Books, 1997.

Selimović, Meša. *Death and the Dervish*. Translated by Bogdan Rakić and Stephen M. Dickey. Evanston: Northwestern University Press, 1996.

Silber, Laura and Allan Little. *Yugoslavia: Death of a Nation, 2nd revision*. London and New York: Penguin Books, 1997.

Sivric, Ivo. *The Peasant Culture of Bosnia and Herzegovina*. Chicago: Franciscan Herald Press, 1982.

Tanner, Marcus. *Croatia: A Nation Forged in War*. New Haven and London: Yale University Press, 1997.

Todorova, Maria. *Imagining the Balkans*. New York and Oxford: Oxford University Press, 1997.

West, Rebecca. *Black Lamb and Grey Falcon: A Journey through Yugoslavia*. London: Macmillan London Limited, 1940, 1941; Canongate Classics, 1993.

Woodward, Susan L. *Balkan Tragedy: Chaos and Dissolution after the Cold War*. Washington, D.C.: The Brookings Institution, 1995.

Zimmerman, Warren. *Origins of a Catastrophe*. New York: Times Books (Random House), 1996.

Index

About the Author

Gale A. Kirking, a Wisconsin native, moved to Czechoslovakia in 1992, immediately after completing a Master's Degree in International Management at the American Graduate School of International Management (Thunderbird). He has worked several years in central and eastern Europe's emerging capital markets as an investment analyst and director of research for a stock brokerage firm.

Untangling Bosnia and Hercegovina was conceived, researched and written during a yearlong personal sabbatical. Kirking, who is single and describes himself as a mediocre but hopelessly devoted student of foreign languages, presently divides his time between Europe and the US.

On the Cover

The cover's blue and yellow background is from the official flag of Bosnia and Hercegovina. Flags have been a source of abundant controversy in the post-Dayton period. As there seemed no other way to resolve a symbolic stalemate, the international community's High Representative ultimately commissioned a design for the theoretically unified country's flag. He aimed to find something that would not offend any ethnonational group. Also shown on the front (in center) is the flag of the Federation. It is flanked by the Croatian (at left) and Republika Srpska (at right) flags. This flag of neighboring Croatia is commonly flown in Croat-controlled areas within the Federation. The Republika Srpska flag, which is a simple Yugoslav tricolor, is used throughout Republika Srpska.

The back cover photo is from Ahmići, a Muslim village in central Bosnia that was systematically decimated in spring 1993. Shown is the toppled minaret from one of the village's two mosques. Photo from Ahmići by the author. Photo of the author by Monika Whalley. Cover design by Gary Cox.